BONDS OF IMPERFECTION

Christian Politics, Past and Present

Oliver O'Donovan *&* Joan Lockwood O'Donovan

WILLIAM B. EERDMANS PUBLISHING COMPANY

GRAND RAPIDS, MICHIGAN / CAMBRIDGE, U.K.

Wm. B. Eerdmans Publishing Co.
255 Jefferson Ave. S.E., Grand Rapids, Michigan 49503 /
P.O. Box 163, Cambridge CB3 9PU U.K.

Printed in the United States of America

08 07 06 05 04   7 6 5 4 3 2 1

Library of Congress Cataloging-in-Publication Data

O'Donovan, Oliver.
Bonds of imperfection: Christian politics, past and present /
Oliver O'Donovan & Joan Lockwood O'Donovan.
      p.   cm.
Includes bibliographical references.
ISBN 0-8028-4975-X (alk. paper)
1. Christianity and politics — History.
I. O'Donovan, Joan Lockwood, 1950-   II. Title.

BR115.P7O36   2004
261.7'09 — dc22
                              2003049483

www.eerdmans.com

Contents

CONTENTS

Introduction

The essays collected here are explorations in 'the political' — in political agency, political action, political institutions, and political society — from a perspective formed by the Bible and the Latin theological tradition. All the essays engage at some level with contemporary understandings and issues, and all bring to bear in a critical and constructive manner the theological resources of the older tradition. There is, nevertheless, a shift of emphasis between Parts 1 and 2: from recovering significant theoretical moments and strands of the Christian political past to analyzing present thought and practice in their light.

This collection forms an accompaniment to our compilation of texts, *From Irenaeus to Grotius: A Sourcebook in Christian Political Thought*[1] which intended to provide extensive access to the tradition with the aid of translations, introductions, and commentary. In that enterprise we were naturally constrained from undertaking more sustained analysis of individual thinkers and more developed arguments about specific issues. It is a selection of these that the following essays offer, with, we hope, a progressively unfolding coherence, even though their composition spanned more than a decade of our intellectual labor. It need hardly be said that the material in *From Irenaeus to Grotius* is capable of inspiring many other discussions than those we have taken up here.

The engagement with contemporary approaches, ideas, and institutions is pre-eminently but by no means exclusively critical, while that with the older tradition is largely constructive. If there is an imbalance here, it may be viewed as a corrective to a consensus within and without the church that regards the prevailing liberal-democratic institutions of the West as wholly normative for

1. (Grand Rapids: Eerdmans, 1999). Throughout these essays, we have noted translations of primary sources referred to in *From Irenaeus to Grotius* (IG).

1

all times and occasions, even while it finds a continual source of vexation in their fallout. This consensus admits a variety of approaches to the older theo-political tradition, from the more flattering to the more dismissive, but hardly allows it to speak with its own voice. It is regarded complacently as the foundation, albeit inchoate, of future political progress, or disowned guiltily as the shadow cast by a theocratic civilization, and in either case it is denied its proper integrity and authority. Taking the tradition seriously implies a confrontational stance, not necessarily towards contemporary institutions but towards the commonplaces which are universally supposed to shore them up — the commonplaces of republican freedom and self-government, of popular sovereignty and the rights of individuals and communities.

The diversity of their subject matter should not obscure the ways in which these essays cohere, in respect both of the pre-modern and of the modern traditions. With respect to the former, they identify the political with the sphere of judgment, divine and human, that gives order to the human community in history. This judgment is demanded as a penultimate response to human waywardness, for the sake of preserving human society and creation against the ravages of sin, rather than to accomplish their redemption and restoration. At the same time, it is the sphere in which human rebellion against God achieves collective solidarity, definitively manifested in the crucifixion of Christ and the persecution of his witnesses. The political remains a morally ambiguous realm, an instrument of God's merciful dealings with humankind and an object of his wrath, subject to the risen Christ on both accounts. It is not insulated from the resurrection conquest of Christ and the signs of the coming kingdom, but it does not belong among them. The justice and peace achieved by earthly politics, while bound to God's law in nature and Scripture, is transient and tragically deficient. Only with the arrival of the heavenly kingdom can the political, purified of its earthly texture, be coterminous with redeemed society under the rule of Christ. Until then, it is not political action but the communion of the church that looks forward to the city of God.

The modern tradition, on the other hand, is portrayed as detaching the foundations of the political from the judgment of God, with one of two results: either the political is merely a *modus vivendi* among self-interested human beings, or, if human sinfulness is also suppressed, it is the powerhouse for collective self-perfection. In this last form it becomes the administrative agent of technological mastery and cultural expression. In either case the overriding political good is the enhancement of human freedom, individual and collective. But this is not the freedom which the older tradition knew as "evangelical freedom": it is no longer law-governed, obedient, and a fitting response to "what is" — to what the Father has made, the Son has redeemed and the Spirit is sancti-

2

fying. Projected as autonomous self-possession, freedom assaults the intrinsic forms of sharing and solidarity that comprise moral community: it assaults not only our communication in the created goods and structures by which we live well but also our solidarity as the object of God's condemnation, forgiveness, and renewal. These essays probe *sub specie libertatis* the intellectual and practical pitfalls of the modern political inheritance.

In their advocacy of the older theo-political tradition, the essays in this volume have not abandoned the constructive political task of the present. They do not recollect the tradition in an antiquarian mood of regret and nostalgia, but attempt to show its perennial relevance. And if this attempt is at all successful, it alters the horizons of present political understanding and opens up possibilities for action. All legitimate criticism illuminates the way forward. The most trenchant form of complacency is acquiescence in contemporary certainties as a *datum* of historical necessity. Only when criticism becomes totalized, as in postmodernist indifference, does it become a council of despair, self-defeating and without point.

*   *   *

The opening essay of the collection, "History and Politics in the Book of Revelation," forms a programmatic introduction. In John of Patmos's apocalyptic overcoming of the political order Oliver O'Donovan discerns an imagined space for hopeful common action. In contrast to readings that see in John's "mythologizing" the negating transcendence of history and politics, O'Donovan construes the three cycles of seven visions of Revelation as a progressive unfolding of God's judgment in history. This judgment is initially depicted as an outworking of historical necessity, but its political features are successively exhibited, in its vindication of order and created goodness, its response to the "demands of outraged justice," and its restoration of individual and communal freedom.[2]

Passing from the pre-messianic politics of the first two cycles to the messianic politics of the third cycle, John projects earthly empire as a phenomenon with two aspects, historical and eschatological. On the one hand it is a perennial phenomenon of sinful politics, naturally fated to self-destruction; on the other, it is a disclosure of eschatological evil, a messianic and trinitarian parody with two totalitarian faces, violent oppression and ideological deception. As a perennial political enterprise, imperial dominion weds military to economic subjugation, until it finally collapses under the weight of massed rebellion. As a

---

2. All quotations in our *Introduction* are from the essays that follow.

disclosure of eschatological evil, it exposes its nihilistic core: devoid of created good, it collapses into pure negation, the assault upon God, the source and principle of being.

John's cyclical unfolding of God's judgment in history is also an unfolding of the eschatological paradox of freedom: the necessity of "immanent justice" which diminishes human freedom is converted by God's Word into "the freedom of the saints' corporate obedience." His concluding vision of divine triumph divides into the victory of the Son in which the saints participate and the judgment of the Father to which they remain subject. But the judgment of God on history is a reconciling and fulfilling one, anticipating the new creation, as emerges from the hidden identity of the opposing cities: the "Great City" and the "Holy City," Babylon-Rome and the New Jerusalem.

Augustine's *City of God,* the shaping text of the Western theo-political tradition, follows Revelation in locating the meaning of history and of politics in terms of the opposing "ends" of the Two Cities. But whereas Revelation and Books 20-22 of *The City of God* consider these ends in a "strictly eschatological sense," Book 19 considers them in a prolegomenal manner: as "horizons of action that generate their contrasting moral characters." According to "The Political Thought of *City of God* 19," the Two Cities comprise for Augustine true and false resolutions of the dilemma for action posed by historical contingency, true and false answers to the question of the "highest good." The City of God is the community of "perfect and eternal peace," the Earthly City the community of "mortal peace." It is with the latter community that Augustine aligns the politics of the *res publica,* denying the possibility of an earthly polity defined in terms of "right" *(ius)* or "common interest" *(utilitas).*

Oliver O'Donovan shows how this alignment is resisted by both the idealist and realist accounts of Augustine's political thought current in contemporary liberalism. While idealists read Augustine as admitting an earthly commonwealth — Christian or (at least) monotheistic — of relative justice, realists read him as admitting a morally neutral commonwealth which, although laying no claim to justice in the strong sense, is unaligned with either city. Central to both accounts is a misunderstanding of the "common use" of mortal necessities by the two cities. Failing to distinguish common use from common utility, they impute a "consensus of wills" *(compositio voluntatum)* between the cities, and attribute membership in the Earthly City to members of the Heavenly City, whereas the latter merely use the Earthly City's own consensus without participating in it. Both accounts, in effect, attribute a greater or lesser degree of "relative justice" to the civil polity, whereas Augustine reserves that for the peace of the earthly church.

Consequently, neither the idealist nor the realist interpretation grasps clearly the implications of the church's justice for civil polity. The justice of sins forgiven issues in civil justice, the just rule of the justified sinner, the Christian prince whose supramundane virtues are of benefit to civil government precisely because they answer to "'the right' as it is generally recognized and universally desired." At the same time, the justice of sins forgiven remains for Augustine a "superimposition" on civil peace that it "can function quite well without." The key to civil rule without justice lies in Augustine's Platonic conception of the predatory dependence of human vice on virtue, of moral disorder on order, which enables even "manifestly vicious communities" to "function as organized societies." On the one hand, the essence of earthly rule — "dominion" — expresses the disordered will of fallen humanity, the individual and collective vice of pride; on the other, the structured vice of dominion fulfills God's providential purpose of curtailing the disorder flowing from pride. The just rule of the Christian emperor, therefore, does not extricate empire from the demonic course of the earthly city envisaged by John of Patmos, but is *a sign* of God's coming judgment and restoration of human society.

The idealist determination to extricate political rule from its demonic history has been a dominant feature of past as well as present treatments of Augustine. The medieval papal tradition of "political Augustinianism" (to use a popular scholarly nomenclature) was a project of Christianizing political authority by assimilating it to God's work of salvation. This followed the twofold route of (a) subordinating civil to ecclesiastical government, teleologically and legally, and (b) juridicalizing ecclesiastical government. In putting his definitive stamp on the project, Pope Gregory VII ("Hildebrand")[3] was fully persuaded (not least by his own experience!) of the demonic character of unregenerate secular rule, and equally persuaded that its redemption lay in strong clerical (especially papal) guidance and oversight. For him it was not a question of making pious use of, or superimposing Christian virtue on, the hellbent path of civil rule, but of redirecting its path heavenward, to Rome's political and legal supremacy. Justice was available to civil as to ecclesiastical judgment and law, but it descended in a seamless garment from Christ's Vicar.

However, while papal political theology habitually blurred the distinction between God's providential and salvific action, medieval Augustinianism never lost sight of the postlapsarian status of human government, or "jurisdiction." It was most jealously guarded in Franciscan theology, on account of the interconnectedness in the patristic inheritance of political rule and property. For Franciscan theology was concerned before all else with expounding and defending the order's Rule of absolute poverty that committed the brothers to the total re-

---

3. *IG*, pp. 240-49.

nunciation of property and of individual and collective ownership, as well as to severe material deprivation. In the third essay, "Christian Platonism and Nonproprietary Community," Joan O'Donovan situates the Franciscan "theology of poverty" within the Christian Platonist tradition of trinitarian and christological moral realism ('realism' in the schoolmen's sense), and explores its historical contributions to ecclesiology and political thought, as well as its contemporary timeliness.

Against the backdrop of a papal church endowed with extensive property and jurisdiction, the Franciscan Minister General, Bonaventure, authoritatively expounded evangelical perfection as the imitation of Christ's freely accepted humiliation of physical destitution, powerlessness, and suffering. His core ethical insight was into the intimate relationship between pride and covetousness in the disordered love of the soul (and analogously, of society): that the soul's "consuming will to possess" other beings and things "is always in order to aggrandize its powers as privately possessed, as belonging exclusively to itself rather than to God." Hence the Franciscan discipline of renouncing "not only the relative abundance of ecclesiastical possession but also the positive legal rights connected with it" was "an efficacious sign that the apostolic wayfarer is not a self-possessor," not a proprietor of his physical and spiritual powers, but rather "possessed by Christ." The discipline both manifested and reinforced the individual's surrender of his own will.

Despite the solitary cast of Franciscan discipleship, Bonaventure conceived non-proprietary existence in communal as well as individual terms, speculatively attributing it (in Augustinian fashion) to the communities of created and sanctified humanity: to Adamic society, on the one hand, and to the communion of saints ('the just') on the other, who live by natural and divine 'right' alone without the need of positive human 'right' (law). It was, however, John Wyclif in the next century who gave extensive theological, metaphysical, epistemological, and ecclesiological development to non-proprietary community. For Wyclif, created and perfected human community was essentially trinitarian — formed by the Father's self-communication in Christ through the Holy Spirit — and as such comprised a freely "communicating and communicable possession and use" of spiritual and material goods. Only sin disrupted this free communication of resources, necessitating humanly contrived and forcibly imposed constraints such as property right. Wyclif accepted the Augustinian thesis that restrictive proprietorship ("civil dominion") had no independent validity apart from righteous communicative possession and use of goods ("evangelical dominion"). However, contrary to the papalist conclusion that the church had superior jurisdiction over all earthly property, Wyclif concluded that the clerical estate as a whole should be non-propertied, concretely manifesting the evangelical dominion of christological community that under-girds all valid civil proprietorship.

At the forefront of the Franciscan-Wycliffite legacy, then, was a more spir-itual, less jurisdictional ecclesiology. In the Franciscan phase this went together with a mystical, christocentric spirituality and asceticism, in the Wycliffite phase with a complex dialectic of divine and human law, right, and community. The legacy presented an evolving undertaking to distinguish and hold in ten-sion the theological moments of created, fallen, redeemed, and sanctified hu-manity. Whatever the shortcomings of the christological, non-proprietary ethic, it was in its time, and is still, a challenge to naturalistic and idealistic po-litical and social theologies that have little sense of the moral ambiguity of in-stitutions belonging to the fallen state. A central contention of the essay is that the prevailing form of idealistic naturalism today is the political language of subjective 'rights' which has universalized a proprietary concept (property right) into a legalistic and individualistic ethic of self-possession. This is the first of a number of critical analyses of liberal rights in this volume.

The consideration of medieval usury theory that follows, "The Theologi-cal Economics of Medieval Usury Theory," is a logical progression from discus-sion of non-proprietary community, in that the early, formative strand of Christian argumentation against usury presupposed the moral ambiguity of property. One intention of this essay is to show the indispensability of the anti-proprietary strand of argument inherited from the Church Fathers to the moral depth and coherence of usury theory. The heart of this Christianized tradition was a vision of creation resurrected in Christ as a participatory sharing in the gifts of God and a common self-giving to meet one another's needs. This vision was invoked to interpret biblical condemnations and prohibitions of usury (i.e., profiting from a loan) and especially Christ's injunction of Luke 6:35 to "lend, expecting nothing in return," and it gave an overall theological orienta-tion to a range of 'natural law' arguments drawing on Roman law and Aristote-lian ideas.

With Thomas Aquinas's treatment of usury, and his economic ethics gen-erally, proposes Joan O'Donovan, there was a pivotal shift away from participa-tory and self-giving community to the natural law issue of commutative justice (justice in exchange), for which property was no longer morally problematic. Thomas's arguments against usury from "the consumptibility of money" and "economic compulsion," together with his handling of the "external titles to in-terest," demonstrated a more sophisticated grasp of the factors determining just equivalence in economic exchange, but at the expense of the evangelical and spiritual aspects of the tradition. While the Franciscan economic synthesizers who came after Thomas re-emphasized the evangelical foundation of the usury prohibition and selectively endorsed traditional natural-law objections, they also attacked core Thomistic-Aristotelian arguments in ways that revealed a more voluntarist, abstract, and even capitalist grasp of the economic field. From the fourteenth century onward both evangelical and natural-law supports of the usury prohibition steadily lost ground in practice and in theory, a significant exception being Luther's recovery of the older theological integration in his writing against usury, which has the last historical word.

The primary aim of this interpretative survey of medieval usury theory is to unfold its theological and philosophical complexities and draw out the admirable balances and dialectical tensions of its moral argument, particularly between sinful and redeemed humanity and between natural justice and christological love. In the present climate of economic theory that has little room for ethical considerations beyond those of contract and competition, it is salutary to be reminded of past Christian aspirations for property and economic exchange. There is scope even today for reaping theoretical and practical gains from the scholastic tradition of economic ethics.

With the transition to Erasmus in the fifth essay we depart from the medieval Platonist tradition in some respects but remain within it in others. Positively, Erasmus shares with the tradition a christocentric, idealist, and ecstatic ethic; negatively, he shares an aversion to philosophical and legalistic naturalism and rationalism. For Erasmus, as for Bonaventure and Wyclif, true discipleship is *imitatio Christi*, real participation in the Savior's moral perfections. He departed from his scholastic predecessors in his humanistic conception of Christian *paideia*, in the central role he assigned to the classical literary and rhetorical arts in evangelical communication. Discipleship, for Erasmus, was a kind of poetic *mimesis*, shaped by the rhetorical representations of Christ in the community of believers, beginning with the representations of Scripture. The ecclesiological, poetic, and humanistic cast of his ethics is quite close to some contemporary thinking, particularly the christocentric social *poesis* of John Milbank. To appreciate Erasmus as a social and political moralist, then, is not without current value.

"The Christian Pedagogy and Ethics of Erasmus" interprets the two most celebrated works of Erasmian ethical poetics: *The Praise of Folly* and *Complaint of Peace*. Joan O'Donovan understands the rhetorical movements of both pieces as representations of a Pauline "renewal of the mind" intrinsic to the moral integrity of the believer's conduct and to social and political judgment. Folly's oration of self-praise carries her listeners from "a fleshly to a spiritual vantagepoint," from complacent indulgence in the social marriage of virtue and vice to encounter with "the divine imperatives of world-denying, self-giving love." This spiritual transition implies a theoretical reorientation, from "a sophistical to a christological understanding of society." Pivotal to Erasmus's depiction of the purification of love and knowledge is the moment of highest satirical intensity in which the authorities of the Christian cultural and political order are displayed in their hellbent, demonic potency as expressions of the "spirit of worldliness."

In a different rhetorical tone the self-eulogizing complaint of Peace moves between two poles: on the one hand, the natural and divine, preserving and saving benefits of Peace for human society, that make her a uniquely suitable object for pious mimesis; on the other hand, men's habitual, compulsive mimesis of the warring demons. At the same time, her complaint moves from the universal cause of social strife in the destructive passions of humankind to the causes of international armed conflict in the destructive passions of princes. Conversion to the Spirit of Christ displays the character of war as an unbridled expression of human lust rather than as a political constraint, and of the principles of 'just war' as moral rationalizations rather than moral reason.

While appreciating the evangelical and prophetic strengths of Erasmian rhetorical pedagogy, the essay voices reservations about its ethical adequacy. It draws attention to moral aspects of created and fallen human community that his christocentric mimesis does not allow Erasmus to thematize, most particularly the lawful use of coercive power, and argues that a fully trinitarian moral pedagogy requires their thematic integration. Moreover, this integration ignores at its peril the contribution of late scholastic thinkers to politics, despite the biting humanist and Reformation criticisms of them (which Erasmian polemics so memorably illustrate), not least because they compose part of the backdrop to modern developments. As the next essay shows, late- and neo-scholastic theologians gave systematic expression to principles and ideas that have been determinative for modern liberal-democratic theory, yet in formulations more coherent with the older biblical-theological tradition than are modern formulations. So in seeking the theological renewal of contemporary political thought, we would do well to attend to them.

"The Challenge and the Promise of Proto-modern Christian Political Thought" explores the possibility of finding "a unified theological foundation for a renewal of liberal-democratic theory and practice" in the thought of the late medieval and early modern periods. To avoid the conceptual slide into arbitrariness that frequently mars such an exploration, Joan O'Donovan begins by clarifying the meaning of 'modern liberal democracy', distinguishing the principles and institutions peculiar to it from those it shares with earlier political forms. She proposes that modern liberal democracy is defined by the two principles of "maximization of individual and collective freedom and the equality of individuals in regard to freedom," and that these principles entail republican self-government, popular sovereignty, and egalitarianism. Moreover, the principles are internally related through the "economic anthropology" of subjective rights, in which individual and collective subjects have a "natural proprietary right over their spiritual and corporeal capabilities and acts" and, consequently, a right to "the outward means of securing and developing their personal property." In view of the social and political corrosiveness of economic rights anthropology, the challenge is to find in proto-modern thought an alternative way of conceptualizing liberal-democratic principles.

Her investigation distinguishes four proto-modern theoretical strands connected with the enlargement of freedom and equality: those of 'evangelical freedom' and 'natural' (or 'civil') freedom pertaining primarily (but not exclusively) to individuals, and 'civic republicanism' and 'mystical corporatism' pertaining to urban and ecclesiastical corporations. She traces the strand of *evangelical freedom* from William of Ockham's attack on papal tyranny and defence of the individual believer's epistemological authority, through John Wyclif's theory of 'dominion by grace' and advocacy of lay Bible-reading, to the Protestant Reformers' concepts of the bondage of the will, justification by faith, and the participation of all the faithful in Christ's royal, priestly, and prophetic offices. Throughout this development, she argues, individual liberty remained "embedded in communal structures of authority" and a balance was maintained between private and public ministries, epistemological and political authorities, the freedom and participation of individuals and their subjection to an aristocracy of the Word. Not democratization but education was the key to an ordered church polity within the proto-modern theological mainstream. Outside the mainstream, the pneumatological and perfectionist movements that cultivated democratic radicalism remained, of necessity, relatively episodic, peripheral, and restrictive in membership.

The strand of *natural* or *civil freedom* is principally about subjective rights, and so engages directly the problem of modern 'proprietary' formulations. In presenting the formative Ockhamist and Marsiglian conceptualizations of rights, undertaken in defence of Franciscan poverty, Joan O'Donovan points to their important non-proprietary features, and as well, to their wedding of subjective right, defined as the "power to perform a lawful action," to objective right, law, obedience, and duty. It was chiefly, she argues, the later Sorbonnist tradition of theorizing rights as 'faculties' (i.e., 'immanent spiritual capabilities' possessed by individuals) that unfolded the voluntarist, subjectivist, and proprietary potential of the concept. Their assimilation of individual freedom to proprietary right paved the way for conceiving political society in contractual terms, as formed by a compact among equal rights-bearing individuals. Nevertheless, late scholastic and early modern compact theory continued to recognize a framework of "divinely established social-moral bonds" constituting "natural patterns of human fellowship," as well as the postlapsarian character of government as divinely ordained and upheld judgment.

By contrast, the strand of *civic republicanism* comprised a more populist and egalitarian elaboration of rights. Its core paradigm was the medieval 'corporation', a social-legal entity that embodied principles of elective representation, delegated authority, collective lawmaking and the equality of its members. Its structure expressed the municipal culture of the merchant guilds, and its fraternal ethos blended well with popular Christian devotion and cultic piety. Theologians, however, were wary of recasting political society on the model of a self-governing corporation, with the relative exception of Marsiglio of Padua who took furthest the republican project in his largely Aristotelian *Defensor pacis*. More influential was Ockham's conservative integration of fundamental corporate rights with the longstanding ideas of Christian monarchy. Nevertheless, the persistent difficulties in harmonizing communal rights and God's rights sustained theological suspicion of the corporational legacy, intensified among the Protestant Reformers.

Less susceptible of republican interpretation was the ecclesiological strand of *mystical corporatism*, which emerged as an interpretation of the Roman church's hierarchy of priestly rule. The attempt of the conciliarist movement in the fourteenth and fifteenth centuries to enshrine corporational principles in the church's political constitution was theoretically coherent only as long as it preserved papal monarchy. When it threatened to undermine the latter, it lost both theoretical coherence and public support.

The essay's conclusion is that none of these theoretical enlargements of individual and corporate freedom, whether in the civil or ecclesiastical realms, offer an adequate foundation for contemporary democracy. Insofar as they achieve continuity with the older theo-political tradition, they resist full-blown republicanism and egalitarian democracy as incompatible with "God's continuing sovereignty over civil polity, the juridical task of civil government, and the waywardness of the multitude." Consequently, they do not resolve the question of whether our contemporary 'rights' polity has a theological justification; but they are not for that reason without critical and constructive import.

The same could be said about the work of Hugo Grotius, the formidable theological, jurisprudential, and political thinker of the early seventeenth century, whose thought on justice and subjective right is the subject of the final essay in the historical section. While Grotius, like many of his contemporaries, accorded a place to subjective rights in political justice, he did not have in mind anything like our liberal-democratic 'rights' polity. There is a current vogue for interpreting Grotius as an early architect of the liberal contractarian tradition of natural rights, along with Hobbes, Pufendorf, and Locke. On this interpretation, he presents a novel humanistic departure from the late scholastic treatment of subjective right shaped by the legacy of Aristotle and Thomas, which situates it within the context of objective right. Grotius is thus read as extending the scope of individual proprietary right, and so, the moral-political dominance of the 'proprietary subject', with the resulting attenuation of divine-human and social bonds. A principal aim of "The Justice of Assignment and Subjective Rights in Grotius" is to show that this reading of Grotius commits the hermeneutical error of divorcing his political from his theological reflection and so neglecting the shaping commitments of his political theory. When the mature Grotius is allowed to speak with his own voice, argues Oliver O'Donovan, he reveals himself as belonging to the post-Reformation revival of an older Christian conception of justice as 'judgment'. Moreover, he reveals himself as constantly wrestling with the Thomistic and Aristotelian tradition and offering original corrections of it, in conversation with Catholic neo-scholastics. These corrections, far from extending the scope of proprietary right, reduce it in favor of the more socially differentiating concept of a 'fitness'.

The essay begins with the lynchpin of the Thomistic-Aristotelian tradition, namely, Aristotle's two sets of distinctions concerning justice: (1) the distinction between a wider and a narrower meaning of the term, referring either to what accords "with virtue as a whole" or to "a partial virtue"; and (2) the distinction, within the second meaning, of two kinds of justice: one pertaining to the distribution of goods among the members of a political community, and the other pertaining to "rectification in transactions." In translating these distinctions into a Christian legal culture, "for which the primary category was *ius*," Thomas boldly spliced the two sets together to produce "a tripod of duties distinguished by the political status of their subjects and recipients." At the same time, he took over Aristotle's two types of relationship of equality — "geometric" and "arithmetic" — to describe distributive and commutative justice respectively.

Grotius's creative reworking of these formulations, of which the most important concerns Aristotle's concept of distributive justice, was driven by his reservations about subjective right. The innovation of his mature rights theory, contained in his major work of 1625, *De Iure Belli ac Pacis,* was to distinguish a 'strict' sense of right as 'faculty' from an 'imperfect' sense of right as 'fitness'. His facultative concept of right (like that of major neo-scholastics influenced by Sorbonnist theory), is proprietary, designating "a *suum*": that is, a "perfect moral quality" that confers a proprietary ('perfect') title to "have something or do something." Distinct from a 'faculty' is a 'fitness', which is a 'less than perfect': a 'potential' rather than 'actual' moral power to have or to do something.

The subject may possess an 'aptitude' or 'fitness' for a thing or action to which he/she has no proprietary claim. From the distinction of 'faculty' and 'fitness' issues Grotius's reinterpretation of Aristotle's two kinds of justice: attending to 'strict' right, he proposes, is Aristotle's "justice of transactions"; attending to 'fitness' is Aristotle's "justice of distribution," which Grotius renames 'attributive' or 'assignative justice'.

This novel alignment discloses certain weaknesses in both Thomas and Aristotle's expositions of the two kinds of justice, including the alignment with arithmetical and geometrical proportion, and in Thomas's case, with the private and public realms. Most importantly, the novel association of 'attributive justice' with relations of 'fitness' undercuts Aristotle's paradigm of geometric equality that "requires four terms, two people, and two treatments meted out," and assigns to each person "a share proportionate to their relative worth." For judging the 'fitness' of persons to actions or things does not always require comparisons, but rather a knowledge of the personal qualifications relevant to the concrete 'business at hand'. What attributive justice requires is a prudential and social judgment that grasps the variety of human actions and enterprises, and the virtues and capabilities they need, while rejecting all attempts to render social goods commensurable, or to achieve uniformity of criteria by applying restrictive concepts of personal merit or worth, egalitarian or not. The logic of attributive justice, suggests the essay, is less proprietary than that of Aristotelian 'distribution' which entails the "curiously abstract thought of unowned resources in search of the right owners"; moreover, it is implicitly critical of any approach to economic justice that seeks to preserve an "existing balance of merit" in society (whether equal or unequal), rather than exploring the various ways of "spending public resources creatively."

In addition, the essay shows how the concept of attributive justice promises a superior account of punishment to that produced by Aristotelian or Thomistic analysis, although Grotius did not himself fulfill this promise. The reason was his failure to understand that 'punishment reaches beyond the existing moral state of affairs to a *prudens dispensatio*, a judicious exercise of discretion in promoting social welfare'. He did not see that the retributive *form* of punishment could allow for society's 'creative initiative' in determining its *content*. Thus, understanding 'punishment as judgment' enables us to conceive it as the 'new act' by which society responds to a crime, 'express[ing] its moral quality truthfully.'

If both parts of natural right, 'strict' right and 'fitness', 'expletive' and 'attributive' justice, express the "rational sociality" of human beings, the second part also expressed for Grotius their rational relation to God. Contrary to the 'secular' natural rights theory attributed to him, the mature Grotius was clear that 'assignative justice' includes the "religious duty of obeying God" quite apart from "the contingent fact of divine revelation." Not that divine revelation is irrelevant to the formulation of natural right: rather, Grotius's thought manifests its indispensability. Not only did his particular insights into attributive justice have a theological origin, but his decision to introduce "a wider account of *ius* by way of Aristotle's second distinction" rather than "through the category of 'general' justice" was "decisively Protestant" in motivation. It expressed his theological conviction that objective (and so subjective) right, in its connection with positive law, cannot be coterminous with virtue, as in Aristotle, but presupposes sin. Right, for Grotius, is the correction of the failure of sociality, "the negation of its negation," not its fulfillment. 'Primary objective right' is "constituted by the prohibition of wrong . . . the negation of injustice."

*   *   *

While the historical studies of Part 1 reflect implicitly, and sometimes explicitly, on the waywardness of modern political thought, the essays in Part 2 address specific impasses of the liberal-democratic tradition. In each case, the forgotten and misunderstood past provides pointers for situating these impasses and indicates avenues through them.

With paradigmatic pride of place, 'Government as Judgment' addresses the peculiarly modern constitutional dilemma thrown up by the separation of governmental powers: namely, that the judicial review of legislation in the service of civil rights "deprives lawmaking of democratic accountability." The problem has arisen, Oliver O'Donovan argues, from the early-modern abandonment of the Pauline tradition of understanding all acts of government as 'judgment', i.e., as applying divine law (natural and revealed) to "the infinite possibilities of human wrongdoing." In the newer political orientation: (1) human lawmaking was elevated to the foundational political act on which subsequent judicial acts depend; and (2) the prerogative of lawmaking was invested in the people as a whole, which thereby became "the primary authorization" for every governmental act. As divine lawgiving was increasingly deemed irrelevant to human legislating, the latter took on the character of a continuous political re-founding *ex nihilo*. Now undertaken by a standing branch of government claiming sovereignty, legislation became the "continuous spring of rationality that sustains political society in being." Our contemporary crisis results from the late-modern reaction to the tyranny of legislative rationality, which is attempting to re-assert a prior, more fundamental 'natural' right by "erecting the courts as counter-legislature, an equal and opposite imitation."

The way out of this paralyzing governmental self-contradiction, the essay proposes, lies in a return to the Pauline model which allows governmental acts to be distinguished as different moments in the giving of judgment, according to narrower or broader public moral parameters. The biblical order of governmental acts reverses the early-modern order: not legislative, administrative, judicial, but judicial, administrative, legislative. The judicial enterprise of 'declaring the law' in particular cases requires the administrative founding and oversight of courts, which in turn requires correction or adjustment of the legal tradition by legislative declarations. The generic scope of legislation calls for a process of public consultation and deliberation, the traditional role of the English parliament as a "court of common pleas." Thus, unification of governmental *activity* within the practice of judgment grounds the unity of governmental *agency* in its ongoing dialogue with the commonweal. Only the restoration of this twofold juridical unity overcomes the idolatrous inflation of legislative power and the jurisdictional rivalries resulting from it, of which the most troubling today arise from independent courts, national and transnational, adjudicating cases under "universal rights" legislation.

The European Court of Human Rights, adjudicating cases under the European Convention, has acted as a rival jurisdiction to governments of signatory countries that have not domesticated the Convention. For signatory countries that are also members of the European Community, such rivalry is part of the larger challenge to good government presented by institutions of European integration. Understanding government as judgment is no less relevant to this larger challenge of determining where in the European political project lie the chief threats to, and opportunities for, good government. Our ninth essay attempts to show this through a critical analysis of Roman Catholic political thought over the past century, which has significantly shaped the aspirations and mechanisms of greater European unity. "Subsidiarity and Political Authority in Theological Perspective" looks at successive formulations of the principle of 'subsidiarity' within the progressive liberalization and democratization of Catholic political teaching, and concludes by situating Pope John Paul II in relation to this evolution.

The course of this evolution, Joan O'Donovan argues, is away from the juridical and toward the administrative and 'directive' (i.e., legislative) conception of government. In the neo-scholastic Thomism revived by Leo XIII at the end of the nineteenth century, the juridical (Augustinian) and directive (Aristotelian) orientations to government are found juxtaposed, as in Thomas's own political thought. On the Aristotelian side is Leo's concept of political society as the *societas perfecta* in the two senses of: (1) self-sufficiency — "possessing all that is necessary for 'living and living well'"; and (2) inclusiveness — "comprehending all other 'particular' communities and their 'private' goods." In that the *societas perfecta,* identified with 'the state', is alone authorized to define and realize the 'common good', the scope of governmental action is coterminous with the "good of the social whole and the aggregated good of its parts" (individuals and groups). On the Augustinian side is the Pope's restrictive characterization of governmental action as that "'required for the remedy of [an] evil or the removal of [a] danger'." Ambiguously (in terms of these contrasting orientations), he places juridical action in the service of natural rights: particularly individual property and familial rights. But most importantly, it is in the context of "juridically qualifying state intervention" that Leo XIII pronounces what will become the principle of subsidiarity: "that the state must not absorb the individual or the family" but rather permit them "free and untrammelled action as far as is consistent with the common good and the interest of others."

In subsequent papal teaching and Catholic reflection the subsidiarity principle becomes increasingly detached from the juridical circumscription of governmental action, and assimilated to systemic visions of the civil *societas perfecta,* such as Pope Pius XI's organic hierarchy of self-regulating corporations and Jacques Maritain's unified culture of public-legal rights. Maritain's polity of civil, political, and social rights completes the liberalizing, democratizing and secularizing of Thomistic theory. Subverting the traditional (Gelasian and Tridentine) 'two spheres' doctrine of church and state, it allows the church as "a universal, supernatural *societas perfecta*" to make "no institutional, communal claims on the body politic," but only such as are mediated by "the natural political rights of the Catholic believer *qua* citizen." Subsidiarity has now come to have less to do with the freedom of fundamental communities from unwarranted governmental intervention than with the instrumental role of government in the protection and advancements of 'rights'. This latter connection is retained by Pope John XXIII's "elevation of subsidiarity into a principle of global political organization" in his advocacy of a "worldwide public authority" to serve the international *societas perfecta* by safeguarding and promoting the equal rights of both persons and political communities.

The critical thrust of this essay is directed against the Thomistic-Aristotelian concept of the civil *societas perfecta* and its liberal-democratic reinterpretation as a framework for expounding the principle of subsidiarity. It argues that this concept, with its aspects of self-sufficiency and inclusiveness, presents a homogenizing and totalizing vision of political society. The concept is homogenizing because it suppresses the inherent disparateness of social goods as well as the divisions and disjunctions of human society under the conditions of human sinfulness. Whether the ideal is one of hierarchical harmony, organic-functional integration, or moral-juridical unification (through the public language of rights), the concept does not accommodate the ontological and moral diversity of postlapsarian associations. It is totalizing because it suppresses the eschatological perfection of society in the communion of divine and human love, which impinges on worldly society as a constant judgment and leaven of renewal. The unification of liberal-democratic society through the individualist and voluntarist language of 'rights' is the modern form of moral monism; for while this language pretends to recognize the moral pluriformity of society, it actually establishes individual self-determination as the overriding moral good. The moral monism of the 'rights' society is exacerbated in a transnational polity removed from the concrete particularity of social and political traditions.

The independent well-being of communities and institutions within society depends on recognition of their origin and end in God's manifold grace towards his human creatures, and their embodiment of binding claims on human action. It is only as they are seen to participate in the unique *societas perfecta* of creation renewed in Christ that their claims can appear in their moral depth and clarity. While papal social teaching over the last century has always proclaimed the eschatological presence of Christ's kingdom in the church as the final revelation of human community, Pope John Paul II has increasingly viewed the civil body politic from a christological-ecclesiological perspective. This provides a powerful antidote to the naturalistic secularism of liberal-democratic theory, but leaves in some obscurity the proper juridical form of political society. The essay concludes that the defence of ordered social freedom in relation to all levels of governmental activity, which the principle of subsidiarity intends, must keep in the forefront the limiting and limited communal bonds of political judgment, justice, and law.

The precise nature of these limiting and limited communal bonds is at issue in our tenth article, "Karl Barth and Paul Ramsey's 'Uses of Power.'" The politico-ethical differences between these two theologians are the more striking as their theological orientations are closer than may appear to a casual reader. Both approach the work of political justice from within the kingdom of Christ, subjecting it to his commanding authority and "the mastery of Christ-like love." They differ theologically in one respect: where Barth situates that work exclusively within Christ's kingdom, understanding it entirely in terms of its teleological completion, Ramsey situates it as well in God's preservation of sinful humankind. Nevertheless, Barth and Ramsey concur in the ambiguity of political justice as a witness to Christ's rule: "That our justice falls short of true atonement; that it fails to sanctify and regenerate while it judges and destroys; that when it kills it cannot raise to life again: there is the tragic gap which separates the authority of Christ from the authority of the witness; there is the 'indirect relation' between the God who alone does right and the right of the 'earthly city of God.'"

17 'casual reader'? Does a 'casual reader' look at any of this?

[handwritten annotation: Herbert ... [illegible] would join him there ... & so would I!]

What separates them, argues Oliver O'Donovan, is not the Augustinian 'gap', but their responses to it. While Ramsey's response appears to remain on the bleak terrain of an 'Augustinian realism' that accepts the tragedy of political judgment with sorrowful resignation, Barth finally turns away from this terrain "to locate a different ground on which a 'normal' politics can function." This ground is pacifist, involving the refusal of coercive power to take human life. For Barth the very deficiency of human justice, standing under the judgment of Christ's cross, dictates the humble renunciation of force, at least in the general course of the state's activity. At the same time, exceptional threats to the state's authority place limits on this normal renunciation — e.g., Hitler's "Revolution of Nihilism", in the face of which defensive measures "honor God."

In contrast to Barth's 'abnormalizing' of the political use of force, Ramsey accepts that its "possible use" is implied by "the ordered disposition of power" *(ordo)* that belongs to "the *esse* of politics," and "is inseparable" from its "*bene esse.*" In conjunction with *lex* and *iustitia, ordo* inheres for Ramsey in the political task of preserving the "proximate order" of earthly community "that is threatened with entropy too soon before the kingdom dawns." But the political vocation is not on that account pre- (or extra-) christological, but is "a fruit of that *provisional fulfillment* which is given us in the advent of Jesus Christ." Ramsey's dialectic of *bene esse* and *esse,* the essay points out, sets politics in the time of Advent, the time of messianic fulfillment marked by an "active struggle" between the new and the old humanity, between Christ's law of love and the deficient justice of fallen human nature. Barth's account of the Christ-event, by comparison, is not historically differentiated enough to leave room for Advent, with the result that political action tends "to disintegrate in an explosive fission of old and new," in the dissociation of an ideal, non-coercive, evangelical politics and an actual, coercive, un-evangelical politics.

Oliver O'Donovan draws attention to Ramsey's discernment of an analogous oscillation in American liberalism between an 'illusioned' inflation and a 'disillusioned' deflation of confidence in "the moral possibilities of political action," the former typically attached to domestic politics and the latter to foreign politics. The key to these oscillations, he suggests, lies in the enduring legacy in Western liberalism of Lockean contract-theory which confines the moral possibilities of politics to communities constituted by association, and relegates all external, intercommunal relationships to "the state of nature." Interpreting Barth's oscillation between a 'normal' and an 'abnormal' politics through the lens of Locke's legacy affords a sharper appreciation not only of the idealistic character of Barth's liberalism, but, conversely, of Ramsey's achievement as a faithful exponent of the older tradition, in which the ordered disposition of political power is situated "between the times."

Of concern to this essay as to the preceding one is the approach of liberal-democratic theory to international order. Ramsey understood that both 'illusioned' and 'disillusioned' liberalism undermine the neighborly cooperation of nations. Inflated political aspirations fuel the demand for global government directly, for only a single political agent can bring about and sustain lasting peace and justice. Deflated aspirations fuel it indirectly, for purely self-interested nations left to their own devices throw up only the most haphazard international order. Or moral deflation may produce the simple-minded *laissez faire* doctrine that "each nation's pursuit of its domestic interest is conducive to a better world." In the last century of Catholic political thought liberal inflation projected a global body politic under global political authority, integrated primarily through the charter of universal rights, as the only fully self-sufficient political community. This global rights-polity, composed of equal nation-states, comes under criticism in the eleventh essay for its defective understanding of "the nation" and, hence, of the community of nations.

While the chief target of criticism in "Nation, State, and Civil Society in the Western Biblical Tradition" is the modern 'civic' construction of the nation as a universal rights polity, the critical net is cast more broadly over the spectrum of modern concepts of the nation: 'romantic', 'functional', and 'civic'. The context for this analysis is the proliferation in the liberal-democratic era of state persecutions of minority populations; and attention is largely focused on the role played by the wedding of 'romantic' and 'civic' concepts in the political dynamic of such perversions. The ideological fusion of community rights and citizens' rights, far from extending justice to cultural, ethnic, and religious minorities, has more often than not exacerbated injustice by rendering political resolutions impossible. The underlying problem, argues Joan O'Donovan, is that government is seen as the instrument of a prior communal will, and this inhibits its proper work of giving judgment.

To overcome the inadequacies of prevailing constructs of nationhood it is necessary to recover the articulation of the nation from the Christian political tradition, in which all the conceptual elements of our fragmented formulations are given a theological coherence. This articulation is grounded in the biblical revelation of political authority and political community in the history of Israel, fulfilled in the "new Israel." It is grounded in God's covenantal election and royal rule of the twelve tribes, in Israel's possession of the land and the law as God's gift, in her political identity as a loyal and worshiping community. But it is also grounded in Israel's repeated rebellions against her divine ruler, in her exilic dispossession, her unfulfilled hope of historical restoration, and her messianic expectancy. And finally, it is grounded in the fulfillment of Israel's political vocation in "the earthly ministry, death, resurrection, and exaltation of Jesus Christ, continued in the earthly witness of Christ's faithful people to his coming kingdom." The passage from the "old" to the "new" Israel effects a profound change in the theological meaning and determination of the nation. As a "concrete territorial order of political power, judgment and tradition," the nation is no longer the vehicle of God's salvific governance of the world through the Spirit of righteousness, but the vehicle of a preserving governance that "sustains a space within the sinful human condition" for the gathering of a faithful people. While the natural and historical elements of the nation persist, they yield definitively to the "primacy of authoritative judgment and communal law."

The community of Pentecost, "the *telos* of earthly polity," reveals the inherent deficiencies and limitations of the earthly nation: of coercive power, of public judgment, and of historical-cultural self-definition. In the Christian formation of Western nations, these deficiencies and limitations have too often been ignored, owing in part to misappropriations of Israel's unique vocation. Inflations of national identity have also been provoked by expansive political pretensions on the part of the church, pursued at the expense of its true christological and eschatological identity. However, the evolving institutional structures of Christendom also facilitated mutual criticism of church and nation. By contrast, in the modern era of immanent nationalisms there has been little efficacious criticism of nation-state ideologies, especially of the secular civic faith that has defined "the nation" in the liberal West since the end of the Second World War, and forms the basis of international order through the United Nations.

The constructive portion of this essay endeavors to recover the twin theological themes that have elaborated the primacy of legal justice and have been the central pillars of the Christian formation of nations: the divine vicariate of rulers and the commonwealth as a body of law. In defending their continuing validity, Joan O'Donovan undertakes to dispel two contemporary misrepresentations of them. One misrepresents the ruler's divine vicariate as a species of state absolutism; the other misrepresents the modern rights polity (at the national and the international level) as a continuation of traditional natural law, and specifically of the *ius gentium*. The outcome of her effort is a sharper appreciation of how late-modern liberal ideology dissolves political tradition as such, and the reality of the nation with it, and conversely, how a liberalism that acknowledges authority beyond itself can renew political tradition even as it judges it.

Our last essay explores the contemporary homogenizing effects of liberal universalism and voluntarism operating in abstract political philosophy, industrial capitalism, and technological standardization, by focusing on the impoverished socio-cultural texture described in the title, "The Loss of a Sense of Place." 'Place' is defined as embodying the "reciprocal relation between nature and culture: geographical space mediating a possibility for human life in community." Since sharing space is the essence of 'place', public or common spaces are paramount in giving concrete expression to a sense of place, whether these are natural, artefactual or both. A sense of place involves participatory possession of public goods, the enjoyment of common ownership rather than actual use. Arising from such possessive sharing is a sense of "belonging to one another" which defines the fellow human being as "neighbor." The sense of place, and of the neighbor as fellow-inhabitant, is closely related to the sense of the nation, which organizes the reciprocal determination of nature and culture over a wider territory.

Our difficulty in recovering a sense of place today is exacerbated by a deep rooted misunderstanding of Christian moral universalism, which opposes it undialectically to moral particularism. Such an opposition places Christian faith on the side of the relentless thrust of technological society towards the universal and homogeneous state. For while the universalist stance perceives the inherent moral dangers in "loving one's own," it does not perceive its moral necessity. It loses sight of the intrinsic relation of "one's own" to "all the others," of the fact that the eschatological perfecting of love has a presupposition in natural ties. To clarify this relationship, Oliver O'Donovan has recourse to two biblical *loci*: the Israelite theology of the promised land as presented by the Deuteronomic historians and the parable of the Merciful Samaritan in St. Luke's Gospel.

The fierce attachment of the Deuteronomic historians to Israel's territorial possessions is, he explains, an attachment to a lost treasure. It arises from the conviction that the occupied land had been "the medium through which YHWH gave himself to his people." As a place consecrated to worship, the land always pointed beyond itself to the meeting of Israel with God. The land was lost, not as a gift not fully given, but as a gift not fully taken: Israel's collective possession of it was a test of faithfulness which "contained the seeds of . . . failure"; for the "rest" that the land offered was never "the rest of total possession in the unqualified, unmediated rule of YHWH, but rather a rest of partial success and qualified obedience."

The universal identity of "your neighbor" as "every man," transcending all natural boundaries and divisions, is often thought to be the moral of Luke's parable, with its profound rebuke to the spirit of Jewish exclusivism. But rather than recommending a placeless universalism, the parable "draws our attention to a particular kind of proximity": a contingent "nearness of pure place, unqualified by any relation or connection"; and in that proximity it discovers the

BE ch... it K your neighbour

Luth.

relation of neighbors. On the roadside, which is a "non-place through which we pass on our way from place to place," the parable finds "the meeting-place between a Jew and a Samaritan, the two historic inhabitants of that land," which through their immediate proximity constitutes the "new holy land." Rather than dissolving "the elect places" into pure universality, the parable (and, indeed, the Gospel) replicates them as "the matrix in which meetings between God and mankind" are shaped. For God communicates his love to human beings in 'relations of particular belonging' without prejudice to its universal scope; and the eschatological perfection of human community is not the abolition of these relations, but of their false claims to autonomy, which prevent them from being of mutual service.

In a society where "the neutrality and openness of passageways" has become a paradigm of social and political relationships, Christians should be in no doubt about the moral propriety of "a sense of place." It may be that the recollection of what has been lost is endemic to our sense of place in the era of liberal, technological homogeneity, in which all the modes of particularity expressive of the richness of human community have undergone erosion. If, however, such recollected loss belongs to our universal Christian pilgrimage through the vale of sin and tears that is fallen society, so the hope of the heavenly city undergirds a patient, courageous, and compassionate striving to discover its prefigurations in the allegiances available to us here on earth.

The 'place' of 'the political', then, that all the essays in this volume have sought to map, is the place of shadowy common allegiance and common action which brings into being both remote prefigurations of Christ's kingdom and immediate manifestations of Satan's. The freedom of common action that gives form to 'the political' may be false or true, depending on the universal in which it is grounded. Our critical energies in these essays have been largely devoted to charting the false universal in which the modern tradition of political freedom grounds itself: the universal self-possession of an abstract humanity. This false universal, we have tried to show, traps common action in a futile and destructive present, cutting it off from the relations to the common past and the common future on which political creativity depends — those of repentance and hope. To demonstrate the true ground of repentance and hope, and so of the genuine freedom of political action, has been the constructive thrust of our forays into the theo-political tradition. This ground is the Christ who has come in Jesus, and who will come again to judge both the living and the dead. The limited and deficient judgment that is the content of 'the political' belongs to the messianic era, but not in the way that the corporate action of the church belongs to it: for the church's action participates in the victory of the resurrected Lord, while political judgment only points to it.

PART 1

Moments in the
Theological-Political Tradition

History and Politics
in the Book of Revelation

OLIVER O'DONOVAN

[handwritten annotation: Bauckham is nearly always right on]

"The most powerful piece of political resistance literature from the period of the early empire." This judgment of the Book of Revelation, from an interpreter whose outstanding literary sensibility and scholarly mastery of its cultural and religious background has put us all in his debt, is not a difficult one to share.[1] The difficulty arises when we ask what we mean by "political resistance litera- ture." Is that a species of *political* literature, or is it *anti-political*? If a prophet contests the whole system of Roman power in the name of the sovereign God of Abraham, Isaac, and Jacob, does he contest all systems of political power what- ever, or does he point to an alternative? Or if, as the same interpreter continues, "Revelation takes a view from the 'underside of history', from the perspective of the victims of Rome's power and glory," how far can those victims see?[2] Only as far as the negation of the order which oppresses them? Or can they discern the outline of a liberating political order as well?

---

1. Richard Bauckham, *The Theology of the Book of Revelation* (Cambridge: Cambridge University Press, 1993), p. 38. Bauckham's work, in this book and in *The Climax of Prophecy* (Ed- inburgh: T&T Clark, 1993) crowns a remarkable century of the recovery of Revelation for Chris- tian understanding. Among the earlier contributors I cannot omit a word of gratitude to the Oxford exegete George B. Caird, whose commentary, *The Revelation of St. John the Divine* (Lon- don: A&C Black, 1966), first opened my eyes, as it opened the eyes of many others, to the signifi- cance of this book.
2. Bauckham, *Theology*, p. 39.

This article originated as the Tyndale Ethics Lecture 1985, delivered at Tyndale House, Cambridge, and published under the title "The Political Thought of the Book of Revela- tion" in *Tyndale Bulletin* 37 (1986): 61-94. It is here substantially revised, taking account of more recent literature.

To this question Richard Bauckham has inclined to give a restrictive answer. Responding to hostile objections from advocates of democracy and feminism to John's depiction of God's universal throne, he replies that what the "political imagery" really has in view is "transcendence." "John's purpose is certainly not to compare the divine sovereignty in heaven with the absolute power of human rulers on earth. Quite the contrary: his purpose is to oppose the two." John's critics seem "unable to understand real transcendence," which is a "relation between God and his creatures which is unique." The imagery has "a kind of apophaticism . . . which purges it of anthropomorphism, and suggests the incompatibility of God's sovereignty."[3] The core message of Revelation for Bauckham, then, is not a political one, but a message about the unique relation of the divine to the human. Political concerns, though powerful, are the object of negative criticism. If in general John "effects a kind of purging of the Christian imagination, refurbishing it with alternative visions of how the world is and will be," we may suppose that it is the images of political power that are purged, setting us free to envisage our relations with God and world apart from them.[4] We are set free to experience the transcendence of the divine in a way not comparable to our experience of political power.[5]

A very different answer is presented by Christopher Rowland. For apocalypticists, he claims, "historical events were the carriers of cosmic significance."[6] John's interest was shaped by the seer of the Book of Daniel, fascinated by the meaning of the succession of world empires in ancient history (though there is nothing in Revelation like Daniel's stories of the prophet in the royal court).[7] And an aspect of Revelation that "has not received the attention it deserves" is the millennium, "a period when the messianic reign will take place *on earth*."[8] In the new creation beyond the millennium, what is important is the coming of the new Jerusalem from heaven *to earth*, so that "the contrast between heaven and earth disappears."[9] There are continuities to be explored be-

3. Bauckham, *Theology,* pp. 43f.

4. Bauckham, *Theology,* p. 17.

5. Bauckham does not, however, speak uniformly in such terms. In saying that "it is precisely the recognition of God's absolute power that relativises all human power" (p. 44), he allows us a glimpse of a positive analogy between divine and human authority.

6. Christopher Rowland, *The Open Heaven* (London: SPCK, 1982), p. 38.

7. Rowland, *Revelation,* an Epworth Commentary (London: Epworth Press, 1993), pp. 50-3. Paul D. Hanson's judgment (*Visionaries and Their Apocalypses* [London: SPCK, 1983], p. 55) that Daniel's sequence of empires "serves one function only in the vision, that of indicating the point when the cosmic event at the centre of the vision would occur," can hardly be taken seriously.

8. Rowland, *Revelation,* p. 147.

9. Rowland, *Revelation,* p. 153.

26

tween God's final unchallenged rule and the possibilities of the present, however much the world is in rebellion against him. The millennium, an era which is not yet the new creation but is already the reign of Christ in his saints, provides a symbol of mediation between them. Rowland stops short of applying this symbol to Christendom, as generations of Christians, following Augustine, did; but he is at one with them in wanting to emphasize its suggestion that Christ holds sway even over an earth still awaiting new creation.

There is, however, a second question to be asked. If John of Patmos's political imagination is to be taken seriously, is it a helpful or a destructive one? A series of studies of apocalyptic as a literary genre which emerged in the 1960s and 1970s argued that the apocalyptic view of world history represented a flight from real society and history. "World history in its entirety," wrote H.-D. Betz in 1969, "is identical with the 'evil eon'. . . . The apocalyptic view of history . . . has . . . dispensed with historical thinking."[10] This thesis was taken up and developed by Paul Hanson in 1971, who contrasted two opposing views of the world, the mythopoeic and the prophetic. The prophetic view "recognized . . . divine activity as involving a movement from promise to fulfilment" and "embraces the flux and movement of history as the arena of divine activity," whereas myth "offers escape from the change of the historical process."[11] The birth of apocalyptic occurred when Deutero-Isaiah reintroduced mythic elements into the prophetic view of history, so resolving a difficulty in which the Deuteronomic tradition had become ensnared in the hopeless conditions following the fall of Jerusalem. Thereafter apocalyptic moved towards the mythic pole, drawing its readers "above the flux of the mundane sphere" to "a salvation won on a timeless, cosmic level."[12] Whereas in classical prophecy "the realm of human history was the realm within which the covenant relationship between YHWH and his people was being carried out," in apocalyptic events are "bound towards a predetermined end," and dynamic history becomes inflexible, "a timetable of cosmic events."[13]

The opposition of 'myth' and 'history' is central to this thesis. The decline of prophecy, Hanson thinks, followed the loss of a perfect balance between the two achieved by the classical prophets; confronted with the fall of Jerusalem, the tradition collapsed into pure history, while a subsequent attempt to recover the balance led to collapse in the other direction. Gerhard Ebeling, in an early

10. Hans-Dieter Betz, "The Concept of Apocalyptic in the Theology of the Pannenberg Group," in R. W. Funk, ed., *Apocalypticism* (New York: Herder, 1969), pp. 201f.

11. Paul D. Hanson, "Old Testament Apocalyptic Reexamined," in Hanson, ed., *Visionaries and their Apocalypses,* p. 40.

12. Hanson, "Apocalyptic Reexamined," p. 50.

13. Hanson, "Apocalyptic Reexamined," p. 57.

(1961) contribution to the discussion, summarized the new orthodoxy in the following revealing way: "The ground on which we are authorised to think God and history together in the right way (that is, differentiatingly) lies not in apocalyptic but in the unapocalyptic fact of Jesus. . . . Thinking God and history together in the name of Jesus leads of necessity to a criticism of apocalyptic, certainly not in the sense of a reinterpretation of apocalyptic in terms of a concept of revelation and universal history that is of Hegelian provenance, but in the sense that through his word God manifests his power over history by putting an end to the power of history."[14] The right way to relate God and history, that is, is to *differentiate* them, allowing history no revelatory status. Yet precisely that denial, he thinks, assures us of history's true importance. History becomes a messenger of God in the "unapocalyptic fact" of Jesus — unapocalyptic in the sense that he conveys no cosmic teleology and confers no perspicuous purposiveness upon history. The significance of the Christ-event for history is negative: it refuses history's claims to meaning and potency. The apocalyptic mistake is to think it can tame history as God tamed Leviathan, conceiving of a world-historical order which escapes from history by refusing the scandal that history poses for faith.

The charge that John is disengaged from history needs to be understood with a certain nuance. It does not mean that John had no interest in history; on the contrary, his critics suggest, his interest was very real, but very unhealthy. He hoped to find in history a direct disclosure of heaven's purposes; what he ought to have sought from history is something different. What is that? History is 'flux', in opposition to the 'timeless' character of myth and to the predetermination of events. Myth embraces every kind of determinism: on the one hand, the motionlessness of eternity, on the other, the foreseeing control of providential direction.

Behind this sharp opposition lies the mid-twentieth-century rejection of historical mega-narrative, associated in the English-speaking world with Karl Popper and in the German context with existentialist hostility to the reviving interest in Hegel.[15] It is rooted in a polar opposition between necessity and freedom, where 'freedom' is characterized negatively as the absence of structure and order. Politics, in this context, is understood as simple power; political freedom is the unconstrained interplay of power-holders, always at risk of breaking down into oppression of some power-holders by others, i.e., tyranny. Since that

---

14. "The Ground of Christian Theology," in Funk, *Apocalypticism*, 64.

15. So Betz conceived his article as a shot across the bows of the Hegelian revival, then led by the young Wolfhart Pannenberg, while Ebeling concluded his essay eccentrically with a four-page quotation from Kierkegaard.

risk would be supremely realized by the operations of a supreme power, faith is reduced to the deistic conviction that God refuses to direct history, so that history, opaque to ultimate values, may afford an open and undetermined space for freedom, indifferent alike to good and evil. Such a vacant and uninterpretable space is the sole alternative, in the view of John's critics, to value-totalitarianism. History must offer no purchase for the ideological interpreter. But could such a vacuum of intelligibility, we may wonder, even support such a thing as a *historian?* The word 'history' itself has become a term of art. For history can be seen as 'flux', as Jean-Yves Lacoste demonstrates, only from a pretended *post*-historical viewpoint: "after history comes nature".[16]

Taking these two questions about John's politics together, we may suggest that his interpreters form a triangle of oppositions. Bauckham and Rowland both intend to defend John against his liberal critics, but they have opposite strategies for doing so. Bauckham accepts in principle the objections to an ideological construction of history, but denies John any such intention; Rowland accepts that such was John's intention, but denies (by implication) the validity of the criticism. The explorations which follow may be taken as providing support for Rowland's general approach. Against Bauckham we shall agree that political criticism is not the deployment of a set of images to disclose a transcendent non-political reality; it is the expression of a hope for a real world order under Christ's rule. Against the liberal critics, we shall argue that their conception of the relation of freedom and necessity is much less plausible than that which John himself displays. In place of their quasi-Newtonian picture of freedom as residing in atomic power centers, he works with a more Einsteinian conception in which the possibilities of agency itself, as well as of society, are constituted by a field of energy. Political order does not rest ultimately on bare power, but on the truth of God's Word; and within the field of this Word "necessity" and "freedom" are mutually complementary and mutually dependent. John combines a diastatic emphasis on the difference of God and the opacity of historical events with a narrative of historical revelation that finds the ultimate meaning of human sociality in the rule of Christ.

The function of political criticism is to stretch the boundaries of the political imagination itself. If John's interest were only to mark the distance between religious proposition and political program, the amount of substantive political criticism he offers would be meaningless; for the pure religious adept

16. Jean-Yves Lacoste, *Expérience et Absolu* (Paris: Presses Universitaires de France, 1994), p. 148: "Après l'histoire vient la nature. Elle intervient comme ordre définitif des choses, comme ce que rien ne critiquera ni n'abolira." The whole discussion of the eschatological legacy of Hegel, pp. 136-65, throws great light upon our theme, and especially the role of Bultmann, for whom "le croyant . . . peut y échapper à toute trouble qu'un avenir . . . puisse jeter sur le présent" (p. 158).

has no more reason to criticize human tyranny than human justice. Criticism, in John's hands, is a discipline for avoiding the banal repetition and imitation of the bad in politics, a device for teaching us to speak of possibilities that we have still to learn how to think of and hope for. The imagination is purged not merely *from* the political, but *for* the political, too.

II

At the beginning of his vision proper, after the introductory letters to the churches, the prophet articulates a decisive question: why and how does the course of *history* impugn the excellence of *creation?* In the fourth and fifth chapters he sees a tableau of creation, in which the throne of God is surrounded by the symbolic representatives of the created order, ceaselessly offering their praise. But their hymns are interrupted by the discovery of a sealed scroll in the hand of the Most High. As a scroll, it represents history; as a sealed scroll, its contents are unintelligible. So the prophet presents his problem: how can the created order which declares the beauty and splendor of its creator be the subject of a world history, the events of which are apparently contradictory and without point? Only if history can be shown to have a purpose can the prophet's tears be wiped away and the praise of the creation be resumed. The words in which the assurance of the Gospel is announced to him are famous: "Weep not; lo, the lion of the tribe of Judah, the root of David, has conquered, so that he can open the scroll and its seven seals." And then, as the prophet tells us unforgettably, "I saw a lamb standing as though it had been slain" (5:5f.). The sacrificial death of God's Messiah is the event to interpret all events. It alone can offer human existence the assurance of cosmic meaning which is required. It justifies creation within history, and justifies history within creation.

With this announcement of his theme the prophet launches into the first of his three cycles of seven visions: the seven seals, the seven trumpets, and the seven bowls, which present us with successive views of the whole course of history, each with a closer focus than the last.[17] Between the second and third of these cycles John places the central episode of the book, around which all turn: the encounter in saving history between the two Christs, the true and the false. The cycles follow a common formal pattern: the Lamb breaks the seven seals, the angel blows the seven trumpets or pours out the seven bowls, and after each one something happens. In the first four visions of each cycle it is a natural or

17. See Bauckham, *Theology*, pp. 40f., and note especially pp. 82f. on the suppressed series of seven thunders.

political disaster. With the fifth or sixth the character of the event changes, exposing some aspect of moral or spiritual evil. The seventh of each cycle represents the victory of God over evil; yet the victory is at the same time the climax of the evils, since it is the exercise of divine judgment, the overwhelming of human wrath by divine (cf. 11:18).

It is not until the third cycle, the cycle of bowls, that John is ready to show us the divine victory emerging immediately out of the historical process, for not until then has he shown us how the course of history has from the beginning been an expression of the battle between God and the primeval serpent, the devil. So in the first two cycles the victorious climax is shown only indirectly, visible to faith but not yet fully disclosed. It still lies outside the reach of history. This is achieved by a simple structural device: before the seventh moment of the first and second cycles, there is an interjected episode which displays the meaning of that victory in terms of the anticipatory triumph of the church, a mirror, as it were, through which we can gaze at the ultimate moment. Thus the cycle of seals ends mysteriously, "When the Lamb opened the seventh seal, there was silence in heaven for about half an hour" (8:1). This silence, which is a space in the unfolding of the divine purposes for the prayers of the righteous, opens the way for the summoning of the angels with the trumpets and a moment of theophany, recalling the thunder of Sinai.[18] On its own this is entirely ambiguous. Only if we have taken note of the interjected episode between the sixth and seventh seals, which showed us the gathered faithful of Israel and the nations, can we take comfort from it; for the content of that episode explains the form of the silent conclusion: the four winds were held back, and the command was given to restrain the forces of judgment while God's servants were sealed on their foreheads (7:1-3). Something similar happens at the end of the cycle of trumpets. A long interval (10:1–11:13) precedes the sounding of the seventh trumpet (11:14-19), which, although it is announced as the "third woe," is only distantly overheard as voices of praise and thunder. But what that praise and that thunder means we have been shown before in the interjected episode which depicts the martyrdom and resurrection of the two prophets.

Richard Bauckham has demonstrated how John has attached the beginning of each sequence to the last scene of the preceding one in what he calls "a technique of overlapping or interweaving."[19] This creates the impression that

---

18. See Bauckham, "The Use of Apocalyptic Traditions," *Climax*, pp. 38-91, especially pp. 70-83.

19. Bauckham, "Structure and Composition," *Climax*, pp. 1-37, especially pp. 7-15. Also "The Eschatological Earthquake," in the same volume, pp. 202-4.

each new sequence of seven visions explores more fully the final stage of the previous one. Yet this carefully crafted relationship is not merely *chronological*. Though the seven trumpets are enclosed within the theophany of 8:5 and 11:19, which itself concludes the series of seals, what they reveal reflects on the content of all seven seals, and shows the course of history as a totality, seen now from the point of view of those who believe in God's action in history. For within the cycle of seals history has appeared as a chain of natural necessity. The four horsemen who open the sequence are summoned, not directly by the Lamb's breaking of the seals, but by a summons from one of the four living creatures out of the vision of creation. That is to say, it is the forces of *nature* that called forth the enterprise of war in its four degenerating phases, from its origin in ambition to its denouement in economic chaos and widespread death. War is undertaken as a form of natural self-assertion; but in its train comes the imperiling of social existence by depopulation and starvation. That is the puzzle of nature and history as the prophet conceives it. Nature carries the seeds of its own destruction. Political strife is the fatal overspilling of natural energies, which must eventually frustrate created nature and bring it to nothing.[20]

The fifth seal engages the question of justice through the unsatisfied cry for vindication which goes up to God from the afflicted righteous — not, however, identified as the church. Yet no divine intervention follows, but only, with the sixth seal, an atmosphere of dread and impending international disaster, in which kings, potentates, and commanders cower before geophysical and astrological disturbances, which may suggest to us, but do not disclose to them, the hand of God. And so the course of history, from which God is apparently absent, reaches its point of theophany only with silence. It conceals the hand that guides it. Yet what *may* be seen in history are the twin communities of praise, Jewish and Gentile.

In the cycle of seals, therefore, we are left with history as a problem; the vision of the elect before the heavenly throne appears rather as a suspension of

---

20. This departs from the time-honored interpretation of the seals as a development of the "signs of the end" in the synoptic apocalypses. See John M. Court, *Myth and History in the Book of Revelation* (London: SPCK, 1979), pp. 43-81, which yields a much more church-oriented reading: the horsemen represent the turbulent background of the first-century church, the martyrs of the fifth seal become Christian martyrs, etc. Without denying a measure of formal dependence on the synoptic tradition, I would doubt whether this does justice to the setting of the seals in the cosmic scenario of chapters 4 and 5. The sealed scroll was *already* in the hand of the enthroned Lord before the Lamb appeared to open it. Nor does it allow for the careful identification of the sealed saints as consisting of *ancient* Jews, the faithful from the twelve tribes of the Old Covenant, the number of which is complete, and of a still indefinite number of *contemporary* Christians of all races.

historical necessity than as a reconciliation of it. But in the cycle of trumpets a new perspective is added. The initiation of the chain of evils lies not with the forces of nature but with the prayers of the saints which ascend from the altar of sacrifice. The disasters — which in this cycle are natural, not political — are called forth by the demands of outraged justice. In the cycle of bowls the initiative is transferred again: it comes directly from God himself, speaking out of his heavenly temple, so that the disasters, which resemble the plagues of Egypt, are seen to be the direct work of divine providence. Successively, we come to see how the horrors of history, which appear at first to be self-contradictory, manifest a purpose.

The sequence of cycles, then, contains a part of the answer to the problem posed by the sealed scroll. Creation is vindicated by the necessity of unfolding events. The ambivalent term, 'necessity', perfectly captures the prophet's idea: necessity is, on the one hand, constraint, which deprives us of our fulfillment; it is on the other hand a form of order which underwrites the good in ruling out randomness and arbitrary meaninglessness. We are invited to read the legend of history by conceiving its tragedies as a progressive loss of freedom within which we may see the purposes of justice and the hand of God. Sheer arbitrariness is already set at a distance; the good is a controlling presence. Yet this answer can only be a partial one. For although divine judgment vindicates order, and created goodness with it, it is a negative vindication when order is imposed at the cost of freedom, not a positive vindication in terms of flourishing and perfection. A universe in which sinful existence is cancelled out by divine wrath has a kind of formal rightness; yet it is not worthy of the creator to be satisfied with such a vindication. What place is there for the restoration of freedom in this presentation of historical necessity as divine justice?

In the first place we see freedom exercised in prayer. The afflicted righteous who, in the fifth vision of the first cycle, cry out from beneath the altar, "How long?" (6:10) are told to wait, not merely in order that the divine purpose for others than themselves may reach maturity, but that their own freedom may be realized in the activity of prayer itself. When we first hear that prayer, it is no more than a cry of impotence. But at the beginning of the second cycle it becomes a prayer of power; for it is this prayer which the angel mingles with the incense on the altar, so that it rises before God (8:3); and it is this prayer which, when cast as fire upon the earth, sets loose the thunder, lightning, and earthquake which presage the seven trumpets. In the second place, freedom is exercised as prophecy, and here we touch on a theme close to John's heart, the theme of his own vocation. The interjected episode which lies between the sixth and seventh visions of the second cycle tells of the two witnesses who prophesy in God's name with great authority, are slain and rise to life again by the power of God. The believer, then, exercises freedom in speech: the speech of prayer which addresses God out of historical affliction, and the speech of prophecy which addresses mankind in the authority of God's word.

So creation is vindicated in two ways: by the judgment of God that is worked out immanently through catastrophe, and by the overcoming of constraint in the utterance of speech. Much of an answer has thus been given us by the end of chapter 11, at the climax of the cycle of trumpets. But it is a dialectical answer: constraint and freedom are present together, but not yet reconciled. The sphere of politics is a sphere of necessity, and the sphere of freedom is an anti-political sphere of prayer and prophecy.

This impression is confirmed in the episode of the two witnesses, in which John speaks of "the great city, which is allegorically called Sodom and Egypt, where their Lord was crucified" (11:8). The city, that pregnant symbol of all political life, is the concrete definition of the human urge to conquer when confronted by the prophetic rebuke of the Word of God. Conquest, which first let loose the horrors of war, has assumed a permanent form; it has embodied itself in an institution, opposed to the freedom of the Word of truth. Politics is power exercised against the Word. Yet John has not neglected to drop a hint of things to come: another view of the city is possible. The episode of the two witnesses began with a solemn ritual of measuring the temple, which was to be kept safe while the city around it, "the holy city," was trampled underfoot by the nations (11:2). This holy city is apparently the same as that called Sodom and Egypt — and it is also, though John will not grant it the dignity of the name Jerusalem, the city in which Christ was put to death. The political institution which appears as the embodiment of opposition to the truth may, below the level of appearances, be something else: it may be the holy city given over to desecration. Behind the phenomenon of power-against-the-Word there is the deeper reality of a political community consecrated to the Word. We are at least permitted to anticipate that the politics of conquest may be countered by an alternative politics of worship.

III

At the beginning of the twelfth chapter, introducing the central section of his work, John presents an allegorical narrative of the birth and triumph of Christ. This is of great importance to our understanding of what has gone before and what is to come after. The content of the first two cycles has been explored, as it were, *remoto Christo*. The souls of the righteous beneath the altar were not necessarily the souls of Christian faithful, but simply the souls of righteous mankind; the two witnesses who prophesied in the great city were not Christian witnesses, but figures from the Old Testament, the olive trees and lampstand of Zechariah, "the two anointed who stand by the Lord of the whole earth" (Zech. 4:14), slain in the appropriate city where every prophet must perish. Naturally, the course of history as seen in these two cycles reaches its climax in "the kingdom of our Lord and of his Christ" (11:15). Since it was the Lamb who opened the seals, we could expect nothing less. But only with the interjected episodes before the seventh stage of each cycle is a distinct reference to Christ introduced: the gentile multitude who have "washed their robes and made them white in the blood of the Lamb" (7:14), and the two prophets slain in the city "where their Lord was crucified" (11:8). Only with the dawning of the kingdom do we see how the righteous in either case have, in fact, been serving Christ all through the vicissitudes of their oppressive and apparently meaningless history.

But from that point on we are in the narrative of the messianic age. The central section of John's vision proceeds from the taking up of the Messiah into heaven to the expulsion and fall of Satan, the persecution of the church, and finally to the memorable description of the summoning of the beasts from sea and land and their oppressive and idolatrous political order. We should reflect on John's intention in situating one of his two chief passages of political criticism at this point, in such decisive relation to salvation history. The mainstream Western Christian tradition does not do this: it understands politics in terms of a providential dispensation *post lapsum,* a mark of Cain, a covenant with Noah, a scattering of Babel. It is not, of course, that John *contests* the relation between politics and providence, already sketched out in the two preceding cycles. But he wishes to identify something distinctive about politics in the messianic age, between the Ascension and Parousia of Christ. In this respect his approach bears comparison with the account of political authority in Romans and 1 Peter. For although these passages are important sources for the providential account, they also display a marked eschatological emphasis. We may innocuously call John's approach 'apocalyptic' and that of the Pauline strand 'secular', provided that we remember that secularity itself ("every human institution," 1 Pet. 2:13) is an idea situated in relation to the expected "day of visitation" (2:12). The Pauline strand, too, knows that we stand between the Ascension and the Parousia, that "the night is far gone, the day is at hand" (Rom. 13:12). If there is a contrast between the two approaches, it lies, perhaps, in the fact that Pauline believers pray for "a quiet and peaceable life" under their authorities (1 Tim. 2:2), whereas John expects those same prayers to let loose an idolatrous empire.

John's image of the blasphemous empire is heavily dependent upon the Book of Daniel. Yet the changes that John introduces into Daniel's pictures are

as important as the points of resemblance. There arises a beast from the sea —
"the sea" representing the abyss of chaos and disorder which was overcome in
the divine act of creation. But John's one beast combines the characteristics of
four in Daniel 7. He is not propounding a *history* of empire, as Daniel does, in
which each of the successive great powers, past and present, has a place. His interest, rather, is in empire as an eschatological phenomenon, evoked by the triumph of Christ. So the order of events in Daniel is turned on its head: where
the Old Testament prophet saw a sequence of historical empires being brought
to its close by the exaltation of the Son of Man, the New Testament prophet sees
empire as appearing in a new, temporarily limited form evoked precisely by the
exaltation of the Son of Man.

John's beast differs also in its relation to the dragon, "that ancient serpent
who is called the Devil and Satan" (12:9). Daniel's four beasts emerge from the
abyss of their own accord, where John's beast is summoned by a force more primeval than itself, which it resembles not only in the possession of ten horns (a
feature which they share with Daniel's fourth beast) but in the possession of
seven heads. The native element of the dragon was heaven. Cast down by
Christ's triumph, he looks for an earthly form in which to operate, and that
form is empire. In various ways the prophet suggests that the relation between
the dragon and the beast is a parodic reflection of the relation between God the
Father and God the Son. The dragon confers upon him "his power and his
throne and great authority" (13:2) in imitation of the enthronement of the Messiah. At the end of the Apocalypse evil is overthrown in two stages: the beast by
the victorious Messiah and the dragon by the all-judging Father. And there is
the feature of the healed wound, the symbol of messianic suffering and triumph, by which the beast parodies the death and resurrection of Christ. By imposing order upon chaos, empire seems to introduce the promise of resurrection into human affairs.[21] Throughout John's presentation of the beast and its
empire we find him absorbed in the pretensions of evil to provide a positive focus for political cohesion. At heart, he believes, evil is simply self-destructive
and provides no ontologically secure basis for community, yet it pretends to do
so. John's critique of that pretence is that it is a mere derivation; it achieves what
it appears to achieve only by crude imitation and distortion. So the authority of
the beast is established by the names of blasphemy which it bears, a parody of
one who has authority by bearing the divine name before mankind.

---

21. The symbol is commonly, and with good reason, taken as a reference to the myth of
Nero Redivivus (cf. Bauckham, "Nero and the Beast," *Climax*, pp. 384-452.) Yet it makes its point
independently of this allusion, simply in terms of the phenomenon of empire itself, which looks
as though it brings political life out of death.

Parodic imitation is carried even further with the appearance of the second beast, the beast from the land also called the "false prophet," which accompanies the false Christ in literal fulfillment of Mark 13:22.[22] The expansion of the Father-Son relation into a fully trinitarian account of evil is quite self-conscious. The Holy Spirit is constantly discussed in Revelation in connection with prophecy.[23] The beast from the land is called the false prophet, and unlike Daniel's he-goat, speaks; it is his *raison d'être* to be the ideologist of empire and to support his speech with miraculous signs. John thus allows that though the essence of political oppression is conquest and the denial of true speech, the falsely messianic empire must conceal its character with a plausible appearance of true speech. The authority of falsehood is of critical importance to the Antichrist's regime, but the only authority which falsehood has is that which it has borrowed from the truth.

The false prophet maintains the claim of Antichrist to possess his subjects wholly, as Christ possesses his saints, by a parody of the baptismal seal. In the light of twentieth-century experience we are fond of seeing here a description of what we call 'totalitarianism', and this is not mistaken, but too limited.[24] The essence of totalitarianism is the assumption of all independent authority, natural or spiritual, the authority of teacher, parent, priest, or artist, into a unified authority of political power. But behind that evil, John would show us, is the more fundamental evil of pseudo-messianic ideology, a claim to ultimate loyalty based on the occupation of a decisive role in history. By posing as the emissary of divine redemption, the empire brings the final condition of hell into history. It provides a concrete form in which mankind can give itself, heart and soul, to a community of evil.

Here we can only underline the contrast with the Pauline approach to politics. The state of government for which Christians are commanded to pray is one in which there is space — "a quiet and peaceable life" — for the issue of ultimate allegiance to be raised and answered through the preaching of the gospel. John does not challenge the suggestion that we *ought* to pray for such a space; yet he does not expect that prayer to be answered in the form in which it is made. Under the pressure of the gospel and the Christian allegiance that it

22. Although the second beast is described in details from Daniel 8:3, its immediate source is the later apocalyptic tradition, which speaks of two beasts, Leviathan and Behemoth (cf. 2 Esdras 6:49ff.; 1 Enoch 60:7f.; 2 Baruch 29:4).

23. On the designations and functions of the Spirit in Revelation, cf. Bauckham, *Theology*, pp. 109-25.

24. I agree on this point with Christopher Rowland, *Revelation*, p. 115. He is on less sure ground, however, when he views the critique generically as directed at 'the state' (cf. also p. 133) — a category of which John, like other ancient thinkers, had no conception.

evokes, political authority comes to demand an opposed and ultimate allegiance. The mutual exclusion of good and evil begins to take shape within history. Those who do not worship the beast are thrust out from the market, the place of 'distanced' commerce, communication without commitment. The closure of the market on ideological lines is a sign of the separation of the communities. Yet even in this development, John would tell us, which is the very opposite of what we have prayed for, we can see God's most direct route towards the day when all our prayers for justice will receive their truest answer.

IV

It is one of those puzzles with which John confronts his interpreters that he has not just one, but two dominant images for the Roman empire. After the reign of the beast from the sea and the false prophet, we meet, in the first of the concluding visions of judgment and triumph, the Great Whore. And as though to force his interpreters to confront the puzzle, John sets the Whore riding upon a beast which, despite its acquisition of a scarlet coloration, is none other than the beast from the sea, still rising from the abyss (17:8).

The best explanation for this dual imagery, in my view, is that the beast represents empire quite specifically as the phenomenon of the messianic age, evoked by the triumph of the Christ-child and the restricted dominion of the devil upon earth. But empire as such had long been the prevailing political pattern of the eastern Mediterranean world. The prophet had, therefore, to bring together empire as a standing feature of world politics and the eschatological heightening of the phenomenon which marked the era of the church. The paradigm of world empire in the Old Testament was Babylon; in giving that name to the Whore, John intends to stress the continuity between the prophets' experience of Mesopotamian empire and the contemporary experience of Rome.[25] The Whore is not Rome *simpliciter.* She is Rome as imperial power, or Babylon transferred to Rome, the old familiar figure brought out from retirement by a new patron, of whose demonic origins she is comfortably unaware, and set up in a new home to be used for ends she cannot begin to understand. Thus John is able to present the political situation of his day from another angle, examining the general features that it shares with empires of the past, yet not withdrawing from the particular claims he has made about the character of empire in the messianic age. And he wishes to stress that empire, simply as a phenome-

25. The name is hardly a device for concealment. When John points out that this Babylon sits on seven hills, the hint is too heavy for the dullest reader to miss.

non of human politics, has a fate coming to it: the Whore, as the prophets said long ago, is destroyed by her lovers. The beast himself, however, has a different end in store.[26]

Already in chapter 14 John has heard from the lips of one of the three angels entrusted with the "eternal Gospel" some words recalled from the Isaianic apocalypse: "Fallen, fallen is Babylon!" (Isa. 21:9) The prophet's hope for an end to imperial bondage is fulfilled by Christ's coming to the world. But the *form* of the quotation at 14:8 deserves closer scrutiny. These words are immediately followed by others from the Babylon oracle in Jeremiah 51:"who has made all nations drunk with her wine." Nowhere is John more careful in his use of Old Testament material than in his presentation of Babylon. Into this composite quotation he further inserts a description of the wine as "the wine of the wrath of her fornication." When we first hear these words, their bearing seems evident enough: the wrath is the wrath of God, seen in the growth of the Chaldean empire, and all nations have been made to experience Babylon's "fornication," i.e., her indiscriminate conquests. But when they return slightly amplified at 17:2, the reader wakes up to what the author has done: into the tissue of Babylon quotations he has woven the prophecy against Tyre at Isaiah 23:17: "At the end of seventy years, the Lord will visit Tyre, and she will return to her hire, and will play the harlot with all the kingdoms of the world upon the face of the earth." But this puts a different complexion upon the word 'fornication'; for the fornication of Tyre is not indiscriminate conquest, but promiscuous trade. And as we read the lament over Babylon-Rome which occupies chapter 18 of the Apocalypse, we find it composed in about equal parts of allusions to military Babylon in Jeremiah 51 and to mercantile Tyre in Ezekiel 27. Details of the Babylon prophecy take on new significance as they are associated with Tyre: the "many waters" on which the harlot sits, for example, began as a reference to Babylon's elaborate canal system (Jer. 51:13), but become the Mediterranean Sea, on which the great commercial city plies her trade.[27]

It is possible to see this merely as a happy use of diverse materials to characterize the hold which Rome has upon the nations of her empire, a hold

26. Bauckham, "The Economic Critique of Rome in Revelation 18," *Climax*, pp. 338-83, distinguishes the Beast from the Whore in terms of the military might of empire and the economic luxury of the city. Plausible enough in itself as a rendering of the images, this interpretation fails, in my view, to do justice to the identity of the beast with that in chapter 13, and to the prophet's interest in the course of salvation history. Furthermore, it forces a rather unnatural distinction between economic criticism, supposedly directed at the city, and the criticism of conquest, supposedly directed at the beast.

27. On the importance and details of the trading aspects in chapter 18, see Bauckham, "Economic Critique," *Climax*.

very much rooted in commercial culture and by no means merely a matter of force majeure. Yet this would underestimate our author, for whom it is no circumstantial detail that the new Babylon has learned the arts of the old Tyre, nor is his use of the description of trade as "fornication" merely decorative. The significance of this marriage of Tyre- and Babylon-motifs is that trade, too, as much as conquest, violates the integrity of communities dominated by the stronger trading power. Trade is a kind of cultural promiscuity by which one power exploits and drains the resources of many others. John is certainly to be counted among those who have seen mercantile enterprise as a tool of imperialism. The tyranny of the beast in chapter 13 was exercised through the market. And he reserves for the conclusion of his lament on Babylon-Rome a quotation from the Tyre-oracle, Isaiah 23:8, to which he gives great prominence: "Thy merchants were the great men of the earth" (18:23). To the ancient world accustomed to government by landowners and military chiefs, it was a paradoxical sight that confronted the astonished Israelite prophet when he looked upon Tyre: a society governed by merchants, an ancient Venice! This paradox was the key to the power of the world empire under which the prophet lived: it ruled over nations by exercising commercial and cultural monopoly.

In Ezekiel's lament over Tyre the wealthy seafaring classes wail and weep at her fall, while the "merchants among the peoples" rather unexpectedly "hiss" (Ezek. 27:36).[28] John allows no such division of opinion over the fall of his Babylon-Rome. Without her there would be no commercial endeavor at all, so that the merchants join the seafarers in weeping at her destruction. Her end means the end of all cultural endeavor: harpists, minstrels, flautists, and trumpeters fall silent; crafts are abandoned; basic cultural activities, such as grinding and lighting lamps, are let go; weddings are not celebrated.[29] But to the list of those who lament the loss of culture John adds the "kings of the earth," the very figures whose independence has been drained away by their fornication with this monopolistic cultural force.

This is a point on which we must linger, for the relation between the empire and its client kingdoms is central to the prophet's view of how empire comes to its destruction. The beast from the abyss boasted seven heads and ten horns, explained in chapter 17 as follows: the seven heads represent both the seven hills of Rome and an unfinished series of emperors, of which, John tells

---

28. Presumably because Tyre's dominance has excluded them from the market share to which they felt entitled. But note the view that this is an apotropaic 'whistling' to ward off ill-luck (W. Eichrodt, *Ezekiel* (London, SCM Press, 1970).

29. Cf. Jer. 18:22f.

us, the sixth is now reigning.[30] Beyond this series the beast is to have a final manifestation as an "eighth." The ten horns are ten kings, but not, as in the model in Daniel, a *series* of ten, for they all act together in concert. They must, then, be the kings of the earth who have committed fornication with the harlot and over whom she exercises dominion; they are the subordinate powers on which her extensive empire of trade and conquest relies. These kings, John predicts, are to receive authority for one hour together with the beast (17:12). We see this moment in closer perspective at 19:19, when the two Messiahs meet in battle. It is the hour of the mystery of evil, in which the beast takes form as an eighth emperor. At this point the ten kings will unite with the beast to make war on the Lamb (17:13-14), and turn against the Whore, devouring her flesh and burning her up with fire (17:16); and this will be according to God's purposes, who has "put it into their hearts to carry out his purpose by being of one mind and giving over their royal power to the beast, until the words of God shall be fulfilled" (17:17). It is a confusing scenario: the kings receive their royal power at the end of history, unanimously renounce it in favor of the beast, then turn upon the empire which has nurtured them, lament the fall which they themselves have encompassed, and finally turn self-destructively against the Lamb. What sense can be made of it?

John's analysis of empire sees it as "fornication," the surrender of individual integrity in undisciplined and destructive commerce. Empire is not simply an extreme case of unified rule; it is a coalescence of powers that drains integrity from all but the dominant partner. The kings are at once the dependents of empire and its victims. Their relation to it is a mixture of resentment and need characteristic of dependents. The climax of the career of empire, then, is its dissolution under the force of the resentment which it has engendered. The 'unity' which it has effected achieves its height in that 'one mind' which unites its dependents in rebellion against the source of their own strength. The ultimate paroxysm of self-destruction is the paradoxical disclosure of the unity engendered by imperial means.

But this general thesis about the end of empire is woven together with an eschatological narrative of the disclosure of evil as messianic pretension. The beast is destined to turn against the empire it has promoted. The mystery of evil may have provisional form in an apparently coherent political structure; but it can complete its self-disclosure only as every positive element borrowed from creation is banished and confronted in battle. Its goal is the vanishing point of unity in pure negation. The logic of the beast's end and the logic of the Whore's

---

30. For an argument that this series should not be taken literally in terms of the Julio-Claudian succession, see Bauckham, "Nero and the Beast," *Climax*, pp. 406-7.

end are the same, predatory power collapsing in on itself. And so the two ends are coordinated. As the client kings discover their unity in turning against its source, they offer the purest worship to the beast; and at that point the beast can make his final throw against the Lamb, carrying the forces of negation against the throne of God himself. But even the unity of evil is a borrowed unity. Its purposefulness was always a sign of predatory dependence on the good which it denied. The diabolical project of claiming sovereignty was a self-contradiction from the beginning. As the collapse of empire, then, reveals the operation of divine providence, so the collapse of this messianic empire will reveal the final rule of God's Messiah over history.

V

Almost every political observation made by John so far has been criticism. The paradigm of political activity has been imperial conquest; the permanent political institution, the city, has merely served to sustain and develop the exploitation of imperial dominion by commercial means. The exercise of human freedom in response to the Word of God has thrown the believer into irresoluble conflict with the organized community. And in these last days empire has taken on a new significance as the form in which the Antichrist lays claim to mankind's ultimate allegiance.

The mainstream Western tradition of politics, derived from Augustine and Gelasius, might expect at this point to see the church introduced as a balancing factor, a form of social life in which the predominance of truth and love is maintained, imperfectly but really, in a form of social organization which points beyond itself to the city of God. Strikingly John refuses to take this path. Not even in the church can we find an alternative form of political existence to that which has taken shape as empire. The faithful believer appears in history as an individual ("him who conquers" in the letters to the seven churches) or as a pair (the two witnesses), standing against organized society. The very word "church" is used by John only to designate those equivocal communities which he addresses in his introductory letters. There is, on the face of it, no place for the church catholic on earth. But this startling silence is not intended as a denial. However equivocal when viewed one by one, those churches add up to *seven*, which, as in the use of the designation "seven spirits" for the Holy Spirit, points to a catholic unity behind them. What John intends is to direct our eyes to the *source* of this new and real political community. We encounter it first in heaven, in the gathered Jews and Gentiles of chapter 7 and in the community of the first fruits of chapter 14.

Worship, for John, characteristically takes place in heaven — which does not mean that worship does not take place on earth, but that it is nourished and facilitated from beyond the resources and from outside the frames of reference that obtain on earth.[31]

John's eschatological approach to ecclesiology has this point in view: the root of any true political order, in which human beings can relate to God and to each other lovingly, is the conspicuous judgment of God. The good order of society is founded upon a judgment *(dikaiōma)*, a declarative act which establishes a justice *(dikaiosunē)*. Without God's judgments we cannot comprehend how we may live together. In judgment the paradoxical conflict beween the freedom of the Word of God and the necessity of immanent justice in history is resolved. God's Word becomes judgment, in that its freedom creates the order of a concrete society; and the necessity of history becomes judgment, too, in that its tragedy is turned into the freedom of the saints' corporate obedience. It is quite clear at what point in the Apocalypse we are permitted to see this coming together of necessity and freedom. It happens in the third cycle of seven visions, which is introduced by the words of those who have obeyed and conquered the beast, "Thy judgments have been revealed!" (15:4), and it is accompanied by a confession of God's justice from the afflicted innocent beneath the altar: "Yea, Lord God the Almighty, true and just are thy judgments!" (16:7). It happens precisely at this point because in the preceding section we have seen the Christ revealed and exalted and have heard the angels proclaiming the eternal gospel, concluding with the vision of the Son of Man coming upon the cloud to judge. We may, then, expect that in the concluding sections of the Apocalypse we shall be shown the outline of a new social existence founded upon the judgments of God. This cannot be a product of history, because it is brought about by the judgment of God upon history. It is given from heaven, descending like a bride prepared for the bridegroom.

We have observed already that the vision of divine conquest, the second of the three concluding sections of the work (19:11-20:15), presents the triumph over evil twice, each time under two aspects, as a battle and as an act of judgment (described by the verb *krinein* this time, not by *dikaiōma*, indicating a reactive, rather than a constitutive judgment.) Before the battle involving the mythical Gog and Magog with Satan, which is resolved by fire from heaven and prepares the way for the universal judgment before God's white throne, there is the engagement conducted by the Messiah, "the faithful and true," riding on a

31. Cf. Rowland, *Revelation*, p. 47: "Heaven offers that alternative 'space' for God . . . the place where God is acknowledged."

43

white horse against the beast. His victory is shared by the faithful, who are seated on thrones with him and reign with him for a thousand years (20:4). This scenario invites us to consider the share in authority and sovereignty which is given to all members of a well-constituted community. Only the victory of the true Messiah over the false can make this possible. The word of truth has first to take form as a sword issuing from Messiah's mouth, to defeat those who live by the sword; then it may take form as a judgment, ennobling and dignifying those whose social hope has been founded upon it. There is, of course, something paradoxical about the picture of the Prince of Martyrs at the head of an army. It is an image which seems to negate itself, canceling, rather than confirming, the political categories on which it draws. It is what Aquinas called the "symbolic predication of proportional analogy." What is less often observed is that the analogy of *judgment* is not merely symbolic, and that here the political language does not negate itself. The idea of an ordered social existence under the authority of divine *dikaiōma*, participating in the exercise of human *krima*, is not a paradoxical form. It conveys to us a hope that in the life to which we are summoned with Christ we may experience as political reality that authority of truth and justice which political society on earth has consistently failed to achieve.

The implication for our question is that if God's word of judgment pronounced in Christ is the foundation for a new order of society, the witnesses who challenged the prevailing political order in the name of Christ were not acting anti-politically or purely negatively, but were preparing the way for a new foundation, one constituted by participation in the exercise of the Messiah's authority. Yet when John turns from the triumph of the Messiah to the triumph of the Father, we are shown a more fundamental act of jurisdiction, in which there is no participation. To be part of an ordered community is to share in the exercise of its proper authority, yet, more profoundly, it is to be subject to God's authority. As from God's true speech flows all possibility of true human speech, so from God's true judgment flows all possibility of true human judgment. The hope of being participators in the exercise of righteous judgment leads back to the hope of being the object of it. For only in standing before the divine throne and being judged there can any judgment of our own be grounded and authorized. John proceeds from the judgment of the saints to the judgment of the Father as from an effect to a cause.

Upon how we read the ecstatic chapter with which Revelation concludes there turns a great deal for our view of John's political perspectives. Although what we see there is *future,* it also descends from heaven *to earth.* That is to say, it is the conclusion of our earthly historical present which awaits it, not a cancellation of it.[32] Part of its impact springs from the fact that we have come all this way, observing nations, races, armies, empires, kings, princes, and merchants, simply to see a city, which we might have thought of as an elementary building-block of human society rather than a crowning accomplishment. We have, of course, met one city already: Babylon-Rome, which was "the Great City," the epithet distinguishing her from the New Jerusalem, which is "the Holy City." John underlines the parallel between the two cities by the close verbal echo of 17:1 at 21:9: "Then came one of the seven angels who had the seven bowls . . . and said to me, 'Come, I will show you. . . .'" In the opposition between these two the whole conflict of good and evil is worked out: the city is the bride and the city is the whore.

But behind the opposition we recall a hint of their fundamental identity. In chapter 11 John was commanded to measure the temple but leave the outer court unmeasured, since it was given over to the gentiles who "will trample over the *holy city* for forty-two months." In this same city, apparently, God appointed his two witnesses to prophesy and be slain, and their bodies to lie "in the street of the *great city* which is allegorically called Sodom and Egypt, where their Lord was crucified" (11:2, 8). Here, then, the two epithets are assigned to the one city, which on this occasion is neither called Babylon nor Jerusalem, though the presence of the temple and the reference to Jesus' death there identify it with the historical Jerusalem. Here is the clearest possible statement of the original unity of the human community, set against the recurrent emphasis on its division. The holy city has lost its name and its sanctity, apart from the temple in its midst. It is corrupted into a denial of itself.

The details of John's heavenly Jerusalem are drawn primarily from the vision of the temple-city which occupies the concluding nine chapters of Ezekiel, but there are significant revisions. Ezekiel's city is built around a temple and set in the midst of the reorganized holy land. John's is a city without temple, and is set in the midst of a redeemed earth. In a highly significant comment on Ezekiel 47:12 John adds that the leaves of the trees beside the river are to heal *the nations* (22:2), so pointing to the restoration of the whole human community, as the older prophet never did. In the light of this we may wonder why, in equipping his guide with a measuring-rod (21:15), John did not follow through the argument of Zechariah 2:1-5 and declare that the eschatological city should be un-walled, a logic he will not hesitate to follow when it suggests the abolition of the temple.[33]

---

32. Cf. Rowland, *Revelation*, p. 47: "In the present age heaven stands over against earth. That is not part of the permanent order of things. God wishes to walk again in paradise in the cool of the day and tend the garden of the created world."

33. That Zech. 2:1ff. was in John's mind is clear from 11:1.

The answer is apparently that he saw the city's walls not simply as a protection, but as a definition. The gates and walls give form: their twelvefold structure confirms the city's continuity both with Israel and the church; but the ever-open gates show the elect community in its appointed openness to the world, providing the light by which the nations walk and the shrine to which the kings of the earth bring their glory (21:24f.). To the reader who is not attuned to John's dialectical use of images, this is a disconcerting moment. How can there be a humanity living outside of the redeemed Jerusalem? As the city of the faithful, the heavenly Jerusalem contains universality in itself. It *is* restored humanity, and outside it there is nothing but rejection (22:15). Yet it is also the elect people, whose destiny it is to shed God's light into the world, and this aspect is of special importance as it balances the resentful and destructive relation of the client kings to the imperial city. There must be a mutuality of peoples and authorities, such as was destroyed by empire; and yet this is compatible with the exclusion of every service of evil.

John's city, like Ezekiel's (48:35), is the place where YHWH dwells (21:3). But whereas Ezekiel expresses this by making the temple dominate the city, John "saw no temple" (21:22). And whereas for the author to the Hebrews the cultic is but the shadow of good things to come, for John the presence of God in the community is unmediated. Therefore the temple "is" the Lord God Almighty and the Lamb, absorbed into their throne. At 16:17 he heard God speak "out of the temple, from the throne, saying, 'It is done!'" but now the voice which was then mediated through the temple speaks from the throne immediately (21:3), no longer in secret communication with mankind, but in open settlement of the affairs of the universe.

Its words (21:3-8) form the climax of the Apocalypse, giving a decisive interpretation to the final vision, which is itself the interpretation of all the visions that have gone before. They consist of two Gospel declarations, one of reconciliation ("Behold, the dwelling of God is with men . . .") and one of judgment ("To the thirsty I will give from the fountain of the water of life . . . but as for the cowardly . . ."). These two flank three short utterances about the beginning and end of history: "Behold, I make all things new!"; "Write this, for these words are trustworthy and true!"; and "It is done! I am the Alpha and the Omega, the beginning and the end." With these three we stand at the *sanctum sanctorum* of history. Everything is stripped away; even judgment and reconciliation stand to one side. God who by his Word created the heaven and the earth now by his word makes all things new, giving creation a history and a fulfillment. The words "I make" and "It is done!" complement each other: there is no futurity about the first and no preterity about the second. History is summoned into being by God's ever-present declarative act, and then and there it is accomplished, reflecting back the glory of the one who summoned it, who is now known as Alpha and Omega.

But in between these two there is the command to the prophet, "Write!" At the heart of the ineffable being and act of God the prophet finds his own vocation, for in God's decision to constitute history, there is the decision that written history should make God known. He who can make himself Alpha and Omega of history, declares himself so through prophecy. The heart of God's self-announcement is that he is the self-announcing God. "In the beginning was the Word" (John 1:1). On that self-announcement mediated through prophetic writing the holy city is founded. At the heart of politics is true speech, divine speech, entering into conflict with the false orders of human society, the guarantor of the only true order that the universe can ever attain.

[handwritten marginalia, left] a most interesting survey — How I really think Snacklam is right!

[handwritten marginalia, right] what can a practising politician or a historian actually make of this? How does the last sentence actually work out for the House of Commons MP?

The Political Thought
of *City of God* 19

OLIVER O'DONOVAN

Book 19 of *The City of God*, one of the high points of patristic literature, has a central place in any attempt to describe Augustine's contribution to Western political thought. The author whose work in this field has for a generation set the standard by which other attempts must be judged, R. A. Markus, entitled his monograph *Saeculum*, giving expression to the view that Augustine was the first theorist of a secular sphere of society, a view which depends heavily on this book for its justification.[1] Yet not all who have written about *The City of God* are agreed that we are justified in looking for political thought within a text that contains more or less nothing about the constitution of political societies or their government.[2] This

1. *Saeculum: History and Society in the Theology of St. Augustine* (Cambridge: Cambridge University Press, 1970). My criticism of this work should not deter any reader from learning at first hand the many valuable things which Markus had to teach thirty years ago, and which have not been taught better; these should, however, be supplemented with the author's later thoughts, which include some constructive dialogue with this essay. Some of these are gathered in *Sacred and Secular: Studies on Augustine and Latin Christianity* (London: Variorum, 1994), where the articles "*De civitate Dei:* Pride and the Common Good" and "Conversion and Disenchantment in Augustine's Spiritual Career" are of special interest to us here.

2. A generation ago R. H. Barrow, in a popular commentary on the book, stressed insistently that Augustine propounded no contribution to political theory: "He is concerned with historical criticism, and not with developing a theory of the state" (*Introduction to St. Augus-*

This paper originated in lectures delivered at the Faculty of Classics in Dalhousie University, Nova Scotia, and in Duke University Divinity School, North Carolina, in 1986; as "Augustine's *City of God* XIX and Western Political Thought," it was published in *Dionysius* 11 (1987): 89-110. Thanks are due to Professor R. A. Markus and to the Most Rev. (then Professor) R. D. Williams for helpful comments in the course of its composition. The version published here is completely revised, taking note of more recent contributions to the discussion.

disagreement as to how Augustine's program should be understood brings to light some underlying assumptions about how the defining limits of a 'political' discourse are to be set. Part of the interest in exploring it lies in exposing these assumptions and in noting how and why Augustine challenges them.

In order to reach an opinion on the nature of Augustine's project, we need first to review the contents of Book 19. It has twenty-eight chapters, of which the last seven are largely devoted to what looks like an Appendix, taking up some unfinished business from Book 2. The role of the book is to provide an introduction to the fifth and last main section of *The City of God* (Books 19-22), which is concerned with the "appointed ends" *(debiti fines)* of the two cities. Books 20-22 will tell of their "ends" in a strictly eschatological sense, treating of judgment, hell, and heaven in that order; the nineteenth book prepares for this by discussing their "ends" in another sense, i.e., their horizons of action that generate their contrasting moral characters. Augustine shares in the classical conception of a thing's end as its "perfection" *(non quo consumatur sed quo perficiatur)*, so that this discussion deals with the supreme end-of-action, the *summum bonum*, "that object for which other objects are sought, but which is sought only for itself," supplemented by a *summum malum,* "that object of repulsion, to avoid which other things are shunned, but which is shunned on its own account."[3]

---

tine: *The City of God* [London: Faber, 1950], p. 249, cf. p. 253). It is a view that has been taken up more recently by Ernest L. Fortin, who, recognizing that what we say about Augustine we shall have to say about other classical political philosophy, observes: "Like that of the classical philosophers, it remains nonpolitical or, better still, transpolitical" (*Augustine, Political Writings,* trans. Michael W. Tkacz and Douglas Kries [Indianapolis: Hackett, 1994], p. xxvi). For a judicious conclusion, see Gerard O'Daly, *Augustine's "City of God". A Reader's Guide* (Oxford: Clarendon, 1999), pp. 209f.: "It comes as near as any work of Augustine's to propounding his political views. But it is important to realize what it does not do. It is not a discussion of the relations between church and state. . . . no details of constitutional practice or theory . . . no programme for the Christianization of Roman political institutions." Note, too, the qualification made by Robert Dodaro, "Church and State," in *Augustine through the Ages,* ed. Allan D. Fitzgerald (Grand Rapids: Eerdmans, 1999), pp. 181f.: "Augustine wrote no political treatise. . . . However, concern for context ought not to limit the range of Augustine's writings that are considered 'political.'"

3. On the complications surrounding the conception of a *finis malorum* for the earthly city, see G. Bardy's note (*Bibliothèque Augustinienne* 37 (1960): 725ff.). Augustine has inherited the antithesis of the *fines bonorum et malorum* from the Stoics, but the antithetical terms cannot be meant in quite the same sense: "Le ciel est un bien sans aucun mélange de mal; mais il reste encore du bien dans l'enfer." The problem is focused in the two different definitions of ultimate evil which Augustine lays side by side in 1.1: "that object of repulsion, to avoid which other things are shunned, but which is shunned on its own account. . . not a cessation of evil, but the damage that is finally accomplished." In the case of the good the two senses of "final" converge: what we desire supremely is what we desire to transpire in the end. In the case of the evil they do not converge so easily: the ultimate disaster is not necessarily the negative goal of all our striving.

The scope of the book, therefore, is broadly moral, rather than narrowly political. It presents its agenda by way of an extended line-by-line discussion of a pagan text, a section of Varro's lost work *De philosophia*.[4] In this text the pagan author identifies six cardinal questions on which moral philosophers are observed to disagree and, by computing the possible combinations of answers to these six questions, postulates a theoretical total of two hundred and eighty-eight different philosophical schools; then by discounting in turn the importance of all but two of the six questions, he reduces the number of serious alternative positions to three. These are: (1) the practice of virtue is valued as a means to attaining the primary goods of nature (health, security, intelligence, etc.); (2) the primary goods are sought as a means to acquiring virtue; (3) the primary goods and virtue are valued each on their own terms and for their own sake (the view that Varro himself prefers).

Augustine then announces his intention of giving the Christian reply, "the answer of the City of God," to these six questions. The way in which he fulfills his promise is rather striking. The first two questions are treated together in a longish passage of 202 lines of *Corpus Christianorum* text (19.4), which declares that the Christian view is different from any that Varro has considered. Virtue cannot be valued for its own sake, any more than can the "primary goods", for neither can overcome the miseries of historical contingency. The final good is eternal life, for only this can provide secure happiness, the true end of action. Augustine then turns to Varro's third question, whether or not the highest good is social, devoting 663 lines to it (19.5-17). The fourth question is dispatched in 17 lines (19.18), the fifth (which is "of no importance") and the sixth together in 40 (19.19). A brief résumé of 16 lines (19.20) sums up his answer to the first three questions, before he proceeds to the apparent Appendix, which runs to 437 lines.[5]

So Augustine has set himself an agenda taken from Varro's discussion of

---

4. W. Geerlings writes justifiably of a "distanziert-ironische Verführung" ("De civitate Dei XIX als Buch der augustinischen Friedenslehre," in Christoph Horn, ed., *Augustinus, de civitate Dei* [Berlin: Akademie Verlag, 1997], p. 219). There is indeed a glint of humor in what is, nevertheless, an over-long exposition.

5. Commentators do not agree on this — to my mind rather straightforward — analysis. O'Daly (*Reader's Guide*, p. 199) marks the end of the discussion of the third question at chap. 13 (without explaining what chaps. 14-17 are doing). Geerlings ("De civitate Dei XIX," pp. 211-33) proposes major divisions after chapters 16, 19 and 25. Both these schemas create major inconveniences. Not only do they ignore the self-conscious flourish with which Augustine brings the long discussion of the social question to a close: *quoniam vita civitatis utique socialis est* — "for the life of the City of God is certainly a social life!" They also create difficulties for the relation of chaps. 14-17 to the program outlined in the "table of peace" in 13, a relation noted by Geerlings himself.

the highest good, but he has treated that agenda with some freedom. He departs from Varro especially in his handling of the third question, "whether the wise man makes it a point of principle to desire and promote the supreme good . . . not only for himself but for a friend." This, for Varro, is "a secondary matter . . . not a matter of the supreme good as such" (1.3). But Augustine makes society central to the supreme good.[6] He subsequently re-visits the definition of the highest good which he offered at the beginning of chapter 4, and reformulates it to incorporate not only an eschatological but a social determinant. It is "peace in eternal life" or "eternal life in peace," where "peace" functions as the most general category of social welfare (11). He could almost, he thinks, simply say "peace" were it not that that word is used also of the relative social conditions of this life. Augustine has challenged the classical account of the supreme good over its asocial way of organizing the question. The capacity of Christian thought to break free of an individualist vision of the good into a social one is, he thinks, distinctive. "Now we turn to the view that 'the wise man's life is social,' which we can support — and *much more strongly than they do*" (5).[7]

6. In *The Problem of Self-Love in St. Augustine* (New Haven: Yale University Press, 1980), p. 115, I carelessly misread this text as though Augustine agreed with Varro on the point. Others have made the same mistake, among them Miikka Ruokanen, *Theology of Social Life in Augustine's "De civitate Dei"* (Göttingen: Vandenhoeck & Ruprecht, 1993), p. 56. Augustine's rejection of Varro's position is, of course, a repudiation of his own earlier positions. See *Problem of Self-Love*, pp. 112-36, and John M. Rist, *Augustine: Ancient Thought Baptized* (Cambridge: Cambridge University Press, 1994), pp. 203-7.

7. *Nos multo amplius adprobamus:* Translation from *IG*, p. 148, where I followed the lead of G. Combès ("nous l'approuvons et bien plus qu'eux," *BA* 37), which supposes the comparison is between the church and the pagan philosophers. H. Bettenson ([Harmondsworth: Penguin, 1972]: "In this we support them much more heartily") and R. W. Dyson ([Cambridge: Cambridge University Press, 1999]: "this is a view of which we much more readily approve") make it a comparison between the church's answer to the third question and its answer to the first two.

A case can be made for the latter reading, according to which Augustine finds more coincidence with the philosophers' views on this point than on the previous ones. It assumes a reference back to the extended statement of Varro's views in chap. 3, where the answer to the third question is stated, not as Varro's alone, but as that of the Old Academy which Varro supports: *hanc vitam beatam etiam socialem perhibent esse* (3.2). The plural subject is echoed in our place by *socialem vitam volunt esse*. On this account *amplius adprobamus* is slightly ironic. Augustine has actually thought the philosophers' answers to the first two questions hopelessly misconceived — *hic beati esse a se ipsis beatificari mira vanitate voluerunt* (4.1) — but here he can find a "greater measure" of agreement. Having supported their judgment, he makes a serious qualification to it: *sed in huius mortalitatis aerumna quot et quantis abundet malis humana societas. . . .* The same determination on the philosophers' part to locate the supreme good immanently within this life vitiates the truth of their reply about society.

On the first interpretation *amplius adprobamus* is a contraction of two ideas: we agree,

Book 19 of *The City of God* is, at the very least, then, an essay to demonstrate that *moral* philosophy must be *social* philosophy. Yet, as in the rest of *The City of God*, the attention paid to society excludes any sustained attention to government. This is all the more striking when we lay the great work alongside other writings in which he advanced a perfectly coherent, if somewhat conventional, Christian account of secular government and its relation to the church (an account which finds its fullest expression in *Letter* 153, of A.D. 414). Here he turns his eyes away from these questions to the moral forces which shape a society and its practices. Can such a concern be accommodated within the scope of the political? It is, perhaps, a terminological decision. But it would be a curiously starved political theory that excluded such reflections upon the moral foundations of human sociality.

The case for a political purpose is sharpened, however, by the curious phenomenon of the Appendix, chaps. 21-6. "This brings me to the point," he announces, having wound up the agenda presented by Varro's distinctions, "at which I must explain as briefly and as clearly as I can what I said, and promised to prove, in Book Two: that by the definitions proposed by Scipio in Cicero's *Republic* there never was a Roman commonwealth." There follows a discussion which turns upon the meaning to be given to the word *respublica* ("commonwealth") and whether "right" (*ius*) is included in its definition.

In Book 2, where Augustine was in the full flood of his polemic against paganism, he argued that traditional Roman religion had no inherent tradition of moral teaching. Those pagan authors who most praised the austere virtue of the early republic witnessed most damningly to the failure of Roman culture to perpetuate its morality in the changing circumstances of growing national security and power. In Cicero's dialogue this view was put in the mouth of a hero from the second century B.C., Scipio Africanus, who argued that the Roman commonwealth was now a commonwealth only in name and

---

and we make the affirmation with more conviction than the pagans. The church can be a more effective and committed advocate of the social character of the good than pagan philosophers can be. In evidence for this assertion he continues: "Here we are with the nineteenth book of *The City of God* in our hands, and how could that city ever set out, advance, or reach its appointed end if the life of the saints were not social?" In other words, the *church* is the proof and the substance of the Christian commitment to a social good. "But," he continues, "in the miserable conditions of this life . . ." the pagan philosophers have nothing comparable to point to. Subsequently he spends a disproportionate amount of space (19.5-17) on this one question. For him it is the essence of the *quaestio de summo bono*, where Varro relegated it to a secondary place. He will refashion his definition of the supreme good to incorporate a social idea, peace. This would seem plentiful justification for his claim that Christians take sociality more seriously. Though either interpretation is defensible, I prefer this one for the explanation it offers of the priorities of the book as a whole.

not in reality. For a "commonwealth" *(respublica)* is "a people's wealth" *(res populi);* and a people implies association both by consent to right *(ius)* and common interest *(utilitas),* two things which, Scipio holds, have altogether disappeared from the later, degenerate republic. To achieve his ostensible polemical purpose all that Augustine needed to do with this passage, the sentiments of which were, of course, Cicero's own, not those of the historical Africanus, was to quote it. It supported his view of the Roman republic entirely. In promising to go further and demonstrate how on Cicero/Scipio's terms the Roman commonwealth had never existed, Augustine indicated that the polemic of Book 2 did not exhaust his interest in the question of what constituted a commonwealth.

He now resumes this discussion, writing a decade or so later. The argument does not appear at first to have advanced very far. True right implies obedience to the true God; for "rightness" (i.e., justice — this slightly arch translation is the best I can do to keep the philological parallel between *ius* and *iustitia)* is the virtue that assigns everyone his due, and there can be no rightness when the worship owed to the creator is offered instead to unclean demons. But if there is no rightness, there is no right. "One should not describe as 'rights' *(iura)* what are merely the unequal institutions of men." And if no right, there is no people associated by consent to right, and therefore, on Cicero/Scipio's terms, no commonwealth. The only important element in this argument that was not to hand when he first broached the quotation in Book 2 was the contention that rightness implies the worship of the true God. But this point was made, in effect, in Book 5, where Augustine argued that good moral qualities *(mores, bonae artes)* can be inspired by fundamentally vicious motivations. The Romans achieved what they did achieve at their best, an austere courage, self-mastery, and adherence to high standards of honor, only because they were driven by an overmastering passion for glory. True virtue is not acquired this way, however, but only by that piety which involves humility. So much was established by the end of the first five books of *The City of God.* Why, then, did Augustine not conclude the unfinished business of those books while he was writing them? We cannot rule out non-philosophical constraints upon the composition of a work composed over so many years, intermittently and without the benefit of notebooks, jottings and revisions.[8] It is conceivable that

8. For a sensitive treatment of the arbitrary features in Augustine's composition, see H. Marrou, *S. Augustin et la fin de la culture antique* (4th ed., Paris: de Boccard, 1938), pp. 59-76. In the earlier published version of this essay I took the view that chaps. 22-23, which discuss Porphyry's *Philosophy from Oracles,* was an example of a digression prompted by pure contingency of composition. Without ruling out an element of contingency, I am now more persuaded of its relevance to the context.

he simply forgot about the promise of Book 2 until years later. However, there is a good case for taking at their face value the confident words of connection which introduce chapter 21: *quapropter nunc est locus,* "This brings me to the point. . . ."

Quapropter refers us back to the short summary (chap. 20) which concludes the discussion of Varro's questions and sums up Augustine's views on the first three, the ones to which he attaches some weight. Three points are made in this summary:

(a) *An eschatological claim:* the supreme good is "perfect and eternal peace." This is the answer to the first question as modified by the answer to the third, which Augustine reached and proposed at the midpoint (chaps. 11-12) of his treatment of Varro's third question.

(b) *A negative conclusion:* in comparison, "this life which we live here, replete as it may be with good things of body, mind, or circumstance, is by comparison the most unhappy." This sums up the answer to the first two questions (chap. 4) and the first part of the answer to the third (chaps. 5-10).

(c) *A positive qualification to the negative conclusion:* we can, nevertheless, speak without absurdity of a qualified happiness here and now if we "make use of this life to relate it to that other life as [our] end." It is the hope of the eternal that makes us relatively happy, for only in hope can we enjoy the true good of the mind, which is to contemplate the eternal. This summarizes the second half of the answer to the third question (chaps. 13-17), which compares the peace of the two cities and their two corresponding households.

The section which then follows is organized in a way that closely parallels chaps. 4-17: a negative argument, denying the possibility of a commonwealth considered absolutely in terms of right (chap. 21); a lengthy central passage, which, like the discussion of peace in chapter 12, has the appearance of a digression (chaps. 22-23); finally, a positive qualification to the negative thesis, affirming the possibility of a commonwealth considered relatively, without mention of right, in terms of common objects of love (chaps. 24-26). This leads back effortlessly into a recapitulatory summary of the discussion of peace (chap. 27). The central passage, a polemical discussion of Porphyry's *Philosophy from Oracles,* aims to exploit the pagan philosopher's favorable references to the Judaeo-Christian God, to suggest that even paganism, when consistent with its own best insights, can acknowledge the importance of monotheism to any conception of justice. Its role is to reinforce the negative thesis of the preceding passage, and in this respect the parallel is not exact, since the role of chapter 12 was to prepare for the positive thesis of chaps. 13-17.

It is clear, however, why the discussion of Cicero's definition was postponed until the nineteenth book. It needed the account of peace which Augustine purposed to write there. His new definition of the commonwealth belonged with his conception of an "earthly peace"(chap. 17), an "unequal peace" (chap. 12), a peace which consists in the "co-operative order for giving and accepting commands among fellow-citizens" (chaps. 13, 17), which secures "community of interest in the resources for this mortal life" (chap. 17). In this earthly peace the city of God has a stake, exploiting its benefits to support it on its pilgrimage, while it cherishes its own provisional peace, though that, too, in comparison, is but a "solace to unhappiness" (chap. 27). It was, I conclude, Augustine's purpose from the beginning to develop his discussion of the social coherence of the two cities around their respective ideas of peace into thoughts on the status of the earthly commonwealth. The idea of a relative earthly peace — "something not to be despised" — affords him a way of conceptualizing the existence of a political society without compromise to his refusal of "right" to a polity without true religion. And so he reaches a *political* assessment of the Roman republic which matches his *moral* assessment: just as Rome had no *virtus,* but only *bonae artes,* so it had no *ius;* but "I would not conclude that Rome was not a people, nor that its people's wealth was not a commonwealth" (chap. 24).

II

Augustine's new definition of a commonwealth excludes the element of "right," or "law," which is often thought decisive to the constitution of a political society. Cicero's definition, "a gathered multitude united by consent to right *(ius)* and common interest" (chap. 21), is replaced by an alternative: "a gathered multitude of rational beings united by agreeing to share the things they love" (24). In their reactions to this proposal interpreters diverge sharply in what we may call 'idealist' and 'realist' directions. Idealist-leaning commentators find it difficult to take the proposal seriously. Can Augustine really mean to save the face of the Roman republic at such an immense theoretical cost? Does he not really insinuate that the true republic, complete with justice, must be a Christian, or at least a monotheist one, while the commonwealth bound together merely by an agreement on the objects of its love is a commonwealth only in name?[9] Realist-

9. Barrow, *Introduction,* p. 253, declared that Augustine "show(s) how empty and vacuous a definition would have to be if it had to encompass all the polities which have been called

leaning commentators, on the other hand, welcome the new definition as anticipating the modern idea of a morally neutral political community, a meeting-
place of those with differing ultimate values.

Augustine is susceptible of being read in more than one way; both approaches to interpreting him can be carried through with careful attention
and delicate nuance, in a way that promises convergence — on grounds we
shall explore shortly.[10] Injudiciously developed, however, either of these approaches can drown out essential aspects of the thought. Commonly found in
idealist accounts is the suggestion that ordinary less-than-perfect states may
evince 'relative', as opposed to 'true' justice; but such a phrase, or any equivalent to it, is stubbornly absent from Augustine's pages, and, indeed, more or
less excluded by his resolute denials of "right" to the earthly commonwealth.[11] Commonly found in realist accounts is the postulate that the two
cities which are the theme of the work are not to be identified with any
earthly communities, but are ideal moral communities, possibilities which all
earthly communities merely approximate in one degree or another.[12] That
Augustine's two cities are *moral* communities, there can be no doubt; yet the
history of the earthly city is supremely that of the Babylonian and Roman em-

---

commonwealths in the history of the world." John von Heyking believes that Augustine adopts a
"rhetorical strategy" of "excessive rhetoric," which serves to discount Augustine's "apparent rejection of politics" (*Augustine and Politics as Longing in the World* [Columbia: University of Mis-
souri Press, 2001], pp. 32, 39). Fortin speaks of Augustine's "most extreme, one is almost
tempted to say 'outrageous' pronouncements" ("Justice as the Foundation of the Political Community," in Horn, ed., *Augustinus*, p. 47).

10. For the realist case, see Markus, *Saeculum,* especially pp. 154-86 and 197-210, finding
points of comparison with Oscar Cullmann and Harvey Cox. For the idealist, cf. Domenico
Marafioti, S.J. ("I frutti della carità: giustizia e pace nel *De civitate Dei* di Sant' Agostino," *Vivar-
ium* 4 [1996]: 271-304); also Rowan Williams, "Politics and the Soul: A Reading of the *City of
God,*" *Milltown Studies* 19-20 (1987): 55-72.

11. There is, perhaps, the hint of such a conception in the two references to just war, 15.4
and 19.7, where the use of the epithet is too established conventionally to admit of terminological innovation. *Summa iustitia* at II.21 is a quotation from Cicero, and even as such has no implication that there might be a relative justice. At *De spiritu et littera* 36.65 Augustine speaks of a
iustitia minor huic vitae competens, qua iustus ex fide vivit. But this, as the relative clause unam-
biguously shows, is a virtue of the Christian pilgrim, not of civil society as mistakenly supposed
by Fortin, "Justice as the Foundation," p. 57.

12. This is maintained in a strong form by Donald X. Burt, who calls the two cities "transcendent cities" and "supra-temporal societies" (*Friendship and Society* [Grand Rapids: Eerdmans, 1999], p. 120). It is also maintained by Ruokanen, *Theology of Social Life,* p. 93, e.g.:
"*Civitas terrena* is not a concept used for the description of any part of created nature. The ter-
restrial city is a spiritual or metaphysical reality, which molds the naturally good being of rational beings."

pires, and the *history* of the heavenly city is that of the faithful in Israel and of the church.[13]

Cicero's Scipio Africanus had proposed not one but two necessary grounds of association in a political community, and Augustine rejects both of them. Most of his attention, and the attention of his commentators, is given to the rejection of "right." We may, however, shed some light on this more controversial move, if we consider his reasons for repudiating the other ground, that of common utility or interest *(utilitas)*. There is, he argues, "no *utilitas* to be shared in impious lives devoted to the service not of God but of demons" (21). This may seem perplexing, since "utility" is a term we commonly use of means rather than ends. To us "utilities" are life-sustaining goods which the community affords, on the basis of which we may pursue our own goals. They perfectly express the thought that ends are private, means shared. And it is probable that Cicero meant something similar. But Augustine, in keeping with his universal practice, will speak of *utilitas* only where the supreme good is in view as an end. He would have liked to impose the same restriction on the term *usus*, more than once observing that there is no "use" of things to wrong ends, but only "abuse," and preferring to describe the wicked as "wanting to make use" of goods wrongly, rather than as actually using them wrongly.[14] But he recognizes that common patterns of speech were against him, so that the carthly city is, after all, said to "use" earthly goods. With *utilitas*, however, he holds the line. "Common use" does not imply "common utility." To derive "utility" from the use of any means, one must use it rightly.

This affects the important question of how the City of God relates to the earthly city in its handling of material goods. In chapter 17 Augustine tells us that the two communities of mankind have a *communis usus* of the necessaries of this mortal life, but that each has its own end in using them. He goes on: "So it is that the earthly city, too, which does not live by faith, aims at an earthly peace, and so fixes the terms of cooperation of its citizens in giving and accepting commands as to ensure some consensus of human wills in respect of the resources for this mortal life." It is the easiest mistake in the world for the casual reader to take the words rendered "so it is that" *(ita etiam)* to refer to what has

---

13. Cf. Marafioti's well-judged statement ("I frutti della carità," pp. 272f.): "Esse non si identificano automaticamente con lo Stato e la Chiesa; e tuttavia la 'città terrena' si rende visibile e reconoscibile, presente e operante nello Stato che si allontana da Dio e perseguita la Chiesa; ugualmente la 'città di Dio', pur non essendo la stessa cosa della Chiesa storica, si incarna nella Chiesa presente nel tempo."

14. For *utilitas*, cf. the early *De diversis quaestionibus* 83.30; for *usus*, cf. *De civ. Dei* 11.25. See my "*Usus* and *Fruitio* in Augustine, *De doctrina Christiana* 1," *Journal of Theological Studies* 23 (1982): 376.

gone immediately before: the City of God and the earthly city get on together by having a common use and differing ends; similarly, the earthly city comprises in itself a multitude of citizens with common use and different ends. But when the passage is read in its entirety, it is obvious that the connective phrase links this sentence not to the sentence about common use and different ends, but to the first sentence of chapter 17: "A household of those who do not live by faith pursues an earthly peace based on resources and benefits of this temporal life. . . . So it is that the earthly city, too, which does not live by faith, aims at an earthly peace. . . ." The comparison is not between the earthly city and the *ensemble* of the two cities, but between the earthly city and the earthly household. Augustine does not think that the earthly city is constituted within itself in the same way as the relation between the earthly and heavenly cities is constituted. He does not say that there is common use but different ends among the members of the earthly city. On the contrary, there is a common end, eternal death, and no "use" at all in the ideal sense of the word, because there is no utility, no final good which gives real value to the pursuit of intermediate goods. The earthly city is not a neutral meeting space, a "naked public square."

Here the difference between Augustine and modern secularism emerges at its sharpest, and it is the single weakness of Markus's fine book to have obscured this difference. "Society," he writes, "becomes intrinsically 'secular' in the sense that it is not as such committed to any particular ultimate loyalty. It is the sphere in which different individuals with different beliefs and loyalties pursue their common objectives insofar as they coincide. His 'secularisation' of the realm of politics implies a pluralistic, religiously neutral civil community."[15] But for Augustine, the earthly city, with its earthly peace, did have an ultimate commitment in which all its members shared, the "love of self to the exclusion of love of God" (14.28). Whatever the difficulties that surround the idea of a *finis malorum* in Augustine, we misunderstand him if we fail to see that he assigns it a seriously ontological status. "Love of self" is no mere circumlocution for diversity of ends. It is the name for a terrible moral unity; and its final state, an eternal cohesion of eternal dissolution, is war, "an opposition of will and passion in which hostilities cannot be terminated by the victory of either" (chap. 28).

Two things follow from this. First, the members of the heavenly city are not members of the earthly city, too, however much they may support and encourage the "consensus of human wills in respect of resources for man's mortal existence"(chap. 17). This "consensus of human wills" *(compositio voluntatum)* is not, as may first appear, a consensus between themselves and the earthly city.

15. *Saeculum*, p. 173. For some second thoughts, see his "*De civitate Dei:* Pride and the Common Good."

This is the second occurrence of the phrase in chapter 17, and on its first occurrence it was simply part of the earthly city's project, the essential condition for the earthly peace to be realized. "So it is that the earthly city, too, which does not live by faith, aims at an earthly peace, and so fixes the terms of cooperation of its citizens in giving and accepting commands as to ensure some consensus of human wills in respect of the resources for this mortal life." On its second occurrence some twenty lines later, then, the phrase must refer to the same thing. The heavenly city's relation to the *compositio voluntatum* is simply an aspect of its "use" of the earthly peace in general. The wills in question are those of the members of the earthly city among themselves, and the heavenly city supports their consensus in the way that Augustine has just explained, by not trying to change their various laws and customs.

In the second place it follows that there is no true *tertium quid* between the two cities, no neutral space on which they meet as equal partners. Markus writes that "membership of either is compatible both with belonging to the Roman, or some other state, and with belonging to the church," but this goes beyond Augustine, for whom, it would seem, true Christians were never true Romans (in the sense of being part of the Roman imperial project) nor false Christians true members of the church (in the sense of being part of a pilgrim society).[16] We observe how Markus reaches in this context for the word 'state'. The difference could be summed up by saying that Augustine had no conception of a 'state'. Rome is not the name of a 'state', but of a *civitas* or 'city', which is a concrete and morally determined body of citizens. Only the "earthly peace," "that temporal peace of the meantime which is shared by good and wicked alike" (chap. 26), is common to both communities, not an institution but simply a condition of order. Each community makes, as it were, its own peace out of it. What Augustine likes to say is that the City of God "makes use of" the peace of Babylon, and then, quoting Jeremiah, "In her peace is your peace."

III

We return, then, to the major change Augustine made to Cicero's definition, the removal of the reference to "right". He was, of course, perfectly aware that the word *ius* need mean no more than a system of law. But one ought not, in Augustine's view, to speak in that way of *ius* without raising the question of its relation to justice. Cicero himself had argued that the loss of *iustitia* caused the Roman commonwealth to cease existing. "They themselves have a saying," Au-

---

16. *Saeculum,* pp. 60f.

gustine comments, "'*ius* flows from the source of *iustitia*'" (21). He had argued in Book 2 that Rome, in lacking a religious morality, lacked a unified public moral culture, having only the heterogeneous elements of a philosophical morality, a tradition of law, and a flagrantly immoral public religion (2.12). So it was that reflective and conscientious Romans such as Cicero ended up with a sense of bad faith in regard to the public culture (2.27). A unified account of justice that related law to religion was philosophically indispensable.

It would have been an obvious step for Augustine to distinguish an absolute justice from a relative justice, and to allow the pagan commonwealth a certain measure of justice which fell short of the ideal. This is, after all, the way he handles the concept of peace: there is the absolute peace of the City of God, and beneath it there is a wide spectrum of relative peace at almost every imaginable level of human or sub-human aspiration. So why not distinguish absolute justice from relative justice in the same way? In fact there is a relative justice in Augustine's thought, but it does not extend far enough to embrace the activities of the earthly commonwealth. We can observe the disparity in his handling of *pax*, on the one hand, and of *iustitia*, on the other, from the last words of chapter 26 and the opening of 27.[17] "He [Jeremiah] meant, of course, that temporal peace of the meantime which is shared by good and wicked alike; though our own proper peace, peace with God, is experienced here by faith, too, and not only by sight in eternity. Yet no peace here, whether that shared peace or our own proper peace, can be more than a solace to unhappiness. There is no delighting in happiness yet." There are, we notice, three kinds of peace mentioned: the final peace of heaven, the interior peace of the City of God enjoyed by faith, and the peace which is common to the two cities.[18] He then continues: "Our *iustitia*, too, 'truly right' as it may be on account of the truly good end to which it relates, is in this life no more than forgiven sin. Virtue is not yet perfected." Here we have only two kinds of *iustitia*, both peculiar to the City of God. There is no third kind which might be common to the two cities.

As the discussion proceeds, it becomes evident why. The Latin *iustitia*, like the Greek *dikaiosunē*, is notoriously translated in theological English by no fewer than three words: 'righteousness', 'justice', and 'justification'. Augustine cannot use the term without being aware of the problematic represented by the third of these, the *iustitia Dei, non qua iustus est sed qua iusti sunt homines quos iustificat*, "not in the sense of his being righteous (just) but in the sense of his

17. The sixth-century chapter division is highly unfortunate, breaking across the logic of a single thought. On the origins of the chapter headings and the divisions they import see M. M. Gorman, "The oldest mss. of *De civitate Dei*," *Journal of Theological Studies* 33 (1982): 398-410.

18. For the significance of the *pax ecclesiae* in relation to the Donatist controversy, see Shinji Kayama, *From Ordo to Pax* (Oxford University D.Phil. thesis, 1996).

justifying mankind."[19] He cannot or will not disengage a separate social or political sense of the word from its theological sense. *Iustitia* must include the forgiveness of sins. That is why chapter 27 takes an unexpected turn onto the terrain of his long-fought controversy with the Pelagians over Christian perfection and forgiveness.

Yet at two places in earlier books of *The City of God* Augustine spoke of *iustitia* in connection with civil government, and from these his idealist-leaning interpreters like to start. There is, in the first place, the famous aphorism of 4.4, which has caused interpreters much work: "Remove *iustitia*, and what are kingdoms but gangs of criminals on a large scale? What are criminal gangs but petty kingdoms?" And there is the brief "mirror for princes" of 5.24, where Augustine speaks of Christian emperors as ruling *iuste*. I think that a consistent account of his view of justice can be given which pays proper attention to these texts as well as to the contentions of the second and nineteenth books. On this account Augustine believed two things: (a) that justice is a virtue of civil government, though not a necessary criterion for it; (b) that this virtue is realized only when civil government is conducted by Christians. On these propositions the idealist and realist approaches may converge. In denying "justice" to religiously defective societies, Augustine meant what he said; yet the "justice" which the heavenly city embodies is not merely supramundane: it answers to "the right" as it is generally recognized and universally desired.

The context of 4.4 makes it clear that Augustine's interest lies in the structural similarities between a *regnum* and a *latrocinium*. He refers to an episode of Roman republican history which seems to have fascinated him (for we find it again at 3.26), the Servile War, in which some gladiators under Spartacus revolted and established a petty kingdom of their own in Campania which lasted for two years. Whatever can be said, Augustine argues, about the rise of Rome, ought to be said *mutatis mutandis* about that *latrocinium*, for there is no formal difference between them (4.5). The point is still in his mind at 19.12, where his first example to show that peace is a universal object of human aspiration is that of the *latrocinium*. Here is the sharpest point of difference between Augustine and the later medieval and Renaissance political tradition influenced by civil and canon law. To Hugo Grotius, for example, it was self-evident that a state may commit injustice without losing political capacity, and that a band of pirates can never become a state. Pirates are bound together solely by the commission of crime, whereas states are associated for the mutual support of lawful right.[20]

---

19. *Ep.* 140.72; cf. *De spiritu et littera* 32.56.
20. *De iure belli ac pacis* 3.3.2.

Augustine's comparison holds only "if you take away justice." But *must* we take away justice? The aphorism is immediately preceded by a contrast between two kinds of kingdom: everybody benefits, Augustine says, from the rule of the good, that is to say, from the rule of those who have no great desire to be rulers, since their piety and integrity are sufficient for their happiness (4.3). At 5.24 just rule means an insusceptibility to flattery, a love of God's kingdom which is stronger than the love of one's own kingdom, a reluctance to punish from personal animosity, a concern for the amendment of wrongdoers, and a gentleness in showing mercy; a mastery of appetite and a readiness to make the sacrifice of humility, compassion, and prayer for what one has done amiss, a point of great importance in Augustine's portrait of Theodosius.[21] And there is only one kind of ruler of whom all this can be true, that is to say, a Christian ruler.

It is a measure of the distance which Augustine has set between himself and the propaganda of the Christian empire that the claims made for Christian rulers in this passage can strike us as something for which we have not felt prepared. Peter Brown described them as "some of the most shoddy passages of the *City of God*," suggesting, I suppose, that they were gratuitous and superficial.[22] This judgment needs some qualification. Simply as a theoretical matter, it could not have been an attractive option to depict the Christian emperor at the head of a gang of terrorists. Augustine needed some account of what the arrival of the Christian regime meant. We have examples from other sources of what was said along these lines in his day. There are the poems of Prudentius, with their theory of civilizational growth and maturity.[23] There is Orosius's historical tribute, written at Augustine's own suggestion, as we learn, and almost certainly the subject of his censure.[24] What most impresses us in the end is how

21. On which cf. Y.-M. Duval, "L'éloge de Théodose dans le Cité de Dieu," *Recherches Augustiniennes* 4 (1966): 135-79.

22. "Political Society" in R. A. Markus, ed., *Augustine: A Collection of Critical Essays* (New York: Doubleday, 1972), p. 319 [= "St. Augustine's Attitude to Religious Coercion," in *Religion and Society in the Age of St. Augustine* (London: Faber, 1972)].

23. *Contra Orationem Symmachi* 2.325-34 (trans. H. J. Thomson, Loeb Classical Library): "By just such stages has the race of men led its changeful life through differing periods of time. Unintelligent in its first efforts and sunk on the ground, it lived as it were on all fours; then in its boyhood, having a mind that could learn and becoming capable of acquiring skills, it attained refinement by trying different novelties. Next it grew up into the hot years of passion, swelling the while with corruptions, till it worked off the excess of vigour and made its strength firm. Now the time is come for it to understand things divine, having skill, with the thought of a mind unclouded, more actively to search out mysteries and at last to watch over its eternal well-being."

24. At 18.52 Augustine rejected the theory that there could be no more persecutions before the final tribulation, pointedly criticizing a proof which Orosius advanced for it, based on the number of the plagues in Egypt (*Hist.* 7.27). In 19.7 he trumps Orosius by deploying an argu-

modest the claims he admits are: the Christian emperor superimposes on the government of his dominions a kind of *iustitia* that it can function quite well without, and which consists principally in his readiness to ask and to offer forgiveness.

In the end, though, we must dissent from the claim that *The City of God* is "in the main a book about justice," and agree that justice is not at the forefront of Augustine's concerns.[25] But before we conclude that Augustine simply paid less attention to political justice than to theological righteousness, we must reckon with what he had on hand to put in its place. Having severed the connection between society and virtue, Augustine takes a very different direction from the early modern theorists who attempted to re-found society on passion.[26] On the contrary, he re-formulates something like the traditional virtue-based concept of society, but in new terms which will give due recognition both to the reality of the moral order which makes social existence possible and to its fundamentally flawed character. He embarks on the radical policy of accounting for societies in terms of their moral *disorders*, which itself provides an account of their political *order*, since, in his decisively Platonic view, disorder is nothing but a failure of underlying order. The famous statement in 19.25, "If the virtues which it thinks it displays in commanding body or [controlling] vice are related to the acquisition or retention of any object other than God himself, they are more properly vices than virtues," is not empty rhetoric, certainly; but it must be read alongside the characteristic anti-Manichean affirmation of 19.12: "Yet even something perverted must be at peace, subsisting in some aspect, deriving from some aspect, relating to some aspect of reality in which or from which it subsists; otherwise it could not exist at all."[27] A vice, in other words, is a perversion of virtue; it is a disorder predatory upon some order. In the twelfth chapter of Book 5 Augustine wrote that the Romans "checked their other lusts with a single huge lust for this one thing," i.e., glory. From this

---

ment he uses to belittle the moral significance of the victories of the republic, to dismiss claims very similar to Orosius's for the internationalism of the imperial *pax Romana* (cf. *Hist.* 5.1, 2).

25. For the first claim, see Fortin, "Justice as the Foundation," p. 47; for the second Miikka Ruokanen, *Theology of Social Life*, pp. 121-30.

26. For what follows, see Fortin, *Political Idealism and Christianity in the Thought of St. Augustine* (Philadelphia: Villanova, 1972). Ruokanen's otherwise persuasive exposition (cf. n. 25 above) is weakened by the doubtful claim that Augustine's use of the verb *diligere* suggests a this-worldly, interest-oriented pursuit. On the dangers of over-weighting the significance of the different vocabulary Augustine used for love, I refer to my discussion in *The Problem of Self-Love in St. Augustine*, pp. 10f.

27. Its resumption of anti-Manichean themes is one more reason, if more be needed, to reject the suggestion that chapter 12 was based on a Varronian model. See Geerlings' critique of this proposal, "De civitate Dei XIX," pp. 222-24.

sprang their "moral qualities" *(mores)* and "good arts" *(bonae artes)*, everything valuable about a civilization, in fact, apart from 'real' virtue.[28]

This theory has evoked some notable echoes in the modern period.[29] It deserves them, since it strikingly combines certain strengths both of ancient and modern political thought. It allows us to understand how manifestly vicious communities can function as organized societies, and apparently function well. And yet it allows us an independent point of criticism from which we can say, as Augustine does, "The better the things [that they love], the better the people; the worse the things, the worse their agreement to share them" (chap. 24).[30] Not the least striking feature about it is its ability to take terrorist groups seriously as political communities and to understand their functioning in terms that are relevant to politics. Peter Brown has drawn our attention to a telling remark in one of Augustine's sermons: it is love that enables a terrorist to endure torture rather than reveal the names of his accomplices.[31] Love, we must note, is not a *passion*. Though the objects of the community's love are as various as sin itself, love is still directed to the good, even if not always to the supreme good. What Augustine's reader finally takes away with him is not a denigration of the role of virtue in politics, though there is a fair amount of deflation of moral pretension, but an ability to discern the shadows cast by virtue in the most surprising places.

28. For the same argument turned against the Pelagians, with another reference to Epicurus' famous dictum about virtues as the handmaids of pleasure, cf. *Contra Iulianum* 4.3.21: *non officiis sed finibus a vitiis esse discernendas esse virtutes.* When not pressing his polemical point, Augustine could occasionally allow the word *virtus* in relation to the ancient Romans. They displayed "civil virtues without religion" (*Ep.* 138.3.17), and at *CD* 1.24 Regulus is spoken of the best *inter omnes suos laudabiles et virtutis insignibus illustres.* The discussion at *CD* 5.12 is of central importance for establishing a restrictive sense for "true virtue," while entertaining, at least, the relative claims to virtue of the greatest Romans. The parallel between Augustine's restrictive doctrine of virtue and the Stoic doctrine of the sage is well drawn by Rist, *Ancient Thought Baptized,* pp. 168-73.

29. Cf. J. J. Rousseau, *Discourse on Inequality:* "This burning desire to be talked about, this yearning for distinction which keeps us almost always in a restless state is responsible for what is best and what is worst among men, for our virtues and our vices, for our sciences and our mistakes, for our conquerors and our philosophers — that is to say, for a multitude of bad things and very few good things."

30. I see no reason to conclude with Rist (*Ancient Thought Baptized,* p. 305) that "all earthly societies would seem to be equally bad *in practice,* not merely in potentiality."

31. *Serm.* 169.11.14; cf. Brown, "Political Society," p. 317.

IV

Augustine's social reflections, then, abstract on the one hand from government and on the other from law. We now notice a third element of political reflection that seems to be absent from his thought: there is no place for a political program and no prospect of progress. A generation ago H. Richard Niebuhr popularized the thesis that Augustine stood for a "transformation" of human culture by Christ.[32] It is a thesis which will garner very little support today. Many heads have been shaken sadly over the complacency with which the institution of slavery is regarded in chapters 14-16.[33]

The context of that discussion is important, and we must allow ourselves some space to explore it. Augustine's theoretical foundation, laid down at the beginning of chapter 14, is that in the earthly city all use of temporal goods is related to the enjoyment of earthly peace, while in the heavenly city it is related to the enjoyment of eternal peace. He expounds this in relation to each of the ascending steps in the "table of peace" at the beginning of chapter 13, in which peace is applied analogously to a range of phenomena, from the structure of a physical organism to the kingdom of God.[34] The *tabula* thus serves as a list of contents for the chapters that follow it.

It runs in a reverse direction from that of chapter 12, where the thought begins with society and descends to the lowest level, the peace of an organism. Here the list starts from (1) the peace of the body and proceeds to (2) the peace of the irrational and (3) of the rational soul, and so to (4) the peace of the body-soul union underlying all animal existence. The sequence then takes a puzzling turn with (5) the peace of man and God, followed by (6) *pax hominum,* from which it runs in an ascent through the orders of society: (7) domestic peace, (8) civic peace, and (9) the peace of the heavenly city. Items (1)-(5) have definitions including the adjective *ordinata* with a variable noun: *temperatura, requies, consensio, vita et salus, oboedientia.* Items (6)-(9) all have a definition involving the *ordinata concordia.* Then, when we think we have reached the top of the ontological ladder, we are surprised to find (10) *pax omnium rerum tranquillitas ordinis.* The *tabula* then concludes with (11) a definition of *ordo.*

32. *Christ and Culture* (New York: Harper & Row, 1951), pp. 206-18.

33. Cf. Rist, *Ancient Thought Baptized,* p. 306: "He had no time for the reform of many human institutions (such as slavery). . . . Yet his own principles could have told him that that is no reason to decline the attempt. . . ." Cf. Ruokanen, *Theology of Social Life,* p. 152: "Augustine has very little belief in the possibility of Christians or Christian rulers improving the miserable state of political society."

34. Cf. Geerlings, "De civitate Dei XIX," p. 228: "Hier spannt sich der Bogen vom Frieden des Körpers hin zum Frieden der civitas caelestis und zur ewigen Ruheordnung aller Dinge."

Augustine postpones his use of this ascending ladder until chap. 14, since he conceives his first task as explaining the place of misery and final punishment within the concept of peace as an all-embracing category. Then he prefaces his treatment with the general statement to which we have referred about the differing principles of use and enjoyment within the two cities; this statement is to be illustrated at every step.[35] The order is then slightly varied: (1) body, (2) irrational soul, (4a) body-soul union of animals (excusing this departure by the explanation that the body-soul union is necessarily implied in the peace of the irrational soul). Then come (3) the rational soul, (4b) the body-soul union in relation to rational beings, and, by way of the assertion that this latter requires a "divine instruction" to be received in faith, we reach, as though coming to a conclusion, (5) the peace of man with God: "That is why we relate every form of peace — body's peace, soul's peace, peace of the body and soul together — to the peace uniting mortal man to immortal God: an ordered obedience of faith governed by the eternal law."

And it is, indeed, a conclusion of a kind, for the next step involves a fresh start, introducing into the hierarchy of body-soul-man-God the new consideration of *sociality*. We are told that divine instruction commends to us our neighbor, and that love of the neighbor is (6) *pax hominum*, 'the peace of the human community', defined, as in chapter 13, as *ordinata concordia* and expounded in the two principles that one do no harm and do good where possible. This is then explored at length in three stages, at each of which Augustine repeats the relevant definition from chapter 13. The discussion of (7) the peace of the household runs from the end of chapter 14 ("Our first responsibility is to our family . . .") to chapter 16. The discussion of (8) the peace of the city runs from the end of chapter 16 ("Now, the household must be the beginning, or the cell, of the city . . ."). At the end of 17, finally, he touches briefly on (9) the peace of the heavenly city ("It relates this earthly peace to a heavenly peace . . .").

It is evident from the way Augustine develops his ascending sequence, that it is in two parts, one concerned with individual organisms, the other with societies. Further, it is clear that (5) belongs in the first part, as the highest expression of the peace of the human being as such; that (6) is regarded as a general characterization of social peace as *ordinata concordia*, which is then given specification in (7)-(9). Finally, one can see that the ladder goes no higher than (9). What, then, of (10) and (11)? Clearly (11) exists to explain (10). The concept of *ordo* invoked in the definition of *pax omnium rerum* in turn requires explanation. Items (1)-(9) have also invoked the concept of *ordo* through the adjective *ordinata*. But (10) is not merely one of these formulations with *ordinata*; it

---

35. *Quapropter* signals the beginning of the ladder of ascent: "To develop this in detail. . . ."

is formally distinct, and, as we have seen, is given no place in the subsequent development. I take it to be the general statement which underlies the whole sequence (1)-(9), just as (6) is the general statement about social peace which underlies the sub-sequence (7)-(9). *Omnium rerum,* then, should not be translated "universe," or in any way that suggests that some kind of eschatological peace is in view. The relations between the terms "peace" and "order" are clearly those of a definition; order, for Augustine, is not something different from peace that enables it or brings it about: "What, then, is peace? The peace of any and every thing is the tranquillity of order."[36]

The household occupies Augustine in chapters 14-16. He discusses it primarily as a Christian household, that is to say, with a believer at its head, seeking to love his neighbor within the social context the household affords. A mere sentence or two about the non-Christian household at the beginning of chapter 17 leads Augustine to the city, which he treats in the opposite order, first speaking of how the earthly city establishes its peace and then of how the heavenly city makes use of it. It is a reasonable inference from the different approaches that Augustine thinks of a Christian household as achieving a concrete form in the way that a Christian city cannot.

"Household" *(domus)* means something political, "an ordered harmony about giving and receiving commands among those who live in the same house." It is the "the beginning, or the cell, of the city" and consequently "derives its rules from the city's laws" (16). That is to say, it is a sphere of punishment and command. Not only do masters command servants, but parents command children and husbands wives. The distinctive feature which Augustine discerns in the Christian household is that commands are given "not from a craving to dominate, but from a readiness to take care, not from a pride which asserts mastery, but from a compassionate acceptance of responsibility" (14). And if Augustine had stopped there, we would have concluded simply that the Christian household differs from any other only by the *motive* for which the authority structure is maintained. But he goes on: "This, of course [i.e., the readiness to take care and the compassionate acceptance of responsibility], is what the arrangements of nature require; it is how God created mankind" (15). Creation order allowed no place for dominion; the patriarchs were shepherds who ruled flocks, not kings who ruled subjects. And that is why before the time of Noah there were no slaves. In this almost offhand way Augustine reminds us of the patristic tradition that government and slavery were a provision of providence for a fallen world and no part of

36. For a different view, cf. W. Geerlings, "De civitate Dei XIX," p. 231: "Hierbei handelt es sich nicht um eine Definition sondern eher um eine Umschreibung der verschiedenen Bereiche. . . . Die Universalität des Friedens ist damit angesprochen."

the order of creation. With it he conveys the message that the practice of the Christian householder is in fact subtly subversive of these institutions in that it reasserts the primal equality of every human being to every other.[37] The righteous patriarchs, he remarks, "made a distinction with regard to temporal goods between the situation of their children and their slaves," but "made no distinction at all when it came to worshipping God, where permanent goods are looked for; rather, they cared for every member of their household with an equal love. This practice," he repeats, "conforms . . . well to the arrangements of nature" (16). And so it is with the Christian householder, who emerges in a form reminiscent of the Christian emperor: strangely detached from the earthly privilege of his position and longing for the heavenly rest where the burden of command will be taken from his shoulders, he makes himself the servant of others — and has more need of patience under his burden than his servants have under theirs.[38]

There is, then, a significant transvaluation of the structures of society, but it would seem to fall considerably short of what is meant by speaking of their "transformation." The authority structure of the household will not change before the coming of Christ's kingdom. What the Christian householder achieves is to superimpose another meaning on the relationships within it, very much as the Christian emperor superimposes the humble justice of his conduct upon the tasks of dominion. They are the sign of God's purpose to restore created innocence, but not the substance. And we may, not unjustly, wish to excuse Augustine for going no further than this by pleading that his political experience did not extend as far as ours. We have seen the effect of that subversion in the slow erosion of slavery and in the birth of law-governed states. Augustine's foreshortened historical perspective prevented him from seeing what kinds of change were possible given the right change in attitudes.

Yet such an excuse, which, however positively meant, concedes the right to modernity against Augustine, does not get to the root of the opposition between his expectations of politics and our own, which are based on an optimistic view of history and a belief in social malleability deriving from the revolutionary traditions of the Enlightenment. For the truth is, Augustine had a strong sense of historical development, and found it inherently ambiguous. The history of the earthly city is the history of the growth of empire. There is an important chapter (18.2) where he claims that the earthly city has taken form "in a

---

37. So easily missed is Augustine's allusion to the patristic tradition here that an early-modern political thinker could cite this passage in support of the doctrine that *imperium* is neutral and for the benefit of all (Althusius, *Politica,* chap. 1).

38. *Quo donec veniatur, magis debent patres quod dominantur, quam servi tolerare quod serviunt.* Combès has understood the idiomatic deferred infinitive correctly: "les pères doivent avoir plus de patience à supporter de commander que les esclaves de servir," *BA* 37, p. 125.

great number of empires," of which two have emerged as the central empires of world history, Assyria (in which he includes the subsequent Mesopotamian empires) and Rome. "All other kingdoms and kings I should describe as something like appendages of those empires." To write the history of the earthly city is to write of a destiny of world government given to Rome. "It was God's design to conquer the world through her, to unite the world into a single community of Roman commonwealth and Roman laws, and so impose peace throughout its length and breadth" (18.22). But this, we exclaim, is nothing other than the Vergilian ideology of the Roman empire! Quite — but with one significant difference, which turns it into a kind of photographic negative of Vergil. Guided by the prophets of Israel and the seer of the Apocalypse, Augustine sees this design of God fulfilled by the growth of Rome's overweening love of glory.[39] God's purpose is achieved by allowing evil to wax great. Within the first lines of *The City of God* he finds an opportunity to quote the famous tag of Aeneid VI, *parcere subiectis et debellare superbos,* and to comment, "This is God's prerogative; but man's arrogant spirit in his swelling pride has claimed it as his own and delights to hear this verse quoted in his own praise."[40]

World history, then, does assume a shape, and the evolution of a pacified and civilized world government is the key to it. Augustine is to this extent a historicist: there are no general questions of political authority left unaccounted for when he has given us his account of the growth of Rome.[41] There are, certainly, counterfactual hypotheses that may be entertained: what if, instead of empire, there were many kingdoms dwelling peacefully together like households in a city (4:15)? What if the Roman empire had been put together by a series of peaceful bilateral agreements and without war (5:17)? But the history turns out in fact to have been a demonic history, which expresses the divine purpose only as providence, following its own hidden course to higher ends.[42] His problem, then, is not to *conceive* of progress within the political realm, but to *distance* himself from it, retaining the perspective that God brings the pretensions of the proud to naught. What appears to be civilizational progress is, in fact, on the moral and spiritual level, self-defeating.

39. Von Heyking (*Politics as Longing,* pp. 21f.; 150-71) stresses helpfully Augustine's distinction between love of glory and lust for domination; but love of glory is not politically innocent. Cf. 5.17: had the empire been formed by peaceful agreement, "there would have been no glory for the victors."

40. 1. *prol.* Augustine's love of Vergil influenced much of *The City of God.* Vergil's great virtue, in Augustine's eyes, was that he could not suppress a "shudder of compassion" at the brutal deeds which made the empire great (3.16).

41. Against Barrow, *Introduction,* p. 249.

42. *Ipse dat regna terrena et bonis et malis . . . pro rerum ordine ac temporum occulto nobis, notissimo sibi* (4.33); *Divina providentia regna constituuntur humana* (5.1).

I conclude by illustrating how he attempts to show this from the most haunting chapters of Book 19, chapters 5-9, the purpose of which is to elaborate in social terms the arguments advanced in chapter 4 — that the final good cannot be realized in this life. Augustine reviews four spheres of society: the household, the city, the world, and the universe.[43] In each case he shows that distress is inseparable from our experience of them, so that none of them can represent the end of human action. The household comes first, and since no one thinks domesticity the goal of all human endeavor, Augustine can afford to be lighthearted, with two cynical quotations from Terence about marriage and love. But the point is a serious one, on which he will build subsequently: "Peace . . . is quite unpredictable, since we do not know the hearts of those we wish to be at peace with; and if we knew them today, we would certainly not know how they would stand tomorrow."

Far from lighthearted is the electrifying discussion of the ills of the city, seen from the point of view of the dilemmas of a judge. This choice of angle is itself striking.[44] Judicial tasks are the hallmark of Roman imperial civilization, and Augustine conceives them as virtually impossible to discharge. Again, it is lack of insight into the heart that lies at the root of the trouble: "What idea can we form of the pitiable predicament of men who sit in judgment on other men without being able to read their consciences?" The judge's well-meaning ignorance is a calamity for the innocent accused, who may be tortured to secure valid evidence for the defence, only to be driven to a false confession and so executed for a crime he did not commit. We shall miss the point of this if we confine ourselves to observations on the barbarous laws of evidence which obtained in the late empire. Augustine himself shows no sign of sharing the view that the Roman legal system grew more brutal as the empire grew old. For him it is a universal problem about judicial process everywhere. It is a guess as to which party is lying and which telling the truth, and any inquisitorial process adopted to reduce the element of hazard may backfire and defeat its own ends. Yet not for that reason do we refuse to lend our best efforts to the judicial process, though we do so with a grim sense of our limitations and a prayer for deliverance upon our lips.[45]

43. That division, attributed unspecifically to "philosophers," may reasonably be supposed to originate with Varro.

44. The personal experience lying behind these reflections has been drawn to our attention by one of the recently discovered Divjak letters (*Ep.* 24*), which concerns a dilemma faced by Augustine as a judge. Yet his authority will never have extended to torture and execution, and the background to this will surely lie in his role as an intercessor, discussed at length in *Ep.* 153.

45. Although Augustine is still in dialogue with the philosophers about the "wise man," he clearly anticipates the discussion of chap. 17 on the City of God's support for the laws of earthly peace.

After the city comes the world, which gives him the occasion to speak directly about the Roman empire. Differences of language create an infinity of misunderstandings, he remarks, and then envisages a reply which can be advanced on behalf of world government.[46] "I shall be told that the imperial city was at pains to impose not only its yoke but its language to pacify and socialize the races that it conquered, with the result that there was no lack of interpreters, but an abundance of them rather." To which he responds: "True enough; but at what cost was this achieved, in constant wars of such a scale, in slaughter and the shedding of human blood!" The gain of world civilization he does not deny; yet he will not permit us to forget how it was achieved. Wars, he continues in a seminal few sentences, are always dreadful, even when they are just; and then he lets fly one last barb at all complacent apologists for "vast, abominable and cruel evils": "Whoever experiences no grief, when they occur or when he simply contemplates them, is without doubt much more unhappy; he thinks himself happy solely for want of all human sensibility!"

If we have followed Augustine carefully up to this point, we shall have no difficulty in situating the next phase in his argument (chap. 8). It is about friendship, a theme which seems to interrupt the expanding sequence of concentric circles from family to universe. But the friendship of which Augustine writes is that which links persons on different continents, that inter-territorial friendship which was to him, as every reader of his correspondence knows, the most precious benefit of the network of imperial communications. But the very possibility of communication means that our affections become engaged in ways that leave us most vulnerable to anxieties evoked by distance. We learn that our friend's land has been overrun by invaders or stricken by famine, or that our friend has died; or, much worse, we learn that our friend has forsaken the faith or has committed some moral offence that threatens death to his soul; and we learn all this impotently at the opposite end of the world. Anyone who has lived in one country and had friends or family in another knows what Augustine means: the very availability of communications crucifies us more perceptibly on the ineradicable fact of absence, which heightens the hiddenness that casts a shadow over the best of our social relations.

Hiddenness is the root of the matter. No one, perhaps, before Kierkegaard was so vexed by the difficulties we experience in displaying our hearts to one another. It is this, rather than the pride of original sin, the dazzle of glory, the

---

46. The voice that speaks is apparently that of Laelius from Cicero's *de re publica.* Cf. 21.2, where the passage is summarized: *Responsum est a parte iustitiae ideo iustum esse quod talibus hominibus sit utilis servitus,* noting the occurrence of the phrase *imperiosa civitas* in both passages. Yet a discreetly concealed argument with Orosius also seems to be intended.

iron rod of power, or the lure of sensuality, which casts a shadow over all social relations. We may be deceived in one another. To follow Augustine to the fourth stage, the Universe, is to see how this inexorable law applies also in our relations with the spirits and demons which imprint their character upon the institutions of the earthly city. Empire, because it unifies us, tempts us to think that this constraint can be overcome; but in winning ground at one point, it loses it at another. While showing little or no interest in the possibilities of life apart from the Roman empire, Augustine could not accept its pretensions, and therefore had to conclude that the story of human progress which it told was illusory. It did not overcome the resistance of the human heart to mutual knowledge. A later political philosophy would distinguish between private and public spheres of communication, making it a criterion for political relevance that something should be capable of emerging into the daylight of public scrutiny, while the domestic sphere, being essentially private, could be dismissed as an irrelevance to politics.[47] We can imagine Augustine replying, "If that is politics, there never was a political community!" For the privacy of our motives vitiates our communications at every conceivable level, and forms a prison out of which in this world there can be no escape. In a wonderful comment on the suicide of the chaste Lucretia (in the first book of Livy), he observes that she sought death because "she was unable to disclose her purity of conscience to the world" (1.19).

These chapters are a microcosm of Augustine's social thought. Either we find that they illumine the constraints of social existence as little else in Western literature can, or we shake our heads in bewilderment and ask, "But why was he so gloomy?" If it does not trouble us that we are ignorant of what our children are thinking, that our spouse may be sleeping with our best friend, that many inmates of our prisons may be innocent of the crimes for which they are being punished, that foreign relations are built upon a capacity to repel sudden and unforeseen attack; or if we think that there are alternative patterns of political life available which are not vulnerable to treachery, stupidity, or simple conflicts of view, then we will find Augustine's somber rhetoric merely perplexing. But in that case, Augustine will say to us, we are hardly fit to be citizens of the heavenly city, in which each will be transparent to all: *patebunt cogitationes nostrae invicem nobis* (22.29.6).

---

47. Immanuel Kant, *On Perpetual Peace* (AA 8.381). The distinction between private and public spheres belongs to the earliest phases of modern thought. Cf. Althusius, *Politica*, chap. 2, who, however, includes the private sphere within the realm of politics. It is to Rousseau (*Discourse on Inequality* Q) that we owe the doctrine that private morality cannot be the subject of public justice.

Christian Platonism and
Non-proprietary Community

JOAN LOCKWOOD O'DONOVAN

The thirteenth and fourteenth centuries witnessed the finest flowering of the medieval Augustinian tradition of trinitarian and christological moral realism. This tradition was Platonist in the sense of having absorbed Platonist elements of mysticism, contemplation, asceticism, illuminationism and universalism.[1] In both centuries, its most accomplished exponents were embroiled in the controversy over the Franciscan practice of "evangelical poverty," the issue of which was whether the most perfect path of Christian discipleship entailed *the absolute renunciation of property* — the renunciation of both individual and communal ownership of earthly goods — as well as the "poor use" *(usus pauper)* of goods — the restricted use of only those goods necessary for personal and communal subsistence. In the 1260s the Franciscan theologian and Minister General Bonaventure defended the friars' twofold poverty of living without property and using only necessities, against vehement assaults from within and without his own order. A little more than a century later the English theologian John Wyclif, although himself a secular cleric, advocated that the whole clerical estate conform to the discipline of evangelical poverty by living "exproprietarily." For both thinkers the matter of evangelical poverty engaged fundamental theological understandings: of the person and work of Christ; of the human community as created, fallen, redeemed and sanctified; of the ethics of ordered love. It is this engagement that I wish to explore.

1. By universalism I refer to the scholastic theory of the independent being of the universals of thought and language.

One earlier version of this paper was published in *Modern Theology* 14:1 (1998): 19-42, and another was presented to the Conference on the Doctrine of God and Ethics, King's College, London, April 1997.

My exploration has two objectives. The first is to show the enduring importance for theological ethics of the medieval theology of poverty. The second is to bring the Franciscan and Wycliffite tradition of christological realism critically to bear on a particular widespread development in contemporary Christian social ethics: namely, its incorporation of the concept of *subjective natural rights,* i.e., of natural moral rights attributable to persons.

For some years now, I have been struck by the proclivity of contemporary theologians of all denominations for moving theologically from the creation of humankind in God's image to the unique dignity of persons in community to their universal possession of fundamental rights. Elsewhere[2] I have argued that this movement is lamentably naïve and misled, given the inescapable association of the concept of rights with the modern philosophical perspective of "possessive individualism" (to use C. B. Macpherson's memorable epithet).[3] This is the perspective bequeathed by the liberal contractarian tradition of Hobbes, Locke, Rousseau, Kant, and the apologists of the American and French Revolutions, and still vigorous, with utilitarian accretions, in the writings of such contemporary contractarians as John Rawls and Robert Nozick.[4] It is not my intention here to retrace the modern philosophical lineage of the concept of natural rights, but rather to illuminate the concept's theological unacceptability, by exploring the antithetical perspective offered by the medieval theology of poverty, that is, of individual and communal non-proprietorship.

My discussion falls into five sections. The first clarifies the antithesis between poverty understood as non-proprietorship and the possession of natural rights by individuals and groups, and suggests the timeliness of investigating this antithesis in the current crisis of liberal rights; the second examines the patristic foundations of the medieval theology of poverty; the third expounds the classical Franciscan formulations; the fourth explicates Wyclif's transformation and application of the Franciscan ethic; and the concluding section draws out the contribution of the non-proprietary tradition to Christian social thought.

Obviously, my investigation is not a comprehensive study of the Christian Platonist, non-proprietary tradition, which would lead us from Wyclif into Hus and various late medieval perfectionist movements, Renaissance Platonists

---

2. "Historical Prolegomena to a Theological Review of 'Human Rights,'" *Studies in Christian Ethics* 9:2 (1996): 52-65; revised in *A Preserving Grace: Protestants, Catholics, and Natural Law,* ed. M. Cromartie (Grand Rapids: Eerdmans, 1997), pp. 143-56.

3. C. B. Macpherson, *The Political Theory of Possessive Individualism* (Oxford: Clarendon Press, 1962).

4. The theoretical continuity of the liberal contractarian tradition from Hobbes to Nozick is persuasively argued by Ian Shapiro in *The Evolution of Rights in Liberal Theory* (Cambridge: Cambridge University Press, 1986).

such as Thomas More, Luther and the Anabaptists, and beyond. Rather, I am foregoing a more complete historical sketch for the sake of concentrating on the theologically crucial expositions of the thirteenth and fourteenth centuries.

The Proprietary Subject and the Crisis of Liberal Rights

The antithesis between poverty understood as non-proprietorship and the individual and collective possession of natural rights is simply this: that the *possession* of rights is always proprietorship; all natural rights, at least in the Western political tradition, originate in property right, so that to reject property right is to reject natural or fundamental rights as such. Indeed, the whole panoply of modern rights (including what are called "entitlements") has sprung historically from the attribution to humankind of two radical proprietary rights: firstly, an original or natural proprietary right over the non-human goods of creation, and secondarily, the person's natural right to dispose of his own acts (i.e., his right of freedom), which came to be explicitly construed as a form of proprietorship. From these radical proprietary rights has evolved the proprietary subject who seeks to dominate his moral and natural environments not only by protecting what he already possesses against any and every other possessor, but by demanding what he does not yet possess as an entitlement that is entailed in his original proprietorship.

It is of historical and theological significance that the attribution to humankind of these two natural property rights did not originate with Hobbes and Locke but with late medieval canon and civil lawyers, canonist popes and theologians.[5] A recognized milestone was Pope John XXII's proposal in a bull of 1329 that, from the moment of his creation, mankind was collectively endowed with full *lordship* in the sense of *ownership* (the Roman legal term being *dominium*) of earthly goods, after God's own lordship/ownership *(dominium)*.[6] While conceding that God's ordination of private, individual ownership presupposed the sin of our first parents, he nevertheless presented divine ownership, mankind's original common ownership, his subsequent private

---

5. For late medieval developments in natural rights theory, see R. Tuck's short summary in *Natural Rights Theories: Their Origin and Development* (Cambridge: Cambridge University Press, 1979) and the longer, more thoroughly researched study by B. Tierney in *The Idea of Natural Rights: Studies on Natural Rights, Natural Law and Church Law* (Atlanta: Emory University/ Scholars Press, 1997). Tierney's study, which is highly critical of Tuck, proposes some important corrections of his historical representations, without, in my judgment, accomplishing the overall refutation of Tuck's account at which he aims.

6. *Quia vir reprobus* in C. Eubel, ed., *Bullarium Franciscanum* 5 (1898): 408-50.

ownership, and finally civil ownership as a continuous vindication of property right, thus anticipating the trajectory of seventeenth-century ideas. As we shall see, John XXII's primary objective in this and other bulls was to discredit the theological and christological foundations of the Franciscan practice of absolute (legal) poverty. Over the next few centuries, influential Paris theologians and their followers[7] explicated man's natural *dominium* as a moral faculty *(facultas)* or power, a subjective right *(ius)*, and assimilated freedom to it, so that men were conceived as having a natural *dominium* in their freedom. This prepared for the full-blown proprietary theory of right in Hobbes, Locke, and the Levellers, which cast the individual rights-bearer as "free in as much as he is the proprietor of his person and capacities."[8]

As the immediate, exclusive proprietor of his/her physical and spiritual being and capacities, and derivatively, of those external objects necessary to their preservation and development, the modern rights-possessor is typically occupied in controlling, acquisitive, and competitive actions — acts of disposing, using, exchanging, commanding, and demanding. The proprietary subject forms social and political relationships through the formal mechanism of the contract, modeled on an economic transaction undertaken from calculations of self-interest. His/her freedom, prior to and within contractual relationships, consists in independence from or non-subjection to other wills, externally imposed obligations, and natural limitations. The associations produced by the binding agreement of self-possessing individuals conform to the commercial logic of investment corporations and consumer groups, always poised on the brink of litigation.

In recent years doubts about the tenability of the liberal rights society have sprung up in many quarters. Even the more libertarian voices of popular culture appear to be disturbed by the proliferation of actual rights-claims and the infinity of potential claims, as the awareness dawns that the content of rights is in fact coterminous with the objects of human desire and possession. There is also growing appreciation of the difficulties of rationally adjudicating disparate and conflictual rights-claims, though too little appreciation of the impossibility of adjudicating them in the light of a common or public good that rests on no other foundation than private rights and the derivative normativity of market processes.

Current rights-claims are limited by only two horizons: the expanding horizon of technological ingenuity and the shrinking horizon of the public

---

7. Most notably, the nominalist Jean Gerson (d. 1429) and his later followers John Mair (d. 1550) and Jacques Almain (d. 1515), who influenced a broad spectrum of sixteenth- and seventeenth-century thinkers, including the Spanish neo-scholastics, Luis de Molina and Francisco Suárez.

8. C. B. Macpherson, *Political Theory of Possessive Individualism,* p. 3.

purse. Both are causes of popular unease, as the gathering clouds of ecological disaster reveal the Faustian character of technological hubris to ever more people, and the cost to taxpayers of meeting the rights-claims of citizens appears ever less feasible in the long (if not the short) term. Discerning that all universal rights are held against government at some level (owing to the implicit terms of the political contract),[9] taxpayers now realize that their political investment is subject to the law of diminishing returns, given the inflationary logic of rights. Efforts of governments to reinforce the political contract by formalizing their obligations to citizens in published bills and charters of rights appear only to aggravate popular discontent and restlessness by increasing the incentives and opportunities of citizens to seek legal redress for public failures in rights provision. It is hardly surprising that the uneasy majority are tempted by the negative libertarian solution of casting off the whole class of welfare entitlements.

In the midst of these perplexities, the more profound and subtle threat to community posed by the moral culture of rights has attracted little notice. The current popular anxiety exhibits little awareness that the shared goods in which the reality of community consists elude the common satisfaction of individual rights. The most credible and consistent Christian theological responses to this threat have come from the dominant natural law traditions, Catholic and Reformed, which have drawn attention to the shared spiritual goods constitutive not only of the political community but of all communities, from the family, the church, and the school to the business, the trade union, and the professional society. Moreover, exponents of these traditions have attributed rights not only to individuals but to institutional communities with stable teleological structures, intending thereby to situate the concept of subjective right firmly within a framework of moral law or objective right. In so responding, they are walking in the footsteps of the greatest Christian natural rights theorists of the sixteenth and seventeenth centuries: Luis de Molina, Francisco Suárez, Hugo Grotius, and Johannes Althusius. But just as the earlier enterprise, having admitted into moral-political discourse *the proprietary will* or *rights-possessing subject,* was unable to prevent the destruction of community entailed in its political ambitions, so too, the contemporary enterprise to reclaim the rights culture may fare no better.

At this juncture, it can only be salutary to entertain the more radical critique of the concept of natural property right arising within the Christian Platonist tradition. It stands alone in developing christological and ecclesiological objections to the proprietary subject.

---

9. The implicit terms are that government meet the rights-claims of its citizens in return for their surrender of some portion of natural rights to, for example, freedom and material property.

Patristic Foundations of Non-Proprietary Community

From the beginning Christian moral thought was sensitive to issues of property and wealth, particularly as concerning the uses made of material possessions. Typically the Church Fathers constructed their morality of ownership around the injunctions to, and examples of, generous giving and sharing of possessions, and conversely, the warnings against covetousness and greed contained in the Gospels, Epistles and Book of Acts. In the third century, Christian writers discovered a paradigm of Christian possession in the community of goods attributed by the author of Acts to the original gathering of Christ's disciples in Jerusalem who "had all things in common" (2:44; also 4:32-37). The paradigmatic status of common possession was reinforced by speculations about the natural (prelapsarian) form of Adamic community fed chiefly from Roman Stoic writers such as Seneca, but also from Plato[10] and the Roman law books.

Echoing older Greek and Latin sources, Seneca described a state of primitive human innocence in which men harmoniously shared the earth's bounty, without violently appropriating it through labor or claiming exclusive ownership of it.[11] Complementing their natural equality of need-satisfaction was their natural equality of freedom. Only when the growth of avarice and lust for power corrupted their natural sociability were private property and coercive power established to curb both possession and freedom. Such speculations found their way into the second century Roman legal philosophy of the *Digest*, with some jurists ascribing common possession of things and equality of freedom to the *ius naturale* in contradistinction to the *ius gentium*.[12] Church Fathers who favored the Senecan position were inclined to conceive of men's communal sharing of material things according to need as an imitation of God's equal beneficence to all his creatures in bestowing the natural gifts of air, sunshine and rain, moon, stars, sea, and the seasons.[13] Some of the most influential concluded from God's intention that the earth and its fruits be the com-

---

10. Influential were Plato's arguments for the communism of the guardian class in his ideal republic, in Book 3 of *The Republic*, 416d-417b.

11. *Ep.* 14.2

12. For a concise discussion of the law of nature in the *Digest* and *Institutes* of Justinian's *Corpus iuris civilis*, see A. J. Carlyle, *A History of Mediaeval Political Theory*, 1 (Edinburgh: William Blackwood & Sons, 1962), pp. 33-44.

13. Cyprian, *De opere et eleemosynis* 25, PL 4:644; Zeno of Verona, *Tractatus* 1.3.6, PL 11: 287; also Clement of Alexandria, *Paidagogus* 2.12, PG 8:541-44; Basil the Great, *Homilia in illud Lucae*, "Destruam . . . ," 7, PG 31:277; Ambrose of Milan, *Commentarium in Epistolam II ad Corinthios* 9.9, PL 17:313-14.

mon possession of all, that support of the needy out of one's abundance was an obligation of divine justice.[14] Moreover, many Fathers endorsed humankind's natural equality of freedom, and viewed the institutions of slavery and coercive rule as postlapsarian divine ordinances that express, even as they remedy, the disordered passions of sinful humanity.[15]

Augustine's apparent reiteration of the Stoic-patristic tradition carried immense authority for later generations, and more importantly, he provided the theological arguments and principles that would furnish a framework for its development — not only by the Franciscans but by their papalist opponents as well! In the first place, Augustine distinguished between two (objective) "rights" on which earthly possession of goods is based: "divine right, according to which all things belong to the righteous," and "human right, which is in the jurisdiction of the kings of the earth."[16] Replying to the protests of the heretical Donatists against the imperial confiscation of their churches and other property, he maintained that they had forfeited their possessions in accordance with both rights: for imperial law enforced what divine law required, that their property be awarded to the truly "just," i.e., to the true (institutional) church. Elsewhere Augustine displays the gulf between the divine and human titles, as when he expounds divine right in terms of God's intention that the earth's abundance should sustain all men and contrasts with it the human property right by which one man presumes, on the basis of imperial law, to claim: "*Haec villa mea est, haec domus mea, hic servus meus est.*"[17] Or when he proposes that the Christian believer alone possesses things justly, since he knows how to use them rightly, and concludes that, however licit (according to the civil laws) the acquisitions of the unfaithful may appear, his possession of things is not just, owing to his ignorance of their proper use.[18]

This last argument reverberates the core themes of Augustine's moral and political theology that would set the future theoretical contours of non-

14. And conversely, that the accumulation of wealth for one's private (exclusive) use contravened God's intention, and amounted to robbing the needy of what belonged to them by divine and natural right. Clement of Alexandria, *Quis dives salvetur* 31, PG 9:637; Basil, *Homilia*, PG 31:276-77; Ambrose, *De Nabuthe* 3, 11, PL 14:734, 747; *De officiis ministrorum* 1.28, PL 16:61-62; *In Psalmum CXVII Expositio* 8.22, PL 15:1303; *Commentarium in Epistolam II ad Corinthios* 9.9, PL 17:313-14; Chrysostom, *De Lazaro* 2.4, PG 48:987-88; Augustine, *Enarratio in Psalmum CXLVII* 12, PL 37:1922; Gregory the Great, *Liber regulae pastoralis* 3.21, PL 77:87.

15. For a survey of the patristic positions on natural equality, slavery, and coercive rule, see Carlyle, *History*, 1, pp. 111-31.

16. *Ep.* 93, *Nicene and Post-Nicene Fathers*, 1st series (Grand Rapids: Eerdmans, 1974), 1: 400.

17. *In Joannis Evangelium* Tractatus 6.25, PL 35:1437.

18. *Ep.* 153.26, PL 33:665; *IG*, p. 130.

proprietary community. Chiefly, it recalls his conception of justice in the individual soul and in the body politic in terms of a rightly ordered love. According to Augustine, love is rightly ordered when the transcendent, universal, and supreme good is loved as such, and all created goods are loved in their determinate relation of dependence on him, their dependence being at once ontological, teleological, and axiological. In a just soul, the movement of its appetite toward an object is ruled by a true apprehension of this manifold relationship of dependence and by consent of the will to it.[19] Correspondingly, in a just commonwealth, "the highest and truest common good, namely, God, is loved by all, and men love each other in Him without dissimulation. . . ."[20] Thus, the *bonum commune* is above all *a sharing in rightly ordered loving — an activity that is entirely common in the sense of inclusive and participatory because entirely spiritual.* This is the theological rationale of Augustine's daring proposal in *The City of God* that Cicero's celebrated *res publica,* intending as it must to unite the substance of justice and right, could not have existed.[21]

By contrast, Augustine conceived the disordered love of the soul as the *privatization of good,* in that it entails the soul's turning away from the "universal common good" to its "private good," that is, to itself as privately possessed. Pride, "which is the beginning of all sin," he defined as the soul's delighting in its powers "to excess," as if "there were no God" and so it were the source and owner of them.[22] From pride flows avarice, for the soul that wills to have its powers from itself loves all other beings excessively, as required by the aggrandizement of its private possessions, and therein misuses them.[23] In the body politic, disordered love is the destruction of community, of the *bonum commune,* because it involves radical loss of the shared spiritual possession of being, meaning, and value. The fragmentary association surviving this destruction Augustine discerns in the late Roman Empire: it is the regulated interaction of private spheres of degenerate freedom, secured by the protection of property and enhanced by the provision of material benefits at the hands of unscrupulous tyrants.[24]

---

19. See Oliver O'Donovan's exposition of the rational aspect of love in Augustine's thought in *The Problem of Self-Love in St. Augustine* (New Haven: Yale University Press, 1980), pp. 29-32.

20. *Ep.* 137.5.17, *Nicene and Post-Nicene Fathers* 1:480.

21. 19.21; *IG*, p. 161. For discussion of this passage, see pp. 55-59 above.

22. O. O'Donovan, *Problem of Self-Love,* pp. 95-96.

23. O. O'Donovan, *Problem of Self-Love,* pp. 95-103.

24. *City of God* 2.20; *IG*, pp. 137-38.

Franciscan Poverty: The Theology
of Evangelical Non-possession

The importance for moral and political theology of the Franciscan development
of this patristic and especially Augustinian inheritance must be understood
against the background of the papalist mainstream, which may be described as a
continuous elaboration of Hildebrandine reforming ideas. These ideas expressed the programme of Pope Gregory VII (Hildebrand, ca. 1030-85) and his
successors to emancipate the church from her vassalage to secular lords and
from the excessive lay interference with clerical offices entailed by feudal property relations, primarily in order to foster a more spiritually-minded and chaste,
less avaricious and corrupt clergy. Their overall strategy was to construct a comprehensive ecclesiastical corporation equipped with a unitary structure of government undergirded by the accumulation and legal consolidation of property.

Prior to the late thirteenth and early fourteenth centuries, ownership of
ecclesiastical property was vested in ecclesiastical corporations for specific religious and charitable purposes, such as administering the sacraments, preaching, teaching, and alms-giving. Corporations were formed at various administrative levels (congregational, parochial, diocesan, archdiocesan etc.) and
included a variety of establishments (churches, monastic houses, confraternities, universities, and hospitals). Every corporation was itself legal owner
(dominus) of the property attaching to it, its 'head' or governing authority occupying the office of proctor or administrator *(procurator, administrator)* of
that property.[25] With the centralization of church government, ownership
(dominium) of temporal possessions came to be vested in the universal church,
the whole *congregatio fidelium,* the pope as earthly 'head' occupying the office
of universal administrator *(dispensator universalis).*[26]

Two biblical models were evoked for the church's corporate property: the
Jerusalem church and the "moneybag of Christ." The first model, the common
possession and distribution of temporal goods in the original believing community, was chiefly applicable to cenobitical monasticism (for which it had
been formative). The second model, the 'purse' or 'moneybag' carried by Christ
(or by a disciple on his authority) to provide for his own and his disciples' sustenance, and for the poor, was more generally applicable to church property:
for the church's *fisc,* like Christ's purse, contained the offerings of the faithful,
held in common by Christ's ministers (the clergy) to meet their own and oth-

25. B. Tierney, *Foundations of the Conciliar Theory* (Cambridge: Cambridge University
Press, 1955), pp. 118-19.
26. Tierney, *Foundations,* pp. 140-42, 165-69.

ers' needs.[27] In the mainstream theological and canonist application of these models to the church's temporal goods, the distinction between *common property* and *common non-proprietary possession* never surfaced.

It was only the Franciscan dispute over poverty that brought this distinction into historical prominence for a time. Originally confined within the order, the dispute spread out to engage the friars' enemies and eventually the papacy. It arose from the adaptation of its founder's discipline to the order's evolving ministry. For the "perfect poverty" practiced by St. Francis and his immediate followers, after the perceived pattern of Christ and his apostles, approached a condition of permanent vagrant destitution. As itinerant preachers, the brothers were to seek only the barest necessities, to labor manually without charge, to beg when their labor was not freely rewarded, and to look upon their churches and houses as shrines and shelters for wayfaring pilgrims.[28] Inevitably, however, the numerical growth of the Franciscans and the accompanying expansion and specialization of their ministries brought about a more settled cenobitic organization, a more reliable provision of a greater range of necessities, and continuous access to commodities such as books and writing equipment indispensable to their work.

Thirteenth-century popes played a key role in legislating and defending these relaxations of the Franciscan Rule. Their central strategy of adaptation consisted in moves to define Franciscan poverty in legal as well as practical terms. The first move was to claim that the Rule bound the brothers not only to a minimal use of goods but to a total renunciation of property, individual and collective;[29] the second move resolved the ensuing problem of who owned the moveable goods used by the Minorites by vesting their ownership *(dominium)* in the pope, while leaving the ownership of non-moveables in the hands of their donors as before.[30] By interpreting Franciscan poverty as an exproprietary state, Rome licenced the brotherhood's steady accumulation of material resources through a machinery for regular economic acquisition and alienation that did not involve the friars directly as legal agents.[31] Not surprisingly, the pa-

27. I am indebted to J. D. Dawson's exposition of the ecclesiological functioning of these biblical models in "Richard FitzRalph and the Fourteenth-Century Poverty Controversies," *Journal of Ecclesiastical History* 34 (1983): 317-19.

28. G. Leff, *Heresy in the Later Middle Ages: The Relation of Heterodoxy to Dissent c. 1250-1450*, 2 vols. (London: Manchester University Press, 1967), 1:57.

29. Pope Gregory IX, *Quo elongati* (1229), cited in Leff, *Heresy,* 1:65-66.

30. Innocent IV, *Ordinem vestrum* (1245), cited in Leff, *Heresy,* 1:67; also J. Coleman, "Poverty and Property" in J. H. Burns, ed., *The Cambridge History of Medieval Political Thought c. 350–c. 1450* (Cambridge: Cambridge University Press, 1988), p. 634.

31. Leff, *Heresy,* pp. 67-68.

pal strategy only incensed Franciscan rigorists, for whom the minimal use of goods *(usus pauper)* rather than their exproprietary use was essential to the order's apostolic vocation.

By the 1260s the Fransciscans were in dire need of a masterful theological treatment of the poverty issue that would reconcile the disputants within the order, preserve its relations with the papacy, and combat external critics.[32] About 1269 Bonaventure furnished the needed treatise under the title *Apologia pauperum*. His work provided an unrivalled theological explication of the Franciscan ethic which vindicated the uniqueness of the mendicant 'way', while situating it within the manifold discipleship of the church.

The *Apologia pauperum* gave clear expression to Bonaventure's overall mission of carrying forward the theological tradition of Augustine, Anselm, the Pseudo-Dionysius, and his illustrious mentor, Alexander of Hales, which made the divine Trinity and the Word Incarnate the *fons* and *finis* of thought and spirituality. His theological mission involved him, as a schoolman, in resisting the rise of Averroism and all species of philosophical naturalism; as a mystic, in charting the mind's ascent to ecstatic contemplation of the Truth; as a pastor, in cultivating and vindicating the discipline of life that undergirded the mystical ascent. He detected a profound unity in the assaults of Averroist philosophy on traditional theology and the assaults of the secular masters on the mendicant way: the former asserted the self-sufficiency of reason apart from faith and the latter, the holiness of worldly strivings of the will after success, wealth, honors, and freedom from ascetical deprivations. Both elevated the distorted structures of sinful humanity into the structures of humankind created *imago dei* and restored in Christ.

For Bonaventure a central aspect of Christ's earthly work of salvation was his revelation of the perfect moral life, the life of "evangelical perfection." This life is the issue of divine-human love which combines perfect will and perfect power of action in the efficacious avoidance of evil, the zealous pursuit of the good, and the patient bearing of trials.[33] Jesus manifested love's threefold work not only in his action but in his counsels: to surrender material goods — to practice poverty (Matt. 19:21); to deny self-will — to practice obedience (Matt. 16:24); and to refrain from sexual activity — to practice chastity (Matt. 19:12).[34]

---

32. Chief among the order's external critics were two secular masters of the University of Paris, William of St. Amour and Gerard of Abbeville, who, giving vent to the resentment harbored by seculars against the mendicant masters, mounted a wholesale attack on the Franciscan constitution, accusing the Minorites of following the heterodox prophecies of Joachim of Fiore.

33. *Apologia pauperum*, ch. 3.5-7, *Opera Omnia* 8 (Quaracchi, 1898); *The Works of Bonaventure*, 4, ed. and trans. José de Vinck (Paterson, N.J.: St. Antony Guild Press, 1966): 40-41. All quotations are from the de Vinck translation.

34. *Defense of the Mendicants*, ch. 3.5, de Vinck 4:40.

Christ showed that these three forms of self-sacrifice assist all the works of love. Chiefly they assist love's first work of overcoming the root human evils of covetousness, pride, and physical lust; but they also facilitate love's second work of pursuing the active good of "caring for our neighbor" and as well, the contemplative good of "lifting up our mind to God" (2 Cor. 5:13); and they assist love's third work of bearing trials with patience and joyful acceptance for the Father's sake.[35]

Bonaventure regarded the order of Christ's "counsels of perfection" in the Beatitudes (Matt. 5:3-12) as confirming the primacy of the practice of poverty in the evangelical life.[36] For this practice overcomes the radical spiritual evil of covetousness, the "root of all evils" (1 Tim. 6:10), by removing temptations to it and by strengthening the habit of resisting it.[37] He followed Augustine in discerning the intimate relationship between the sins of covetousness and pride in the disordered love of the soul: that the soul's excessive love of other beings and things, its consuming will to possess them, is always in order to aggrandize its powers as *privately possessed,* as belonging exclusively to itself rather than to God; the coveting soul apprehends, wills, and desires itself, other selves and things, not according to their divinely ordained being, meaning, and worth, but according to an arbitrary measure reflecting its inflated self-love.

In the extreme poverty freely adopted by Christ and enjoined on his disciples during their missionary journeys (Mark 6:7-13; Luke 9:1-6), Bonaventure and his fellow Franciscans found the divinely prescribed remedy for the sins of covetousness and pride. By seeking and using only the barest necessities and giving away all superfluous goods, by depending for their daily sustenance on the free alms of believers, and by renouncing altogether the legal ownership of the goods that they used, the brothers sought to participate most fully in "the nakedness" of Christ's "naked Cross": that is, in Christ's earthly humiliation and suffering even unto death, in which he proved obedient to his Father's will.[38] To surrender not only the relative abundance of ecclesiastical possession but also the positive legal rights connected with it was, for them, intrinsic to the destitution of the Son of Man and his disciples, because they regarded just that possibility of claiming temporal goods *for oneself* and *against another,* created by legal property right, as disruptive of the human response to divine love.[39] Bonaventure recognized that the proprietary demand of the right-bearing will,

35. 3.5-7, de Vinck 4:40-41.
36. 7.1, de Vinck 4:125.
37. 9.14-17, de Vinck 4:200ff.
38. 7.21, de Vinck 4:145.
39. Indeed, it is legal rights defensible in the courts that define for Bonaventure temporal dominion in all its forms, whether (as in Roman law) "ownership," "possession," or "usufruct."

seeking to impose obligation on others, involved it in a degree of self-possession, separation from other wills and self-referential attachment to the material good at issue that approached selfishness and covetousness.[40]

Thus the renunciation of proprietary right as well as even transient wealth was an efficacious sign that the apostolic wayfarer is not a self-possessor, not a proprietor of his physical powers, but rather is possessed by Christ, receiving immediately from Him all the good that he is, has, and does. The external sign is efficacious because it both manifests and reinforces the self-surrender of the individual will to Christ's.[41] At the same time, by maximizing the disciple's dependence for his daily necessities on other (human and non-human) creatures and minimizing his control over them, the discipline trains his spirit in receiving the truth, beauty, and goodness of the world as Christ's gift, and in responding to the generosity of its giver. His "simple use" of necessities assists the friar to pass beyond the distorted utility judgments of sinful human community to find Christ in the physical world and the physical world in Christ.[42]

Bonaventure construes the exproprietary use of goods owned and conceded by others as use according to natural and divine right: for by natural right all creatures have a share in those material things necessary to sustain them in life;[43] and by divine right the whole earth and the Lord who made it are possessed by the universal congregation of "the just" in their "communion of love."[44] Neither natural nor divine right permits of renunciation by any Christian person or community, and together they circumscribe the original and just use of the earth's bounty belonging to Adamic community.[45] The Franciscan recovery of the original community of goods is not, however, a direct return to created, prelapsarian human nature, but a restoration mediated by participation in the Cross of Christ, by the strictest conformity to his counsels of self-sacrificing love.

---

40. While he does not systematically set out his objections to litigation, their logic is clear enough from his exposition of the evangelical counsels of Christ in terms of the Augustinian ethic of rightly ordered love.

41. Bonaventure shows how the Franciscan renunciation of property-right exhibits the spiritual meaning of the monastic vow itself. In that the vow (to poverty, obedience, and chastity) creates the obligation to perform "perfect acts," it is subjection to Christ's law not only of one's acts but of one's will. He invokes Anselm's comparison of the religious state created by the vow to one's offering to God both the fruits of a tree and its *ownership*. See 3.11-12, de Vinck 4:45-46.

42. The primacy of the mystical or contemplative use of nature in Franciscan spirituality is a central feature of Bonaventure's celebrated work of theological mysticism, *Itinerarium mentis in Deum.*

43. 10.13, de Vinck 4:232.

44. 10.14, de Vinck 4:233.

45. 10.13-14, de Vinck 4:232-33.

While commending the way of "evangelical perfection" to all Christians, Bonaventure strenuously denies that a less stringent conformity to Christ is necessarily sinful and requiring of forgiveness:[46] he argues that every grade of perfection and, equally, every "state of the church" is "worthy of its proper praise."[47] Every Christian, in whatever ecclesial estate, participates in the "nakedness" of Christ's "naked cross": the laymen by obeying the law's command to strip himself of "every perverse attachment of avarice and cupidity"; the secular cleric by living from "altar offerings" and rejecting "every superfluity and private possession" in administering "the church's purse"; the regular and cenobite by further surrendering both "the *right* to possess anything privately" and his "own will"; and the "apostolic men" by renouncing even the church's "purse" for the perfection of poverty.[48]

The success of Bonaventure's monumental venture of reconciliation barely survived his lifetime. As the poverty dispute progressed into the late thirteenth century, all parties perceived more clearly the potential Minorite challenge to the propertied church. An unbridgeable chasm opened up between the mendicant and papalist ecclesiologies and their underlying Christologies, owing largely to the exaggerated dimensions taken on by papal proprietary right toward the turn of the century. In the course of a protracted and bitter controversy between Pope Boniface VIII and King Philip IV of France over church administration and finance, Roman publicists such as Giles of Rome and James of Viterbo invested the pope not merely with the universal administration of the church's purse but with the supreme legal ownership of all worldly goods and possessions, whether held by ecclesiastical or secular collectivities, or by individual churchmen, lay or clerical.[49] By virtue of Christ's purported exercise *as man* of universal and immediate lordship over property, and his transmission of this "plenitude" of lordship *(dominium)* to his earthly vicars, the pope was deemed to have both supreme enforceable jurisdiction over temporal goods (i.e., judgment concerning the justice of their possession) and supreme right of use (i.e., the right to tithe and to tax possessors).[50] Propagating a positivist ecclesiological reading of Augustine's theology of "just possession," these papalists argued that only proprietors judged worthy by the Roman Church

46. 2.15, de Vinck 4:33-34.

47. 1.3, de Vinck 4:7.

48. 7.21-22, de Vinck 4:145-47.

49. Giles of Rome, *De ecclesiastica potestate*, ed. R. Scholz (Weimar: Böhlau Verlag, 1929); H.-X. Arquillière, ed., *Le plus ancien traité de l'Église: Jacques de Viterbo, De regimine christiano, 1301-1302* (Paris: Gabriel Beauchesne, 1926).

50. Giles of Rome, *De ecclesiastica potestate* 3.11; trans. R. W. Dyson (Woodbridge, Suffolk: The Boydell Press, 1986), pp. 197-203.

possessed their goods justly, according to divine law, while all others — heretics, excommunicates and infidels — possessed their goods unjustly, without divine right, and so were liable to be justly deprived of them by the church.[51]

In this climate of doctrinal antagonism Pope John XXII (1316–1334), upon concluding a successful campaign against the heretical Franciscan Spirituals and Beguins, undertook to rid the church of the menace of supreme poverty. His assaults on the Minorite "way" between 1322 and 1329 set the stage for subsequent theoretical and terminological developments, in the work of William of Ockham and Marsiglio of Padua as well as John Wyclif. The pope first attacked the concept of non-proprietary use, arguing that all morally licit use of things entails a right of use *(ius utendi),* and in the case of things consumed in use, *dominium.*[52] From the identity of moral and positive legal right, he contended that Christ and his disciples used nothing without legal right.[53] He next proposed that property and *dominium* are intrinsic to evangelical perfection, which consists in spiritual rather than practical renunciation of possessions.[54] To complete his case, the pope ascribed to Adam from the moment of his creation full ownership *(dominium)* of earthly goods, after God's own *dominium,* and pointed to God's repeated post-lapsarian confirmations of human ownership, prior to the appearance of customary and statute law.[55] The practical strategy of John XXII's legislation was to render the Franciscans a partially propertied order by renouncing papal ownership of all temporalities used by the brothers, apart from churches and goods dedicated to divine use.[56]

Wyclif's Ecclesiological Revolution: "Evangelical Lordship" and Clerical Dispossession

It is ironic that the theological cogency of Wyclif's radically anti-papal church reform owed a great deal, historically speaking, to the nagging doubts of Pope John XXII's successors about his cavalier treatment of earlier papal pronouncements on Franciscan poverty. Twenty years after John's legislation, Pope Clem-

---

51. Giles of Rome, *De ecclesiastica potestate* 2.7.10, Dyson, pp. 65-70.

52. *Ad conditorem canonum* (1322), Eubel 5:233-46.

53. *Cum inter nonnullos* (1323), Eubel 5:256-59.

54. *Quia quorumdam mentes* (1324), Eubel 5:271-80.

55. *Quia vir reprobus* (1329), Eubel 5:408-49. See the reproduction of the key passages of this bull in Ockham's polemical response, *Opus nonaginta dierum* 2, 26-8, 65, 88, 93 in A. S. McGrade and J. Kilcullen, eds., *A Letter to the Friars Minor and Other Writings,* trans. J. Kilcullen (Cambridge: Cambridge University Press, 1995), pp. 19-117; also Leff's summary in *Heresy,* 1:247-48.

56. Leff, *Heresy,* 1:164.

ent VI, responding to interminable ecclesiastical wrangling over the Friars' ministries, appointed a commission to resolve apparent discrepancies between the decretals of John XXII and his predecessor, Nicholas III, who had enshrined the Bonaventuran theological settlement. This otherwise futile committee inspired one of its archiepiscopal members, Richard FitzRalph, to bring fresh theological insight to the issue of apostolic poverty.

In his *De pauperie salvatoris,* written between 1351 and 1356, FitzRalph synthesized the high-papalist, Augustinian argument that *true property right is by grace* with Bonaventure's (essentially patristic) thesis that *common possession by right of nature is non-proprietary,* to propose that all civil property rests on an original non-proprietary *dominium* that is at once "by grace" and "by natural right," in that Adam's *dominium* over the earth already presupposed justifying grace. He proposed, moreover, that natural human lordship can be abolished only through sin, and is merely curtailed in its exercise by human law, which confers no additional right to the divine title. While insisting that positive legal distributions of property must always intend to conform to natural and divine right, he conceded that they normally and inevitably express agnosticism about the spiritual states of proprietors, and so have just an "interim validity" until God pronounces his certain judgments.[57]

The pivotal thesis of FitzRalph's treatise for Wyclif was the continuing universal force of natural, non-proprietary dominion by grace as the only just title to possession. Determined to rescue this thesis from an inconsequential fate, Wyclif argued that non-proprietary possession belonged not only to Adam's original rectitude, Christ's earthly ministry, and the apostolic witness, but to the apostolate of the whole clerical estate, and not just the Friars Minor. In Holy Scripture he found revealed the eternal model of the non-possessing church militant: the post-resurrection gathering of disciples in Jerusalem that formed a spiritual community of belief, moral practice, and preaching, and a physical community of equal sharing in the use of goods without civil ownership.[58] Following FitzRalph, Wyclif departed from the moderate Franciscan and papalist view of the primitive church as having a "double profession": of common property (the church's "purse") and of non-proprietary use of necessities (the apostolic missions). The church has a single profession of apostolic non-proprietorship.

However, given the divinely ordained historical growth of the church to include all of political society and its diverse estates, the governing and laboring

---

57. Dawson, "Richard FitzRalph," pp. 336-37.
58. Wyclif, *De civili dominio* 3.6, J. Loserth, ed., 4 vols. (London: Wyclif Society, 1885-1904), 3:77-81.

as well as preaching estates, it is the latter which, according to Wyclif, continues in time the original apostolic society by its literal practice of the church's single profession.[59] Only to this estate, whose office is to study and teach God's revelation in Christ and the Scriptures, belongs the apostolic vocation of displaying in thought and action the church's eternal essence in which every member and estate participates. Its high office of "spiritual lordship" requires of its members the most literal imitation of Christ's life of poverty, chastity, humility, contemplation, and charity, which every lay person is also bound to imitate, but in a less literal mode.[60] In expounding the "spiritual" priesthood, Wyclif provided the most comprehensive theological account of non-proprietary community from within the Augustinian tradition, surpassing even Bonaventure. For Bonaventure was hampered by the strongly eremitical cast of the Minorite vocation, to which communal features were incidental, if not threatening. His spiritual inheritance was inseparably wedded to the pattern of the wandering apostle — vagrant, destitute, suffering perpetual humiliation and deprivation — and to the towering figure of St. Francis who, in addition, communed miraculously with non-human nature and enjoyed an almost continuous state of ecstatic contemplation. Thus he failed to place his idealistic and christological epistemology and his Augustinian ethic of ordered love directly in the service of expounding *apostolic community* as distinct from the apostolic "way."

Wyclif's starting point was FitzRalph's understanding of divine lordship (*dominium divinum*), with its Thomistic and Roman legal as well as Augustinian aspects. FitzRalph agreed with John XXII that God's lordship over the world flows from his creation of it and entails his full right of freely possessing and using it and all it contains.[61] He conceives God's possession of creation as his maintenance (*conservacio*) of it and his use of creation as his "delight" (*delectio*) in it and governance (*gubernacio*) of it.[62] From the universality, immutability, and (hence) inalienability of divine lordship, FitzRalph concludes that God's gift of lordship to Adam is *a communication or sharing of himself and his lordship* rather than an alienating transfer of lordship, which would diminish God. Moreover, he conceives of Adam's "lent" lordship as an imperfect, derivative, and dependent reflection of God's own, and so, *a communicating and communicable possession and use of things according to rational necessity.*[63]

59. 3.12, Loserth 3:206; also *Sermones* 2.3, J. Loserth, ed., 4 vols. (London: Wyclif Society, 1886-89), 2:175-76.

60. 1.11, Loserth 1:73-80.

61. FitzRalph, *De pauperie salvatoris*, Appendix to Wyclif, *De dominio divino*, ed. R. L. Poole (London: Wyclif Society, 1890), pp. 283-91.

62. Poole, pp. 283-91.

63. Poole, pp. 306-11, 315-17.

For Wyclif the essence of the church's "evangelical" lordship, which is the renewal of Adamic lordship, is God's gift of himself as the love of Christ and the fellowship of the Holy Spirit (2 Cor. 13:13).[64] God's trinitarian self-giving is the archetypal cause of all divine and human communication of both spiritual and physical goods. All the justified, says Wyclif, who "coexist" in Christ's love, share (*communicant*) in lordship that is held not from one another but directly from Christ.[65] This lordship is, before all else, their spiritual possession (possession in knowledge and love) of themselves, of one another, and of the non-human creation in Christ. Wyclif's core Augustinian insight is that just lordship over (i.e., possession and use of) earthly goods involves rightly ordered love toward them, which in turn depends on the true knowledge of them available only in Christ. For in Christ, says Wyclif, is contained the intelligible being, and therefore the potential and actual being, of every creature.[66] From this primary intellectual and ethical possession of the non-human creation flow the manifold spiritual and physical uses made of it by humankind, in contemplative enjoyment, aesthetic appreciation, and in the fulfillment of material needs.[67] Evangelical dominion is, therefore, the just communal possession and use of earthly goods that shadows God's own dominion by conserving the being of non-human creatures and assisting them to realize their divinely appointed purposes. There is a parallel in Wyclif's thought between the principal human act of communicating spiritual dominion, namely, drawing others into the revelation of God's love and grace through preaching, and the principal act of communicating physical dominion, namely, drawing others into the rational use of the same material goods. In both cases the human act is merely instrumental to God's own action.[68]

Wyclif's universalizing of evangelical lordship as the christological form of the church from the time of creation brings it into an important theoretical and practical relationship with civil lordship (*dominium civilis*), i.e., positive legal proprietorship, typical of the relationship between divine and human law in his thought. There are at once the starkest opposition and the closest proximity between the two types of lordship. His voluminous *De civili dominio* (1375-6) is full of contrasts unflattering to civil lordship. He characterizes evangelical lordship as divinely instituted, founded on righteousness, communicable without limit, inalienable (except through sin), secure of tenure, free of anxiety and

64. *De civili dominio* 1.7, Loserth 1:47-50; also *De dominio divino* 3.2, Poole, pp. 207-13.

65. *De civili dominio* 3.13, Loserth 3:230.

66. *De civili dominio* 1.7, Loserth 1:49-51; *De dominio divino* 3.3, Poole, p. 219.

67. *De civili dominio* 1.8, Loserth 1:52-53; 3.8, 10, 12, Loserth 3:113, 152, 204-5; *De dominio divino* 3.2, Poole, pp. 212-13.

68. *De dominio divino* 1.10, Poole, pp. 74-75; 3.1, Poole, pp. 206-7.

temptation, and oriented to the service of God and the neighbor.[69] By comparison, civil lordship is a deficient form of communicating earthly goods, being occasioned by sin, severely limited in distribution, alienable at will, insecure of tenure, loaded with anxiety and temptation, and oriented chiefly to the service of private interests and the common utility of civil lords.[70] As unflinchingly, if not more unflinchingly than Bonaventure, Wyclif ties civil ownership to the sins of pride and avarice, arguing that if ownership does not necessitate venial sins, it renders them all but inevitable.[71] For the separate interest of each in his property and his relative liberty of disposing of it, safeguarded by coercive human sanctions, enmesh the possessor in an inordinate attachment to worldly goods to the detriment of the love of their Giver.[72]

At the same time, civil lordship stands in the closest proximity to its universal underlying title. Wyclif accepts the Augustinian thesis that civil proprietorship has no independent right or validity apart from the righteous dominion over earthly goods granted to those whom Christ has justified,[73] while rejecting the papal gloss that aligns righteous dominion with obedience to the Roman church. Precisely because civil property is a remedial institution approved by God for sinful humanity, it remains within the purview of divine law, divine right, and divine justice. Were this not so, lay proprietors would not belong to the divinely ordained composition of the church militant, in a relation of organic complementarity to the clerical estate. They too must conform their lordship to Christ's law of love by holding and using earthly goods righteously within the constraints of private ownership.[74] In part they achieve such conformity by surrendering the use of some portion of their property to the clergy and the needy for no worldly gain. By this surrender they not only make possible the literal practice of evangelical lordship by the clerical estate (who use what they do not own), but approximate this practice in their own lives. Relinquishing the use of their property in a permanent loan is a less rigorous conforming to the evangelical standard of non-proprietary sharing of temporal as well as spiritual goods. Moreover, since evangelical lordship is the ethical structure of all just possession, every just use of lay property accords with Christ's sovereign and complete command. Indeed, the civil laws of property are just when and where they faithfully fulfil, under the conditions of human sinfulness, Christ's law of justified nature.

69. *De civili dominio* 1.18-19, Loserth 1:126-33.
70. *De civili dominio* 1.18-19; also 1.11, Loserth 1:76-77.
71. *De civili dominio* 3.10, Loserth 3:161-62.
72. *De civili dominio* 1.18, Loserth 1:129-33.
73. *De civili dominio* 1.4, Loserth 1:25-33.
74. *De civili dominio* 1.6, 41, Loserth 1:39-42, 317-24.

Moreover, a final ecclesiastical service of civil lordship is suggested to Wyclif by the fitness of the civil law for promulgating the Gospel law to the "mixed society" *(societas permixta)* of regenerate and unregenerate members comprising the earthly church: namely, that of coercive discipline. Civil jurisdiction, to which material wealth and power are intrinsic, is God's remedy for incorrigible sin in his church, even in the clerical estate.[75] The pervasive, flagrant defiance of Christ's teaching by the papal hierarchy requires the lay lords forcibly to reform it, chiefly by disendowing and dispossessing the clergy. In that English law prescribes "free alms" as the form of ecclesiastical donation, it entitles the lay magistracy to compel the clergy to live "exproprietarily," without compulsory tithes and exactions, perpetual alms, the practice of simony, and the machinery of ecclesiastical litigation.[76]

Thus does Wyclif move with astonishing deftness from the Franciscan/papalist synthesis inherited from FitzRalph to a thoroughly Marsiglian programme for reducing the Hildebrandine church to a state of evangelical perfection.

Conclusion: Non-proprietary Community of Right as an Antidote to the Liberal Rights Society

It is all too easy to allow the glaring pitfalls of the Christian Platonist theology of non-proprietorship to obscure its profound and abiding contributions to political thought. To dismiss the Franciscan and Wycliffite ethics of evangelical perfection as crypto-Manichean or Pelagian or elitist, and to dismiss Wycliffite ecclesiology as Erastian or worse, Donatist, are plausible, but, I would venture, superficial and shortsighted theological judgments. A more worthwhile task is to extract the sound theological insights of this tradition in their challenging import for the present, while taking care to avoid the pitfalls.

The most fundamental insight of this theological ethic is that *we are not our own but Christ's* (1 Cor. 6:19): we are not self-possessors, not proprietors of our physical and spiritual being and powers, but rather are possessed by Christ and receive all the good that we are, have, and do from him, as a "loan." (Bonaventure and Wyclif prefer "loan" over "trust," perhaps to emphasize our dependence on the Lender rather than our executive power over what is held in trust.) As we are possessed by Christ and receive ourselves from him, the central act of our willing is one of conforming to his will, of surrendering and going

75. *De civili dominio* 1.37, Loserth 1:265-74.
76. *De civili dominio* 1.41, Loserth 1:325-28; 3.16, Loserth 3:303-6.

out of ourselves. The self-transcending of our wills in obedience to Christ is preeminently our encounter with the Supreme Good as absolute claim on us, but also, in many cases, our encounter with lesser, created goods as existing prior to and independently of our willing. In encountering created goods we first "possess" them in their essential being, through knowledge illumined by the love of Christ, before answering *the demand or claim that they present.* Of all creatures, but especially of human individuals, this ethic affirms that they *are claims,* not that they *possess rights:* as objects of God's self-communication in Christ persons are claims upon the wills of one another. Each, in conforming his/her will to Christ's, recognizes and responds to the claim that the other is. Each, in obedience to Christ's law of love, fulfills the demands of justice, *but not the demands of one another.*

Bonaventure and Wyclif saw the practice of evangelical non-possession as both manifesting and reinforcing the surrender of the individual's will to Christ. By maximizing his dependence on others and minimizing his control over them, the practice was to train the disciple's spirit to receive the truth, beauty, and goodness of the world as Christ's gift and to respond to the generosity of its Giver. For their daily sustenance the Friars were to be at the mercy of others' free exercise of charity and to exercise little discretion in their use of the bare necessities. Similarly, Wyclif's dispossessed clergy, while not physically hard-pressed, were also to be at the mercy of lay charity, and especially of the un-coerced judgments of lay donors as to their fitness for the ministry of God's Word.

In regard to the claims of non-human creatures, Bonaventure and Wyclif conceived even our most practical use of them to satisfy our most pressing needs as guided by our possession of them as intelligible and worthy in themselves, that is, as objects of God's knowledge and love. They considered humankind's natural and christological lordship over the rest of creation to be primarily one of contemplative enjoyment rather than creative work, of losing our wills in delight at the non-human creation rather than of imposing them in the physical transformation of nature through labor and technology. They had no need, as does the modern ethic of natural rights, to make credible the claims of non-human creatures on the human community by ludicrously portraying them too as proprietary wills, as rights-bearing subjects.

A second insight of the non-proprietary ethic is that righteous human lordship is communal chiefly because it is spiritual: that is, righteous human community is a sharing in or communication of spiritual goods before physical goods. Only the fellowship of the Holy Spirit entered into through the divine-human communication of Christ crucified and resurrected makes possible an inclusive communion in the use of physical goods: a communion that admits no claims of mine and thine, or equally of ours and yours. Not that community of use, as envisaged by Bonaventure and Wyclif, allows for no "private" use, as, for example, the continuous use by one person of an item of clothing. Rather it admits no claims by individuals or groups to the defensible right or power of disposing of goods so as to determine the use made of them by others, no legal exclusivity of possession and/or use. Common possession means that no one acts as if any good belongs to him/her in any excluding or even particularizing sense. In this regard the sharing of divisible goods mirrors humankind's sharing in the indivisible physical goods of nature — air, sun, rain, etc. — which in turn mirrors the sharing by all in the indivisible spiritual goods: the indivisible communication of the love of Christ and the fellowship of the Holy Spirit, and the common intellectual possession, ethical appreciation, and aesthetic delight in the whole creation and every creature in and through that communion. The natural and evangelical use of physical goods without proprietary division is physical use in the image and service of spiritual use.[77]

Bonaventure and Wyclif were right in supposing that in christological community each individual's use of earthly goods is so mediated by common spiritual participation as to render superfluous the constraints of property. They were, however, overly sanguine about the durable realization of non-proprietary community under the conditions of human sinfulness, as was evidenced by the convoluted and even bizarre legal arrangements adopted by the Franciscan order to sustain its non-proprietary use of goods, and equally, by the prospect of a state- and lay-oppressed church that loomed over Wyclif's advocacy of a dispossessed clergy. Nevertheless, the unrealities and dangers posed by the practice of evangelical poverty do not undermine the theological understanding of it as the form of created, redeemed, and sanctified community to which all members of Christ's body are called and empowered by the Holy Spirit to conform, both spiritually and materially, within the constraints of legal proprietorship, and not without sacrifice and deprivation.

77. Here we should note a parting of ways between the Franciscan/Wycliffite vision of natural non-proprietary community and the Thomistic conception of property as natural in its distributive aspect (Aquinas, *Summa Theologiae* 2a2ae.66.1, 2). From the Christian Platonist perspective, distribution *as such* is less natural than common use, for the reason that natural (and Christological) community is *a real unity of spiritual participation* in every human pursuit, individual and collective. It is the extent to which the individual's use of earthly goods is mediated by common spiritual participation that renders unnecessary not only private "directive" lordship *(dominium)* over things but also public "directive" lordship *(dominium)* over men. By contrast, Thomas in his mature thought considers both property and political rule as belonging to the human community by nature, arguing that the latter is necessary to keep individuals from neglecting the common good in their pursuit of the private (*De regno* I.1.8). To Bonaventure and Wyclif, such disregard of the common good by individuals is unthinkable apart from human sinfulness.

Moreover, Wyclif's universalizing of evangelical lordship as the structure of the church accomplished two further feats for political theology. On the one hand, it maximized the distance between the earthly church as the revelation of eschatological community and the civil polity of property and coercive jurisdiction. It forcefully opposed the undertaking of the papal church to *construe the church's divine-human essence in terms of the remedial institutions of sinful human society.* Thus, those who preached God's Word in Christ had to live after Christ's pattern — without property and the power of jurisdiction. Wyclif's failing, like the early Luther's, was to underestimate the necessary involvement of the institutional church in the divinely ordained remedial structures of sinful human nature. But he addressed headlong the problem which liberal Christianity constantly suppresses: that of institutionally distinguishing the evangelical action of the church from the action of civil society. The perennial truth of his ecclesiology is that the community of faith is bound to a more exact and complete conformity to Christ's evangelical law of love than the civil community; that the church polity, ruled immediately by the Spirit of Christ, constitutes a more perfect common good and fabric of relationships than the civil polity. So we may conclude that even if the civil polity were properly constituted as a system of proprietary, civil, political, and social "rights," the church's essential action would still embody the non-proprietary *dominium* of self-surrendering love.

On the other hand, Wyclif brought the revelation of eschatological community most closely to bear on civil society. In Augustinian fashion, he refused to accord civil possession, civil law, and civil justice any right or validity, except as a reflection of divine possession, divine law, and divine justice. Although the civil economy of property and the polity of coercive rule were tainted by the very sins that they were divinely instituted to remedy, they remained marred reflections of the economy and polity of created and justified humanity. Wyclif distinguished, however, degrees of distortion, and saw the work of civil justice as precisely that of reducing the distortion, of rendering civil institutions more transparent (or, perhaps, less opaque), to divine justice. For him, the enterprise of civil justice hung on two necessary and sufficient conditions: a Bible-reading laity and an apostolic (preaching) clergy. Without either it was doomed to futility.

I have thus far reserved comment on the fact that Wyclif (following FitzRalph) placed at the center of his moral and political theology a concept — namely, *dominium* — that in the civil law expressed both property right and jurisdictional right belonging to individuals and corporations. It may be argued that his pivotal use of this term gave impetus to the proto-modern development of 'natural rights' political theories. (The argument gains in plausibility if we assume that his contemporaries read him with as much inattention as do some modern historians.) But Wyclif's remarkable accomplishment was to furnish a concept of natural and evangelical *dominium* devoid of proprietary and jurisdictional content. Within the next century, however, the concept of *dominium* was redeveloped along naturalistic lines, with proprietary and jurisdictional content; and it was this that undermined the truth of evangelical dominion by substituting concepts and structures of sinful human nature and society for the perfection of life revealed in Jesus Christ.

The modern tradition of natural rights, which has universalized property right into an original and permanent ethical datum of humanity, is a further phase of theological naturalism, at least on the lips of theologians. In so elevating a restraining institution of civil society, the concept of natural rights blurs the distinction between civil and eschatological community, concealing both the remoteness and the proximity in their relationship. Consequently, instead of allowing civil society to be opened by the Holy Spirit to the demands and reality of evangelical community, this concept closes civil society to those demands and that reality, enveloping it in sinful complacency. The effects of this closing can only be deleterious for both civil and ecclesial communities; for from the unlimited proprietary powers of sovereign subjects spring a morality that is at once lawless and legalistic, a culture at once Manichean and materialistic, and a society of contractual relationships at once precarious and potentially totalitarian.

The Theological Economics
of Medieval Usury Theory

JOAN LOCKWOOD O'DONOVAN

The Medieval Contribution to Christian Economics

There is no area of medieval economic thought that has elicited more expressions of exasperation and contempt from modern economists than the theory of loans constructed around the prohibition of usury or profitable lending. When considered against the expanding range of financial and commercial opportunities and institutions characterizing the period, the medieval arguments against usury have appeared to be as analytically bizarre as they are morally sophistical. While economic historians have hailed the scholastic theory of "the just price" (whatever its imperfections) as the solid achievement of medieval economic thought, they have regarded usury theory as its permanent embarrassment.

One outstanding accomplishment of Odd Langholm's scholarship in medieval economics over twenty years has been to challenge the dismissive assessment of usury theory within his discipline. In a series of studies he has matched the detailed textual research of his scholarly predecessors, and brought to the texts an exceptionally sympathetic intelligence.[1] While he has attempted in the

---

1. Langholm's studies include: *Wealth and Money in the Aristotelian Tradition* (New York: Columbia University Press, 1983); *The Aristotelian Analysis of Usury* (New York: Columbia University Press, 1984); *Economics in the Medieval Schools: Wealth, Exchange, Value, Money and Usury According to the Paris Theological Tradition, 1200-1350* (Leiden: Brill, 1992); *The Legacy of Scholasticism in Economic Thought: Antecedents of Choice and Power* (Cambridge: Cambridge University Press, 1998). Among his predecessors in the field, B. W. Dempsey, *Interest and Usury*

A short version of this paper was presented to the Society for the Study of Christian Ethics (Oxford, 2000), and the present essay (with minor changes) was subsequently published in *Studies in Christian Ethics* 14:1 (2001): 48-64.

course of his expositions to give due weight to all the theological and philo-sophical elements of usury theory, he has been particularly concerned to dem-onstrate the analytical consistency and moral relevance of the Aristotelian ar-guments. His most recent study, *The Legacy of Scholasticism in Economic Thought: Antecedents of Choice and Power,* commends the scholastics' Aristote-lian conceptualization of freedom and compulsion in economic exchange as their lasting contribution to the discipline of economics, and of vital impor-tance to the restoration of *personal (moral) agency* in contemporary economic discussion.

However, Langholm's interpretative and constructive orientation as an economic historian displays a deep-seated ambiguity that bears on his treat-ment of scholastic usury arguments. On the one hand, he wishes to affirm an analytical and ethical continuity between the scholastic thinkers and those con-temporary critics of classical and neoclassical economics who have challenged the 'freedom' of market exchanges by demonstrating the coercive nature of eco-nomic bargaining.[2] On the other, he wishes to portray modern economics as resting on theoretical foundations that are antithetical to the scholastic para-digm of just exchange, and as pursuing analytical methods that undermine moral agency in the economic sphere. While this portrayal implies that no in-jection of Aristotelian moral reasoning can save the modern discipline, Langholm, nevertheless, offers the Aristotelian ethic of just exchange as a way forward for his profession.

What is lost in Langholm's selective enthusiasm is the theological complex-ity and depth of medieval economic thought, which is nowhere better illustrated than in the theory of loans. For the arguments against usury in early and high scholasticism brought together concepts and principles of natural economic jus-tice indebted largely to Aristotle, with elements of patristic economic teaching in-tegrated into a christocentric ethic of perfection that drew heavily on the Stoic-Platonic tradition. In the most theologically complete treatments of the usury prohibition, these distinct conceptual strands sustain the interdependence in fruitful tension of the 'natural law' of the Decalogue and the evangelical law of Christ's Sermon on the Mount. Nevertheless, the full reception of Aristotle's ethi-cal and political works in the thirteenth century, and especially the work of St. Thomas, brought into sharper focus the differently nuanced attitudes of the Phi-losopher and the Church Fathers toward poverty, wealth, and property right, that

---

(London: D. Dobson, 1948) and J. T. Noonan, *The Scholastic Analysis of Usury* (Cambridge, Mass.: Harvard University Press, 1957) are especially worthy of note.

2. J. R. Commons and R. L. Hale, writing between the wars, and their successors in the 1970s and 80s.

were bound up with broader differences in understanding moral and spiritual community. The patristic teaching on which the medievals principally drew, resting on the polarity of opposing loves of spiritual and worldly riches, viewed avarice as the root of all evil, property right and the economic exchanges presupposing it as morally tainted, and money as the most seductive of possessions. The Thomistic-Aristotelian ethic viewed moderate wealth as an instrument of individual virtue, property as a natural condition of communal order and harmony, economic exchanges involving money as morally hazardous (on account of the seductiveness of money) but also potentially comprising a sphere of social reciprocity. The patristic ethic envisaged community primarily in terms of a common participation in indivisible goods and a charitable sharing of divisible goods by its members, whereas the Aristotelian ethic gave a larger communal role to the just distribution and exchange of property.

From the mid-thirteenth century onward, usury theory (and economic thought generally) was dominated by the Franciscan and Dominican orders, some of whose incessant quarrels involved perceived divergences between the christocentric economic ethic of evangelical perfection and the Aristotelian natural-law ethic. Although the formidable Franciscan economic synthesizers spurned the overt use of Aristotle, they nevertheless incorporated Aristotelian, along with other natural-law arguments, within an evangelical and christocentric approach to usury. Their synthesis, however, proved unstable, in part because of the distance they perceived between the rule of christological love through the evangelical "counsels" in restored and sanctified community and the "commands" of natural justice in fallen community. As the evangelical counsels lost their purchase on the economic conduct of the laity, becoming the preserve of the monastic (and especially the mendicant) way of life, so the traditional natural law restrictions on economic conduct lost much of their force before the rising tide of economic voluntarism and scientism. The late scholasticism of the fifteenth and sixteenth centuries preserved certain of the Thomistic-Aristotelian formulations of justice in exchange, but only by rewriting them to accommodate free-market principles, so that they no longer operated as severe restraints on profit-seeking, in loans and other transactions. It is of more than passing interest, therefore, that Luther's restoration of the earlier theological balance to usury theory should entail an assault on the theological-ethical distinction between 'counsels' and 'commands'.

The following exploration will trace medieval usury theory through the early scholastic and penitential works, Thomas's definitive use of the Aristotelian arguments, and later Franciscan revisions of this inheritance, and will conclude with a consideration of Luther's thought on usury that must be counted among the late flowerings of medieval economic ethics, despite its theological adjustments. Let me begin with some brief remarks on the canonical development of the usury prohibition in the medieval economic context.

Canonical Development of the Usury Prohibition

The fountainhead of the canonical exposition of the usury prohibition in the Middle Ages was Gratian's systematic compilation of church law completed by 1140 and known as the *Decretum*. Two loci in the *Decretum* treat of usury, the second offering a fairly full determination of what usury is[3]: it is to demand, to receive, or even to expect to receive more in a loan *(mutuum)* than the sum lent (the capital). This excess may be in money or in kind (e.g., in wheat, wine, or oil) or in some other favor (e.g., a gift of merchandise from a merchant). In establishing that usury violates divine and natural law, Gratian invokes a conciliar tradition reaching back to the Council of Nicaea and beyond.[4] The assembled canons reflect the church's traditional preoccupation with condemning and punishing as *turpe lucrum* the practice of usury by priests — usurers can neither receive holy orders nor remain in them. However, in some places, the laity is also forbidden usury, along with other avaricious commercial practices, under the threat of less severe punishments.

Complicating the canonical prohibition of usury was the discrepancy between civil and canon law. Not until the Carolingian period was the usury prohibition enacted into the imperial law of the land. The corpus of Roman civil law compiled by the Emperor Justinian in the sixth century, notwithstanding its confirmation of the canons of Nicaea, contained numerous texts contradicting the canonical prohibition, including Justinian's own legislation to reduce the legal rate of interest on loans.[5] While canonist and civilian commentators were

3. Part 1, Distinction 46, chaps. 8-10 — Distinction 47, chaps. 1-5; Part 2, Causa 14, Questions 1-6; *Corpus Iuris Canonici*, ed. A. Friedberg (Leipzig: Tauchnitz, 1879), I: 169-71, 732-74. The core definition is in II. C.14.q.3; I: 735. Over the next centuries, these loci attracted an industry of canonist scholarship that sought to bring clarification and precision to Gratian's text and to extend its legal application, often with reference to civilian scholarship on the corpus of Roman law and subsequent church legislation. Further exposition of the usury prohibition came from the canonical collections of the popes Gregory IX, Boniface VIII and Clement V and the massive decretalist scholarship generated by them. For the development of canonist usury theory, see T. P. McLaughlin, "The Teaching of the Canonists on Usury (XII, XIII and XIV Centuries)," *Mediaeval Studies* 1 (1939): 81-147; 2 (1940): 1-22.

4. II. C.14, q.4, c.7; I: 737.

5. Novella 34, c.1, in the Code following 4.32.16. Like the *Decretum*, the *Corpus iuris civilis* collected legal material from earlier periods, its earliest commentaries belonging to the second century A.D.

largely agreed that imperial usury laws contravening divine and natural laws were without force,[6] both were keen to define usurious practice with increasing legal precision and to discriminate cases falling outside of it.

Through the clarifications of lawyers and theologians, the church's official teaching and legislation underwent several important developments. In the first place, the church recognized two extrinsic titles to interest (i.e., indemnity) on loans in the case of delayed repayment: initially, the title of damages sustained *(damnum emergens)* and eventually that of profit foregone *(lucrum cessans)* on account of the delay. Secondly, she gave her approval to types of investment contracts distinguishable from loans, the most common being the *locatio,* the *societas,* and the *census.* The *locatio* was a rental contract on property such as a house, horse, or agricultural implement that could be borrowed for use over a period and returned intact. The *societas* was a partnership in a profitable enterprise in which both the profit and the risk were shared. Athough ideally each partner would invest both money and labor, it was licit for one partner to supply the money as long as the risk were shared. The *census* in its most acceptable form was the sale or purchase for life of a rent-charge, i.e., a regular income in money or other goods from a fruitful real estate base. While resembling a loan secured by a mortgage, it differed importantly in that the rate of return varied with the productivity of the agricultural base. Thirdly, the church judged certain ostensibly non-loan contracts to be either covertly usurious or usury-evading *(in fraudem usurae),* the most widespread being simulated sales (e.g., where A purchases a field from B to reap a profit on its fruits with an agreed resale to B after a period) and buying and selling on credit *(venditio* and *emptio ad tempus* or *ad terminem)* wherein the seller either defers payment for his merchandise and on that account raises the price, or defers delivery of his merchandise and consequently lowers the price. Numerous practices of international exchange dealers and bankers involving the extension of credit through bills of exchange (e.g., where a *de facto* loan in one currency is repaid in another at a profit to the dealer) were similarly condemned.

In these developments the church gave moral license to limited opportunities for investment and credit that, on the one hand, favored the welfare of the poor, the vulnerable, the distressed, and the clerical estate — those who by reason of age, infirmity or spiritual vocation were unable to provide for themselves

---

6. Some civilians, however, accepted the Justinianic argument that the emperor, in permitting modest interest, was equitably interpreting the divine prohibition under the conditions of human sinfulness in which men were too lacking in charity to loan freely. McLaughlin, "Teaching of the Canonists," p. 92.

through labor and those whose immediate sustenance or livelihood depended on a loan. On the other hand, these avenues did not serve the ongoing needs of merchants, manufacturers, and financiers. Sufficient testimony to their inadequacy to feed an expanding commercial economy is furnished by the increasingly harsh papal and conciliar legislation against usurers from the twelfth to the fourteenth centuries.[7] Unrepentant Christian usurers by occupation were denied not only the sacraments but Christian burial and their wills were declared invalid; they and their heirs were required to restore usurious gains and their alms were pronounced unacceptable. And although Innocent III and the Fourth Lateran Council (1215) accused the Jews of depriving the church of necessary tithes and oblations by their steady acquisition of the property of Christians, their pawnbroking was, in the longer term, very 'small fry' compared with the lending operations of Italian exchange-bankers, and soon to be overtaken by Cahorsine and Lombard competition.[8] When in 1311 the Council of Vienne, guided by Clement V, imposed sentence of excommunication on ruling authorities who would enact laws holding debtors to the payment of usury and disallowing claims for restitution of usury paid, it had in mind municipal statutes all over Europe, and especially in northern Italy.[9]

Not surprisingly, the papal church was less vocal and somewhat inconsistent in condemning debtors who paid usury. While a letter of Pope Alexander III, included in the Decretals of Gregory IX, ruled that borrowing at usury, even for the best of causes, was a crime admitting of no dispensation,[10] other texts require that debtors under oaths to pay usury, keep their oaths,[11] implying that paying usury was not in all cases a mortal sin (for if it were, the oaths would not be binding). These discordant rulings led canonists to discriminate motives and circumstances of the borrower as well as of the lender. They concluded that borrowing at usury is not sinful only when undertaken out of necessity, to satisfy pressing need or sustain one's livelihood, and not for purposes of pleasure or business utility — to accumulate superfluous wealth, or where alternative sources of income were available. It was not simply that the hard-pressed borrower was judged to have chosen the lesser of two evils: it was argued that he "does not intend to participate in the crime" of usury even if he offers an occasion for it; unless, that is, he entices a lender into usury or hinders

---

7. For a concise summary of this legislation, see T. F. Divine, *Interest: An Historical and Analytical Study in Economics and Modern Ethics* (Milwaukee: Marquette University Press, 1959), pp. 59-64.

8. Divine, *Interest*, pp. 39-40, 61-62; also McLaughlin, "Teaching of the Canonists," p. 110.

9. McLaughlin, "Teaching of the Canonists," p. 84.

10. X.5.19.c.4, cited in McLaughlin, "Teaching of the Canonists," p. 108.

11. McLaughlin, "Teaching of the Canonists," Section 4.

his repentance and reform.[12] The relationship between necessity and intention will receive further clarification below.

While the church's condemnations and concessions in the sphere of investment and credit cannot easily be dismissed as willful, hypocritical, and self-serving, they are open to the charge of inconsistency on several fronts. The first concerns the complexification over time of the contracts of *societas and census* in ways incompatible with the usury prohibition, so that later scholastic endorsement of these modifications unquestionably undermined the church's position. Consistency required the church to condemn the fully insured partnership contract with a fixed interest (the "triple contract")[13] and the personal, mutually redeemable *census* contract,[14] but condemnation was not always forthcoming. Likewise, commercial pressure for interest titles to cover the original loan period was not always resisted. Secondly, the church's investigations into usurious practices concentrated in some areas rather than others, being slow to penetrate the sphere of exchange banking, upon which, it has to be said, the centralized finances of the papal church depended. Yet even here the more blatantly usurious practices drew official condemnation, and the church strenuously resisted the idea that money was a commodity with a market price. Thirdly, later apologists for capitalist practices contended that they were only applying principles recognized implicitly in earlier concessions: e.g., to concede that one party investing only capital in a joint enterprise could claim a share in the profit implied that money was productive — a principle that flew in the face of usury theory. Such failings, however, make it imperative that the principles and arguments of usury theory be understood in an integral rather than piecemeal fashion, within their broader theological and philosophical context.

The Earlier Medieval Treatment of Usury

The earlier medieval treatments of usury were dominated by the Church Fathers' handling of it, and were integrated through the leading themes of patris-

12. McLaughlin, "Teaching of the Canonists," pp. 108-10. Also Langholm, *Legacy of Scholasticism*, pp. 66-69.

13. In defending the popular 5% contract, John Eck of Augsburg famously analyzed it into three separate contracts: the original contract of partnership, a contract ensuring the principal, and a contract in which uncertain future profit is sold for a lesser certain profit (i.e., a guaranteed fixed return of 5%). J. T. Noonan, *Scholastic Analysis*, pp. 209ff.

14. Founded not on specific property but on the entire returns of a serf or debtor's labor or all the goods of a merchant, guaranteeing temporary, life, or perpetual rights to money, and redeemable by the purchaser as well as the seller; Noonan, pp. 159-60, 230-31.

tic economic ethics. Among the Greeks, Clement of Alexandria, Cyprian of Carthage, Basil the Great, Gregory of Nyssa, and John Chrysostom charted the economic landscape within which usury was understood, and among the Latins, Ambrose, Jerome, and Augustine. The early medievals followed the Fathers in combining the Old Testament condemnation of usury as an avaricious oppression of the poor that feeds on their misfortune[15] with the exhortation of both Testaments to merciful, generous, and self-sacrificial giving to the needy neighbor, the fulcrum of which was Christ's injunction in Luke 6:35 to "lend, expecting nothing in return."[16] Gratian's influential texts on usury set the tone by situating the Savior's injunction within his other exhortations to the fullness of evangelical love that gives to everyone who begs and does not withhold the tunic from him who takes one's cloak (Luke 6:29-30), that does not seek after and cling to possessions, but sells all that one has and gives to the poor (Matt. 19:21).[17]

Paramount for Gratian and his readers, as for their patristic mentors, was the conformity of merciful and charitable giving with God's original will for the human community, manifested in the fellowship of Christ: that its members make common use of the goods of creation to relieve material want. The preeminent paradigm of this common use was the sharing of humanity with other creatures in God's indivisible bounty of nature — of air, sun, rain, sea, the seasons — goods divinely created as *koina*, unable to be privately appropriated and possessed.[18] To this paradigm it was thought that the common use of divisible goods should approach, as much as use itself allowed. For the earlier medievals even more than for the Church Fathers, this original common use, restored in Christ, did not entail private ownership, which was occasioned by the sinful impulses and disciplinary needs of fallen humanity.[19] Within the

15. Exod. 22:25; Prov. 28:8; Pss. 14:4-6; 72:13, 14; Ezek. 18:5-18. In his review of Old Testament texts concerned (implicitly or explicitly) with the practice of usury, T. F. Divine distinguishes those that (1) prohibit usurious loans to the poor and distressed within the Jewish community, including sojourners (Ps. 14:4-6; Exod. 22:25; Lev. 25:35-38, and the supporting example of Neh. 5:1-13); (2) prohibit usurious loans to Jews while permitting them to foreigners (Deut. 23:19-20), and (3) castigate those who enrich themselves by oppressing the poor with usury (Ezek. 18:5-18), *Interest*, pp. 5-11.

16. Also Lev. 25:35-38; Deut. 15:7-11; 24:10-13; Ecclus. 29:1-3, 10-14.

17. II. C.14, q.1, Friedberg, 1:732.

18. Borrowed from Greek and Roman Stoic sources, this paradigm was influentially transmitted through such patristic works as: Clement of Alexandria, *Paidagogus* 2.12, PG 8:541-4; Basil the Great, *Homilia in illud Lucae, "Destruam,"* 7, PG 31:277; Ambrose of Milan, *Commentarium in Epistolam II ad Corinthios* 9.9, PL 17:313-14.

19. Following Gratian's lead (*Decretum* I. D.1. c. 6), the mainstream of medieval theologians before the mid-thirteenth century systematized the theory, indebted chiefly to Augustine

practice of the church, the original use was more perfectly approximated by the communal ownership and distribution of goods throughout the clerical and monastic estates, but was also reflected in the giving away of superfluous property to the poor by all estates of the church. As much as the Fathers, the medievals viewed the private amassing of wealth, retained and preserved by property right for exclusive use, as a violation of the divine owner's intention that the earth's abundance be shared in charity and distributed justly for the sustenance of all, love and justice being bound together. They concurred in their predecessors' indictment of avaricious accumulation as robbery of the needy, taking from the poor what belongs to them by divine and natural right.[20]

It is within this vision of participatory sharing in material as well as spiritual goods, in which property right plays a secondary, morally ambiguous, and rigorously circumscribed role, that the severe condemnation of usury bequeathed by the Church Fathers must be set. For usurious lending compounds the injustice of keeping from the needy neighbor what is rightfully his — namely, one's superfluities,[21] and further, it compounds the uncharitableness of not sacrificing of one's necessaries to relieve his distress. To hope for the return of one's possessions may be justified by one's own need, but to enrich oneself at the expense of one's needy neighbor is to deny the moral community of use to which property is subject. If economic exchange — that is, the transfer of property for the sake of supplying necessities — is always prone to perversion in the direction of profit-making, usurious gain is an especially offensive illustration, in that it openly perverts the form of the just and charitable act com-

---

(*In Ioannis Evangelium,* 6.25, *PL* 35:1437), that pre-lapsarian community possessed goods in common by natural law, while private property presupposed the post-lapsarian discipline of human government. Langholm, in *Economics in the Medieval Schools,* demonstrates the consistent adherence of early Paris-linked theologians to this position, including in his survey: Thomas Chobham, Robert de Courçon and William of Auxerre; Roland of Cremona, Hugh of St. Cher, Peter of Tarentaise and Albert the Great among the Dominicans; John of La Rochelle, Alexander of Hales, and Bonaventure among the Franciscans.

20. See, e.g., Robert de Courçon, *Summa* 16.5; William of Auxerre, *Summa aurea* 3.24.5.1, 3; Hugh of Saint-Cher, *Postilla in Lucam* 12:24. Among the frequently used patristic sources were: Clement of Alexandria, *Quis dives salvetur* 31, *PG* 9:637; Basil the Great, *Homilia, PG* 31: 276-77; Ambrose, *De Nabuthe* 3, 11, *PL* 14:734, 747; *De officiis ministrorum* 1.28, *PL* 16:61-2; *In Psalmum CXVII Expositio* 8.22, *PL* 15:1303; *Commentarium in Epistolam II ad Corinthios* 9.9, *PL* 17:313-14; Chrysostom, *De Lazaro* 2.4, *PG* 48:987-88; Augustine, *Enarratio in Psalmum CXLVII* 12, *PL* 37:1922, Gregory the Great, *Liber regulae pastoralis* 3.21, *PL* 77:87.

21. Alexander of Hales in *Quaestio de superfluo* gives a typical definition of *superfluum* as "that which one can be without according to just necessity and pious utility." *Quaestiones disputatae antequam esset frater* I. q. 17; cited in Langholm, *Economics,* p. 127.

manded directly by Christ.[22] While medieval theologians were drawn to the patristic disapproval of commercial exchange (*negotiari* = to do business) as almost inevitably embodying avarice, they nevertheless condemned only lending at usury, and not buying and selling, as *essentially* rather than *accidentally* "fifthy lucre" *(turpe lucrum).*[23]

Among the natural law arguments against usury popular with early scholastic theologians, none speaks more eloquently of the Stoic-Platonic inheritance of the Fathers than the argument that the usurer sells time. While this argument was the church's foremost weapon in attacking higher prices in credit sales, its hold on the medieval theological imagination exceeded any purely practical expediency. In providing its first developed statement, William of Auxerre (1160-1229) dwells not only on the commonality of time to all creatures, but on the universality of self-giving in created community:[24] "each creature," he says, invoking Augustine, "is compelled to give himself; the sun is compelled to give itself to illuminate; similarly the earth is compelled to give whatever it can, and similarly the water. Nothing, however, so naturally gives itself as time: willy-nilly things have time." Thus, in selling what belongs to all creatures freely and universally, the usurer injures them all, "even the stones," who "would cry out" against him, were men to be silent. William's objection to the usurer's selling time is not only that time is the property of God alone, as universal owner of his creation — which later scholastic rehearsals of the argument would emphasize; but rather that time is a *koinon*, indivisibly and inclusively shared by the whole community of creatures, and exclusively appropriated by none.

This central thrust of the objection to "selling time" must be kept in mind when interpreting the cluster of arguments that show usury to be unjust, and even, robbery, in its violation of the loan contract. The medievals were no more adverse than the Fathers to condemning usury as 'robbery' in the positive legal sense of taking another's property against the owner's will. Nevertheless, like

---

22. Peter of Tarentaise makes this point succinctly in the argument reported by Langholm (*Comm. Sent.* 3.37.3.4, ed. Toulouse [1652], p. 309): as "a loan is meant to be made to relieve the need of one's neighbour, . . . it is wrong that that which was instituted as a favour should be turned into an injury." Langholm, *Economics,* p. 107.

23. Drawing on an influential exegesis of Jesus's cleansing of the temple (Matt. 21:12) incorporated in the palea *Eiciens* of Gratian's *Decretum* (I.88.11), Hugh of Saint-Cher in his *Postillae* on the Four Gospels interprets Christ's driving out of the traders as his condemnation of, firstly, venial simoniacs conducting a commerce in ecclesiastical offices and services and, secondly, unjust merchants making a profit by reselling goods "whole and unaltered" (that is, without expending labor on them to justify the higher price). Langholm, *Economics,* pp. 102-3.

24. *Summa aurea* 3.21, f.225v:a, cited in Noonan, *Scholastic Analysis,* pp. 43-44.

the Fathers, they viewed the usurer's violation of commutative justice and human property right in the context of his graver violation of the divine laws of neighbor love, and justice in the evangelical sense. Behind the narrower, 'proprietary' meaning of 'robbery' loomed its more profound theological and 'trans-proprietary' (even 'anti-proprietary') meaning.[25] Still, the explication of usury as a violation of the seventh commandment of the Decalogue was a large and indispensable part of scholastic usury theory from its inception, drawing impetus from the authority of Gratian[26] and Peter Lombard.[27]

While the biblical inspiration for identifying usury with robbery was somewhat imprecise, coming from their close association in the prophet Ezekiel's pronouncements of divine vindication and condemnation of the righteous and unrighteous,[28] the Roman legal element in the identification was very precise. In the Roman contract of loan *(mutuum)*, as explicated by both ancient and medieval jurists, ownership of a fungible good — i.e., something that can be counted, weighed, or measured — is transferred from lender to borrower.[29] Ownership is transferred because the borrower is not obligated "to repay the identical thing which is consumed in use, but the same quantity of a similar kind."[30] In assuming ownership, the borrower also assumes the risk of loss and is bound to repay the loan, even if the good is fortuituously lost.[31] (Roman law, before canon law, distinguished the *mutuum* from the contracts of *commodatum* and *locatio,* in which the lender retains ownership of, and bears the risk for, a good given to another for use, and the borrower is obliged to return the identical good after use.)[32] On this legal basis, the medieval theologians and canonists could argue, in the first place, that the usurer charges the debtor for what the debtor already owns; and moreover, that he seeks to profit

25. This duality is evidenced in the key patristic usury texts for the medieval thinkers, including Basil, *Hom. II in Ps. 14,* PG 29:264-80; Ambrose, *De bono mortis,* 12.56, *CSEL* 32/1, 752; *De Tobia,* PL 14:591-622; Chrysostom, *Hom. in Matt.* 56.5-6, PG 58:555-58.

26. Gratian's *Decretum* incorporated a line from Ambrose (*De bono mortis* 12.56) identifying usury as robbery: *Si quis usuram accipit, rapinam facit, vita non vivit.* II.14.4.10, Friedberg, 1:738.

27. Lombard subsumed usury under robbery in expounding the seventh commandment (*Sent.* 3.37.5): *Hic etiam usura prohibetur, quae sub rapina continetur.* Cited in Langholm, *Legacy of Scholasticism,* pp. 59-60.

28. Ezek. 18:5-18; 33:14-16.

29. The Roman law texts are *Digest* 44.7.1.2 and 4; 12.1.2; *Institutes* 3.14, preface and 2. For the evolution of canonist commentary on the contract of *mutuum,* see McLaughlin, "Teaching of the Canonists," pp. 100-104.

30. McLaughlin, "Teaching of the Canonists," p. 100.

31. *Institutes* 3.14, preface and 2.

32. *Institutes* 3.14.2; 3.23; cf. *Digest* 44.7.1.3 and 4; 19.2.

from the debtor's property without himself undertaking any labor or assuming any risk. He therefore robs the debtor of the fruits of his labor and exploits his neighbor's suffering and fear of loss, having refused to share in them.[33]

To these arguments from the transfer of ownership and risk were added two discernibly Aristotelian ones. One concerns the debtor's payment of usury under duress or compulsion, and raises the issue of his consent to the loan contract. The borrower was said to pay usury with a "comparative" or "forced" will (*voluntate comparativa, coacta*) rather than with an "absolute will" (*voluntate absoluta*) — a distinction with theoretical roots in Aristotle's concept of a "mixed act."[34] That is to say, he pays it with a will compelled by his need and by the lender's refusal to lend for nothing, and against his absolute will to repay the loan without usury. The borrower's compulsion mitigates, even eliminates, the sinfulness of his act, while the usurer stands accused of theft, of taking another's property against his will.[35] This is the argument, let us recall, concerning freedom and compulsion in exchange, that Langholm singles out as the core scholastic contribution to economic analysis and ethics.

The second argument, that usury transmutes species unnaturally, or makes sterile coin breed coin, either originated in Book 1 of Aristotle's *Politics* or was influentially transmitted by it, being well known to the Church Fathers and incorporated by Gratian.[36] Playing on the pun provided by the Greek word for usury, *tokos,* which means literally "offspring," Aristotle condemned usury as the *most unnatural* form of "wealth-getting" *(crēmatistikē)* for the reason that an increase of money from money runs counter to the natural purpose of money, which is to be a medium of exchange.[37] Significantly, Aristotle also disapproved of trade as a perverse form of "wealth-getting" (as compared with the economic exchange that serves household management), because money (i.e.,

33. For this argument see: *Glossa ordinaria* to *Decretum* C.14, q.3, c.1 at *Plus quam;* Thomas of Chobham, *Summa confessorum* 7.6.11.1; Robert of Courçon, *Summa* 11.4; Albert the Great, *In evangelium Lucam* 6:35, *Opera* 22.

34. Langholm traces this distinction back to Aristotle's concept of "mixed acts" (*Nichomachean Ethics* 3.1: 1110a4-19, b1-7) through the long history of the concept's appropriation. "Mixed acts" are acts performed "from fear of greater evils," which are said to be voluntary in that they are "worthy of choice at the time when they are done" and in the agent's "power to do or not to do," yet also involuntary, abstractly considered, in that "no one would choose any such act in itself." *Legacy of Scholasticism,* p. 17; see chaps. 1-4.

35. Thomas of Chobham, *Summa confessorum* 7.6.11.4; William of Auxerre, *Summa aurea* 3.48.1.2; Roland of Cremona, *Summa* 3, q. 397; John of La Rochelle, *Summa de vitiis* ff.34vb-35ra; Alexander of Hales, *Sum. theol.* 4. 914-15; Bonaventura, *Comm. Sent.* 3.37. See Langholm's review of the scholastic argument from compulsion in *Legacy of Scholasticism,* pp. 59-66.

36. *Decretum* I. 47. 8, Friedberg, 1:171.

37. *Politics* 1258a-b.

coin) is simultaneously the means and the end of the enterprise; and the end is without limit, because human avarice, wedded to vitalistic and hedonistic desires, is unlimited.[38] Aristotle, then, not only concurred with future generations of Christians that money is the most seductive and distracting of possessions, the most "craved by cupidity," as one Franciscan put it;[39] he taught them (albeit sometimes indirectly) that usury is the extreme practical expression of the avaricious profit motive, in that it converts the 'medium' of commercial exchange into its 'terminus': not C-M-C (commodity-money-commodity) but M-M (money-money).[40]

The Thomistic-Aristotelian Treatment of Usury

Compared with his Franciscan and Dominican predecessors (including his economic teacher, Albert the Great), Thomas Aquinas's treatment of usury moves more completely within the ambit of Aristotle's economic ethic, at the expense of the patristic, Stoic-Platonic legacy. At the same time, Thomas places an emphasis on the issue of commutative justice that exceeds Aristotle's in his discussion of usury. In his two extended treatments of usury in *De malo* 13.4[41] and in *Summa Theologiae* 2a2ae.78,[42] Thomas's natural-law arguments begin and end with usury as a sin against justice in exchange, a violation of the requirement of equality of value in the things exchanged. Significantly, they do not include the objection to selling time.

Thus, his natural-law arguments presuppose property right in a morally unambiguous manner. This is consistent with his Aristotelian orientation to property and to wealth more generally; with his endorsements of the benefits of ownership for communal peace, productive efficiency and social order, without reference to the exigencies of fallen humankind or the perfection of prelapsarian community of goods;[43] and with his view of moderate possessions as an instrument of virtue as much as an impediment to it.[44] Of course, Thomas holds to the traditional theological subordination of privately owned goods to "common

38. *Politics* 1257b-1258a 15; cf. *Nichomachean Ethics* 1121b.

39. Bonaventure, *Expositio regulae* 4.2; cited in Langholm, *Economics,* pp. 162-63.

40. Henry of Ghent and Alexander Lombard, cited in Langholm, *The Aristotelian Analysis of Usury,* pp. 64-65.

41. *On Evil,* trans. J. Oesterle (Notre Dame: University of Notre Dame Press, 1996), pp. 400-409.

42. Trans. M. Lefébure (London: Blackfriars, 1975), 38:232-53.

43. *Summa Theologiae* 2a2ae. 66.2, also 57.3.

44. *Summa Theologiae* 1a2ae. 4.6.7; 2a2ae. 55.6 ad 1; 55.7.

use" in the sense of requiring that superfluous possessions be distributed to the needy.[45] Similarly, he holds to the Aristotelian and patristic view of usury as *necessarily* motivated by avarice, in its specific meaning of an inordinate desire for money — which he shows to be potentially idolatrous and destructive of charity, and as such, a mortal sin.[46] Nevertheless, he confines his consideration of usury proper to the objective violation of justice that avarice commits, omitting the disturbance in the affections of the soul that usury manifests.[47]

In demonstrating this injustice, Thomas expounds Aristotle's theory of the sterility of money as a theory of the consumptibility of money. Both of his analyses of usury begin by defining the class of fungibles (that are the object of the Roman contract of *mutuum*) as those goods the proper use of which consists in their substance being consumed. He offers the conventional examples of wine and bread, which are consumed in use by being drunk and eaten respectively. In that the use and substance of these goods cannot be estimated or transferred separately (as, for example, can the use and substance of a house or a horse), the loan of their use must involve a transfer of ownership (the Roman legal argument). To charge separately for the thing and its use, says Thomas, is to sell "something non-existent" *(id quod non est)* or to sell "the same thing twice over" *(eandem rem bis).*[48] Passing to money, he argues that it is also consumed in use in the sense that its proper use is to be spent in exchange for other things.[49] The implicit idea is that to exchange money for a good is to change its substance, as happens in all consumption, the form of money being replaced by the form of the good purchased. Money is thus conceived as coin in the hand, intervening between valuable things, ordered always to the acquisition of necessities.

Moreover, as a medium of exchange, money is a means of measuring equivalence in exchange: it is a conventional or "accidental" measure of the value of goods in exchange; according to Thomas, it quantifies their aggregate utility or usefulness for supplying needs, while having no utility itself.[50] But money can establish equivalence between things only if it is formally equal to

---

45. *Summa Theologiae* 2a2ae.66.2. Arguably, the distributivist conception of "common use" has less of *communal sharing* about it than Aristotle's in the sense that Aristotle entertains the communal sharing of some domestic and agricultural 'tools,' i.e., of some instruments of production. *Politics* 1263a 30-35.

46. *De malo* 13.1-3.

47. Thomas's approach may be contrasted with that of his Dominican mentor, Albert the Great, who interprets Aristotle's objection to money breeding money as an objection to the avaricious desire to lend for profit, which "makes it seem as though money reproduces itself." Cited in Langholm, *Economics*, p. 195.

48. *Summa Theologiae* 2a2ae. 78.1; *De malo* 13.4.

49. *Summa Theologiae* 2a2ae. 78.1; *De malo* 13.4.

50. *Comm. Sent.* 3.37.1.6c; cited in Langholm, *Economics*, p. 240.

itself in exchange, so that in a loan £10 lent equals £10 returned, regardless of (what would today be called) variations in the purchasing power of money.[51] Usury, says Thomas, "diversifies the measure" because it upsets this formal equivalence of money in exchange.[52] In other words, usury treats as a vendible commodity that which is non-vendible.

Two further arguments presuppose the sterility of money as a medium and measure of exchange. One is the objection from compulsion: that the usurer inflicts on the needy borrower a kind of moral violence in subjecting him to the onerous condition of returning more than he was lent. Thomas compares the usurer's extortion to that of a seller forcing a needy buyer to pay more for a good than it is worth.[53] Along with other thinkers, he distinguishes the lender's compelling of the debtor from his acceptance of a spontaneous gift of gratitude. The latter, he says, even if grounded in the natural obligation of friendship, cannot be made a matter of legal obligation, because "the note of necessity" introduced by law "stifles any spontaneous return."[54] The other argument is that human industry and not money is the principal cause of profit. In addressing the question of whether the usurer is bound to restore to the borrower any or all gains made out of his usury, Thomas confines restitution to the actual goods extorted from the borrower, on the principle that all profit made from money (or from other consumable/sterile goods) "is the fruit, not of [the good] itself but of human industry."[55]

Despite his demonstrations of the injustice of usurious gain, Thomas makes notable concessions to current practice. His less significant concession, theoretically considered, is that borrowing at usury and even depositing money with an established money-lender, when undertaken for some good purpose such as the relief of need, may be permitted as a case of "turning [. . .] sins to some good," provided that the borrower or investor not induce the lender into a sin that he would otherwise not have committed.[56] His more significant concession, allowed in *Summa Theologiae* but not in *De malo,* is that the lender is entitled to interest *(interesse)* for actual loss sustained *(damnum emergens)* apparently from the beginning of the loan, and not only in delayed repayment, and, moreover, may settle the terms of compensation with the borrower beforehand.[57]

51. Langholm, *Economics*, p. 240; also Noonan, *Scholastic Analysis*, p. 52.
52. Langholm, *Economics*, p. 240.
53. *De malo* 13.4 ad 7.
54. *Summa Theologiae* 2a2ae. 78.2 ad 2; *De malo* 13.4 ad 5.
55. *Summa Theologiae* 2a2ae. 78.3. However, the usurer is bound to recompense the borrower for any loss of property that has resulted from his payment of usury.
56. *Summa Theologiae* 2a2ae. 78.4; *De malo* 13.4 ad 18.
57. *Summa Theologiae* 2a2ae. 78.2 ad 1.

In *De malo* Thomas subscribes to the majoritarian position of his predecessors and contemporaries, that the lender should "have guarded against incurring a loss" from the outset and the borrower "ought not to incur a loss" because of the lender's lack of foresight.[58] Traditionally, however, theologians were concerned to situate the lender's obligation to the needy borrower within the whole range of his earthly responsibilities, the moral point being that he may not in all circumstances be called to the high discipleship of self-sacrificial lending. Strikingly, Thomas omits such theological-ethical considerations in favor, it would seem, of the economic one of achieving symmetry between usury and just price theory. In proposing that the borrower is not obliged to indemnify the lender for losses incurred, he cites the commercial parallel that the buyer of an article is not obliged to indemnify the seller, but only to pay what the article "is worth" (in the market place).[59] Although later, when arguing *for* the indemnification of the lender, Thomas does not again have recourse to the market parallel, he has nevertheless brought his theory of *interesse* into line with his mature "double rule of just pricing" that bases it on labor and costs criteria (indemnification of the seller) supplemented by aggregate need (current competitive market price).[60] Finally, it is worthy of mention that Thomas follows the conventional line in disallowing the lender's claim to indemnification for potential loss of profits *(lucrum cessans)*, as distinct from actual loss of property (income); but he argues entirely from the speculative character of potential profit rather than from the vicious character of the speculation.[61]

Post-Thomistic Franciscan Developments before 1350

In the wake of the economic contributions of Albert the Great and Thomas Aquinas, the Aristotelian teleology of money formed the core of the natural-law assault on usury as a violation of justice in exchange. However, the ascendancy in the field of Franciscan and, to a lesser extent, Augustinian thinkers meant that the theological and evangelical emphases of the patristic legacy remained in the forefront, balancing and containing the issue of commutative justice. Ethical concern continued to turn on the sin of avarice, expressed in usury, which removed men from the community of christological love in which

58. *De malo* 13.4 ad 14. Recent dating places *De malo* around 1266-67, just prior to Thomas's labor on 1a2ae of *Summa Theologiae*. Preface to *De malo*, xx.

59. 13.4. ad 14.

60. *Summa Theologiae* 2a2ae. 77.1; See Langholm's explication of Thomas's "double rule of just pricing" in *Economics*, pp. 231-32.

61. *Summa Theologiae* 2a2ae. 78.2. ad 1; *De malo* 13.4.14.

all shared in spiritual and material goods on the basis of free self-giving. All injustice in economic exchange, and not only in usury, had to be brought back to the idolatrous distortion of the human will that chooses Mammon over Christ. The challenge of discipleship in the economic sphere was to overcome the craving after gain that sets economic transactions against faith in Christ and the communion of saints, and against natural friendship and society.

Two outstanding Franciscan economic thinkers, Peter Olivi and John Duns Scotus, combined evangelical spiritual and moral rigor with an unrivalled level of analytical sophistication, and so their writings may plausibly be regarded as the high-water mark of scholastic economic ethics. In the area of commodity exchange, they achieved impressive clarifications of the conditions of free bargaining, the basis of value and the criteria of just pricing, demonstrating alertness to the subjective as well as objective features of transactions.[62] While Olivi recognized community as a psychological and moral presence in the determination of market judgments,[63] Duns Scotus brought out the ethical reciprocity of market transactions. Interpreting the Thomistic/Aristotelian theory of just equivalence and mutual profit in exchange through the analogy of the free giving and receiving of property, he argued that all parties to an economic transaction should "remit some of that rigorous justice" (of strict equality), so that "a gift may be said to accompany every contract."[64] Across the whole range of economic exchange, these formidable Franciscans aimed at the integration of love and justice, of evangelical and natural laws, that characterized the earlier medieval tradition.

In their usury theory we find most of the traditional Roman-law and natural-law arguments faithfully rehearsed: that the usurer demands more than he gives, that he sells to the borrower his own property and industry, that he profits without risk or labor, that he makes money breed money, and that he renders money inconsistent as a measure of value in exchange by not applying that measure to money. In addition, Olivi endorses the Thomistic argument that the usurer sells what does not exist or sells the same thing twice; and Duns Scotus, the patristic argument that he sells time which is common to all creatures. Nevertheless, their thought contains elements of direct and indirect at-

---

62. The bulk of Olivi's economic thought is found in his "triple treatise," edited by Todeschini under the title *Tractatus de emptionibus et venditionibus, de usuris, de restitutionibus* (Rome, 1980); the first part is edited by Spicciani under the title *Tractatus de emptione et venditione* (Rome, 1977). The economic contribution of Duns Scotus is found in *Opus Oxoniense* 4.15.2.3-34, *Opera Omnia*, ed. Vivès (Paris, 1891-5), 18:256-341. See Langholm's expositions in *Economics*, pp. 355-65, 409-13.

63. E.g., about the utility value of commodities, the elements of cost in their production, and the conduct of economic negotiations. Langholm, *Economics*, pp. 360-65.

64. *Opus Oxoniense* 4.15.2.15, pp. 283-84; cited in Langholm, *Economics*, pp. 410-11.

tack on the Thomistic and Aristotelian core of the natural law objections, which reflect significant adjustments in their vision of the economic field.

Both Olivi and Duns Scotus, for example, concur that the lender is entitled to seek compensation *(interesse)* for potential loss of profit as well as actual loss sustained, in the event of delayed repayment. Olivi, furthermore, extends compensation to the duration of the loan in cases where the good loaned is clearly intended for a profitable purpose and, instead, lent out of charity to the needy or out of compulsion to the government. In describing such a good as "capital," he makes luminously clear the logic of *lucrum cessans:* "that which in the firm intention of its owner is ordained to some probable gain does not only possess the character of money or a thing straightforward, but beyond this a certain seminal reason of profitability which we usually call capital."[65] By "seminal reason of profitability" Olivi means to convey a potency for, or germ of, profit inhering in some property (whether grain, wine or money) that its owner will intentionally bring to fruition in time.[66] In that lending prevents his bringing to fruition this inherent potential of his property, the lender may claim compensation for profit foregone.[67] It should be evident that such a conception of fungible goods as economically fertile, i.e., as containing the seeds of profit, runs contrary to the Roman juristic and Aristotelian conviction of their economic sterility (at least in a loan contract). In it Olivi is condoning a spiritual orientation to property, especially to money, repudiated not only by Aristotle but by the Church Fathers and the earlier medieval theological tradition. Moreover, his conception undermines the whole objection to usurious loans from equivalence in exchange by implying that property intended for a profitable purpose is worth more in exchange than it would otherwise be, so that, e.g., £100.00 lent has an exchange value of £110.00. To whatever extent Olivi and Duns Scotus actually grasped the challenge to usury theory presented by the title of *lucrum cessans,* acceptance of it manifested their occasional tendency to acquiesce in the inevitable avarice and self-contained rationality of commerce.

65. *De usuris, Dubium* 6, pp. 84-85; cited in Langholm, *Economics,* p. 371: *Illud quod in firmo proposito domini sui est ordinatum ad aliquod probabile lucrum non solum habet rationem simplicis pecuniae seu rei, sed ultra hoc quamdam seminalem rationem lucrosi quam communiter capitale vocamus.*

66. In a *quaestio* devoted to the neo-Platonic and Augustinian theory of "rationes seminales" in his commentary on Book Two of the *Sentences,* Olivi expounds "seminal reasons" as "the potentialities of matter to forms that are to be educed from it by an extrinsic agent." Editor's summary in Index, *Comm. Sent.* III, ed. Jansen, quoted in Langholm, *Economics,* p. 373.

67. Ironically, as lost opportunity for gain had to be demonstrated, merchants and money lenders were in a better position to claim compensation than were widows, orphans, and the infirm.

A more theoretically persuasive and historically interesting attack on the Thomistic position was presented by Duns Scotus's objection to the moral-legal inseparability of consumption and ownership of goods proposed by Thomas. His objection emerged from the Franciscan defence of the order's theology and discipline which made "absolute poverty" central to the imitation of Christ's perfect love shown on the cross. The practice of absolute poverty not only restricted the brothers to a minimal use of goods, i.e., to using the "bare necessities," but denied to them ownership (either individually or collectively) of the necessities that they used. The brothers renounced all legal right to possess and use goods, in favor of (what in their view was) the natural and charitable use of the earth's abundance belonging to created and sanctified community. Practically, this meant that ownership of goods consumed in use by the Friars Minor remained with the pope (as representing the universal church), thus contravening Thomas's argument that in the case of consumable goods, ownership and use could not be transferred separately. Against the Dominican case Duns Scotus could cite the bull of Nicholas III, *Exiit qui seminat* (1279), confirming the papal ownership of consumable goods used by the Franciscans.

The longer-term impact of Duns Scotus's argument was considerable, even if its short-term impact was lessened by Pope John XXII's anti-Franciscan legislation of 1322 overturning his predecessor's judgment on the separability of ownership and use in the case of consumables. Most importantly, his argument both reflected and reinforced the more voluntaristic and abstract conception of property-right generated by the Franciscan commitment to its total renunciation. Before too long, a fellow Franciscan, Gerald Odonis, would argue that in a contract of *mutuum,* the creditor retains ownership of the money lent, in the sense of retaining the property-right to a certain sum of money which the debtor is obliged to repay, and may licitly charge for the right of using this sum.[68] He thus distinguishes ownership of an abstract sum from ownership of the actual coins, which in the *mutuum* passes to the borrower. While his wholesale demolition of usury theory found only limited acceptance with his contemporaries, the idea of *property-right in an abstract sum* played a key role in scholarly vindication of the popular *census* investment. The *census* (i.e., the purchase of a rent-charge from a fruitful base, real or personal) was almost universally interpreted as the purchase of a *right to money* rather than the purchase of money, so (arguably) respecting the non-vendibility of money.

The thought of Odonis gave dramatic expression to the gathering theoretical forces arrayed against the natural-law justifications of the usury prohibition. He systematically refuted Olivi's mature formulation of these justifica-

---

68. Gerald Odonis, *Tract.,* q.13; f.91v.; Langholm, *Economics,* p. 528.

tions, showing instead that the principles of indemnification and equality in exchange allow the creditor to charge in excess of the principal: not only for the right to use his money, but also for the cessation of his own industry entailed in making the loan. In response to the traditional accusations that the usurer sells what is not his, but God's or the borrower's, Odonis argues that the lender sells precisely what is legally and morally his own, and not another's.[69] His admission of a version of Aristotle's finalistic argument about money as well as the argument from compulsion hardly mitigates the damage already inflicted on the natural-law approach. It is to Christ's command to lend freely, to the constraint of divine love for the neighbor, that Odonis points as the indestructible foundation of the church's usury prohibition. In the next centuries, the vulnerability of natural justice in the market-place will become increasingly apparent, as the traditional theological restraints on property and economic exchange lose their persuasiveness.

at last he pops up!

Luther's Restatement of the Medieval Inheritance

By the sixteenth century the relaxation of the usury prohibition in theory and practice was well underway. The title of *lucrum cessans* was so widely accepted as to be almost interchangeable with that of *interesse*.[70] While the majority of theologians and canonists still required delayed repayment and proof of lost opportunity, some powerful voices urged against these conditions; and in any case, the time span of the gratuitous loan was normally short. The *societas* had largely been transformed into the triple contract, in which the principal was insured and a specified gain guaranteed, thus undermining risk as a test of non-usurious investment. The mutually redeemable, personal *census* was becoming entrenched as a means of temporary, life, or perpetual rights to money, so giving respectability to the practice of making a moderate profit from extending credit. Finally, it was widely conceded that capital was as fertile as a field which bears fruit through human industry, or, alternatively, was a requisite 'tool' of the merchant's trade, of which he should not be deprived without compensation.

For the most part, Luther's reflections on usury fly in the face of these developments, exhibiting a startling fidelity to the older theological ethic. Indeed, it is scarcely an exaggeration to remark that the only comparable rehabilitation

69. For Odonis's refutations of Olivi's natural-law objections to usury, see Langholm, *Economics*, pp. 523-29.

70. Divine, *Interest*, p. 55.

of the earlier evangelical rigor by a similarly influential public figure was Pope Sixtus V's bull *Detestabilis* (1583). In his *Long Sermon on Usury*,[71] Luther prefaces his ethical analysis of the prevailing *census* contract (the *Zinskauf*) with an exposition of the Christian modes (or degrees) of economic exchange drawn from Christ's exhortations to perfection. In the spirit of the Fathers, he presents these modes of "dealing fairly and righteously with temporal goods"[72] as the evangelical foundation of lending and all other commercial and trading practices, departing importantly from his medieval predecessors, however, by insisting that they are *Christ's commands of all believers* rather than *counsels for the zealous few*.[73]

The first or highest degree of "righteous dealing" is to permit the unjust seizure of one's property without rancor, resistance, or retribution, as Jesus commands his disciples in Matthew 5:40: "'If anyone would sue you in court to take your coat, let him have your cloak as well [Luther's rendering]!'"[74] If moral pleading fails to bring the robber or would-be robber to repentance, the Christian lets go of his possessions, and neither demands their return nor "take[s] back what is his" by initiating a suit in court.[75] The second degree of righteous dealing is "to give freely and without return to anyone who needs our goods or asks for them," according to Christ's exhortation in Matthew 5:42: "'Give to him who begs from you.'"[76] This is selflessly to bestow alms on the needy neighbor, whether friend or foe, virtuous or vicious, grateful or ungrateful. Likewise, the third degree involves no reciprocal favors: it is "willingly and gladly [to] lend without charge or *Zins*," in accordance with the will of Christ and God revealed in both Testaments (Luke 6:35, Matt. 5:42, Deut. 15:7-8). To charge for a loan violates three laws: the law of Christ that lending be gratuitous, the law of natural equity that we do not seek in our own profit our neighbor's loss, and the law of love that commands us to love our neighbor as ourselves.[77] While these laws permit the creditor to accept a spontaneous gift of gratitude from his debtor,

---

71. Originally published in 1520, Luther's *Long Sermon on Usury* was reprinted with a short supplement in 1524 as an addition to his recently completed treatise on trade, the whole being known as the treatise on *Trade and Usury*. Translated by C. M. Jacobs, revised by W. I. Brandt, *Luther's Works* 45, ed. W. I. Brandt (Philadelphia: Fortress Press, 1962), pp. 245-310.

72. LW 45.273.

73. LW 45.256, 275.

74. LW 45.273.

75. Such restraint, observes Luther, is contrary to the principle of natural justice affirmed by canon and civil law, that "it is all right . . . to meet force with force" *(vim vi pellere iura sinunt)*, p. 275.

76. LW 45.280.

77. LW 45.292-3.

they do not permit him to desire or exact *"interesse,"* by which Luther means compensation for loss of profits during the loan period.[78]

Beneath these three "Christian" modes of transferring temporal goods lies the "fourth" mode, of commercial exchange or "buying and selling." Permitted rather than commanded by God, this mode occupies a perilous moral territory where avarice runs riot.[79] While trade can never be fully conformed to the evangelical law of love, it must, nevertheless, be conformed to natural equity. Luther conceives natural equity in buying and selling along scholastic lines, incorporating the conventional elements of 'just price' — cost, labor, "trouble," and risk, on the supply side; utility and scarcity on the demand side — that allow the seller to seek, within reason, to indemnify himself against loss, while not exploiting the buyer's need. Distinctive of his thought is the moral centrality in commercial exchange of the element of risk, which expresses the divinely ordained structure of humankind's relation to temporal goods. He sees strategies for the overcoming of risk as endemic to the avaricious corruption of exchange, and condemns all practices that enable the merchant to "make safe, certain and continual profit out of unsafe, uncertain, and perishable goods."[80]

In assessing the contract of *Zinskauf*, i.e., the mutually redeemable sale (purchase) of a regular income on the whole personal estate (including the labor) of the seller, the decisive consideration for Luther is that the buyer draws a guaranteed annual income (normally 5% of the capital investment), regardless of the profits and losses of the seller. Any contract, objects Luther, that permits an investor to reap "interest in the profit" from his capital while remaining "wholly and always free from the interest of loss . . . has no actual basis"[81] — no basis in the universal condition of business risk. It is the intervention of risk between capital and profit that defines the "sterility of money" for Luther. "You cannot make money just with money" means "[you cannot] do business only in this one kind of interest": in "buying the interest of profit," you are actually "paying for it with the interest of loss, . . . other people's losses."[82] Money put out at *Zins* has an unnatural base in the whole person and property of the seller, unnatural because "constantly growing and producing profit out of the earth."[83] The only contract of *Zinskauf* acceptable to Luther is one where the base is specifically defined and itemized real estate and where the purchaser's return varies with the profitability of the base, so that his property is subject to

78. LW 45.292-4.
79. LW 45.245-6.
80. LW 45.271.
81. LW 45.299.
82. LW 45.299-300.
83. LW 45.300.

all the "risks by which [the seller's] labor may be hindered," and thereby "subject to the power of God."[84] Moreover, "the fear of God" should make the buyer always anxious about "taking too much rather than too little," disposed to settle for a smaller percentage of the profit. And even if the contract satisfies the law of natural justice, Christ's commandment of love may require the potential *Zins* buyer to make a free gift or loan to his needy neighbor.[85]

It would seem, therefore, that the argument about risk occupies the pivotal place in Luther's usury theory that the arguments about selling time and the consumptibility of money occupy in the early scholastic and Thomist theories. This may suggest a difference between Luther's ethical approach and the earlier ethic that he appears to reinvigorate: namely, that Luther gives somewhat less centrality to the communal, communicative, and participatory qualities of economic activity than to its individual spiritual profile.

Conclusion: The Contribution of Usury Theory to Economic Ethics

The pivotal place occupied by the usury prohibition in medieval economics was owing to its wedding of the claims of evangelical love and natural justice in the command of Christ to "lend, expecting nothing in return." In explicating the prohibition, theologians and canonists envisioned a redeemed and sanctified community of christological participation in spiritual and material goods: a community of sharing and self-giving, of mutual enjoyment and fulfillment in the use of the earth's abundance, a use free of cupidity and possessiveness and all the attending vices and anxieties about present and future satisfaction of needs. Within this vision of the deepest telos of rational love and desire in regard to collective economic existence, they conceptualized the just exchange and distribution of material goods under the conditions of fallen human and non-human nature: conditions of scarce resources, arduous labor, uncertainty and risk of acquisition and possession, of human avarice and the remedial institutions of property (including contracts of transfer and money). At their best they situated the baptized believer in both communities, subjecting him to the claims of both, ordering those of fallen nature to those of redeemed and sanctified nature. In usury theory, this ordering achieved a singular transparency, owing to the directness of the evangelical and Mosaic commands, which made lending inescapably an occasion for selfless generosity as well as unprofitable

84. LW 45.303.
85. LW 45.304.

justice. In repudiating the profit motive in loans, usury theory focused on the dangers to loving and just economic relationships: the dangers of avaricious wealth accumulation, the exercise of economic coercion, the reduction of economic reasoning to calculation of private self-interest and of freedom to the making of binding covenants; the dangers of money as a stimulus to unbounded desire and the will to power over the future, and as a mechanism of the perverse human valuation of material goods under the species of profitability. It is to all these dangers that economic ethics must perennially attend, and never more so than when the prevailing economic theory is undermining the moral dimensions of personal agency in economic transactions.

A favorite argument of economic historians has been that the more plausible medieval objections to lending at interest are overcome by the presence of a competitive market for money that establishes a just common estimate of value. This implies that the only plausible objection is to the monopolistic exploitation of borrowers in the absence of credit institutions. In singling out the Aristotelian argument from compulsion as the enduring contribution of scholastic usury theory, Langholm endorses this view. But he also points out to his fellow economists that, according to Schumpeter's analytical model, the competitive market rate of interest in a stationary economy (like the medieval economy) tends toward the "zero position," an insight that the medieval theologians "could not deduce" (in modern theoretical terms), but "stated nevertheless, in the Aristotelian terms of duress and sterility."[86] Langholm knows perfectly well, however, that the medieval vision of economic society runs counter to the modern vision of a growth economy: of a system of ever-expanding production and consumption financed by credit. And we would add (not without support from Langholm)[87] that, while the medieval theologians and canonists did not always adequately understand nor consistently address their changing economic environment, they could boast an enviably balanced, penetrating, and, most of all, faithful theological comprehension of economic life.

How does this relate to a common . . . borrowers? What would . . . make of it? (handwritten marginal note)

86. Langholm, *Aristotelian Analysis of Usury,* p. 148.
87. Langholm's concluding chapter of *Economics in the Medieval Schools* is his most balanced appreciation of the scholastic tradition.

The Christian Pedagogy and Ethics of Erasmus

JOAN LOCKWOOD O'DONOVAN

It is fascinating to observe that, in the wake of the modern and postmodern assaults on classical Christian thought and culture, theology appears to be undergoing something of a northern humanist Renaissance in the work of John Milbank. His collection of essays entitled *The Word Made Strange: Theology, Language, Culture*[1] has a distinctly Erasmian feel in its use of the classical-Christian tradition in ethics, politics, and rhetoric to develop a trinitarian and christocentric, ecclesiological ethic with a highly contemporary cast. Milbank's understanding of human society as a dynamic of poetic creativity that has its *telos* in the Incarnate Word as divine-human "poesis" resonates with Erasmus's cultural christocentrism. He, like Erasmus, conceives the redemption of society in terms of communicating participation in the perfections of Jesus Christ who is the final exemplar of the good and the beautiful. Both he and Erasmus regard the church's communication of Christ as preeminently a social *paideia*, an education of the larger community in the *imitatio Christi* through poetic persuasion. They both see the tragedy of sin in terms of humanity not realizing the original spiritual powers of reconciled community.

Equally fascinating are the Erasmian overtones in Milbank's theological polemic against the Western political tradition, most notably, against the Western tradition of natural law, Stoic and Christian. Admittedly, Milbank's criticism is primarily aimed at the modern construction of an autonomous, secular reason as the mechanism of individual and collective will to power: to sovereign, self-

---

1. (Oxford: Blackwell, 1997).

A shorter version of this essay was presented to the Conference on Church and Politeia: English and German Theological Contributions (Oxford, May, 2000).

possessing mastery of non-human nature and human society. However, he views medieval scholastic and canonist theory of natural law as continuous with the modern project, and so contrary to an ethic of Christic poesis, to cultivation of the Christian virtues. Indeed, he regards law as such to be problematic for an ecstatic Christian spirituality and sociality. Erasmus too stresses the ecstatic structure of active Christian love, and looks upon the labored discriminations and deductions of scholastic moral theology as ensnared in "Jewish legalism," and its natural-law premises as dangerous digressions from the way of discipleship.

In drawing attention to these similarities of theological orientation, I am not raising the question of Milbank's dependence upon Erasmus, for such correspondences are largely traceable to their common enthusiasm for certain Church Fathers, most notably Origen, Gregory of Nyssa, and Augustine. Nor am I embarking on a comparison of the Renaissance and postmodern intellectual and cultural milieu to which their respective writings are both polemical and constructive responses. Rather, I am suggesting that in the present climate of theological interest in Milbank's Christian poetics, an engagement with Christendom's most celebrated rhetorician promises to be a fruitful enterprise. This is especially so in the sphere of social and political ethics where Milbank's constructive thought has made only sketchy forays beyond the foundational stage, while Erasmus's pedagogy exhibits a most detailed engagement with social and political realities.

In the following I wish to examine appreciatively and critically the two most celebrated and widely-read works of Erasmian ethical poetics, the *Moriae encomium (Praise of Folly)* and *Querela pacis (Complaint of Peace)*, which have long been regarded as both eloquent exercises in Christian moral *paideia* and significant contributions to Christian social and political understanding. At their best, they are outstanding examples of christocentric and trinitarian rhetoric; but they are not without theological weakness. Their weakness, I will argue, lies in a twofold failure to discriminate with sufficient clarity, firstly, the goods of created human community from their disordered condition, and secondly, God's providential work of preserving the common goods of sinful humanity through structures of political authority and human law. These failures, it seems to me, may fairly be laid at the doorstep of Erasmus's Platonism combined with a narrow ecclesiological slant and a rhetorician's disdain for precision in ethical argumentation and communication.

Of course, from a purely literary point of view, to criticize the theoretical imprecision of a rhetorical mode is circular nonsense, insofar as such imprecision is characteristic of the mode. But theologians cannot rest content with literary assessments of Christian pedagogy: in the end, the rhetoric of Christian *paideia* must adequately represent the Word of Christ revealed through the words of Scripture to the church. Moreover, while these writings of Erasmus comprise only a tiny portion of his published corpus, they represent, alongside his editions, translations, and annotations of the New Testament, the core of his vision of Christian renewal. Let us now turn to the texts.

The Rhetoric of Folly

The monumental popularity of the *Moriae encomium* with Erasmus's contemporaries and with subsequent generations into the present owes a great deal to the kaleidoscopic quality of its wit: its subtleties, ambiguities, constantly shifting postures, complicated ironies and multi-layered intentions. At least some of the rhetorical complexity for which the work is famous may be attributed to the author's protracted labors of revision. In one of Erasmus's own accounts (which is not entirely above suspicion), the book originated as a *jeu d'esprit* dashed off during a spell of convalescence in the home of Thomas More — a diversion from his complaints and an intimate literary joke with his cherished companion in letters.[2] Alternatively, in his prefatory dedication to More, he locates the book's inception during his tedious journey on horseback from Italy to England, when his anticipated delight in renewing their friendship prompted him to reflect on the paradoxical association of More with the Greek "folly" *(mōria)*.[3] These accounts are particularly plausible for the first part of the *Encomium,* consisting of Folly's light-hearted banter of self-praise in the burlesque style of the Greek satirist, Lucian, whom More and Erasmus had been translating together in 1509. However, the first published edition of 1511 already exhibits the tensions of a tripartite structure in which elegant jesting gives way to more stinging social and religious satire, which in turn gives way to meditation on the paradoxes of Pauline soteriology and spirituality.[4] Most of the subsequent revisions contained in the 1514 edition involved Erasmus in expanding and sharpening both his criticism of the papal church's theology and piety and his exposition of Paul's ecstatic theological ethic.[5]

2. Erasmus offered this account in a letter of 1515 to Maarten van Dorp (*Collected Works of Erasmus* [*CWE*] 3: 111-38), responding to the Louvain theologian's criticisms of the 1514 edition of *Moriae encomium.* From 1516 onwards, the letter was regularly prefixed to the work, possibly as a strategy for deflecting hostile reactions. M. A. Screech, *Ecstasy and the Praise of Folly* (London: Duckworth & Co., 1980), pp. 4-6.

3. Ep. 222, *CWE* 2:161-64.

4. Cornelis Augustijn, *Erasmus: His Life, Works, and Influence,* trans. J. C. Grayson (Toronto: University of Toronto Press, 1991), pp. 65-70; *CWE* 28, ed. A. H. T. Levi (Toronto: University of Toronto Press, 1986), pp. xx-xxi.

5. Augustijn, *Erasmus,* pp. 65-69.

The mature work, then, has something of a symphonic texture in which the thematic unity of the movements must be discerned through their tonal diversity. While the obvious unity is rhetorical, residing in the figure of Folly praising herself, the work's pedagogical and theoretical significance depends, nevertheless, on a coherence of theological argumentation in the space opened up by Folly's encomium. Our approach to *this* coherence must be through Folly's critical moments of self-identification that, one might say, establish the controlling keys of the distinct movements.

At the outset, it should be observed that the three movements of the work are contained within the formal rhetorical structure of the classical oration, with its internal division into exordium, narration, partition, confirmation, and peroration. Within these divisions, the subject of the declamation — the proposition that "folly deserves the praise of all" — is introduced, defended, defined and divided, confirmed at length and concluded.[6] In terms of this structure, all three of our movements comprise the lengthy argumentation of the confirmation.

The key signatures to the first movement are given in the preface material, at the movement's beginning, and near its end. When Folly (by way of exordium) steps onto the stage to deliver her encomium, she gaily remarks that the youthful "frolic" and "affectionate smiles" with which her audience greets her *mere appearance* are proof beyond any that the rhetorical craft can furnish of her claim to be the divine cause of gods and men rejoicing (7). She defends (by way of narration) the propriety of praising herself publicly by pointing to men's ungrateful refusal or negligent omission to do so (8), and goes on to spurn the rhetorical exercise (partition) of "circumscribing" (defining) and "dissecting" (dividing) herself, whose nature "extends so universally" and whose worship unites "every order of being" (9). She opens the first movement of the confirmation by announcing her pedigree: born of Plutus (money) and Youth in the Fortunate Isles, she was suckered by Drunkenness and Ignorance, and attended in all her endeavors by her household servants, Self-love, Flattery, Forgetfulness, Idleness, Pleasure, Madness, and Sensuality (11). Toward the end of the first movement, she boasts that, without her, no society or union can be either pleasant or permanent (22).

In the intervening flow of playful banter, Folly implicitly discloses that she is the passionate attachment of humanity to all the worldly goods bestowed by nature and fortune and, conversely, the passionate aversion to their loss.

---

6. See Hoyt Hopewell Hudson's formal analysis of the encomium in the appendix to his translation in the Wordsworth Classics of World Literature edition (Ware, Hertfordshire: Wordsworth Editions, 1998). All quotations are from this edition.

Among these goods are the enchantment of helpless infancy, the grace of ignorant adolescence, the forgetfulness and "uninhibited garrulousness" of declin-
ing old age, the seductive beauty of the body, the glamour and gentility of
women, the partisan pleasures of romantic love and friendship, and the "domestic associations" of the sexes (12-22). All the goods to which Folly directs
humankind are intrinsically social, yet bound up with individual self-love. In
their enjoyment, natural virtues are invariably mingled with natural vices: only
rarely do virtue and vice stand forth less equivocally, as, respectively, in mater-
nal forgetfulness of the pain of childbirth (12-13) and the amorous chase of the
elderly after youth (31-32). Friendship and marriage are paradigmatic of the
moral equivocality of all community: friendship is kept alive by the friends'
"conniving" at each other's faults, "passing them over, being blind to them, and
deceived by them, even loving and admiring [them] as if they were virtues"
(20); while the "indivisible bond" of marriage is "propped up and fostered by
flattery, by jesting, by pliableness, ignorance, dissimulation," all "satellites" of
Folly (21-22).

The final key signature of the opening movement of Folly's declamation, which also, one might say, modulates to the key of the second movement, is her outburst of philosophizing on the paradoxical duality of appearance and reality "in human affairs" — an outburst that flows from her claim
to hold sway over the preeminently political virtue of prudence (27-28). Under the two metaphors of the Sileni of Alcibiades, the grotesque and con-
temptible figures that open out to reveal the gods within, and the theatrical
play in which the actors strut across the stage in disguise, Folly conveys the
reversal of the order of appearance by the order of reality (28-29). The wise
man, she declares, who has "dropped down from the sky" to dispel the shadows on the stage by confronting both players and onlookers with reality, is
considered "insane and raving" by the crowd, and as well, by the "truly prudent" who will either "pretend not to notice anything or affably and compan-
ionably be deceived" (29). Of course, madness too, she reminds us in a scholastic moment, is a genus comprised of two species, of which one
comprehends the furiously destructive passions from hell, and the other, the
"amiable dotage" of a careless and delighting spirit — in other words, the
anti-social and the social passions (38-39).

In the wake of her Platonic outburst, Folly dwells on the indispensability
of delusion to human happiness, arguing that human nature is fulfilled in being
deceived (33), and so recapitulating the many aspects of her influence under the
principal aspect of deception. As she canvasses the spectrum of delusions,
good-natured mockery gives way to increasingly acerbic satire, culminating in
her deriding of Christian superstitions: of counterfeit pardons for sin, purgato-

rial punishment measured "as if with an hour glass," prayers uttered as charms to secure the goods of nature and fortune, purchase of the soul's purification from the "cesspool of . . . Life," and manipulation of the saints for private and public ends (42-44). Then, in an ironic tour de force, Folly holds up the delusion of delusions: echoing her opening speech, she expresses herself satified with men's worship of her, despite their refusing her a formal cult with temples, sacrifices, and paeans of praise. For, she observes, the worship they universally accord her is that "specially approved by our divines": they "take me to their souls, manifest me in their actions, and represent me in their lives" (49). Folly is preparing for her demonstration that even the wisest in human society, practitioners of professions revered for their wisdom, are engaged in a pious mimesis of her divine self.

Indeed, she reveals that it is in the learned professions that the spirit of worldly society achieves a focused and reflective representation: in the practice of the arts and sciences, the deceit of fleshly existence becomes objectified conceit. Folly's demonstration traverses the insipid and vapid productions of grammarians, poets, rhetoricians, and writers, the convoluted glosses of lawyers, and the fantastical speculations of natural scientists, sustaining throughout a level of satirical dispassion (52-57). When, however, she arrives at the theologians and monks, the secular and ecclesiastical princes, she abandons herself to an intensity of scathing unbecoming to a literary *divertissement*. She exposes not only to ridicule but to extreme loathing the arrogant presumption of the theologians who not merely cloud but eclipse the shining forth of the apostolic Gospel of Christ by means of the formalities and subtleties of scholastic method and their arcane and trifling *quaestiones disputatae* (57-62). Likewise the monks, who substitute for true discipleship an obsessively legalistic cult of unwholesomeness, and for preaching, absurdly pedantic and chimerical orations designed to impress and to entertain their hearers.

In treating of kings, bishops, cardinals, and the Supreme Pontiff, Folly slips into a plainly sermonic style, contrasting the spiritual requirements of their public offices with their worldly inversion in contemporary Christendom. Her treatments are all admirable miniatures of the political 'mirror of princes' genre, but there are notably different slants for secular and ecclesiastical rulers. Folly portrays the kingly office in an entirely classical manner with both Byzantine and Ciceronian overtones, contrasting the demeanor of the prince — superior in virtue, exemplary in conduct, law-abiding and ever solicitous for the common welfare, with the vices of the tyrant — lawless, unjust, profligate and always self-aggrandizing. With princes of the church, however, Folly places in the foreground their representation of Christ, portraying their sacred offices through the symbolism of their vestments (and so revitalizing a tired tradition of ecclesiological rhetoric). Echoing Bernard of Clairvaux[7], she bids the bishop, cardinal and pope to "consider" the knowledge of God's revealed word in the two Testaments and the emulation of Christ's perfections signified by their attire, pointing to the vestiary symbols of purity of heart, victory over the "carnal affections," self-sacrificing solicitude for Christ's flock, the apostolic stewardship of spiritual things, living in poverty, and "the burning love of God" (71-72). Conversely, she exhibits the degrading deflection of these symbols onto the clerical hierarchy's worldly strivings after wealth, honor, sensual pleasure, and power, even to the point of shedding blood in battle (72-75).

Thus, in claiming as her own the highest authorities (both epistemological and political) of Christian society, Folly demonstrates no affection for them, nor anything lovable about them; rather she simply holds them in derision. As representing the spirit of worldliness, they are hell-bent, and not only they but also the symbolic tradition that has been deflected onto worldly things through generations of rulers educated into evil habits of thought and action. The message of Folly's sermon is clear: the urgency of a spiritual renewal of the traditions of Christendom wherein they become communicative again of the plain teaching of Christ disclosed through the New Testament text. Fortunately for Folly, this plain teaching lies within the purview of her oration, provided only that she resume her eulogizing, interrupted by her deviation into satire. She must pass beyond her self-righteous anger in unmasking sinful folly to the spiritual delight of praising the unsurpassed representation of her divine self. This representation is provided chiefly by St. Paul's First Letter to the Corinthian Church.

Folly prepares her audience to receive Paul's testimony as simply true, beyond rhetorical ambiguity, by placing a particular gloss on his bitterly ironic, self-deprecating remark in 2 Corinthians, that he speaks "as a fool."[8] She explains that, lest Paul's apparent arrogance in boasting offend the Corinthians, he covers himself by "the suggestion of folly [. . .] — as if he would say that it is the privilege of fools that they alone may speak the truth without offence" (80). Throughout her encomium Folly has repeatedly invoked this privilege of truthtelling uniquely accorded to the simple-minded in order to bring her listeners to precisely this juncture where the Gospel truth is proclaimed. This is the teaching of God's folly in saving the world through the incarnation of his Son,

---

7. In his *De consideratione* composed as a spiritual 'mirror of princes' for the former Clairvaux monk, Pope Eugenius III.

8. "I repeat, let no one think me foolish; but even if you do, accept me as a fool, so that I too may boast a little. (What I am saying I say not with the Lord's authority but as a fool, in this boastful confidence; since many boast of worldly things, I too will boast.) For you gladly bear with fools, being wise yourselves!" (2 Cor. 11:16-19, *RSV*).

of Christ's folly in suffering and dying on the cross, and of the folly of Christ's disciples in imitating their master. Folly is *finally and authoritatively praised* as the single movement of divine love in which God in Christ ecstatically united himself with sinful humanity so that sinful humanity might be ecstatically united with him in the Holy Spirit (83-85).

Folly's last arguments are reserved for the happy foolishness of Christian discipleship: for the joyful disengagement of the human soul from worldly passions in surrender to the single passion of divine love (86-90). She points to the several moments of Christian folly: first, to the soul's laying hold on natural simplicity, on her original instinctive trust in God and delight in worshiping him (86); second, to the soul's discipline of death in which, by participating in Christ's sufferings, she is released from the fetters of worldly attachments (86-89); and third, to the soul's foretaste of the eternal happiness of living wholly in the Supreme Spirit (90). Then, in a sudden rhetorical flourish, Folly demurs from a peroration, on the excuse that she has already forgotten everything that she has said, so leaving her audience unmistakably in the oblivion of Plato's cave.

Only in reading and rereading the *Moriae encomium* attentively does its pedagogical and theological accomplishment come fully into view. With consummate rhetorical skill, Erasmus seeks to foster the "renewal of mind" advocated by St. Paul in his admonition to the Romans: "Do not be conformed to this world, but be transformed by the renewal of your mind, that you may prove what is the will of God, what is good and acceptable and perfect" (Rom. 12:2). As Christian exhortation, Folly's self-praise carries the reader from a fleshly to a spiritual vantage point: from complacent acquiescence in the ethical ambiguities of daily life in which vice and virtue seem inextricably wedded, to an awakening at the foot of the cross to the divine imperatives of world-denying, self-giving love. Erasmus achieves with breathtaking subtlety the transition from mimesis of the sinful world to mimesis of its purification and reconciliation through the Spirit of Christ. Intrinsic to this transition is the moment of satirical intensity in which Christ's earthly representatives are shown to be worldly authorities in all their demonic potency. Folly's self-praise effects a parallel theological transition from a sophistical to a christological understanding of society: from society understood as a complex balance of vices and virtues to society understood as the body of Christ, the bond of trinitarian love.

In her rhetorical "turning around" of her listeners from the shadows in the cave to reality in the light of the Son, Folly leaves certain practical matters in relative obscurity. There is the matter of natural human virtues cultivated in the soil of natural earthly attachments: marital and familial love, the enjoyment and representation of sensible beauty, care for and use of the material world. In the blaze of the *summum bonum,* their moral contours as created nature dissolve: they become the undifferentiated occasions for, or objects of, an *imitatio Christi* circumscribed by Christ's "counsels of perfection" in the Sermon on the Mount; so that, e.g., one's earthly father can only be loved as a "good man" (88-89). There is also the matter of civil rule: how to derive its moral contours from the Spirit of Christ, incarnate, crucified and resurrected. Folly's classical portrait of the royal office in terms of virtue, law, and the common good offers little theological explication of it as Christian mimesis, and her contempt for legal casuistry casts a shadow over the realm of public justice. In all fairness, however, the gathering concentration on individual spiritual renewal in Folly's oration excuses her from a more strenuous engagement with political authority and order.

We do not have to look far in Erasmus's corpus for that more strenuous political engagement. His most sustained political works, the *Institutio principis christiani* and *Querimonia pacis* (now known as *Querela pacis*), were both published in 1516 during a period of intense literary productivity which saw his first edition of the Greek *New Testament* along with a fresh Latin translation. Composed in 1515, *The Education of a Christian Prince* appeared in print a few months after Erasmus had been appointed as counsellor to Prince Charles of Burgundy and Aragon (the future Emperor Charles V), a grateful offering of advice and homage to his royal patron. His *Complaint of Peace,* written at the request of the chancellor of Burgundy and Castile,[9] had the practical object of encouraging a negotiated peace between France and the Anglo-Burgundian alliance. While both pieces aspired to universal political pedagogy beyond the circumstances that elicited them, the *Complaint of Peace* comprises the more theogically integrated and original, as well as rhetorically powerful, work. Nevertheless, a few remarks about the *Institutio* are pertinent, as it was Erasmus's first serious attempt at a Christocentric political ethic.

In its rhetorical form and style, the *Institutio* is in the Hellenic-Byzantine 'mirror of princes' tradition, setting forth the ideal of princely government in a series of aphorisms addressed to the young Charles by way of praise and exhortation. While its presentation of the ruler's moral equipment and the principles of government is, for the most part, classically derived (drawing on Plato, Aristotle, Xenophon, Isocrates, Plutarch, Seneca, and Cicero), Erasmus self-consciously attempts to bring this content under the sway of Christian mimesis. He repeatedly holds up Christ as the archetype of kingship and his teaching as the royal philosophy; so that, for example, the prince's sacrifice of

---

9. Jean le Sauvage was "a leading advocate of appeasement with France" in the interests of peace in the Netherlands. *The Education of a Christian Prince,* ed. and trans. Lisa Jardine (Cambridge: Cambridge University Press, 1997), p. 109, note 190.

himself to the common good is his taking up his cross, his chief virtues are selfless care for others, forbearance, and peaceableness (in the spirit of pater-familias), his rule is ministerial rather than dominative (as laid down by Matt. 20:25-26), and his fellowship with his subjects is grounded not principally in natural equality but in their common redemption by Christ. Nevertheless, Erasmus does not wholly succeed in theologically grounding the elements of classical statecraft, nor even always reconciling them with Christian sensibilities.[10] He still declines to situate the salient political elements of law, justice, judgment, and punishment within a framework of divine government and continues to ignore the Old Testament resources for understanding civil rule. Understandably, it is in grappling with the morality of war that he confronts the theological challenge most acutely.

The Rhetoric of Peace

On several occasions, spanning more than a decade, Erasmus mustered his most impassioned and arresting rhetoric in denouncing war. Not even in the *Querela* does he surpass the depictions of war's immediate and lasting evils in his early *Panegyric to the Archduke Philip,* father of Charles (1504), and his essay, *Dulce bellum inexpertis* ("War is sweet to those who have never tried it"), first published in the 1515 edition of his *Adages.* While reproducing a good deal of argumentation from the latter in the *Complaint,* Erasmus nonetheless intends it to be a declamation of similar rhetorical and theological stature to the *Moria.*

Indeed, just as the figures of *Folly* and *Peace* are allegorical companions and counterpoints, so are their orations. The figures are companions inasmuch as both signify most eminently the ecstatic communion of redeemed humanity with Christ through the Holy Spirit; they are counterparts in as much as *Folly* is transmuted in the course of her eulogy from the spirit of worldliness, of the earthly city, into the Spirit of Christ's mystical body, whereas *Peace* undergoes no such transmutation. Consequently, her *complaint* displays a uniform tone of "moral earnestness"[11] without subtle or dramatic shifts, and her style is plainly

10. For example, the cynical twist of Aristotle's advice (*Politics* 5.9.16) that "a prince who wants to escape his people's hatred and to develop their good will will delegate to others the tasks which the people resent and will carry out personally those that are well received" (Jardine, p. 70). Likewise, the skeptical import of Plato's counsel that: "To persuade men not to break the law, you must first use reasoned arguments, then, as a deterrent, the fear of divine vengeance against criminals, and in addition threats of punishment" (p. 82).

11. G. Thompson, *Under Pretext of Praise: Satiric Mode in Erasmus' Fiction* (Toronto: University of Toronto Press, 1973), p. 101.

sermonic, without ironic texture and parodic color. Her rhetoric achieves moments of inspiration throughout, but the whole does not comprise the polished masterpiece of *Folly's* encomium. It almost appears that Erasmus lost interest in the declamatory and allegorical form of the *Querela* as he became absorbed by the vehemence of its content.

In the opening lament of Peace, the reader is drawn irresistibly into contrasting her complaint with that of Folly: whereas Folly complained of men's neglect of her cultic praise and worship, as distinct from the pious mimesis that they duly render her, Peace complains that men forever neglect to honor her in act, while praising her loudly in words.[12] They constantly laud her as "the fount and source, the sustainer, amplifier and preserver of all good things of heaven and earth," but their minds, energies, and desires are bent on spurning her (293). As a lover of humankind, she laments men's ingratitude for her universal provision, chiefly on account of the misery that they incur in depriving themselves of her benefits (293). Since "war is a kind of encircling ocean of all the evils," men's devotion to it of "so much expenditure and application, of such great effort and artifice" must be pitied as "the height of madness" (293). Ironically, "the height of madness" to which Peace refers is the antithesis of the ecstatic love to which Folly finally leads us. Indeed, in terms of the two species of madness distinguished by Folly midway through her encomium, war draws on the "furiously destructive passions from Hell" rather than the pleasantly delusive passions that sustain society.

From her exordium, Peace launches into the argument of her declamation, loosely structured in two parts. The first part is an exercise of self-eulogizing in which she displays her benefits; the second is a denunciation of war in which she exhibits the evils inhering in its causes, conduct and effects.

In displaying her benefits for humankind, Peace appeals to Nature and to Christ. Her first argument is that men are uniquely drawn to her by their singular endowments of both spiritual capabilities and needs. She points to their "reasoning power" and "divine insight," their "gift of speech," "the seeds of learning and the virtues implanted in [them]," their inclination "toward good will" and their "capacity for tears" — all of which comprises their humanity. These capabilities, when reinforced by "ties of kinship and affinity" and combined with individual weaknesses and inequalities of mind and body, render mutual love and service not only possible but necessary (294-5). How paradoxi-

---

12. *The Complaint of Peace Spurned and Rejected by the Whole World,* trans. Betty Radice in *CWE* 27, ed. A. H. T. Levi (Toronto: University of Toronto Press, 1986), p. 293. All quotations are from this translation. Also *IG*, pp. 572-80.

cal, then, sighs Peace, that these bonds should be insufficient to "check [men] in their frenzy for mutual extinction" (296).

Beyond and above nature, Peace appeals to Christ, the author of concord, who came to earth to "reconcile the world with the Father, to bind men together with . . . indestructible love, and . . . to make man his own friend" (300). She reminds us that the angels heralded Christ's birth by proclaiming peace to men of good will, that Christ manifested peace, commanded it and prayed for it, that he bequeathed and promised peace to his disciples, leaving a "final testament" to it in the communion of bread and wine (299-302). With perplexity and sorrow, she ponders the prevalence of strife among those who confess Christ's name and are united in his body by common sacraments, and even more, among those who in a special way represent the Prince of Peace to his people (296-7). Everywhere, Christ's representatives are engaged in unholy warfare: priests in ecclesiastical litigation, monks in factional quarrels, theologians in scholastic disputes, princes in armed conflict. And more shameful still, monks and clerics of every rank instigate, fuel, and exacerbate the wars of princes, and on occasion bloody their own hands in battle.[13] All deny Christ and violate his commands by acting out of the worldly ambitions that he sought to extirpate (302). Blinded by passion, they debase the community of divine love into an "armed camp" (303) wherein "the cross fights the cross and Christ makes war on Christ," so that his ministers "deserve not the crucifix but crucifixion" (309). Contrasting the complacency of Christians with killing one another to the abhorrence of civil war by the Greeks, Peace pleads: "Are men less than blood brothers when they are united in Christ?" (310). Then, comparing sacrificing to demons of which Christians accuse the Turks to Christians sacrificing one another in war, Peace observes bitterly that in the latter case "the wicked demons . . . enjoy a double sacrifice, since the killer and the killed are both equally their victims" (310).

It is more pointedly to the princes that Peace addresses her depiction of war's evils, for the princes are most implicated in the evil causes of war, as they are most implicated in its prevention. If princes were not enslaved to "base passions" but wholly devoted to the common welfare, they would, she claims, pursue peace at almost any cost (311). Out of greed, fear, vanity, and lust for power, they plunge their kingdoms into war on "disgraceful and frivolous pretexts": a "mouldering, obsolete title" to lands, "some trifling omission in a treaty covering a hundred clauses," a neighbor's "interception of an intended spouse or a

13. Erasmus undoubtably had in mind, among others, the English friars that had preached on behalf of Henry VIII's planned expedition in 1512 to invade France, abetted by Rome and Venice, and most eminently, the warrior-pope, Julius II, whose military campaigns and oppressive taxation of conquered territories he had experienced at first hand.

careless word of slander" (305). At the worst they use war to consolidate their despotic rule (305); at the least they confuse "private grievance" with "public concern" (314, 318). They either disregard the public good altogether or culpably misjudge it, making erroneous calculations of the relative benefits and evils for their subjects of fighting a war.

Peace insists that, whatever the justice of its cause, war is inevitably unjust in its conduct: being "the cesspool of every iniquity," it destroys popular happiness and virtue (317). In assaulting a foreign enemy, the prince assaults his own subjects by bringing about their material and spiritual impoverishment, through crippling taxation, the curtailment of business and commerce, the interruption of education and other cultural enterprises; but chiefly, through placing them in the power of "the worst people," "the criminal dregs of hired mercenaries" who spread violence, immorality, lawlessness, and irreligion throughout the land. All this in addition to their defilement with the blood of others! Moreover, the damage inflicted by war is lasting on both sides (317-18).

With her peroration in sight, Peace returns to praising her universal benefaction and appeals again to nature and to Christ. She appeals to the humane pleasures of harmonious intercourse within and among nations and to the true city that Christians possess and occupy, "high on a mountain top, in full sight of God and man" (319). She reminds Christians of the reproach to their faith posed by war-mongering and savagery among themselves, and particularly, their hindrance of the most urgent missionary task of converting the Turks (319). She concludes by summoning all of Christ's ministers in church and state to forsake the "madness" of war and embrace his manifest will for peace, holding up as exemplary the inclinations toward peace of the principal royal and imperial parties to the present negotiations.

Not surprisingly, the *Querela* has been widely read and admired as an exhortation to Christian pacifism. Erasmus himself regarded its "pacific ethic" as his most original contribution to political reflection.[14] Beyond the power of his anti-war rhetoric, pacifists have extolled his effective demolition of scholastic "just war" theory developed from natural-law premises. Roland Bainton, for example, congratulates Erasmus on demolishing "the analogy between war and the administration of justice within the civil state" by showing rulers to be incapable of acting as "impartial judges" in international disputes, not least because the ethical ambiguities of such disputes permit of no clear resolution outside of negotiation.[15] While we would agree with the pacifist reading of the *Querela*

---

14. G. Faludy, *Erasmus of Rotterdam* (London: Eyre & Spottiswoode, 1970), p. 148.
15. *Erasmus of Christendom* (London: Collins, 1969), pp. 151-52. Bainton's remarks have a wider reference to Erasmus's anti-war writings.

that its achievement as Christian moral pedagogy can only be measured in relation to the scholastic just-war tradition, we would propose a more nuanced interpretation of that relation.

Our first consideration is that the *Querela* continues the Pauline exhortation of the *Moria* to "renewal of mind" in conformity with the Spirit of Christ.
Conversion from the fleshly to the spiritual perspective is just as central here. In
the light of christological love, war is revealed to be more a disease of humankind to be cured than a remedy to be administered: the object of an insatiable,
perverted lust. Illuminated by Christ's earthly life and commandments, armed
conflict appears as a demonic parody of self-sacrifice, giving unbridled expression to hellish passions. In that created human nature is ordered to its perfection in Christ, war threatens to frustrate and destroy even man's natural endowments for society, rationality, and friendship.

Inasmuch as the exhortation is directed to those in political authority and
their advisors, Erasmus is also carrying forward his presentation of rule as
Christian mimesis, with more consistency than in the *Institutio*. Given the overriding ethical imperative of war avoidance, he defines the prince's moral orientation more strictly by the evangelical virtues conveyed in Christ's precepts of perfection than the classical language of the cardinal virtues. For Erasmus, the
inflated dynastic and territorial ambitions driving Europe's ruling houses — the
Medici, the Valois, the Tudors, and the Hapsburgs — evidence the enslavement
of princely wills to the passions of private self-aggrandizement rather than of
public service for Christ's sake. In a decade of wars he sees not one undertaken
by a ruler in defense of the common good of his subjects. When he holds up the
"disgraceful and frivolous pretexts" on which wars have been enjoined, he is in-
dicting particular parties whose identity his contemporary readers would know.
The issue for him is not whether princes are able, in principle, to judge impar-
tially in international disputes, but whether Christian princes are, in fact, seeking in their judgments the true welfare of those entrusted by Christ to their care.

It is more accurate to say that Erasmus in the *Querela* sidelines rather
than repudiates just-war theory on account of (what he perceives to be) the
ambiguous relationship of its principles to the argument of Peace. He perceives
that in the academic as in the political forum the guiding principles of just war
are, more frequently than not, pressed into the mould of worldly mimesis: employed to vindicate the marriage of virtue and vice, or worse, pure vice. Such he
judges to be the case with the natural-law principle of the Roman jurists that
"force may be repelled by force" *(vim vi repellere)*.[16] Misconstrued as pro-

16. This principle entered the church's tradition through Isidore of Seville (ca. 560-636)
whose formulations of natural right in his *Etymologiae*, based on Roman juristic sources, were

pounding a universal right of self-defense belonging to individuals and communities,[17] the principle had sanctioned increasingly worldly and un-Christ-like conduct on the part of clerics, from traveling with entourages of armed guards to carrying weapons and leading a triumphal army of occupation, as Pope Julius had done. Likewise, princes regularly abused the natural law requiring that crimes be punished and injuries be made good by inflicting brutal and crippling penalties and reparations on conquered territories, as Pope Julius had done. Nevertheless, Peace does not entirely banish just-war principles from her argument:[18] she passes by them on the path of Christian mimesis without attending to them as important features of the ethical landscape, except to express her skepticism about the possibility of their implementation.

Limitations of the Rhetoric of Christian Mimesis

Erasmus's Christian rhetoric makes imitation of Christ's earthly perfection, as mediated through the apostolic teaching, the form and telos of its pedagogy — pedagogy undertaken within and for the church as the community of Christian representation. Its movement is structured by the Pauline dichotomy of flesh and spirit, of conformity to the deceiving world of carnal affections and conformity to the truth of Christ's self-giving love. Despite the judgment on human society and culture entailed in this movement from world to Christ, Erasmus's intention was not to deny the full flowering of created human nature and culture. His intention was humanist as well as perfectionist, one of purifying social and cultural representations of their demonic and idolatrous self-love. The rhetorical power of his Christian moral pedagogy is directed to manifesting the Spirit's work of purification.

It is evident from the *Moria* and the *Querela*, however, that this rhetorical movement does not equally illuminate all features of the Christian moral landscape. If Folly's encomium leaves the common affections and virtues of created human nature in ill-defined shadow, the complaint of Peace leaves the morality of waging war in a similar theoretical twilight. In both cases, Erasmus's determination to avoid the pitfall of worldly complacency into which scholastic developments of natural law have fallen causes him to settle for something less than

---

incorporated into medieval canon law collections, the most influential being Gratian's *Decretum* (1140).

17. *Dulce bellum inexpertis* (Adage 3001) 4.1.1.

18. For example, she declares that "if war is unavoidable, it should be conducted in such a way that the full force of its calamities must fall on the heads of those who gave cause for it" (312).

theological completeness in his moral pedagogy. In refusing to thematize moral aspects of created and fallen human community apart from Christ-centered mimesis, he refuses to thematize them within a fully trinitarian practice.

His rhetoric of civil government particularly suffers from theological incompleteness in its failure to recognize as a distinct trinitarian work *ad extra* the Father's preservation of the sinful human community by the lawful use of coercive power and to relate this work to the universal rule of the risen Christ through the Holy Spirit. Thus he fluctuates (despite his avowed intentions) between handing over civil rule to pagan writers and assimilating it too closely to the spiritual rule of Christ in the church. His rhetorical aims also make him reluctant to recognize the contribution of a discursive conceptuality of moral principles and 'laws' to interpreting Christ's rule over earthly powers and principalities. To thematize principles of just war under the sway of a christocentric rhetoric of peace is properly to relate God's works of preservation and sanctification as two moments of divine love in and for his human creatures.

Returning to the postmodern Renaissance of Christian humanistic *paideia* in the work of John Milbank, we may appreciate with more precision its likeness in both theological aspiration and method to Erasmian moral rhetoric, whose achievement lies in the christocentric, ecclesial, Pauline, and neo-Platonic *mimesis* at its core. We may also, without intrepidity, anticipate similar weaknesses in Milbank's theological ethics to those of Erasmian pedagogy. However, one striking difference between Erasmus and Milbank is the latter's more pronounced philosophical sophistication, conveyed by the succession of meta-philosophical-historical analyses that characterize his work. While alerting him to certain dangers and temptations that Erasmus did not entirely resist, this sophistication also inclines him to a serious temptation that Erasmus never faced — that of making of poetics yet another philosophical foundation for Christian pedagogy. Succumbing to this temptation would lend an ominous finality to any other theological and methodological weaknesses.

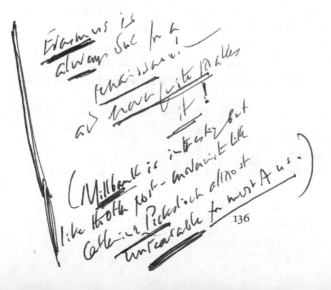

The Challenge and the Promise of Proto-modern Christian Political Thought

JOAN LOCKWOOD O'DONOVAN

A perennial argument of political theorists and politicians in liberal democracies is that democracy and liberal economics are inseparable, in fact and in principle. In the English-speaking world, where formulations of their inseparability continue to wax powerful, the coming to be of democratic political culture and institutions appears to have gone hand in hand with the expansion of market capitalism. While the historical connections are not beyond scholarly dispute,[1] it is the present relationship that attracts the most wide-ranging controversy, in which *de facto* and *de iure* elements are inevitably intertwined.

Contemporary opponents of their inseparability, and especially Christians, are more likely to have doubts about capitalism than democracy. While democratic principles and institutions are the objects of more or less universal approbation in the advanced West, anxieties are rife about the evils resulting from unrestrained market forces, not only social and environmental, but also political evils. It is widely perceived that excessive corporate profit and inflated managerial salaries flout the democratic ethos of social equality, that the coercive features of market exchange diminish individual economic freedom, and that the influence on governmental policy of powerful financial and commercial interests threatens the commanding role of the democratic majority. In-

---

1. The complexity of the theoretical connections and some of the issues arising are conveyed by C. B. Macpherson's careful correlation of phases of modern liberal economic thought with successive models of democracy from Jeremy Bentham and James Mill to the present, in *The Life and Times of Liberal Democracy* (Oxford: Oxford University Press, 1977).

This paper grew out of a seminar presentation at The Institute of Christian Studies (Toronto, Canada) in 2001. My thanks to Dr. Jonathan Chaplin and his students for a valuable discussion. ——

137

deed, there is a mounting sense among democratic populations that the global flow of investment capital seeking larger profit margins, favorable tax benefits, and speculative gains is robbing the majority of the world's citizens of effective political controls over their economic and social future.[2] Many recognize the urgent task of redressing the economic democratic deficit, of reinserting individual and communal economic responsibility into the otherwise ineluctable processes of global capitalism.

While this raft of doubts about domestic and global capitalism are well-placed at the practical level, they somewhat cloud the deeper issue of how democratic and liberal economic principles are related. Serious-minded Christians too easily assume that democratic principles have an independent moral rationale that is consistent with, if not required by, their faith. They participate in the remarkable post-Christian consensus about the superior benefits of liberal democracy over other modes of political and social organization, which has remained relatively unscathed by the not-inconsiderable disaffection within intellectual circles. The tenacious attachment of Christian thinkers to democratic forms and ideas is especially startling, given the animosity of the bulk of the Christian political tradition to them. Modern Christians have proved immensely adept at inoculating themselves against the illiberal and anti-democratic judgments of their revered forefathers, either by dissociating them from the more authoritative elements of their theological contributions or by recasting them in a more liberal and democratic mould. Today, illiberal and anti-democratic arguments are instinctively shunned as dangerous, if not sinful, improprieties.

But Christians must move beyond conventional sensibilities and platitudes if they are to act politically with intellectual integrity and practical wisdom. Their labors for truth and justice in the public realm must be informed by a sober assessment of present hindrances. This requires a more penetrating grasp of the inner logic of liberal democracy: that is, of the common anthropology that binds the principles and practice of modern democracy to those of modern economic liberalism. Their labors must also be informed by past understandings of political ends and political order: preeminently those contained in Scripture, but also those contained in the theological tradition that, precisely because they involve a different (and typically more wide-ranging and

2. While for many of us, this sense of political impotence in the global market of corporate capitalism retains a good deal of vagueness, William Greider in *One World, Ready or Not: The Manic Logic of Global Capitalism* (Harmondsworth, Middlesex: Penguin Books, 1997) furnishes it with a generous amount of sharp analysis and vivid factual detail. His own manic journalistic style should not fatally undermine for the discriminating reader the combined strength of his observations and arguments.

intensive) employment of biblical texts, enable us to break through the narrowness of contemporary political interest in, and interpretation of, the Bible.

For the renewal of our political minds, the thought of the late-medieval and early-modern periods, from the fourteenth to the seventeenth centuries, is a particularly resourceful terrain for this reason: that it contains the seeds of modern theoretical developments, but their conceptualization is, for the most part, more tightly controlled by biblical exposition and a consistent theological legacy. Therefore, it is beneficial for us to inquire whether concepts and principles that have been determinative for modern political thought come to expression during this period in ways that are more theologically coherent and compatible with biblical foundations than are later formulations and, moreover, whether these earlier formulations can furnish a unified theological foundation for a renewal of liberal democratic theory and practice in the present. The following must necessarily be a tentative and modest contribution to such an inquiry.

Our first task, however, is the critical one of demonstrating the inner unity of modern democracy and economic liberalism in a common anthropology.

The Economic Anthropology
of Modern Liberal Democracy

Let us begin by distinguishing the political principles and institutions that are peculiar to modern liberal democracy from those which it shares with earlier political forms. Failure to do so frequently expresses a dogmatic attachment to democracy that inhibits intelligent assessment of alternative polities. For example, modern liberal democracy entails the rule of law: the principle that government is not its own law but governs according to laws publicly enacted by recognized authorities and consented to by the governed. It entails the principle of the equality of all — governors and governed — before the law or under the law. It entails the principle of participation of the governed in legislative and judicial processes, either directly (as in the jury system of trial) or representatively (as in elective and appointed legislative bodies). It entails the principle that the governed enjoy a freedom of action guaranteed against routine governmental interference. These principles, while intrinsic to modern liberal democracy, are by no means peculiar to it, belonging as much to constitutional monarchies or aristocracies, past and present. They may be said to embody the political liberalism of the Western Christian tradition.

Rather, the principles peculiar to modern liberal democracy are two, one teleological and one formal: *the maximization of individual and collective free-*

dom, and *the equality of individuals in regard to freedom.* The end served by modern liberal democratic polity is maximization of the freedom of its members: their freedom to think, to choose, and to act, in independence of one another, and in collective independence of external forces. Government that maximizes the freedom of the governed is self-government, the governed governing themselves: thus, democracy is inherently *republican.* In that the governed comprise the whole people, democratic government is inherently *populist:* it is government "of, by, and for the people." The whole people is both the original and the immediate source of democratic political authority, which may be delegated to chosen representatives who act as instrumental agents of the popular will. The unified political will is formed by the free contracting together of equal individual wills, the terms of the civil contract specifying the internal organization and external limits of governmental authority. Thus, democratic polity is inherently *contractarian* and *egalitarian.* These liberal-democratic principles of *maximizing individual and collective freedom* and *egalitarianism* (entailing *republican self-government, popular sovereignty,* and *political contractualism*) are institutionalized in pervasive mechanisms of popular accountability and choice, the most critical of which are frequent elections with universal adult suffrage, legally guaranteed individual and group freedoms of inquiry, speech and assembly, political parties, an omnipresent public press, and the separation of governmental powers in a system of mutual surveillance and restraint.

It is the equality accorded to individual wills as the source, agents and objects of political authority that expresses the economic anthropology of democratic theory and practice. For this equality of wills is economic before it is political: behind the multitude of naturally self-governing individuals that bind themselves to the civil contract is a multitude of naturally self-owning individuals: individuals who have a natural proprietary right over their spiritual and corporeal capabilities and acts, to dispose of them in whatever way they choose. Thus, for example, the moral and religious freedom of proprietary subjects or rights-bearers consists in their absolute lawful power of spiritual self-determination, expressed in the idea of 'conscience' as the inner agency of untrammeled, idiosyncratic, private judgment. Although individuals are not equal in their personal resources, in the strength or scope of their passions and capabilities, they are equal in their proprietary right over them: equal as proprietors.[3]

However, as self-proprietors are naturally acquisitive as well as naturally self-protective, they are disinclined to be contented with merely formal equal-

---

3. For a more extensive discussion of the relationship between subjective rights and self-ownership, see pp. 73-96 above.

ity: hence, the liberal-democratic tradition has been blighted by an inexorable tension between the freedom and the equality of rights-bearers. On the one hand, the most fundamental arena for maximizing proprietary freedom is market exchange, the laws of which government is obliged to safeguard. On the other hand, the outworking of market exchange continually generates extreme economic inequality and a class of individuals who lack the economic independence of owning productive property (e.g., the unemployed and low-paid wage earners). Over the historical course of liberal democracy, the conceptualization of this dilemma has shifted. Until the establishment of universal suffrage, the issue concerned the political equality of economically unequal individuals: whether economically dependent individuals of little or no property were truly self-proprietors, capable of self-government. Subsequently, the problem has shifted to concern with the social inequality of politically equal citizens: the issue being whether all self-proprietors who exercise equal political authority should have more equal access to economic independence and productive property, that is, to the material means of securing and developing their personal property.

More corrosive of liberal democratic polity than the conflict between freedom and equality is the denial of a *common moral universe* in which objective spiritual goods (apart from the good of promise-keeping) mediate and determine the self-transcending of individual wills in their mutual relationships. In that the rights-bearing subject participates in political society as a contractual creation to secure the good of unbounded self-possession, the public realm is structured solely by the legal terms of the civil contract that express the binding 'empirical' conditions of each individual's freedom as a player in the social and economic market. Only consensus on these conditions is politically unproblematic — all further moral consensus smacks of oppression to libertarians who wish public discussion to be confined by this utilitarian agreement.

If we as Christians reject the economic anthropology of modern liberal democracy, then the question of an alternative theoretical framework for liberal-democratic principles has some urgency. We do not know whether these principles are separable from this anthropology until we actually integrate them into a more adequate theological framework. Let us, therefore, turn to the conceptualization of freedom and equality within the late-medieval and early-modern periods.

The Expansion of Individual Freedom:
Evangelical and Civil

In the time span under consideration, two distinct strands of thought about freedom can be traced: one concerns "evangelical freedom" and the other "natural freedom."

(a) Evangelical Freedom

In the first half of the fourteenth century, William of Ockham presented the most weighty theological defense of individual freedom against papal tyranny.[4] Disputing papal claims of absolute jurisdiction over Christian believers in both ecclesiastical and civil domains, Ockham conceived "evangelical freedom" as having spiritual and temporal dimensions. Theologically considered, evangelical freedom consisted in the individual's active obedience to Christ's commands which comprise the law of salvation for each believer. Regarding this law, Ockham admitted the authority of the clerical hierarchy to promulgate it, and to judge and punish violations of it: in other words, he accepted the church's discipline and spiritual jurisdiction. But he argued that her spiritual requirements should not exceed the explicit commandments of Christ necessary for salvation. He objected to papal imposition of further requirements as "arbitrary," "excessive," and "burdensome."[5] Legislation of the individual's spiritual life was Christ's prerogative and not man's: the first bishop was authorized to be only a mouthpiece and guardian of Christ's explicit law. While not denying the pope's authority as ruler and judge in Christ's place, Ockham argued that an excessive and tyrannical papal discipline impeded rather than facilitated Christian obedience. Thus evangelical freedom included for him the freedom of individual obedience from unjustified external impositions.

While Ockham's fellow polemicist against papal tyranny, Marsiglio of

---

4. The *loci* for this defense are *Breviloquium* 2.3-6, 17-18, A. S. McGrade, ed., *A Short Discourse on Tyrannical Government*, tr. J. Kilcullen (Cambridge: Cambridge University Press, 1992), pp. 21-8; *Octo Quaestiones* 1.6, H. S. Offler, ed., *Opera Politica*, 3 vols., 2nd ed. (Manchester: Manchester University Press, 1974), 1:29-30; *Dialogus* Part 3, Tract 1, bk. 1, chaps. 5-8, M. Goldast, ed., in *Monarchia S. Romani imperii*, 3 vols. (Frankfurt: Conrad Biermann, 1614), 2:776-80; *De imperatorum et pontificum potestate* 2.1-9, R. Scholz, ed., in *Unbekannte kirchenpolitische Streitschriften aus der Zeit Ludwig des Bayern (1327-1354)*, 2 vols. (Rome: 1914), 2:456-66.

5. *Breviloquium* 2.3-5, A. S. McGrade, *Discourse*, pp. 21-28.

Padua, never thematized evangelical freedom in the same way, he contributed substantively to the concept's development by his radical christological denial of papal jurisdiction (i.e., this-worldly coercive judgment) as such, whether spiritual or temporal. Indeed, Marsiglio removed spiritual jurisdiction alto gether from the earthly priesthood, identifying it exclusively with Christ's judgment and punishment of sinners in the "future world."[6] Although he left intact the church's penitential discipline, he laid stress on the purely declarative character of priestly "judgment" — its authority to declare God's prior judgments through which sins have been remitted or retained — and on the voluntary character of submission to it.[7]

The concept of evangelical or "gospel" freedom as the individual's free obedience to Christ's law in the absence of oppressive external exactions continued to be an important moral-political principle throughout the late-medieval and early-modern periods. After Ockham, it underwent a trinitarian and christocentric intensification in the writings of John Wyclif, who emphasized that the freedom enjoyed by the individual believer is the freedom of the crucified and risen Christ imparted by the Holy Spirit, the agency remaining with the Spirit of the Son and the Father.[8] Despite its elements of high Platonic realism, Wyclif's concept of evangelical freedom — of the believer's spiritual lordship of the material world in conformity to Christ — was wholly communal and communicating, having at its core God's trinitarian sharing of himself with his creatures.

The coping stone of this christocentric development was the Protestant Reformers' denial of the individual's moral freedom and insistence on justification by faith in Christ alone, which involved a more penetrating and complex understanding of the meaning of law in relation to sin and salvation than was offered by the late-medieval theologians. The Reformers' rejection of the medieval penitential discipline as "works righteousness" was, on the moral plane, rejection of a legalistic and juridicalized ethics: i.e., an ethics that dissolved the moral life into conformity to a multiplicity of legal exactions, distinguishing various grades of non-conformity and corresponding grades of punishment. Notwithstanding its corporate dimensions, the penitential discipline of the papal church had become excessively individualistic, voluntaristic and rationalis-

6. *Defensor pacis* 2.4-7, trans. A. Gewirth (Toronto: University of Toronto Press, 1980), pp. 113-56.

7. According to Marsiglio, God cleanses the truly contrite sinner from his guilt, absolves him from the debt of eternal death, and reconciles him to the church prior to his intended confession to the priest in the sacrament of penance, pp. 140-46. In addition, an erroneous priestly judgment carries no consequence for the penitent in the future life, p. 148.

8. For textual documentation of Wyclif's theological ideas, see pp. 89-90 above.

tic, and what the Reformers did was to re-emphasize the transcendent, social, participatory and communicative character of the Christian moral life. While the core of Christian freedom for the Reformers was the individual's enjoyment through faith of Christ's righteousness, of the Spirit's dominion over all things, that liberates from human ordinance, they nonetheless saw those who shared in Christ's resurrection glory as comprising a single communion of prayer, praise, and loving service.[9]

All the magisterial Reformers recognized a *visible, corporate aspect* to the universal participation of believers in Christ's royal, priestly, and prophetic offices, Luther's early presentation being the most thoroughgoing. In sundry places[10] he affirmed the *equal power* of believers to preach and teach the word of Christ and to judge doctrinal questions,[11] to declare absolution to the penitent,[12] to administer the sacraments of baptism and the Eucharist,[13] to intercede for fellow Christians,[14] and to offer pastoral support of counsel, exhortation, and consolation. At the same time, he affirmed the basis of the church's *public ministries* in communal "consent and election," in the congregational "call," which restrained individuals from arrogating the "common priesthood" to themselves.[15] It was the principle of communally appointed and representative ministry that dominated his later ecclesiology and that of the other magisterial Reformers, who were quick to emphasize the distinction between "possession" of the priestly power and its "regular exercise."[16] While Melanchthon, Bucer and Calvin espoused with Luther the equal standing (spiritually and vo-

---

9. Luther's 1520 treatise, *The Freedom of a Christian* (WA 7.20-38 = LW 31.329-77), remains the centerpiece of Reformation theological reflection on the subject.

10. Most notably, in *To the Christian Nobility of the German Nation* (WA 6.404-69 = LW 44.123-217), *Babylonian Captivity of the Church* (WA 6.497-573 = LW 36.5-126), and *Concerning the Ministry* (WA 12.169-195 = LW 40.7-44).

11. LW 30.55; 40.21-23, 32-36; 44.134-36; WA 8.423; 11.96 (cf. 12.521; 49.139); 15.720.

12. LW 3.124; 36.88; 39.89f.; 40.26-28; WA 2.189f.; 10.iii.395; 41.546.

13. LW 36.116; 40.9, 24f.; WA 6.566; 15.720.

14. LW 30.55; 36.50-1; 40.29-30, 35; WA 7.54; 12.307.

15. LW 30.55; 36.112-13, 116; 40.11, 34-38; 44.129.

16. See Gert Haendler, *Luther on Ministerial Office and Congregational Function*, ed. E. W. Gritsch, trans. R. C. Gritsch (Philadelphia: Fortress Press, 1981), pp. 77-90; Harro Höpfl, *The Christian Polity of John Calvin* (Cambridge: Cambridge University Press, 1982), pp. 103-21. Bucer makes a revealing comparison between clerical and civil political authority when he explains that, while the church's power belongs to all of Christ's people, the authority of the ministry belongs to bishops and pastors, just as in a civil republic, power and dominion belong to the people and authority to the senate. *Scripta duo adversaria*, 155, cited in W. Van 't Spijker, *The Ecclesiastical Offices in the Thought of Martin Bucer*, trans. J. Vriend, L. D. Bierma (Leiden: E. J. Brill, 1996), pp. 295-96; also Bucer's earlier comparison regarding the "power of the keys," cited on pp. 131-32.

cationally) of Christians before God, they were all the more rigorous in defining the qualifications of public offices and ministries.[17]

A continuously developing dimension of Christian freedom pivotal to the "common priesthood" concerned the dialectic of faith and understanding in the individual's free obedience to Christ: that individual reasoning presupposes the obedience of faith but is also active in obedience. An important milestone here was Ockham's insistence that individual Christians hold their beliefs not on ecclesiastical authority alone, adopting them or surrendering them merely at the behest of the church hierarchy, but rather on the basis of sound scriptural demonstration and argumentation that fully engages their powers of reasoning.[18] And, moreover, that every believer exercises epistemological authority in maintaining the purity of the church's faith, not only by professing right belief, but also by detecting erroneous belief (even among his/her clerical superiors) and bringing it to the attention of the community.[19]

This diffusion of epistemological authority among individual believers was a key feature of both Wycliffite and Reformation ecclesiology, and the chief impetus for biblical translation, Christian education and the growth of lay offices within the church. For Wyclif as for the Protestant Reformers, the restoration of the believer's access to God's Word in Christ through the words of Scripture, purified from wayward, self-aggrandizing human traditions, liberated him for faithful thought, judgment and action in the service of God and his neighbor.[20] Nevertheless, as much as the mature Luther and Calvin, Wyclif conceived of an informal epistemological authority of "private individuals" mediated and contained by public church offices and documents, catechetical and creedal, through which the church's collective response to God's Word in Scripture was formed and disseminated.[21]

17. For example, whereas Luther permitted midwives to baptize infants in emergencies (*LW* 40.23), Calvin opposed the administration of baptism by women, regardless of circumstances (*Institutes* 4.15.20ff.).

18. See Ockham's discussion of the correction of "erring" believers in *Dialogus de Imperio et Pontifica Potestate*, pt. 1, bk. 4, chaps. 13-14, 21, in *Opera Plurima* (London, 1962) 1:xxvi-xxix. Translation of 1.4.13 in *IG*, pp. 457-60.

19. Of course, Ockham endorses an institutional order of precedence for the initiation of public action against offenders, the prerogative descending from ecclesiastical prelates to academic doctors and masters to monastic heads to secular rulers and nobles to simple lay Christians. *Dialogus* 1.7.35-36.

20. *De Veritate Sacrae Scripturae*, ed. R. Buddensieg for the Wyclif Society, 3 vols. (London, 1905-7), 2:129ff.

21. Despite Wyclif's confidence (often polemically expressed) in the capacity of untutored laymen to grasp scriptural meaning in its "simplicity," he strongly upheld the authority in the church of truly learned and disciplined exegetes. See my exposition of Wyclif's eccles-

In the established Lutheran and Calvinist churches, the complex relations between political and epistemological authority precluded radical democratization of the latter, even if the reception of reform had sometimes in its earlier stages depended on the democratic initiatives of urban and rural citizenries. Undoubtedly, the patrician and guild patronage of urban churches and control of urban government, combined with the solidarist and populist aspects of civic culture, were decisive for the establishment of the Reformation in many European towns and cities.[22] Moreover, many elements of Lutheran and Reformed theology and preaching held a special appeal for the burgher classes, not least because they exhibited the influence of civic ideas and sentiments.[23] By and large, however, the Reformers perceived that Christian polity, ecclesial as civil, was served less by democratizing epistemological authority than by raising the communal profile of those offices to which epistemological authority was attached — those of preaching and teaching.[24] In regard to church polity, they fostered congregational freedoms and participation within the context of an aristocracy of the Word, that is, of educated and regulated clerical oversight.

Broadly we may observe that the theological mainstream throughout the period under discussion never enlarged individual liberty to the detriment of communal liberty, but regarded the former as embedded in communal structures of authority and not regularly in conflict with them. Among early-modern formulations of evangelical freedom, Calvin's thought well illustrates the complex interweaving of the individual and communal aspects. For Calvin, Christian liberty included not only emancipation of the individual conscience

Moeller

---

iology in *Theology of Law and Authority in the English Reformation* (Atlanta, GA: Scholars Press, 1991).

22. See, e.g., P. Blickle, *Die Reformation im Reich* (Stuttgart: Ulmer, 1992); *Gemeinde-reformation: Die Menschen des 16. Jahrhunderts auf der Weg zum Heil* (München: Oldenbourg, 1987), trans. T. Dunlap, *Communal Reformation: The Quest for Salvation in Sixteenth-century Germany* (Atlantic Highlands, NJ: Humanities Press, 1992); B. Moeller, *Reichstadt und Reformation* (Gütersloh: Vandenhoeck & Ruprecht, 1965), trans. H. Midelfort and M. Edwards, Jr., *Imperial Cities and the Reformation: Three Essays* (Durham, NC: The Labyrinth Press, 1982); H. Schilling, *Religion, Political Culture and the Emergence of Early Modern Society: Essays in German and Dutch History* (Leiden: Brill, 1992).

23. Moeller, *Imperial Cities*, pp. 69-90. Although Zwingli may provide the most striking evidence of civic influence, Luther's ecclesiology abounds in corporative nuances, while Bucer and Calvin's ecclesiological and political thought displays the influence of a more classical Aristotelian and Ciceronian/Senecan civic republicanism.

24. Even those magisterial theologians that raised the profile of pastoral discipline to a central ecclesiastical activity (e.g., Zwingli in Zurich, Bucer and Capito at Strasbourg, Calvin in Geneva) still admitted the primacy of preaching the Gospel as a 'mark' of the church, and emphasized the catechetical dimension of discipline, i.e., the inseparability of instruction and admonition.

from the law's condemnation and of individual judgment from oppressive external exactions, but also the liberty enjoyed by dutiful rulers and subjects in a morally ordered polity,[25] and the liberty of Christian churches to use for their common edification various human traditions (of external practice) in matters "indifferent to salvation," in opposition to any demand for strict uniformity of practice across the Reformed churches.[26]

The exceptions to the theological mainstream throughout the late-medieval and early-modern periods were the apocalyptic, illuminationist, and anarchic movements that experimented, to various degrees, with epistemological and social egalitarianism. Typical were the movement of "the common man" that culminated in the Peasants' War of 1524-26 and the overlapping movements of Anabaptism and other types of sectarian radicalism, all of which stressed the workings of the Holy Spirit in the minds of ordinary believers. Although outcroppings of spiritualist individualism and antinomianism dotted the sectarian landscape, more usually the perfectionism of these regenerate churches required a marked homogeneity of piety, belief, and conduct which, combined with the presence of strong, if not dictatorial, leadership, issued in constant communal fissuring and fragmentation. Of these ventures in epistemological democratization within close communities, it has to be said that, apart from the doctrinal oversimplifications and occasional heterodoxy that beset them, they were hard pressed to resolve satisfactorily the tension between pastoral leadership and democratic equality of insight.[27]

(b) Natural and Civil Freedom

We have already remarked that Ockham's concept of the Christian believer's evangelical freedom had temporal and spiritual dimensions, being wedded to a concept of civil freedom. In that civil freedom rested for Ockham on a foundation of natural freedom and rights, his concepts of evangelical and natural freedom and rights interpenetrate. It is apparent that, between "rights" and "freedom" or "freedoms" (liberties), rights is the more developed concept in

25. A point helpfully developed by John Witte in his article, "Moderate Religious Liberty in the Theology of John Calvin," in N. B. Reynolds and W. Cole Durham, Jr., eds., *Religious Liberty in Western Thought* (Atlanta, Georgia: Scholars Press, 1996), pp. 83-122.

26. *Institutes* (1559) 2.7.8-9; 2.19.14-15; 3.19.1-8, 14-15; Comm. on 1 Peter 2:16, CO 55:206.

27. For a survey of the development of the Anabaptism movement, see H.-J. Goertz, *Die Täufer, Geschichte und Deutung*, 2nd edn. (Munich: C. H. Beck, 1988) and for a good collection of radical sectarian readings, M. G. Baylor, ed., *The Radical Reformation* (Cambridge: Cambridge University Press, 1991). *H Williams.*

Ockham's thought. Along with Marsiglio of Padua, he was a key figure in the late-medieval integration of the language of subjective rights into Christian political theory.[28] Of the two, Ockham is the more theologically weighty and Marsiglio the more philosophically exacting.

While both thinkers operated with a similar philosophical concept of subjective right, it was Marsiglio who defined it in precise distinction from (what we would term) objective right. Significantly, he proceeded from the objective to the subjective meanings of "right" *(ius)*, as from the primary to the secondary senses.[29] In its primary or objective sense, then, right means a dictate of law, whether divine or human, and (adjectivally) the conformity of any action or omission to the law (i.e., an action is right when it conforms to the law).[30] In its subjective meaning, right denotes a "human act, power, or acquired habit" that conforms to right in the sense of law (to objective right).[31] Ockham agreed with Marsiglio in understanding subjective right as the *power* of an individual to perform a lawful action, or in other words, as a "lawful" or "licit" power.[32]

In view of my argument that the idea of subjective moral power in the modern natural rights tradition involves the notion of self-ownership — that one's moral powers are one's property — we must inquire whether this is also true of Marsiglio and Ockham's thought. What we find is that Marsiglio's more voluntarist and less theological elaboration of subjective right more clearly anticipates the proprietary paradigm. Most strikingly, he introduces into his treatment the concept of human freedom — that is, of the relation of the individual's will to his acts — as a form of ownership.[33] By contrast, we encounter the most effective defenses against the proprietary subject in the theological details of Ockham's elaboration, only some of which are found in Marsiglio's exposition.[34]

28. This is not to overlook the earlier appearances of subjective rights primarily in thirteenth-century canonist discussions, about which Brian Tierney has done much to inform us, most recently in *The Idea of Natural Rights* (Atlanta, Georgia: Scholars Press, 1997).

29. *Defensor Pacis* 2.12, Gewirth, pp. 187-95.

30. Marsiglio stresses the volitional and coercive character of both divine and human law, and distinguishes the three forms of command (prescription), prohibition, and permission, Gewirth trans., pp. 187-90.

31. Gewirth, pp. 190-91.

32. The "power" may be in conformity with positive divine or human law (custom, pact, or ordinance), or with natural right or "right reason." *Opus nonaginta dierum* 2, 65, A. S. McGrade and J. Kilcullen, eds., *Letter to the Friars Minor and Other Writings*, trans. J. Kilcullen (Cambridge: Cambridge University Press, 1995), pp. 19-33, 48-59.

33. *Defensor pacis* 2.12.16, Gewirth, p. 193.

34. This theological detail appears in Ockham in two polemical contexts which he shares with Marsiglio: (1) the Franciscan controversy with Pope John XXII over the order's absolute

Drawing on the Franciscan tradition,[35] Ockham ascribed rights to human beings universally on two accounts, on account of their creation by God in his image and on account of their fallen, sinful state. It is of crucial importance that the "lordship" *(dominium)* over the non-human creation granted by God to Adam and Eve is not a property right in any sense, for all God's creatures are exclusively his property. Rather it is the power *(potestas)* of rationally ruling *(regendi)* and managing *(gubernandi)* the non-human creation for its welfare and for the welfare of the human community, which includes the power of using the earth's resources for the sustenance and comfort of human beings.[36] Following his Franciscan predecessors, Ockham defended the patristic and earlier medieval tradition of understanding Adamic society as a community of sharing in the earth's abundance according to individual need without ownership of any kind.

Accordingly, it was the fall into sin of the first parents that occasioned God's grant to individuals and communities of the power to appropriate temporal goods as their own, for the sake of restraining the avarice of the wicked and of ensuring the proper care and management of material things (the Thomistic-Aristotelian argument). Subsequently, "exclusive human lordships" or private properties were established either by divine or human ordinance.[37] Although in the post-lapsarian condition, Ockham tell us, human beings are normally under divine obligation to exercise this power, it may be renounced, and is renounced in the holiest way of life that participates most fully in the perfection of Christ. By contrast, the Adamic power of using the non-human creation for human sustenance and benefit can never be renounced without, as Marsiglio points out, violating the divine prohibition of homicide.[38] The original *right* of use, then, conforms to the *duty* of sustaining life, even if it encompasses more than its fulfillment. Property right is 'natural' only in a secondary sense, and not in the primary sense of the original, non-proprietary right of ra-

---

poverty, in which both thinkers defend the brothers' renunciation of all property right in the donated necessities of which they make use (see earlier discussion, pp. 81-87); and (2) the controversy of the German emperor with the Roman papacy over imperial rights, in which both thinkers defend the universal political rights of communities (Christian and infidel) and their rulers.

35. As defined by such works as Bonaventure's *Apologia Pauperum* and Bonagratia of Bergamo's *Tractatus de Christi et apostolorum paupertate.* See my discussion of Bonaventure, pp. 83-86 above.

36. *Opus nonaginta dierum* 26-28, McGrade, Kilcullen, pp. 34-48; *Breviloquium* 3.7, McGrade, pp. 88-89.

37. *Breviloquium*, 3.7, 8, McGrade, pp. 89-92; cf. *Dialogus* 3.2.3.6, McGrade, pp. 286-88.

38. *Defensor pacis* 2.13.5, Gewirth, p. 199.

tional use by which Franciscan brothers sustain themselves with temporal goods owned and conceded by others.[39]

Nevertheless, Ockham was intent on securing the civil rights of property (rights of disposal, inheritance, and litigation) and other freedoms of ordinary subjects against arbitrary interference from secular as well as spiritual rulers. And his defense, although concentrating on the natural rights of individuals, also invoked their natural liberty (singular), by which he meant that individuals are not to be coercively used by anyone for merely private advantage (they are not to be made slaves).[40] Natural liberty seems also to be connected with his understanding of the purpose of public law. Aligning himself with Augustine, he objected to any communal law compelling individuals to do good rather than forbidding them to do evil, except on evident public necessity.[41]

The next important figure for the theory of subjective right after Ockham and Marsiglio is the late fourteenth/early fifteenth century Paris theologian, Jean Gerson, a follower of Ockhamist nominalism, but also steeped in Aristotelian and Thomistic thought. While his theological interest was more with corporate than individual rights (as we shall see), he and his mentor, Pierre D'Ailly, inspired a Sorbonnist tradition of theorizing about individual right which continued into the sixteenth century, with far-reaching influence on humanist, Catholic neo-scholastic, and Protestant legal and political thought, well into the seventeenth century. Gerson's theoretical legacy included: firstly, his definition of individual right as a "proximate faculty *(facultas)* or power" conforming to the dictate of "right reason" or "primary justice";[42] secondly, his assimilation of the *facultas* of individual freedom to

39. It is important to understand that for Ockham (following the Franciscan line), the extra-legal, non-proprietary right by which the brothers use goods conceded by donors is a continuing remnant in the fallen human community of the original power belonging to Adam's lordship of using the non-human creation for human sustenance and comfort. Although, Ockham tells us, this "natural right" of use may be "limited and in some way restricted and impeded" by positive laws of property, these restrictions/and or impediments are lifted by the "mere permission" or "license" of the owners of temporal goods. Moreover, in the case of dire need, the brothers (or anyone else) may use by natural right whatever goods are necessary to sustain life, with or without their owner's permission. McGrade, Kilcullen, pp. 55-56. When the extent and persistence of Adamic "lordship" is not properly understood, Ockham's account of the Franciscans' *regular* use of donors' goods by natural right appears to lack logical coherence, as in Annabel Brett's discussion in *Liberty, Right and Nature: Individual Rights in Later Scholastic Thought* (Cambridge: Cambridge University Press, 1997), pp. 64-8.

40. *Dialogus* 3.1.2.6, McGrade, Kilcullen, p. 139; *Breviloquium* 2.5, McGrade, p. 26; *Octo Quaestiones* 3.6, McGrade, Kilcullen, pp. 317-18.

41. *Breviloquium* 2.5, McGrade, p. 30.

42. *De vita spirituali animae* [Lectio Tertia], P. Glorieux, ed., *Oeuvres complètes* 3 (Paris: Desclée, 1962) 141; also *De potestate ecclesiastica* 13, *Oeuvres complètes* 6:242; *IG*, p. 528.

Adam's natural *dominium*[43]; and thirdly, his proposal that a theory of "primary justice" would assign to everything its proper "right," in the sense of "title" or "possession."[44]

Some of his followers took the "faculty" concept of right further in a voluntarist, subjectivist, and proprietary direction.[45] As property-right or ownership (*dominium* in the civil-legal sense of having unrestrained power of disposal over something) eclipsed non-proprietary use (Adamic *dominium*) as fundamental natural right,[46] it shaped subjective right in a twofold way. In the first place, rights were conceived as immanent spiritual capabilities possessed or owned by individuals, so that their relation to divine command and authorization lost immediacy or transparency. One consequence was that individual freedom was considered by some thinkers (including the later neo-scholastics, Luis de Molina and Francisco Suárez) to be a property alienable by agreement or contract (as when someone sells himself into slavery).[47] In the second place, the relation of individuals to the external objects of their rights (even objects which they did not own) took on a proprietary character, so that the individual's claim-right *to something* (as distinct from *in something*) was construed as a form of *dominium*.[48] Thus was the individual a moral proprietor (*dominus*)

43. 3:145.

44. *De potestate ecclesiastica* 13, *IG*, p. 527.

45. But not all: Jacques Almain, for instance, continued Gerson's alignment of *facultas* with obligation and law, as Brett shows in *Liberty, Right and Nature*, pp. 116-22.

46. At one level, this signaled the eclipse of primary natural law (the moral structure of created community) by secondary natural law (the moral structure of fallen community) expressed in the 'law of nations' *(ius gentium)*. The Spanish neo-scholastic, Francisco de Vitoria, for example, conceived Adamic '*dominium*' over the rest of creation in proprietary terms, as an unfettered power of disposal by which mankind "could use any object he like and even abuse it according to his pleasure, as long as he did not harm other men or himself." Comm. *ST* 62.1.13, cited in Brett, *Liberty, Right and Nature*, p. 130. Brett rightly indicates the close relationship in Vitoria between *dominium* and *libertas*, the individual's spiritual *ius* (authority) of disposing of his own acts (pp. 130-34); but she also distinguishes from *dominium* a more Gersonian alignment of *ius* with obligation and law, in the manner of Almain.

47. E.g. Mazzolini da Prierio, *Summa Summarum quae Silvestrina nuncupatur* 1 (Lyons, 1539), p. 256v, cited in Richard Tuck, *Natural Rights Theories: Their Origin and Development* (Cambridge: Cambridge University Press, 1979), p. 49; Luis de Molina, *De iustitia et iure* 1 (Mainz, 1614), cols. 162-3; Francisco Suárez, *De legibus et Deo Legislatore* (1614), Carnegie Endowment edition, 2 vols. (Oxford: Oxford University Press, 1944), 1:160; (translation) 2:279, also cited in Tuck, *Natural Rights Theories*, pp. 54, 56.

48. Says Conrad Summenhart, arguing for a more encompassing concept of *dominium* equivalent to *ius* (*Septipertitum opus de contractibus* [Hagenau, 1515], sig. E5, cited in Tuck, *Natural Rights Theories*, p. 28): *Et autem possit ita large accipi ut convertitur cum iure; probo: quia quiscunque habet ius in aliqua re; potuit dici dominus illius rei; igitur illud ius poterit dici dominium. . . . Si ei surripietur vel subtraheretur res illa eo invito surripiens diceretur furtum*

not only of what he actually possessed but also of what he demanded as an entitlement.

It is hardly surprising, then, that in later scholastic thought, social relationships were increasingly viewed as contractual, or that contract became the overriding moral bond in certain types of relationships. In economic life the complex theological-moral framework of exchange characterizing earlier medieval thought gradually gave way throughout the fourteenth and fifteenth centuries to a more impersonal, mechanistic view of the market dominated by the principle of promise-keeping.[49] And from the mid-fifteenth century onward, political society itself was quite regularly viewed as formed by a compact among rights-bearing individuals. But it has to be said that neither the objects of individual rights nor the terms of compacts entered into by individuals were severed from objective right defined by divine and natural law (even if the moral content of the latter was attenuated at times). Limited contracts of exchange, and even the compact establishing political society itself, recognized divinely established social-moral bonds transcending them. All the major late scholastic thinkers affirmed the natural sociability of individuals and natural patterns of human fellowship (which could not be said of the Renaissance humanists — especially the jurists).[50]

Let us look more closely at why late scholastic theologians in the Sorbonnist tradition and later theologians indebted to them found it necessary to posit a compact of political society, by which I mean a binding agreement establishing the collective right of the compacting individuals to institute a government (whether or not the compact precedes the institution of government or is simultaneous with it). The several elements of an answer were cogently set out by the late-sixteenth-century Anglican divine, Richard Hooker, whose thought, while only partially indebted to the Sorbonnists, has the virtue of being less radical in important respects than that of influential Gersonians such as Jacques Almain and John Major or later Spanish neo-scholastics, such as Domingo de Soto, Luis de Molina, and Francisco Suárez; and the differences are instructive.

The first part of the answer has to do with the purpose and nature of political rule: under the influence of Ockham, Sorbonnist thinkers conceived political rule along Augustinian lines, as a remedy for those disordered tendencies of sinful

---

commisisse; & si sic; quomodo surripiens contrectavit rem alienam invito domino; tenet consequentia per diffinitionem furti . . .

49. See my discussion of Franciscan usury laws, pp. 114-16 above.

50. Within humanist jurisprudence, which regarded law and civilization as coterminous, the ancient idea of a pre-social state of nature had some currency, being adopted by such eminent jurists as Andrea Alciato and Mario Salamonio.

human beings that undermine the unity and harmony of society. In Book 1 of *Laws of Ecclesiastical Polity,*[51] Hooker distinguishes the purpose of "politic society," which is to supply the material and spiritual needs of individuals that they cannot supply solitarily, from the purpose of "public government," which is to remove the "mutual grievances, injuries, and wrongs" arising from their sinful depravity. The second part of the answer has to do with the efficient cause of political rule: it is not only divine providence that ordains government as an institution and appoints particular rulers, but men who establish government on the basis of rational principles (arrived at with and/or without biblical revelation). According to Hooker, these rational principles include: that individuals may defend themselves against assault, that injuries perpetrated by one on another should be punished, that no individual is impartial enough to "determine his own right" against another, so that (the last principle) all should consent to recognize a common judge, which is the ruler. The third part of the answer has to do with the form that establishment of political rule must take. It must take the form of a compact, because the compact embodies universal consent, the consent of each and every individual to the common judge. Without it, Hooker maintains, no ruler has complete lawful power (unless he is immediately appointed by God). It is the consent of all that finally justifies the lordship of one individual over others, regardless of the natural right to rule that some "judicious men" have accorded to those who are "noble, wise, and virtuous." And (although Hooker was not as explicit as certain of his contemporaries on this point) the compact is necessary to express the *equality of individual liberty, the equal natural rights of all the parties.* So the three planks of the late scholastic compact theory are: sinful human beings caught up in conflict and mutual injury, rational human beings finding the resolution in a common judge, and free human beings who are to be ruled only with their active consent.

Hooker followed his Sorbonnist predecessors in regarding the original compact as establishing a definite "order of union" or "form of regiment." Its terms comprise the "fundamental" (we would say "constitutional") law of the commonwealth. Unlike his predecessors, he does not require that the form of regiment express the permanent authority of the communal will through structures and mechanisms of ongoing public consent (e.g., parliaments, councils, assemblies, elections, etc.). While such structures are usually salutary to good government, they are not necessary to the *right of rule* (i.e., its legitimacy): this depends on the original acts of communal consent alone, because, says Hooker, "corporations are immortal" — we were alive in our predecessors and

---

51. 1.10.4, A. S. McGrade, ed. (Cambridge: Cambridge University Press, 1989); reprinted from the Folger Library Edition, ed. W. Speed Hill (Cambridge, Mass.: Harvard University Press, 1977), vol. 1, pp. 89-91.

they still live on in us; their consent is our consent. Interestingly, however, it is precisely because the Sorbonnist thinkers also regarded political society as a corporation that they insisted on structures of ongoing consent. Corporations evidently had features for them that they did not necessarily have for Hooker, and it is to these corporative ideas that we now turn.

But first, a final remark about the Sorbonnist tradition of individual natural rights and political contractualism. We cannot fully understand this late scholastic tradition and its neo-scholastic continuation apart from the polemical pressures on certain of its key representatives to repudiate the 'heresies' first of Wyclif and then of Luther. Both Wyclif and Luther gave moral centrality to gospel freedom and divine right: indeed, they viewed all right as God's in Christ and refused to develop an independent concept of natural law and subjective rights. It was Wyclif and Luther's use of this evangelical perspective to attack the proprietary and jurisdictional powers of the papal church that called forth polemical resistance from the Sorbonnist and later neo-scholastic thinkers (both pre- and post-Tridentine). In surveying modern-looking developments over this period, we should keep in mind that there persisted an older strand of political thought, more biblical and patristic in inspiration than the late scholastic mainstream, for which the origin, purpose, and limitations of political authority lay immediately in God's reason and will rather than in human rationality and will, whether individual or communal. And it is this strand which Luther, Calvin and the earlier English Reformers revived.

The Expansion of Corporate Freedom

(a) Civic Republicanism and Populism

The twelfth and thirteenth centuries saw the proliferation over western Europe of cities enjoying a large measure of political independence. They shared many communal, corporate, and republican features: legal structures defined by charters; guaranteed equal freedoms and equal obligations for their citizens; citizen participation in municipal administration, either directly or through representative bodies (chiefly guilds); and local churches under some degree of municipal control. While these features were frequently a cause of discomfort to territorial overlords, episcopal and princely, open conflict was largely avoided by practical and legal accommodations. The situation was somewhat different, however, in the northern Italian city-republics where the full-blown theory as well as practice of popular self-government came to early expression. Here a more systematic challenge to the traditional authorities presented itself.

Perhaps the single most important institutional source of urban republican developments, whether incipient or full-blown, was the corporation as a juridical and a social reality. Loosely definable as a "sworn fellowship in pursuit of common aims,"[52] the medieval corporation had roots in Germanic social, military, and craft guilds, and in various Roman associations — guilds, towns, and mercantile societies. From the eleventh century onward, it was progressively developed in canon and civil law. Whether founded principally for economic, social or religious purposes, whether public or private, established by oath, contract, or charter, the Roman "corporation" comprised a collective "legal" (sometimes called "fictive") subject to which legal rights and obligations were attached, collectively and distributively, i.e., to its individual members, usually on an equal basis. The corporation typically had a head *(syndicus, rector, tutor)* elected by the whole body *(universitas)* and a representative at law *(proctor)* authorized to act for it in various transactions, frequently to carry out its express will. Certain prerogatives such as corporate rule-making remained with the assembled members.

Urban communities and corporations interpenetrated in various ways. Not infrequently, towns and cities developed out of mercantile guilds which already exercised wide-ranging legislative and judicial control over local trade and commerce.[53] Towns and cities were themselves established as comprehensive corporations with jurisdiction over lesser guilds. In the course of the fourteenth century, municipal corporations absorbed leading guilds into their political structure, resulting in popular representation or in power-sharing between the patrician and artisan classes.[54] While landed aristocrats and merchant bankers often kept control of the ruling council, the larger corporation of burghers or burgher guilds exercised considerable electoral, consultative, and legislative powers.

Thus medieval urban society was politically homogenized along corporative principles and, moreover, integrated through a more embracing civic ethos in which natural loyalties and social virtues blended with popular Christian devotion and cultic piety. Not only were there confraternities dedicated entirely to pious and charitable purposes, but in mercantile, professional and craft guilds, works of love and piety intermingled with concerns of economic justice and self-interest, social reciprocity and mutuality. Correspondingly, urban churches took

---

52. A. Black, *Guilds and Civil Society in European Thought from the Twelfth Century to the Present* (London: Methuen, 1984), p. 49.

53. H. Berman, *Law and Revolution: The Formation of the Western Legal Tradition* (Cambridge, Mass.: Harvard University Press, 1983), pp. 333-403.

54. Less frequently, guilds wrested control of the ruling councils away from the local oligarchy, as happened in some northern Italian, Flemish, and west and south German cities during the thirteenth century. Black, *Guilds and Civil Society,* p. 66.

on not just congregational but civic features, as ecclesial fellowship merged with guild solidarity and the culture of corporate rights and obligations.

Not surprisingly, many theologians of the period viewed the republican and populist features of urban corporatism with more suspicion than did the powerful and aspiring burghers. Alarmed by this apparent break with the past, they continued to draw on the earlier tradition of royal and imperial rule in which political society was not construed as a self-governing body, nor government as an instrument of the corporate will, constituted by it to carry out its express purposes. But they were not ill-disposed to integrating corporative principles and ideas into their thought, often inspired by the Thomistic-Aristotelian notion of the 'perfect society' *(societas perfecta)* which enabled its members not only to live but to live well. This reality became for them the prior political reality, the pre-existing collective moral subject in which political authority resided. Depending on their more conservative or more radical bent, they attached to this prior corporate subject some or all of the rights belonging to other corporate subjects in positive law: rights to make corporate rules and to elect, advise, correct and even remove corporate governors (administrators). And as they construed the political community as the natural source of political authority, so they construed these corporate rights as natural. While a theologian like Ockham, however, was clear that all communal political rights were divinely imparted, post-lapsarian rights, a theologian like Marsiglio neither made the distinction of pre- and post-lapsarian nor mentioned God's authorship.

Marsiglio carried through most consistently the theoretical project of republicanism, combining urban corporatism and Aristotle's *Politics* in the starkest defiance of the older tradition. He laid down the power (right) to make laws as the principal political power, and then set up the political community *(universitas, populus)* as the primary, permanent *legislator* that acts either immediately or mediately, through the (secondary) agency of a chosen ruler. He granted to the communal *legislator* an ongoing right of political judgment, to be exercised in the periodic election, correction, and (if need be) deposition of rulers, either immediately or through representatives. While Marsiglio intended his abstract corporative framework to accommodate a wide range of polities, from the elective monarchy of the empire to the northern Italian city councils and communes,[55] he never intended it to accommodate hereditary

55. It is fair to say that his model could accommodate the Roman *imperium* only by a theoretical slight of hand in which the communal *legislator* underwent serious attenuation. This attenuation is most noticeable in regard to election of the emperor where the six prince-electors of the Empire were the sole representatives of the Roman corporation. In regard to legislation, the Imperial Diet was a more plausible, but still defective (on Marsiglio's terms) mechanism of corporate representation.

monarchy, for which the *populus* was not an ongoing constitutive source of political authority. We should note, however, that he repudiated democratic republicanism. Although he admitted the "common mass" *(vulgus)* of artisans, farmers, and traders to membership in the political corporation *(universitas civium)*, he assigned them less political weight than the nobility *(honorabilitas)*[56] and never entertained rule by the *vulgus*, despite their numerical majority.[57] Inclusive democracy on our contemporary scale was for Marsiglio, as for Aristotle, a diseased polity.

Ockham, by comparison, avoided the full-blown republican project of Marsiglio by qualifying the framework of corporate rights so as to facilitate their integration into the older theological tradition. Chiefly, he did not make lawmaking the preeminent political act,[58] nor invest the people as *legislator* with the ongoing, inalienable right of political judgment. Rather he proposed that, in electing a ruler (or a dynasty), the people conferred on him jurisdiction over itself, so that the ruler ruled under God and under law (divine, natural, and communal), but not under the people.[59] In other words, political authority was acquired from the people, but held from God. Moreover, Ockham admitted forms of communal consent other than election in the establishment of political rule — e.g., simple acclamation of a ruler by the people or their acknowledgment of his title over time,[60] and justified the forcible removal of rulers by the natural law of necessity (that is, by the natural right of self-defence), to preserve the common good under dire threat, rather than by an inalienable right of corporate self-government.[61] In such collective emergencies, he balanced communal appeal to a higher political authority (e.g., in the case of a corrupt king, an appeal to imperial or papal jurisdiction) with the orderly initiatives of subjects.[62]

When we consider the positions of later scholastics and neo scholastics

---

56. Following Aristotle, Marsiglio allows the agricultural, financial, and artisan classes *(vulgaris)* is a "part" of the *civitas* only in a loose sense, and not in the strict sense in which the *honorabilitas* is a "part." 1.5.1, Gewirth, p. 15.

57. Marsiglio explains that the "weightier part" *(valentior pars)* of the citizen body in which its political authority may reside is to be defined qualitatively as well as quantitatively, taking into account the "quality" of citizens as well as their numerical weight. 1.12.3, p. 45.

58. Rather, it is the restraining of evildoing by coercive judgment and punishment. *Dialogus* 3.2.1.1, McGrade, Kilcullen, pp. 237-43; *Octo Quaestiones* 3.8, McGrade, Kilcullen, pp. 319-20.

59. *Breviloquium* 4.5-8, McGrade, pp. 113-17.

60. *Breviloquium* 4.10-11, McGrade, pp. 122-27.

61. This argument even applies to the removal of ecclesiastical rulers, including the pope. *Dialogus* 3.1.2.20 and 28, McGrade, Kilcullen, pp. 171-77, 200-203.

62. *Breviloquium* 6.2, McGrade, p. 162; *Dialogus* 3.2.1.1, McGrade, Kilcullen, pp. 243-44.

in the light of the different handling of natural communal rights by Ockham and Marsiglio, we can see that they present various combinations of their pre-decessors' positions, some leaning toward republican, others toward more tra-ditional theological treatments. It may be said, however, that the pure philo-sophical republicanism of Marsiglio remained something of an anomaly until the impact of southern Renaissance classicism was more broadly felt, in the sixteenth century — and even then it remained a minority position. The ma-jority of thinkers indebted to classical republican and corporative ideas made a serious attempt to harmonize them with the theological tradition of Chris-tian monarchy. Of vital importance for this harmonisation was the continuing theoretical centrality of the ruler's judicial function that seemed to many, in the light of the biblical testimony, to require the immediate dependence of hu-man on divine political authority, whatever the community's original and continuing powers. In summing up the "common opinion" of his neo-scholastic predecessors and contemporaries,[63] Francisco Suárez presented a most elegant statement of the more conservative "dual source" theory of gov-ernment:

> The general opinion appears to be that this power is given immediately by God as author of nature. Men, as it were, provide the material, producing a candidate for holding the power; God imports the form and confers it.
>
> The argument for this is . . . : given that men decide to come together in a single state, it is not in their power to prevent there being such a jurisdication; which is an indication that it does not flow directly from their decision as its efficient cause.[64]

Nevertheless, the project of harmonizing communal rights and God's right was fraught with tensions, especially when communal freedom was iden-tified with 'self-government'. Perhaps the thorniest problem was how the di-vinely bestowed form of political authority related to the constitutional form dependent on communal choice. It seemed evident to some, but not to all, that radical republican theory and practice obscured the true dependence of human on divine rule. Thus, the coolness of many Protestant Reformers (continental and English) to the Aristotelian/Ciceronian legacy, to the juristic corporatism and self-conscious independence of towns and villages, cannot be put down entirely to the political needs and pressures of church reform. Their theological turn back to Scripture and the Latin Church Fathers provided substantial

63. Suárez provides references to the works of Cajetan, Covarruvias, Vitoria, and de Soto.

64. *De legibus ac Deo Legislatore* 3.3.2, in *IG*, p. 734.

grounds for suspicion. We cannot fully understand their struggle with urban republicanism, however, without examining the rise of corporative theory and practice within the papal church.

(b) The Church's Political Constitution as a Divine and Human Corporation

Of the traditional Christian polities — church, kingdom and empire — that by the late Middle Ages had integrated a multitude of lesser corporations and were integrating corporative ideas into their theo-political self-understanding, the church was by far the most precocious. It had been developing its corporate identity over several centuries through the assiduous labors of canon lawyers, some of whom were also popes.

Papal unification of the church as a "spiritual corporation" — at once the "mystical body of Christ" *(corpus mysticum)* and a political body *(corpus politicum)* — comprised a sustained undertaking to ensure her juridical and proprietary independence of civil rulers. Three centuries of papal reform had produced an ecclesiastical "corporation of corporations," a hierarchy of relatively self-governing, property-owning, corporate units formed at various administrative levels (congregational, parochial, diocesan, archdiocesan etc.) and including a variety of establishments (e.g., monastic houses, confraternities, universities and hospitals).[65] According to historian Brian Tierney, the cathedral chapter composed of a diocesan bishop and diocesan canons offered the central ecclesiastical paradigm of corporate government, with governmental authority distributed between bishop and canons. The bishop as chapter head, elected by the canonical members, exercised some governmental powers entirely on his own, others he exercised with the consultation and consent of his canons (the corporate members), still others were exercised by bishop and canons as equal partners. Hence, the corporate organization of the cathedral chapter exhibited the principles of election, consultation, consent, and equal rights.[66]

This model of corporate government was, however, embedded in a divinely ordained hierarchy of priestly rule in which all powers descended from Christ through his apostles and disciples. The corporative identity of the medieval church was a clerical identity: the administrative powers of the clerical hi-

---

65. See my description of the administration of church property, p. 81 above.

66. *Foundations of the Conciliar Theory: The Contribution of the Medieval Canonists from Gratian to the Great Schism* (Cambridge: Cambridge University Press, 1955), pp. 106-27.

erarchy belonged to their overall jurisdictional powers which were distinct from, but wedded to their sacramental powers. While priests were equal in the exercise of most of the sacramental powers — e.g., consecrating the host, administering absolution and penance, and preaching, they were not equal in the exercise of jurisdictional powers — having to do with the external government of the church, or in the exercise of those sacramental powers underlying the jurisdictional ones — e.g., powers of clerical ordination and episcopal consecration. So, for example, only a bishop could ordain clergy within his diocese; only an archbishop could consecrate a bishop, and so on, up to the pope and cardinal archbishops. Thus, insofar as corporative principles entered into the overall political constitution of the church, they expressed the more fundamental community structure of christological powers.[67]

The influential movement of constitutional reform in the fourteenth and fifteenth century church known as "conciliarist" was, first and foremost, a movement to clarify the distribution of christological powers of jurisdiction.[68] It was chiefly occasioned by the Great Schism (1378-1417) in which, as the result of a disputed papal election, rival claimants to the papal office established separate obediences from Rome and Avignon. The first urgent objective of conciliarist writers, therefore, was to justify resolution of the schism by the decision of a general church council. But their wider objective was, through the authority of a general council, to reform the highly centralized, corrupt, and venal papal government of the church by restoring episcopal jurisdiction and curtailing papal and curial powers. While the doctrinal and juridical supremacy of the general church council was a long-established tradition, it had always included papal authorization, whereas now conciliar action to reunite the church and effect binding reforms had to proceed without papal authorization and against Roman opposition.

The Council of Constance (1414-18), under D'Ailly and Gerson's theological sway, based the council's jurisdictional supremacy on "a plenitude of power" held directly from Christ by virtue of its representing the mystical body of the

---

67. A concise summary of priestly sacramental and jurisdictional powers is given by John of Paris, *De potestate regia et papali* (1302) 12, trans. J. A. Watt, *On Royal and Papal Power* (Toronto: Pontifical Institute of Mediaeval Studies, 1971), pp. 142-50; *IG*, pp. 405-7.

68. On the conciliarist movement, see A. J. Black, *Monarchy and Community: Political Ideas in the Later Conciliar Controversy 1430-1450* (Cambridge: Cambridge University Press, 1970); *Council and Commune: The Conciliar Movement and the Fifteenth-Century Heritage* (London: Burns and Oats, 1979); C. M. D. Crowder, *Unity, Heresy and Reform 1378-1460: The Conciliar Response to the Great Schism* (London: Edward Arnold, 1977); F. Oakley, *Natural Law, Conciliarism and Consent in the Late Middle Ages* (London: Variorum Reprints, 1985); B. Tierney, *Foundations of the Conciliar Theory*.

Heiko Oberman mention: news to a

church.[69] Invested by Christ with the power of the corporate whole, the universal council was not merely a latent potency to be exercised in rare emergencies, but an ongoing regulative, advisory, and disciplinary authority to be convoked at regular intervals.[70] Representation of the universal church by the council was, first and foremost, the real, spiritual presence of the church in the episcopal representatives, each of whom embodied the sacramental and jurisdictional unity of his local church. The same plenitude of power was representatively held by the pope "in its height" and by the council "in its breadth."

Such was the principal theological argument of Gerson's *De potestate ecclesiae*,[71] which is of theoretical moment for offering possibly the most satisfactory harmonization of communal right and divine right in the constitution of political rule. Gerson's formulation that the universal council is invested immediately by Christ with the same power that resides in the whole church as Christ's body provides a *tertium quid* to the rival versions of the transference theory of political constitution, in which the community's power (conceived as property) is either *alienated* to the ruling representative or *delegated* — i.e., lent, with the community retaining ownership.[72] But — and this must be decisive! — the identity of communal and conciliar power depends on the indivisible presence of Christ's divine spirit in the universal church and in its ruling council. This means that Gerson's formulation is not equally applicable to civil rule, where the older theo-political tradition implied a non-identity or disparity between the political authority of the community and that of its ruler.[73] In justifying the council's action, however, Gerson and his Sorbonnist colleagues introduced a note of ambiguity by appealing also to the natural rights of political corporations: e.g., the corporate right of self-defense and the right of representation, implying a communal delegation of jurisdictional powers. In con-

---

69. *Haec Sancta* (1415), J. D. Mansi, ed., *Sacrorum conciliorum nova et amplissima collectio* (Venice, 1759-98), 27 (1784): 590; also B. Tierney, "Hermeneutics and History: The Problem of *Haec Sancta*" in T. A. Sandquist and M. R. Powicke, eds., *Essays in Medieval History* (Toronto: University of Toronto Press, 1969), p. 356; Crowder, *Unity, Heresy and Reform*, p. 83.

70. *Frequens* (1417), Mansi, 27: 590.

71. P. Glorieux, ed., *Oeuvres complètes* 6; translated portions in *IG*, pp. 520-29.

72. The concept of delegation can also be understood in a participatory way: i.e., the ruler participating in the community's political power.

73. It is this disparity that Francisco de Vitoria attempts to protect in his much-disputed neo-Thomistic distinction between the political authority *(auctoritas)* that the community confers on its ruler and the royal power *(potestas)* conferred by God. Vitoria muddies the water by reserving the divinely bestowed *potestas* for monarchs alone instead of allowing it to all government. *Relectio: De potestate civili* (1528) 1.5, trans. J. Lawrence, *On Civil Power* in A. Pagden and J. Lawrence, eds., *Francisco de Vitoria: Political Writings* (Cambridge: Cambridge University Press, 1991), pp. 16-17.

struing the church as a natural as well as a supernatural corporation, they never resolved the theoretical tensions between the diverse jurisdictional bases: natural corporate rights and christological powers.

While not resolving these tensions, the Council of Basel gave a more radical endorsement to the principles of political corporatism: elected and more inclusive representation, and delegated authority. Exasperated with a recalcitrant pope, its members pushed beyond the earlier paradigm of constitutional monarchy to render the pope a subordinate minister of conciliar policy, with jurisdiction inferior to the council, and liable to correction, suspension, and deposition by it. Contributors explicated the infallible and divine grace of the church assembled in council in such a way as to undercut papal infallibility and the pope's christological representation of the whole body. Their corporative theology was reflected in the council's constitution and conduct: e.g., in the equal status of all incorporated members (including laity) and the practice of majority voting.

The most distinguished theologian of Basel, Nicholas of Kues (himself a moderate), undertook a systematic integration of the two bases of ecclesiastical jurisdiction: corporate (and individual) natural rights and christological powers. Employing neo-Platonic ideas of harmony, consent (consensus), and the coincidence of opposites, he produced a humanistic political mysticism in which the natural and divine common good is achieved in church and civil commonwealth through an ascending and descending coincidence of human wills. His political system (like Marsiglio's, which he knew) was versatile in outline and detail: while principally a vindication of elective, constitutional monarchy, it could also provide support for urban aristocracy with popular representation. Despite its argument for the complementary independence of civil and ecclesiastical rule, the structural parallelism of the two orders (albeit imperfect) could reinforce the kinds of interpenetration typical of the period, whether prince-bishopics or municipal churches. Of all late-medieval theologians, Nicholas expresses the idealistic voluntarism and rational optimism characteristic of much modern Christian political thought which invests every liberal democratic polity (and only liberal democratic polities) with the "soul of the church," the power to realize the fullness of communal right.

Conclusion

In our search for a more adequate theo-political foundation for liberal-democratic polity in the late-medieval and early-modern periods, we have explored four theoretical strands concerned with the expansion of individual and corporate freedom in church and civil community. As we have tried to show, these various strands and the positions within them are not equally susceptible of integration into the older theo-political tradition that emphasized the divine establishment, appointment, and maintenance of rulers, and the juridical office of civil magistrates, as executors of God's law for a sinful human community, requiring not only superior virtue and education for rulers, but a permanent subordination of the ruled. Moreover, the older tradition consistently distinguished civil and ecclesiastical rule according to the moral and spiritual ends and cohesiveness of the two polities, giving primacy to the epistemological authority of spiritual rulers, while retaining the centrality of coercion in the secular sphere. We have tried to indicate those enlarging formulations of freedom that respected the parameters of the theo-political tradition. We may summarize them in the following way.

The core formulations concern the enlarging of evangelical freedom: of individual and communal freedom in, for and to Christ; of free inquiry into the truth of Christ revealed in Scripture and in nature, unhampered by excessive pressures to dogmatic conformity; of free obedience to the dynamic claims of Christ's love on human action, unhampered by oppressive spiritual, moral, and ceremonial exactions. The enlarging conceptions of gospel freedom that run from Ockham through Wyclif to Luther and Zwingli, Bucer and Calvin increasingly grasp free conformity to truth and righteousness as belonging to Christ alone and to sinful human beings only through the power of the Holy Spirit of Christ. The equality of Christ's faithful is the equally condescending presence of his spirit to each — forgiving, justifying, purifying, illuminating and directing — empowering their mutual ministry of forgiveness, exhortation, consolation, illumination, and guidance.

At the same time, there was in these formulations an ongoing dialectic between the ministry of all believers and the communally recognized ministries of the church. While the enlarging formulations of freedom greatly modified the traditional ecclesiological distinctions between, e.g., lay and clerical, fraternal and authoritative, private and public, the terms of the dialectic were never simply collapsed. There remained an established rule in the church, a common order of authority that constituted the church as a divinely appointed polity. This order of common ministry was seen to connect the present church with the past of her collective witness, belonging essentially to the divinely assured continuity of her proclamation. It fulfilled its telos in the witness of the individual believers who stood under it, while their witness continually invigorated and purified it. The witness of individual believers was not denied a public role, but the role was chiefly prophetic rather than governing.

While the proto-modern period saw a growing stream of democratic radicalism in the massing of pneumatological movements, as previous periods of the church had seen, these remained, then as before, relatively episodic, peripheral, and restrictive in membership. Their ecclesiological self-understanding as well as their historical vicissitudes exhibited two important principles: that egalitarianism in church polity requires a perfectionist ethos with its rigorous internal and external discipline; and that a perfectionist ethos requires a high degree of separation from the larger ecclesiastical and civil communities. The course of evangelical freedom during the period provides no ecclesiological model for an inclusive, democratic polity.

By contrast, the rival corporative model of papalist ecclesiology offered the maximum integration of spiritual and jurisdictional offices. As we have seen, it early developed the organisational principles of republican and democratic polity — those of election, consent, consultation, delegation, and the equal rights of incorporated members — which conciliarist theologians would later consolidate in a theory of communal supremacy. However, as the structure of interpenetrating ecclesiastical rights (sacramental and juridical, administrative and proprietary) was almost exclusively clerical and hierarchical in its christological constitution, corporative ecclesiology did not, in its integrity, furnish a paradigm of democratic polity. Albeit in a more radical moment, Nicholas of Kues suggested that the equality of created and redeemed humankind in Christ found expression in the democratic elements of church polity. Such a suggestion was only partially acceptable to Luther and Calvin for whom human equality is realized only eschatologically, in the spiritual fellowship of the church and not in any jurisdictional polity, ecclesiastical or civil — which is not to deny that the principles of equality, consent, and representation are indispensable to just and lawful jurisdiction. While admitting moral equality as an implicit end of Christian discipline, Luther and Calvin resisted the late-medieval blend of civic populism and piety in which the equality of believers was an immanent corporative and spiritual given. The frequent association of such an egalitarian ethos with the language of "the common good" rendered this traditional scholastic term suspect to them, even apart from its Aristotelian overtones.

In the civil realm corporative principles encountered less consistent theological restraint, with the result that rights-based, contractual accounts of political society and government entered the late scholastic mainstream. Although the Sorbonnist tradition gave increasing scope to property right and permissive natural law — the lynchpin of modern economic liberalism — it was indebted to and also fostered more conservative theological syntheses. The early formulations of Ockham and Marsiglio, embedded in quarrels with Pope John XXII over Franciscan poverty and papal plenitude, supplied a non-proprietary rationale for subjective right that highlighted its relationship to divinely given obligation. Moreover, Ockham unequivocally located proprietary and political rights in the post-lapsarian human condition of coercive law. While the conformity of subjective right to objective right, i.e., to moral law and divine authorization, lost transparency in Gersonian "faculty" theory, it was reinvigorated by the more traditional Thomists among the sixteenth-century neo-scholastics. Indeed, this neo-scholastic reinvigoration lay behind the papal revival of natural rights over the past century, which has sought to overcome the escalating arbitrariness and subjectivism of libertarian rights by planting them firmly in the soil of natural and evangelical morality.

While all of the proto-modern exponents of individual and communal rights carried some corporative baggage, the theological mainstream, for the most part, resisted full-blown republican and democratic developments as contrary to traditional understandings of God's continuing sovereignty over civil polity, the juridical task of civil government, and the waywardness of the multitude. Their enlargements of freedom stopped short of affirming corporate self-government, popular sovereignty, and the equal political authority of citizens. They did not allow the corporative conception of political society to turn the ruler into the instrumental manager of common projects and administrator of common property. Their novel level of concern with the right of political society to protect itself against the lawlessness of rulers (against their insupportable violations of divine, natural, and positive laws) was a concern with *the right of political society to be governed,* the intention of which was to reinforce rather than undermine the theo-political tradition of rule.

Neither in the civil nor in the ecclesiastical realms do proto-modern enlargements of freedom provide a coherent basis for the democratic culture and institutions of the modern era. Consequently, they do not provide a theoretical route to detaching liberal rights and democracy from liberal economics so as to resolve the question of their interconnectedness. Contemporary Christian thinkers who wish to rescue rights and democracy from the clutches of economic liberalism must take on board this negative evidence from the past. It is striking that, in rescuing liberal rights, modern Catholic thinkers have repudiated neo-liberal, anomic individualism with a consistency that Protestants may envy, but that their endorsement of democracy, like that of most Protestants, has lacked a critical theological edge. This endorsement has not reflected mere acquiescence in the inevitable, or in the lesser of possible political evils, but rather an underlying confidence in the moral-political judgments of "the people" and its elected representatives, and particularly, the openness of both Christians and non-Christians to moral guidance from Rome. During the reign of Pope John Paul II such confidence has been sorely tried. But whereas the

Pope's later encyclicals may reveal a waning enthusiasm for the language of "rights," they do not reveal a waning enthusiasm for democracy.

In exposing the theological weaknesses of modern liberal democracy, earlier traditions of freedom help us to understand its practical moral failures. At the same time, in assisting our discrimination between democratic principles and their broader theoretical interpretation, the earlier traditions open the way for a more adequate theological interpretation of contemporary principles and practice. Moreover, once the residual theological problems posed by democratic principles and institutions are grasped, then the prospect of ameliorating alterations may come into sight.

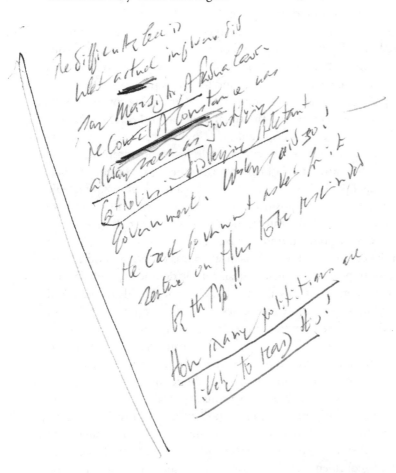

The Justice of Assignment and Subjective Rights in Grotius

OLIVER O'DONOVAN

In the early pages of the fifth book of the *Nicomachean Ethics*, the book on justice, Aristotle introduces two distinctions. The first is between a broader and a narrower sense of the words "just" and "unjust."[1] They can apply to whatever accords or disaccords with virtue as a whole, in all its aspects; or they can name a specific part of virtue or vice, different from other specific parts such as temperance-intemperance, courage-cowardice etc. Aristotle displays this distinction by taking the negative case. A man may be called unjust either because he is "lawless" or because he is a "grabber" *(pleonektēs)*. Since the laws deal with everything that produces happiness in a political community, the lawless man falls short in relation to the whole range of moral requirements, but the grabber falls short in a specific way which differentiates him from the intemperate or cowardly man, by wanting more than his fair share of the goods of fortune. He is "unfair" *(anisos)*.

The second distinction follows Aristotle's announcement that he will set to one side the wider sense of justice and confine his examination to justice as a partial virtue. He then distinguishes two kinds of justice in that sense: "one species that is found in the distribution of honors or wealth or anything else that can be divided among members of a community who share in a political system; for here it is possible for one member to have a share equal or unequal to another's. A second species concerns rectification in transactions."[2] Aristotle differentiates these by the way they understand *isotēs* (usually, though problematically, translated "equality"), which he takes to be the essence of justice. In either case equality is a kind of "proportion" *(analogon)*, a relation not of two but

1. *EN* 1129a26-30b29.
2. *EN* 1130b30-31a1, trans. Terence Irwin (Indianapolis: Hackett, 1999).

of four terms: the *treatment* that is meted out to *one* person is equivalent to the *treatment* that is meted out to *another*.[3] But equality in distribution is marked by a "geometric proportion," by which the treatment meted out to one person differs from the treatment meted out to another in proportion to the difference of the two persons; equality in rectification is marked by an "arithmetic proportion," which strikes a mean between gain and loss so that neither party scores off the other.[4]

In what follows our concern will lie largely with what, for ease of reference, we shall call "Aristotle's second distinction"; but since in the history of Christian Aristotelianism the second has been closely interwoven with the first, a passing observation is in place about the way in which they relate to each other. The mode of dividing the category justice-injustice in each case is quite different. The first presents two ways of *applying the terms*, a more general and a more specialized; the second distinguishes two different *ways of acting* justly or unjustly. The unfair man is, simply by being unfair, lawless, too, since unfairness is included in what is meant by lawlessness, as a part is included in the whole; but the unfair distributor is not necessarily an unfair transactor (a point on which contemporary political debate between neo-liberals and social-democrats has turned), and someone who scores negatively on both fronts has to be unfair twice over, as it were, *both* in transactions *and* in distributions. The implication of this is that the two types of "special" justice do not, when taken together with "general" justice, compose a triad of types of justice. For justice-as-the-whole-of-virtue is not, in Aristotle's account, a *type* of justice at all; it is a way of applying the word that embraces the two types of special justice along with all the other moral virtues in bringing out the importance of every virtue for the good of the community.

Like most of Aristotle's moral and political theory, the second distinction made no impact upon Christian thought until the thirteenth century, when Latin translations of the *Nicomachean Ethics* and *Politics* helped create that wave of Christian Aristotelianism which we associate with high scholasticism. Since then the division of justice into two kinds has never been absent from theological and philosophical discussions, and it is easy to see why. It gives expression to an insight naturally congenial to Christians who reflect on Jesus' parable of the laborers in the vineyard and on Paul's doctrine of justification: there is more to justice than the fair exchange of property rights. That insight is

---

3. *EN* 1131a29ff.

4. *EN* 1132a1ff. What the four terms in rectification are is not quite clear. Probably they are the two parties to the transaction before and after: "τὸ ἴσον ἔχειν καὶ πρότερον καὶ ὕστερον" (1132b19f.).

of great potential significance today for resisting the neo-liberal tendency to construe all justice questions in transactional terms.[5] But if the idea of justice is not exhausted by fair exchange, what precisely is the content of the surplus? Aristotle's proposal that it consisted in *just distribution* proved to be one of the most influential and problematic aspects of his doctrine.

The influence of the distinction was not confined to moral theory in the narrow sense; it also made an impact upon jurisprudence, for the thirteenth century was the age *par excellence* in which law, ethics, and theology moved hand in hand. In its Aristotelian context the discussion of justice belonged to a treatment of the virtues;[6] but now it was incorporated into a framework of Christian Roman Law, for which the primary category was *ius*, "Right"; justice was thus construed in relation to institutional questions about the functions of government. Its transformation in this new context is well illustrated by its treatment at the hands of Saint Thomas, who neatly splices the two Aristotelian distinctions together to produce a tripod of duties distinguished by the political status of their subjects and recipients. *Iustitia commutativa* (his equivalent for rectificatory justice) governs the relations private persons have with each other; *iustitia distributiva* governs the treatment of private persons and other partial interests by the community as a whole. These comprise the two parts of "particular" justice, while *iustitia generalis*, or *legalis*, corresponds to the duties owed by the partial interests of the community, as directed by the law, to the social whole.[7] Thomas's innovations here follow a hint in Aristotle that justice as the whole of virtue is to be understood in terms of the *law's* interest. Nevertheless, they are a striking example of Thomas's virtuosity in reshaping the Aristotelian legacy as it suited his requirements, not least in reconciling Aristotle's observation that justice-as-the-whole-of virtue is especially a virtue of *rulers* with his own need to make it a virtue of the subordinate *parts* of the political community, i.e., subjects.[8]

---

5. As an instance of its interest for twentieth-century thinkers, we may cite Emil Brunner's enthusiastic declaration: "In this way he established a fundamental rule for all time, and we can understand why the theory of justice has at all times taken its stand on these Aristotelian definitions" (*Justice and the Social Order*, trans. Mary Hottinger [London: Lutterworth Press, 1945], p. 31). More recently, and more moderately, Wolfgang Huber: "der Unterschied zwischen der *iustitia distributiva* und der *iustitia commutativa* läßt sich nicht einfach aufheben. Mit dem Prinzip des Äquivalententausches allein lassen die Probleme der Gerechtigkeit sich nicht lösen." *Gerechtigkeit und Recht* (Gütersloh: Kaiser, 1996), p. 157.

6. Cf. 1129a6ff. It has been doubted whether the relation of Book 5 to the surrounding material in the *EN* is original, since it is one of three books common to the *EN* and the earlier *Eudemian Ethics*. However, its context in the *EE* is similar to that in the *EN*, so the point stands.

7. *ST* 2-2.58.5, 61.1.

8. Cf. *EN* 1130a1-5 and *ST* 2-2.58.6. In this article Thomas Aquinas effectively neutralizes Aristotle's understanding that justice-as-the-whole-of-virtue is a general predicate that em-

We should not dismiss the Roman legal remolding of the doctrine as a purely extraneous influence upon Christian thought. The family of ideas surrounding the medieval concept of *ius* did not spring fully armed from the head of Cicero, but grew out of a long institutional cohabitation between Roman law and the Christian church. The institutional questions that now framed Aristotelian justice arose from a theological impulse, derived from both Old and New Testaments, to understand the concept of justice *performatively,* as "judgment."[9] The presence in Thomas's treatment of justice of a prominent article on *iudicium,* which he describes as "the act of justice," is a mark of his perspective as a theologian of Christian institutions.[10] The question of how Aristotelian justice could be accommodated to Roman legal ideas was only the outer clothing of a deeper question: how comfortably it would comport with the theological notion of justice as judgment.

The purpose of this paper is to explore the critical and creative reworking which distributive justice receives at the hands of the great and still largely neglected jurist-theologian, Hugo Grotius (1583-1645), in three passages of his major work *De Iure Belli ac Pacis* (1625). Grotius's treatment has a special interest in that it brings the Aristotelian distinction into connection with another important notion which preoccupies us today, that of subjective rights. His use of the second Aristotelian distinction has been overlooked or misunderstood by the small company of scholars who study his contribution to rights theory, despite the fact that he identifies it as one of the three crucial distinctions that govern his treatment.[11] In this exploration I have two interests. One is a systematic concern for how we may articulate a Christian conception of justice-as-judgment. Grotius's correction of the Aristotelian tradition has rather more to offer us, I would suggest, than alternative ways of appropriating Aristotle's key thought. The other is to engage with a prominent contemporary interpretation of Grotius as to how this theological and juristic humanist is properly to be read.

In a series of concentrated studies on the political thought of the seventeenth century, Richard Tuck has pursued an account of Grotius that presents him (as earlier generations presented him, though with less credibility), as a key

---

braces partial justice as a special predicate: even "general justice" or "legal justice," to give it Thomas's preferred name, is "essentially a special virtue," "general" only with reference to its political effect on the common good.

9. On this see my *Desire of the Nations* (Cambridge: Cambridge University Press, 1996), especially pp. 37-41, 226-42.

10. *ST* 2-2.60.1.

11. *IBP* Proleg. 41. The other two are the distinction between Natural Right and Right of Nations, and the distinction within Right of Nations between a right and an impunity.

figure in the birth of modernity.[12] The debt English-speaking scholars owe to Tuck for treating Grotius as an important object of study in his own right, rather than as a mine for familiar phrases in the genealogical section of an encyclopedia article, and for setting him vividly against the complex background of the intellectual world of the turn of the seventeenth century, justifies the adaptation of Samuel Johnson's compliment to Grotius himself, as "him from whom perhaps every man of learning has learned something."[13] Reacting against a historiographical tradition that he traces to Gierke, of seeing the medieval use of subjective right as the source of a constructive modern liberal tradition in opposition to *raison d'état*, Tuck now takes up a counter-thesis of Leo Strauss that claims with plausibility to discern a radical new development in the seventeenth century. Liberal "natural rights" and conservative *raison d'état* are closer than appeared, both springing from that moment when humanist scepticism, with its conception of the wise man as a "stripped-down psyche," flowed into the older scholastic discussions of natural right and watered down its substantial porridge of human sociality into the thinnest *consommé*. Like Strauss, and surely correctly, Tuck sees Hobbes as the high June of this skeptical early-modern rights tradition. Unlike him, and problematically, he sees Grotius as the spring swallow that announced it, and who "fundamentally revised Western political thought itself."[14]

To state briefly at this point the two cautions that I believe must hold us back from endorsing Tuck's reading of Grotius: first, it is hazardous to read the mature Grotius of *De Iure Belli ac Pacis* principally through the eyes of the twenty-one-year-old author of the *De Indis* (1604).[15] Second, it is worse than

12. Thus G. A. Finch sees in *IBP* "the growing force of the trend away from the theological and dialectic concept of law, towards secularism and modern positivism" ("Introduction" to *De iure praedae*, Carnegie edition [Oxford: Oxford University Press, 1950], vol. 2).

13. Letter, in James Boswell, *Life of Johnson*, 19 July 1777.

14. Richard Tuck, *The Rights of War and Peace: Political Thought and the International Order from Grotius to Kant* (Oxford: Oxford University Press, 1999), p. 81. For earlier treatments, see *Natural Rights Theories: Their Origin and Development* (Cambridge: Cambridge University Press, 1979), pp. 58-81; *Philosophy and Government, 1572-1651* (Cambridge: Cambridge University Press, 1993), pp. 154-201. The interpretation of Grotius has followed a consistent pattern in Tuck's successive treatments, but has become more sharply defined: earlier allowed a "passionate desire for peace," Grotius now comes to support "the right to inflict violence on barbaric peoples" (*Natural Rights*, p. 74; *Rights*, p. 89). He is justly described by Rousseau, in a quotation that Tuck relishes, as "a child, and what is worse, a dishonest child."

15. Tuck deserves credit for demonstrating the theoretical interest of this early work, unpublished in the author's lifetime except for the chapter entitled *Mare Liberum*. I follow him in using Grotius's own title in preference to that of the nineteenth-century publication, *De iure praedae*. Footnote references, however, are to *IP*; page numbers refer to the manuscript, reproduced by collotype in vol. 2 of the Carnegie edition, each with an obverse and a reverse. Slips stuck into the ms. subsequently are numbered a, b, etc.

hazardous to underestimate the increasing strength of theological elements in the mature Grotius's intellectual culture. On the first of these two demurrals we shall have more to say as we proceed. By way of introduction a few comments are in place upon the second, which will point in directions that we cannot travel in this essay.

Between the composition of *De Indis* and *De Iure Belli ac Pacis* there transpired Grotius's dramatic career in a Rotterdam dominated by the Remonstrant controversy, a stormy period culminating in his imprisonment after the Synod of Dordt, which elicited a series of works addressed to the theological battles of the time, and which contain constant indications of his evolving thoughts on law and politics. These works have largely to do with determining the line between Christian doctrine and heresy (especially the recently discovered *Meletius*), and with the relative powers of church and state in that determination (notably the *Ordinum Pietas* and *De Imperio*). Notwithstanding his renaissance consciousness of the multiplicity of scholarly disciplines, Grotius did not pursue each of his several interests separately. Throughout the Remonstrant controversy it was a cardinal point of his Erastian ecclesiology that the business of lawyers lay with the law of God.[16] *IBP* is a work of mature synthesis that constantly draws together the various elements in Grotius's mind: humanist, theological, legal, and political. He makes this point for us himself in the "Prolegomena," where, after debating the problematic character of the Aristotelian legacy, his next methodological question is how the Scriptures of the Old and New Testaments are to be used.[17]

Tuck's evaluation of Grotius's theological views is broadly sympathetic to an older view recently revived, that paints Grotius as the forerunner of theological liberalism, ethically oriented and anti-dogmatic, tending to Unitarianism, as typified by the later Remonstrant communities in the Netherlands.[18] Such a view maximizes the naturalism and minimizes the doctrinal elements in Grotius's mind, though it does not, I think, make very intelligible his later inter-

---

16. Cf. *OP* 110b: *Ipsa iurisprudentia sine cognitione rerum non humanorum duntaxat sed divinorum quoque manca est et mutila.*

17. *IBP* Proleg. 48-50.

18. Here we must mention the name of G. H. M. Postumus Meyjes, the value of whose discovery and edition of the *Meletius* puts all criticisms in perspective. However, doubts must be raised about the bold conclusion he reached from his study of Grotius's preparatory notes for the *Meletius,* a conclusion on which others have relied: "To Grotius the dogma of the Trinity as well as problems concerning free will and predestination were *adiaphora.*" ("Some remarks on Grotius's *Excerpta Theologica,*" in *Hugo Grotius — Theologian: Essays in Honour of G. H. M. Postumus Meyjes,* ed. Henk J. M. Nellen and Edwin Rabbie [Leiden: Brill, 1994], p. 16.) This is a heavy conclusion indeed to hang on the evidence offered us.

ests in Protestant-Catholic union, a cause inconsistent, then as now, with doctrinal indifferentism. It is, of course, true that this interpretation corresponds to the suspicions nursed against him in strict Calvinist circles; but these were not formed on the basis of any deep sympathy for his work and struck him as unjust.

The test of any such characterisation must be its ability to explain the *De Satisfactione Christi* (1617), a work which was to become Europe's most popular handbook for the substitutionary theory of the atonement. It is in many ways an exceptional element in Grotius's output, bringing together his powerful architectonic and systematizing bent, otherwise exercised mainly in jurisprudence, with his commitment to patristic norms of doctrine, otherwise evidenced mainly by his persistent marshalling of quotations from the Church Fathers. Grotius's mind was not *anti*-doctrinal, but it was usually rather *un*-doctrinal. This treatise, however, was an intensely concentrated work of doctrine, and little as one so resistant to new doctrinal standards would have liked to be told so, an innovative one. No other such was to come from his pen; those who were disappointed at not finding something similar in the *De Veritate* were told that it would have been unsuitable for an apologetic work.[19] Although reasons for its composition have been suggested from within the circumstances of the failing cause of the States of Holland, they hardly account for the content of the book, and so tend to create the suspicion that it was dissimulation, another evidence of the dishonest child.[20] But at the time Grotius took a quiet pride in the *De Satisfactione,* and it could hardly have appealed so widely and shaped the course of Protestant theology so thoroughly, had it been simply a demonstration of political correctness.

More difficult to assess is the influence on Grotius of contemporary Catholic theologico-legal writing, especially that of the Salamanca school. It is a point of some importance to Tuck that "in general (it is fair to say) he was not well versed in the modern scholastic literature."[21] This reverses an older fashion that stressed his continuities with the Thomists of the second scholastic, and joins the current consensus that he owed much to the jurists of the sixteenth century, especially Gentili and Vázquez de Menchaca. That such influences operate on Grotius, especially on matters of detailed legal judgment, has been established beyond doubt.[22] Scholastic influences from the first half of the six-

19. Cf. Jan Paul Heering, "Hugo Grotius' *De Veritate Religionis Christianae,*" in *Grotius — Theologian,* pp. 41-52.

20. Cf. Edmund Rabbie's "Introduction" to his edition (Maastricht: Van Gorcum, 1990), pp. 10-19.

21. *Rights,* p. 81.

22. On the debt to Gentili see Peter Haggenmacher, "Grotius and Gentili: A Reassessment of Thomas E. Holland's Inaugural Lecture," in *Hugo Grotius and International Relations,* ed.

teenth century, however, are equally certain, not least in helping Grotius form the systematic framework of his presentation, which he felt to be one of his chief contributions. A dismissive reference in *De Iure Belli ac Pacis* to earlier treatises on war by "theologians" and "jurists," including Vitoria's ground-breaking *relectio*, complains that they failed to distinguish *ius divinum, ius naturae, ius gentium,* and *ius civilis.* A fuller and more complementary reference to *scholastici,* which observes a studied silence about names and conveys the vague impression that they are all medieval, probably has in mind St. Thomas and his commentators right up to Grotius's day.²³ The long-unknown early sketch, *Commentarius in Theses XI,* written with the complex aim of defending the Dutch Revolt in terms more acceptable to monarchists than those deployed by such Calvinist theorists as Beza and the author of the *Vindiciae,* draws freely on arguments from Cajetan and Vitoria; the *De Imperio,* also unpublished in Grotius's lifetime, makes considerable reference to Suárez, too. A reticence about Thomist contemporaries from the late sixteenth and early seventeenth centuries is not hard to explain in a child of the Dutch Reformation, especially when the Europe-wide tension between Catholic and Reformed had been exacerbated by Suárez's inflammatory views on the British crown.²⁴ We shall find further reason to believe that Grotius read in these quarters.

I

One of the features which Tuck finds novel in the *De Indis* and believes to be sustained in the *De Iure Belli ac Pacis* is its handling of the second Aristotelian distinction, which he supposes is conflated with the first: "universal justice should be regarded as the commutative justice of the Aristotelian tradition, and

---

Hedley Bull, Benedict Kingsbury, and Adam Roberts (Oxford: Clarendon Press, 1990), pp. 133-76. In the Prolegomena Grotius mentions Alberico Gentili and Balthazar Ayala as the authors of the two best treatises on the right of war (38), while citing Fernando Vázquez de Menchaca as well as Covarruvias as the only two humanist lawyers who ventured into the field of natural rights (55). A more enthusiastic commendation of Vázquez, the inspiration for Grotius's doctrine of the *mare liberum,* had appeared in the *De Indis.* The general question of sources is much illumined by the discovery of the early *Commentarius in Theses XI,* and the reader is referred to Peter Borschberg's survey of the sources of that work in the first published edition (Berne: Peter Lang, 1994), pp. 47-101.

23. *IBP* Proleg. 38, 52. In the letters of advice on reading addressed to his brother Willem (Sept. 28, 1614) and to B. J. du Maurier (May 11, 1615), *scholastici* almost certainly refers to Thomas and his commentators.

24. Similarly, Grotius concealed his use of Socinus in composing the *De Veritate.* See Heering, *loc. cit.*

justice was solely distributive justice."[25] From *De Indis,* then, we begin, before attending to the three passages of *IBP* in which the distinction is expanded.

The general character which Tuck gives to the *De Indis* is well deserved by its opening chapters. It is a swaggering defense of the Dutch capture of a Portuguese treasure ship in 1602, deploring the poor-spiritedness of domestic critics, uncompromising in spirit and full of youthful pretension. Arguing wholly from the classics, Grotius pleads in his introductory chapter that justice is a mean: it is bad to do wrong, but bad, too, to be the victim of wrong. (This very doctrine is singled out for criticism in the Prolegomena of *IBP* as a "hallucination.")[26] In the second chapter, also called "Prolegomena," the whole content of "Right" (i.e., jurisprudence) is elaborated systematically in a series of normative "laws" and theoretical "rules" which begin formally from the commands of God, but substantially from the impulse to self-preservation, that "ancient and divine self-love, wholly praiseworthy."[27] Onto this is built, "as though by an eternal covenant," mutual care, which is the content of "justice strictly so called," i.e., as distinct from self-preservation.[28] By generating laws of non-maleficence and respect for property, mutual care constitutes justice as a "social virtue" with "equality" as its object, since "as much as" is the next best thing to "the same." There follow two further laws, that injuries must be rectified and benefits repaid, which are the source of retribution, restitution, and everything to do with commutative justice (decked out in fashionable humanist Latinity as *iustitia commutatrix*). Exchanges are of two types, he proceeds in Aristotelian fashion, voluntary and involuntary, and from there, by the standard medical analogy, he explains how inflicting evil on a criminal may be a social good.[29] The exposition proceeds with a discussion of liberty in self-binding compacts to the creation of political society, judgment, magistracy, and finally the *ius gentium.*

That, at least, was how Grotius first conceived the chapter. The mention of a "strict" sense of justice, on the one hand, and the passing reference to commutative justice, on the other, was his only doff of the hat to the two Aristotelian distinctions. But in the course of extensive revision to the manuscript some new paragraphs were added (not contiguously), the first two of which introduce the contrast between "assignative" and "compensatory" justice. Their most striking feature, apart from the new terminology, is that they present the

---

25. *Rights,* p. 88.

26. *IBP* Proleg. 45.

27. *IP* pp. 3, 5.

28. *IP* p. 6: *Hinc illa iustitia propria dicta incipit, quam Aristoteles aliique circa bonum alienum versari tradiderunt.*

29. P. 8: *Unde nascitur talio,* τὸ ἀντιπεπονθός, *restitutio scholasticis, opus iustitiae commutatricis* (the last word subsequently crossed out and replaced with *compensatricis*).

distinction not in Aristotle's but in the scholastics' terms, with reference to the part-whole analysis of society and the role of different political agents within it. Assignative justice is described in terms of the activity of heads of societies, i.e., the *paterfamilias,* or God, and compensatory justice is said to belong to private transactions and not to concern the good of the whole.[30]

Here, then, at the first appearance of the Aristotelian distinction in Grotius, an afterthought in a context otherwise influenced by a Ciceronian humanist tradition, Grotius does not follow the *Nicomachean Ethics* directly but its scholastic interpreters. We can only speculate on the immediate source, but when a decade later Grotius wrote a characteristic letter of advice to B. J. du Maurier on a course of reading, he counselled him not to spend time on "the scholastics" except for the *Secunda Secundae,* advice which probably had questions 57ff. in view.[31] In this backhand way Grotius acknowledged the importance to him of a section of St. Thomas that attracted consistent attention from sixteenth-century scholastics. It is tempting to suppose that the amendments to *De Indis* arose immediately from his first encounter with Thomas's treatise on justice.

In a third insertion we find Grotius facing a problem of interpretation posed by St. Thomas and recognized by his commentators: how was the practice of *punishment* to be fitted into the idea that commutative justice was the justice prevailing between private parties?[32] His answer to this question is that the public whole can relate to a private party not *as* a whole but as another interested party. It can be the recipient of benefits and injuries, and can rightly demand repayment or have repayment demanded of it, just as any other party can. Indeed, in any private injury there is a public interest, too. To this Grotius recurs in a fourth insertion. His exposition has now reached political society:

30. P. 8: *Itaque hic quibus alicuius totius procuratio convenit, iustitia utuntur proportionali, quae et assignatrix dici potest. Haec paterfamilias domesticis suis, pro diversa aetatum ac conditionum ratione, dimensum pensumque assignat. Hac Deus ipse universum ordinat. . . . Altera autem iustitia, quam nunc compensatricem placet dicere non in communibus sed in propriis cuiusque versatur, ideoque partes ad totum non refert.* It should be observed that Grotius's paradigm for justice by assignment includes natural rulers. Tuck's attempt to connect the compensatory-assignative distinction with the state of justice before and after the contract of civil government falls on this point.

31. *Epistulae,* to du Maurier 11.5.15. Question 40, on just war, also attracts considerable attention in the *Commentarius.*

32. P. 8. For Thomas restitution, rather than punishment, was the matrix of commutative justice (q. 62). Molina, noting that Thomas postponed his treatment of *vindicatio* to q. 108, thought punishment was an imperfect form of restitution (*De iustitia et iure* 1.12).

Within this political society, which is a kind of summary of that great society of all mankind, we can observe with much greater clarity the functions of the two kinds of justice. Assignative justice allots public possessions to owners according to the standing of each, and distributes duties and burdens among the citizens according to their capacities. Compensatory justice, on the other hand, not only ensures the equal standing of individual parties in their mutual relations, but honours and rewards those who deserve well of the state, and punishes offenders against society. Compensatory justice, indeed, instructs us how individual claims are in fact the business of the whole community: not only military, but civic honours are in its gift, while its public courts are not limited to dealing with treason, but impose criminal sanctions upon murderers, forgers, and criminals of that type.[33]

The claim that rewards and punishments belong to the sphere of compensation has generated some further thoughts on the state's interest in seeing that private deserts are met. Not only is the state itself a recipient of benefit and harm, owing something to its military saviors and being owed something by its traitors; it is a party in its own right to the punishment of offences against citizens and the rewarding of benefits conferred on citizens. This seems to extend compensatory justice to the point where assignative justice has nothing left to do. Having introduced the distinction, Grotius is, after all, at something of a loss as to how to apply it to rewards. To this he will return.

As regards the general thrust of the argument of *De Indis,* Tuck is certainly correct in saying that commutative justice is the matrix within which the exposition develops. But that is not because Grotius has transformed the Aristotelian distinction; it is because the distinction is superimposed upon an argument devised independently of it. Twenty years later it would be different. The distinction would have assumed an important role in the doctrine of "right", and Grotius would deal very freely with many features of the scholastic exposition.

---

33. P. 11a: *In hac autem universitate, quae magnae illius velut compendium est, opera illa utriusque Iustitiae multo clarius apparent. Nam assignatrix possessiones publicas pro dignitate cuiusque dominis adscribit et officia oneraque in cives pro viribus dispertit, compensatrix vero non tantum inter singulos aequalitatem tuetur, sed et bene de patria meritos honore et praemiis remuneratur et in commune nocentibus ad poenas utitur. Quomodo autem quae in singulos fiunt ad cunctos pertineant, eadem docet, cum praeter triumphos etiam coronas civicas donat nec intra maiestatis reos publica iudicia coercet, sed homicidas quoque et falsarios et id genus sontes ad supplicia deposcit.*

II

We meet Aristotle's second distinction early in the first book of *IBP*, in the middle of a passage which expounds three senses of the term *ius* as used in the title. To this framework we shall have to return; but for the present we join him at the second sense which he ascribes to *ius*:

[4] A right is a moral quality attaching to a subject enabling the subject to have something or do something justly. . . . <So called "real rights" still attach to the person, not the thing.> A moral quality may be said to be "perfect," in which case it is called a "faculty," or it may be less than perfect, in which case it is called a "fitness." These two categories correspond to the categories of *act* and *potency* in metaphysics.

[5] The lawyers call a faculty a *suum*, i.e., "one's own"; we shall call it simply "a right in the strict sense." . . . <Division into a power, a domain and a credit. Further division into vulgar and eminent right.>

[7] A fitness (*axia* in Aristotle, i.e., "dignity") is interpreted by Michael of Ephesus as *to prosarmozon* or *to prepon*, i.e., that which is suitable.

[8] To a faculty corresponds *expletive justice*, i.e., justice in the technical or strict sense of the term. This is what Aristotle calls *sunallaktikē dikaiosunē*, the justice of transactions, but that name is too restrictive. When somebody who holds some property of mine returns it to me, that is not a *sunallagma* or "transaction"; yet the kind of justice that governs it is the same. His other name for it, *epanorthōtikē* or "corrective" justice, is happier. To a fitness corresponds *attributive justice*, which Aristotle calls *dianemētikē*. This is associated with those virtues which serve the interest of other people, such as liberality, compassion, prudent government.

Aristotle's assertion that expletive justice attends to "simple" or "arithmetic proportion," attributive justice to "compound" or "geometric proportion" (though mathematicians use the term "proportion" only for the latter kind of relation), is one of those doctrines that may often hold true, but not always. The essential difference between expletive and attributive justice does not lie in these different types of proportion, but, as we have said, in the different types of right to which they attend. So a contract of partnership is discharged *(expletur)* by observing geometrical proportion; on the other hand, a solitary qualified candidate may be appointed to a public office, an act of attributive justice but using simple commensuration.

No more persuasive is the popular doctrine that attributive justice has to do with public affairs, expletive justice with private. Disposing of one's property by will is an act of attributive justice; and when the state reimburses expenses that citizens have incurred on public business, that is an act of expletive justice. This distinction was correctly remarked by Cyrus's tutor. Cyrus had proposed to give the smaller boy the smaller tunic, though it was not his own, and the larger boy the larger tunic; but his tutor told him: "That is the way to proceed when you are commissioned to decide what would be suitable. But when you have to judge whose tunic it is, then you compare the rival claims to ownership: ought the person who stole it to have it? or the person who made it or bought it?"[34]

The Aristotelian distinction has been subjected to a simple but radical revision: "to a faculty corresponds expletive justice . . . to a fitness corresponds attributive justice." A "faculty" is "a right in the strict sense," that entitles one to claim something as "one's own" — clearly an allusion to the Roman-law definition *suum cuique tribuere*, "to render each his own." A fitness, on the other hand, is a moral quality that is "less than perfect," one which does not consti-

---

34. *IBP* 1.1. Translation from *IG*, pp. 797-99 My abbreviating summaries are placed between parentheses <. . .>, *Ius est qualitas moralis personae competens ad aliquid iuste habendum vel agendum. . . . Qualitas autem moralis perfecta, facultas nobis dicitur; minus perfecta, aptitudo: quibus respondent in naturalibus illi quidem actus, huic autem potentia. Facultatem iurisconsulti nomine sui appellant, nos posthac ius proprie aut stricte dictum appellabimus. . . . Aptitudinem vero ἀξίαν, id est dignitatem vocat Aristoteles (NE 1131a24ff). Michael Ephesius id quod secundum eam aequale dicitur interpretatur τὸ προσάρμοζον et τὸ πρέπον, id quod convenit. Facultatem respicit iustitia expletrix, quae proprie aut stricte iustitiae nomen obtinet, συναλλακτικῇ Aristoteli, nimis arcto vocabulo, nam ut possessor meae rei eam mihi reddat, non est ἐκ συναλλάγματος et tamen ad eandem hanc iustitiam pertinet: itaque ἐπανορθωτικήν idem felicius dixit. Aptitudinem respicit attributrix, quae Aristoteli διανεμητικῇ, comes earum virtutum, quae aliis hominibus utilitatem adferunt, ut liberalitatis, misericordiae, providentiae rectricis. Quod vero idem Aristoteles ab expletrice ait respici proportionem simplicem, quam ἀριθμητικήν vocat, ab attributrice autem comparatam, quam γεωμετρικήν appellat, quae sola apud mathematicos nomen habet proportionis, ex eorum genere est quae saepe locum habent, non semper: neque vero per se iustitia expletrix ab attributrice differt tali proportionum usu, sed materia circa quam versatur, ut iam diximus. Itaque et contractus societatis expletur proportione comparata, et si unus tantum aptus inveniatur ad munus publicum, non alia quam simplici commensione attributio fiet. Neque magis verum est quod a nonnullis dicitur, attributricem versari circa res communes, expletricem circa res singulorum. Contra enim si quis de re sua legare velit, attributrice iustitia uti solet: et civitas quae de communi reddit quod civium quidam in publicum impenderunt nonnisi expletricis iustitiae officio fungitur. Recte hoc discrimen notatum a Cyri magistro: nam cum Cyrus puero minori minorem tunicam, sed alienam, attribuisset, et maiori contra maiorem, docuit eum magister: Tunc quidem ubi constitutus esset arbitrator eius quod cuique conveniret, ita agendum esse; at ubi iudicandum esset utrius esset tunica, id spectandum utra possessio iustior, eumne rem habere qui vi abstulisset, an qui fecisset aut emisset.* I have imposed on the reader the quotation of this and subsequent passages at length, since decontextualized quotation, from which our author has suffered ever since his first readers fell on the *etiamsi daremus* clause in the Prolegomena, poses great risks to the understanding of Grotius.

tute a right in the strict and proper sense. The difference between the two types is quite simply that the one corresponds to a "strict" right, the other does not. Aristotle rightly intuited the distinction between two types of justice, but described it wrongly: his division of the field between transactions and distributions is not exhaustive, since there are just acts which fall into neither of these categories, and the names he used were inadequate.[35] In a first decisive departure from the *De Indis*, Grotius thinks Aristotle wrong to have grounded the distinction on the basis of geometric and arithmetic proportion, which may hold true much of the time, but does not always do so. In a second, the scholastic proposal of St. Thomas to distinguish the two in terms of their political subjects as acts of the community and acts of private citizens, is held to be unsustainable.

This distinction is situated within the category of what we call "subjective right" and Grotius calls "right attaching to a subject." The perfect moral quality, the faculty, is a right that entitles one without further ado to "have something or do something justly." If the right is proven, the moral "power" is actual, and the thing or action laid claim on is already the claimant's "own," needing only to be "filled out" by being given effect. *Suum cuique tribuere* allows no scope for the exercise of imaginative discretion, as the story from Xenophon about Cyrus and the cloak makes clear. Grotius's new preferred name for rectificatory/commutative/compensatory justice, *iustitia expletrix,* is best explained by the phrases *expletio iuris* and *explementum iuris,* which mean compensation in a sale.[36] The *expletio* of a right is its satisfaction or completion.

But subjective right has now been stretched to allow not only for "perfect" rights but for "imperfect" ones. Its general definition, therefore, is not in terms of an *entitlement (facultas),* a time-honored way of defining subjective right, but in terms of a *moralis qualitas,* which we may plausibly paraphrase a "qualification." The imperfect qualification is described as an *aptitudo,* or "fitness."[37] If one has a fitness for having or doing something, it is a qualifying factor for

35. Grotius takes exception to the name that he imagined Aristotle used for the stricter type of justice, συναλλακτική or "transactional" justice, on the ground that it is not only transactions that require one to render each his own. The alternative, "rectificatory justice" (ἐπανορθωτική), is, he thinks, rather better. In this he supposes that Aristotle used these terms as names, as the scholastic discussions did. In fact the phrase τὸ ἐπανορθωτικὸν δίκαιον should be translated, as in Irwin's translation, "the just in rectification" (1132a18).

36. *IBP* 2.7.2.

37. He connects the term with the mention of "merit" (ἀξία) which occurs as an aside in Aristotle's discussion of geometric proportion (1131a24-9). There is, however, no hint in Aristotle of the difference between an entitlement and a fitness.

having or doing it, but not a complete qualification.[38] The difference between the perfect and imperfect is equivalent to that in metaphysics between an act and a potency. In a right proper the moral "power" to do this or that is actual, in an aptitude merely potential. It imports no proprietorial relation to the thing or the act, does not entitle one to regard it as one's own.[39] So attributive justice lies *outside* the scope of the *suum cuique* formula. This is a signficant innovation, for the unanimous tradition of Latin Christian jurisprudence had treated this phrase as a definition of justice as a whole. So had Grotius in the *De Indis*.[40]

There is, then, a surplus in the notion of right that goes beyond proprietorial exchange. That surplus is defined as something like a *prima facie* claim falling short of an entitlement. The important thing to appreciate about Grotius's designation of a "strict" sense of right is how much of central importance to the notion both of justice and of subjective right he thought unaccounted for by it. The meaning of "strict" *(proprie aut stricte dictum)* is "narrow," "exact," or "technical"; it does not mean that Grotius thinks this sense to be the more important or decisive, nor the other "improper."[41] The opposite assumption is, in fact, central to the whole project of *De Iure Belli ac Pacis*, which is replete with reminders that *mera iustitia expletrix* will never yield an adequate account of the law of war.[42]

One example of attributive right that Grotius offers is the appointment of a sole qualified candidate to a post, an example that it is rewarding to explore a little further. Take the case (A) that someone is well qualified for appointment to a vacant post; it is "right" and "just" that that person should be appointed rather than someone less qualified. We could speak of the appointment of an unqualified candidate over the head of a qualified candidate as a "wrong" without any hint of metaphor or analogy. But in what does the wrong consist? Clearly not in denying the qualified candidate his right. The qualified candidate

---

38. A common use of subjective "right" in this "imperfect" sense arises in a linear cognatic system of succession, where a monarch's eldest child, if a daughter, has a "right of succession" that is subject to no son being subsequently born and surviving to succeed. Cf. *IBP* 2.7.28.

39. In *IBP* 2.2 Grotius will use the phrase *id quod nostrum est*, "what is our own," and subdivide it into goods and persons *(res et personas)* and acts *(actus)*, on the one hand, and into "common right" and "singular right" on the other. "Property" *(proprietas)* is vested in goods and persons both of common right (which we can enjoy without excluding others) and singular right (which excludes other proprietors). I use the epithet "proprietorial" more widely, however, to include every aspect of *suum/nostrum* ownership.

40. *IP* pp. 6, 6r.

41. Grotius has his own way of saying that a usage is "improper": *per abusionem*, *IBP* 1.1.10.3.

42. See a series of important passages: *IBP* 2.1.9.1; 10.1; 11; 3.1.4.2.

does not *possess* a right, as is easily shown by supposing the case (B) in which *two* well-qualified candidates are passed over in favor of an unqualified one. In case B the wrong is precisely the same as in case A, yet it is impossible to say which of the two qualified candidates was cheated out of his or her right to the post, and they cannot both have had a "perfect" right to it! Even the best-qualified candidate has no actual moral power over a post; the post is not any-body's "own." Yet appointment can be just or unjust, and its quality of justice or injustice could count in law. For though a disappointed candidate cannot sue for restitution of his property, a failure to appoint qualified people to posts can lead to charges of negligence or corruption.

In Grotius's view this example scotches Aristotle's claim that equality in justice requires four terms, two people and two treatments meted out to them. Grotius does not here take issue directly with the scholastic translation of Aris-totle's term, "distributive justice," but offers yet another new name of his own, *attributrix,* which suppresses the sense of the prefix dia-, *dis-*. The point of the preference is clear enough: he criticises Aristotle for linking this type of justice to geometric proportion, i.e., assigning each person a share proportionate to one's relative worth. The justice in the sole candidate's appointment is simply the *fit* between his qualifications and the post. Justice does not always imply comparisons between one person and another.

III

In the course of his chapter on punishment in the second book (2.20), a little treatise of great significance comparable in importance to the section on "Unrecht" in Hegel's *Grundlinien der Philosophie des Rechts,* Grotius revisits the question to which of the two types justice in punishment belongs.

[2] But it is controversial whether justice in punishment belongs to the assignative or expletive type. Some argue that it is assignative justice on the grounds that graver punishments are given for graver offences, lighter for lighter, and that punishment is handed down by the community as a whole to its members. But behind this lies a fallacious assumption, that assignative justice is in question wherever proportionate equality has to be achieved among more than two terms. In the opening section of this work we have shown this not to be so. Furthermore, the fact that graver punish-ments are given for graver offences, lighter for lighter, is a consequence, not a goal of penal practice. The immediate goal is that the punishment should fit the crime. <Illustrative quotations>.

No less mistaken, as will appear, is the other assumption, that punishments are handed down by the community to its members. We have already shown that the essential principle of assignative justice is neither, on the one hand, this kind of proportionate equality nor, on the other, the activity of the community towards its members; it is the respect due to that kind of "fitness" which does not amount to a "right" in the strict sense, but gives an occasion for right. Certainly the person punished must be "fit" or "meet" for punishment, but the point of punishment is not that he should be awarded something, which is what assignative justice requires.

Yet those who maintain that punishment belongs to expletive justice (or "commutative," to use the common term) hardly make a better case. They often describe the business as though something has to be returned to the offender, as in a contract. The common, and evidently loose, expression, that some punishment is "due" to an offender, has misled them. When something is due to someone in the strict sense, that person may claim it as a right against someone else. But to call a punishment "due" is simply to say that it is fair.

It is, however, true that the primary and essential exercise of justice in punishment is expletive. For punishment to be correctly executed, the punisher must have a right to punish, a right which originates in the offence. And there is something else that makes punishment like contract: namely, that like a vendor who is deemed to have accepted all the natural obligations of a sale without explicit statement to the effect, the offender is deemed to have freely accepted punishment. Since no serious crime can go unpunished, one who directly wills the crime, wills to deserve the punishment.[43]

43. *Sed an ad assignatricem an vero ad expletricem iustitiam poena pertineat, diversi diversum sentiunt. Quidam enim quia qui plus peccavit gravius, qui minus levius puniuntur, et quia poena quasi a toto parti datur, ideo ad assignatricem iustitiam poenas referunt. Sed quod primum illi ponunt, assignatricem iustitiam toties locum habere quoties inter terminos plures duobus instituitur aequalitas, verum non esse in principio operis huius ostendimus: deinde quod magis nocentes gravius, minus nocentes levius puniuntur, id per consequentiam duntaxat evenit, non quod hoc primo ac per se spectetur. Nam primo ac per se spectatur aequalitas inter culpam et poenam. . . . Sed nec alterum quod illi ponunt magis verum est, poenas omnes venire ex toto ad partem, quod ex his quae dicenda sunt apparebit. Tum vero ostensum a nobis supra est, veram iustitiae assignatricis rationem nec in tali aequalitate, nec in processu a toto ad partem proprie consistere, sed in habenda ratione eius aptitudinis, quae ius stricte dictum in se non contineat sed occasionem ei det. Quanquam vero is qui punitur aptus aut dignus esse debet puniri, non eo tamen id spectat ut ipsi accedit aliquid quod assignatrix iustitia postulat. Nec tamen qui expletricem iustitiam, quam vulgo commutatricem vocant, in poenis exerceri volunt, magis se explicant. Ita enim negotium hoc considerant, quasi nocenti aliquid reddatur, sicut in contractibus fieri solet. Decepit eos vulgaris locutio, qua dicimus poenam deberi ei qui deliquit, quod plane est ἄκυρον: nam cui proprie debetur aliquid, is in alterum ius habet. Sed cum deberi alicui poenam dicimus, nihil*

First he considers, and rejects, two arguments for treating justice in punishment as assignative. The first attaches weight to the fact that punishment is assigned proportionately to the gravity of the offence, the second to the fact that it is administered by the community. These two, therefore, correspond to the two accounts of distributive justice which he found wanting in 1.1.8, those of Aristotle and St. Thomas. We must suppose that they come from a scholastic source; yet that source is neither Aristotle nor St. Thomas, both of whom clearly treat punishment as an instance of rectificatory justice. Although the authority of St. Thomas was strong, there was an awareness among scholastics that the answer might not be as simple as it appeared.[44] In refuting the former of these two arguments he repeats his rejection of the Aristotelian thesis that justice consists in an equality among more than two terms. It is not the relation of one person's punishment to another's that concerns us, but the relation of punishment to offence.

He then dismisses an argument on the other side, in favor of treating punishment as an instance of expletive justice. The idea that punishment is *due* to the offender, who is to be "paid" for his crime, is, he thinks, merely a confusion induced by taking a commercial metaphor literally. If the offender were really owed punishment, he would have a right to it, which is absurd. But does Grotius then embrace the inverse form of the commercial model, in which it is the offender who owes something and must pay? In *De Satisfactione Christi*, he had criticised this view very sharply. God's role in punishing human sin was that of a judge; Socinus's error arose from thinking that God acted in the capacity of injured victim, who could simply waive his right, rather than as vindicating the lawful order of the universe.[45] At first glance it may seem that Grotius now takes the view he then rejected; but that impression is quickly dispelled. Certainly, the punishing authority must have a right to punish, and that right is conferred upon it by the offender. But it is not the right of a victim to vengeance or restitution. It is conferred through a tacit understanding which the offender shares with society as a whole, that offence merits punishment, an account anticipating Hegel's "right established with the criminal, in his objec-

---

volumus aliud quam aequum esse ut puniatur. Verum tamen est in poenis primo ac per se exerceri expletricem iustitiam, quia scilicet qui punit, ut recte puniat, ius habere debet ad puniendum, quod ius ex delicto nocentis nascitur. Atque hac in re est aliud quod ad contractuum naturam accedit: quia sicut qui vendit, etiamsi nihil peculiariter dicat, obligasse se censetur ad ea omnia quae venditionis sunt naturalia, ita qui deliquit sua voluntate se videtur obligasse poenae, quia crimen grave non potest non esse punibile, ita ut qui directe vult peccare, per consequentiam et poenam mereri voluerit. Translation from *IG*, pp. 802-3.

44. Cf. L. Molina, *De iustitia et iure* 1.12.

45. *De satisfactione Christi* 2.4-15.

tively embodied will."[46] In punishing, then, as in performing a contract, one is implementing a state of affairs which morally already exists. But that state of affairs is not a private relation between offender and victim, but a social relation between offender and society. The victim, indeed, is hardly noticed.

In a passage of the *De Indis* to which Tuck has frequently drawn attention, Grotius argued that the state's monopoly of punishment in civil society supposes an antecedent private right of punishment. In this important passage private punishment is distinguished from private self-defence or self-compensation, as well as from what we would call "vengeance." Private punishment is undertaken for the common good of the whole human race, which we conceive as a "world-republic," and it poses fewer perils when not undertaken in respect of one's own wrongs.[47] In observing correctly that Grotius still maintains this doctrine in *IBP*, Tuck draws the conclusion that "natural society . . . wholly lacked a genuine community of interests or resources. Its sociability extended only as far as was necessary to justify the private right of punishment."[48] But how far was that? Grotius's point — in both texts, I would judge, but certainly in *IBP* — is that it extends natural sociability quite far. Natural society *foreshadows* civil society; in it, he quotes Plutarch as saying, we view all other human beings "as citizens."[49] Nature, he continues in *IBP* [3], leaves the subject of the right to punish indeterminate, but indicates that "most appropriately" it is a superior, which is to say, it anticipates a structured social context in which representative authority arises. (Grotius's recurrent instance of natural authority is the *paterfamilias*.) Punishment can never be administered by one human being on another without some social utility in view [4], and can never be undertaken for the sake of simple retaliation alone [5]. The substantive account of punishment places it wholly within the context of responsible government. The point of rooting it in "nature" is not to belittle the sociality of pre-civil society (which includes the relations of sovereign states) but to magnify it, showing, as Grotius is always concerned to do, that the whole content of civil jurisprudence derives from the natural terms on which human beings relate to one another.

We may keep open the critical question whether Grotius served his own purpose well by refusing the answer that he toyed with, that punishment could be considered as an exercise of assignative justice. That would have afforded not

---

46. *Grundlinien der Philosophie des Rechts* §100: "Die Verletzung, die dem Verbrecher widerfährt, ist nicht nur an sich gerecht . . . sondern sie ist auch ein Recht an den Verbrecher selbst, d.i. in seinem daseienden Willen, in seiner Handlung gesetzt."

47. *IP*, pp. 39-41. For this argument, phrased in terms of *potestas iudicandi*, cf. also *Commentarius* 42.

48. *Rights*, p. 88.

49. *IP*, p. 41.

a *right,* but a *duty* to punish, arguably a better tool for defending his account of God's dealings. The arguments that he found for such a position were, he judged, weak, but he might have found stronger. He needed only to resolve that punishment responds to a "fitness" in the offender to be punished. Grotius's objection to this takes us to the very heart of the problem: "certainly the person punished must be 'fit' or 'meet' for punishment, but the point of punishment is not that he should be awarded something *(ut ipsi accedat aliquid),* which is what assignative justice requires." The suggestion refused here is not that punishment could be awarded as a *benefit,* for Christian Aristotelians were quite aware that distributive justice encompassed the distribution of burdens.[50] It is that punishment reaches beyond the existing moral state of affairs to a *prudens dispensatio,* a judicious exercise of discretion in promoting social welfare. A true asignee must be put in a position of benefit or burden that is *new,* not already implied in the balance of his moral rights and obligations. At the beginning of the chapter Grotius offered a traditional definition of punishment as *malum passionis quod infligitur ob malum actionis,* "suffering harm for having done harm," and it is this retributive concept of a "return" to the offender of the evil put forth that he cannot reconcile with the thought that punishment is "awarded" as a new burden.

It is worth asking how he might have judged differently. The formal structure of punishment-as-return allows creative initiative in determining the *content* of the return. Like other scholastics Grotius believes that the fixing of any punishment in particular is an act of judicial discretion. Natural law requires, but does not determine punishments.[51] Furthermore, a return may, as such, be a new act, not merely an implementation. Punishment is judgment, and judgment is enacted speech. Its matrix is not that of the market exchange, but of discourse, in which a question or a proposition is "returned" to the speaker in the form of a reply. The offence requires the community, or its officers, to formulate and undertake a truthful answer, returning it to the offender in a new act which expresses its moral quality truthfully. What the offender gets back is different from what he put forth, not an echo. In this way we could indeed say that something new is conferred on the offender in punishment, even punishment understood as *malum passionis ob malum actionis.* Society accords him its judicious attention and its response.

---

50. Cf. Thomas Aquinas, *ST* 2-2.61.3: *est quaedam distributio laboriosorum operum.*
51. *IBP* 2.8.20 for this commonplace of scholastic theory.

IV

We turn, thirdly, to the decisive passage from the Prolegomena to *IBP*, written, it is supposed, after the body of the work was completed, in which Grotius's theory of Natural and Positive Right is expounded from the ground up, starting with behavior common to animals and ending with the most culturally specific forms of law. The general direction of the exposition reminds Tuck of the "Prolegomena" of the *De Indis,* and in their concern to provide a map for the various divisions of jurisprudence they are certainly to be compared. Yet the plan on which the two are constructed is quite different. Here the decisive passage is based on Aristotle's second distinction, though Grotius, writing in apologetic rather than definitional style, avoids the technical terms. Another departure from the pattern of the older "Prolegomena" is the disappearance of that "ancient and divine self-love, wholly praiseworthy" and of the continuity it was supposed to afford between mankind and other animal species, the foundation of the earlier exposition of Natural Right. To the extent that self-preservation appears as a theme at all now, it is on the lips of a chosen adversary, the ancient sceptic Carneades. He was represented in Cicero's *De re publica* as arguing that since laws *(iura)* varied from time to time and place to place, there was no Natural Law *(ius naturae),* but only the self-interested inventions of *ius* by men for their own convenience, a claim supported by appeal to the animal kingdom, in which every creature fights for its own survival.[52] Grotius replies to this that the human race, unlike most animal species, is marked by an "appetite for society" or "identification" with each other. Actually, there are traces of this to be seen in other animal species, too, but in humans it is quite definitive, and is marked especially by the unique power of spoken communication. So rational sociality is now the foundational platform of Natural Right, not, as formerly, a secondary development within it.[53] Grotius continues:

52. This argument occurred in a lost section of Cicero's work, known to Grotius, as to us, through its treatment by Lactantius in *Divinae institutiones* 5.

53. At various points in *IBP* Grotius refers to a "natural" level of behavior which is directed to the agent's safety rather than to the social good, and so lies *below* the level of Natural Right: e.g., 2.1.4.1 of trampling innocents down in the course of flight; 2.5.8.2 of sexual partnerships without fidelity. It is explained at 1.2.1.2. that an investigation of natural right must proceed in two stages: first, what is congruent with the *prima naturae* or *initia naturae,* the "first natural instincts," and then what is *honestum,* dictated by right reason, which should be "dearer" and "by all means pursued." Self-preservation by every means is natural in the primitive sense, common to men and animals, as is demonstrated by our instinctive use of the hands; but it is compatible with natural right only in so far as it is rationally consistent with the nature of society, 1.2.1.4, 5. The use of *naturaliter* at 1.5.1, 2, is comparable, despite the reference to *ius: naturaliter quemque sui iuris esse vindicem: ideo manus nobis datae. Sed et alteri prodesse quae*

[8] This social instinct characteristic of the human intelligence, which we have sketchily described, is the source of *a right in the technical sense of the term*. Here we include: not touching others' property; restoring others' property, if we have it, as well as any gain we may have made from it; the obligation to keep promises; making good damage for which we are to blame, and deserving punishment (as it applies to human relations).

[9] From this sense of Right there flows *a second, wider sense*. It is not only the capacity for society, which we have discussed, that distinguishes human beings from other animals, but the capacity to exercise judgment, not least in calculating future as well as present joys and harms and the courses of action likely to lead to either. To use one's human intelligence in such matters, to act upon a well-formed judgment, without the distorting influence of fear or some immediately attractive pleasure and without being swept away by sudden impulse, is considered appropriate to human nature. Correspondingly, action inconsistent with such judgment is considered "contrary to natural Right" — which means, the Right of human nature. [10] To this belongs the prudent allocation of resources in *adding* to what individuals and collectives own; so that sometimes a wiser person is favoured over someone less wise, sometimes a neighbour receives preferential treatment over a foreigner, sometimes a poor man is treated more generously than a rich man, depending on what is being done in each case and what the business in hand requires. There is a long tradition of treating this as an aspect of Right in the technical and strict sense of the term. But that Right which is technically so called is actually quite different, since it consists in letting someone keep, or have, what is already his.

[11] These observations would have a place even were we to accept the infamous premiss that God did not exist or did not concern himself with human affairs. As it is, however, rational reflection and unbroken tradition combine to inculcate the opposite presumption, which is then confirmed by a range of arguments and by miracles attested in every period of history. From this there follows *a further principle:* that we must obey God without qualification, as our creator to whom we owe ourselves and all that we possess. Especially must we do so since he has shown himself by many means to be both Supreme Good and Supreme Power. To those who obey him he is able to give the highest rewards, eternal rewards, indeed, since he is himself eternal; that he is willing to, is something we should anyway believe, but all the more so if he has promised it explicitly. And that, as we Christians

---

possimus non licitum modo, sed et honestum est. That is to say: natural right prior to political society cannot solely be a matter of *right vindicated,* founded in the same natural instinct, but must also be a matter of *duty discharged* to the neighbor through assistance.

believe with an assurance based on proofs of unquestionable reliability, is precisely what he has done.[54]

As at 1.1, the point is to elaborate the content of *ius*, though now with a polemic aim directed against the contention that there is no *ius* in war. The capacity for society conjoined with a mind capable of framing and understanding general laws is the basis of "a right in the technical sense of the term" *(eius iuris quod proprie tali nomine appellatur)*, which consists generally in the recognition of the difference between one's own and another's; specifically, it includes the prohibition of theft, the keeping of promises, the restitution of damage, and the ideas of desert and punishment. In *De Indis*, too, this was "what is called strict justice," *iustitia propria dicta*.[55] In that context, however, the contrast was with a more basic *ius naturae* constituted by self-preservation. Now it is with an extended, developed sense of "right," a "second and wider sense of *ius*" which springs from different human powers. What Grotius has so far described is, though not named as such, expletive justice; now he contrasts it with the justice of assignment.

The human mind can judge in general terms what benefits and what harms human society; it can anticipate as well as recognise. This second and wider aspect of justice has to do with the prudent ranking of priorities and with

54. *Haec vero quam rudi modo iam expressimus societatis custodia humano intellectui conveniens fons est eius iuris quod proprie tali nomine appellatur: quo pertinent alieni abstinentia et si quid alieni habeamus aut lucri inde fecerimus restitutio, promissorum implendorum obligatio, damni culpa dati reparatio, et poenae inter homines meritum. Ab hac iuris significatione fluxit altera largior: quia enim homo supra ceteras animantes non tantum vim obtinet socialem de qua diximus sed et iudicium ad aestimanda quae delectant aut nocent, non praesentia tantum sed et futura, et quae in utrumvis possunt ducere: pro humani intellectus modo etiam in his iudicium recte conformatum sequi, neque metu aut voluptatis praesentis illecebra corrumpi aut temerario rapi impetu, conveniens esse humanae naturae; et quod tali iudicio plane repugnat etiam contra ius naturae, humanae scilicet, esse intelligitur. Atque huc etiam pertinet in his quae cuique homini aut coetui propria sunt elargiendis prudens dispensatio, ut quae nunc sapientiorem minus sapienti, nunc propinquum extraneo, nunc pauperem diviti, prout actus cuiusque et rei natura fert, praeponit: quam iuris proprie stricteque dicti partem iam olim multi faciunt, cum tamen ius illud proprie nominatum diversam longe naturam habeat, in eo positam, ut quae iam sunt alterius alteri permittantur, aut impleantur. Et haec quidem quae iam diximus locum aliquem haberent etiamsi daremus quod sine summo scelere dari nequit non esse Deum aut non curari ab eo negotia humana: cuius contrarium cum nobis partim ratio, partim traditio perpetua inseuerint, confirment vero et argumenta multa et miracula ab omnibus saeculis testata, sequitur iam ipsi Deo ut opifici et cui nos nostraque omnia debeamus sine exceptione parendum nobis esse, praecipue cum is se multis modis et optimum et potentissimum ostenderit: ita ut sibi obedientibus praemia reddere maxima, etiam aeterna, quippe aeternus ipse, possit, et voluisse credi debeat multoque magis si id desertis uerbis promiserit; quod Christiani indubitata testimoniorum fide convicti credimus.* Translation from *IG*, pp. 793-94.

55. *IP*, p. 6.

the forming and sustaining of long-term policies. Good judgment includes prudence, and this also, Grotius thinks, belongs to the content of *ius naturae*.[56] For the purposes of the treatise on war, this allows him to embrace in the scope of justice the widest possible considerations of general welfare. We find it necessary for the sake of justice to make decisions that could seem unjust on purely expletive criteria, preferring one person to another. Grotius identifies three such types of preference, and by these we can measure how far he stands from Aristotle's notion of proportionate distribution κατ' ἀξίαν. Sometimes we prefer a wiser person to a less wise one (when we admit students to a University, for example); sometimes we prefer a neighbor to a connection with a stranger (at Passport Control, or in issuing invitations to a wedding); sometimes we prefer a poor person to a rich one (in offering welfare benefits). Of these the first fits easily into Aristotle's pattern, the second and third do not.[57] But the key element in Grotius's reconstruction lies in the phrase, *prout actus cuiusque et rei natura fert,* "depending on what is being done in each case and what the business in hand requires." Where Aristotle admitted simply that people could disagree about the criteria for preference, Grotius thinks that these criteria can actually vary from one enterprise to the next. There is no one ground on which we always prefer one person to another; there are many grounds, and the right ground at any moment depends on what it is that we prefer someone *for.* The wider justice, then, comes in innumerable forms corresponding to the innumerable types of action we may prudently undertake.

It is at this point that we meet the words on which Grotius's reputation as an advocate of secular natural right rests: "these observations" *(haec quae jam diximus)* "would have a place even were we to accept the infamous premise that God did not exist or did not concern himself with human affairs." Commentators who discuss every other aspect of this sentence usually fail to ask precisely what is referred to as "these observations." On a more extensive reading it may include everything from paragraph [6] on, i.e., the fact of a human appetite for society, the content of expletive justice and as much of the content of assignative justice as has been expounded so far. On a more restrictive reading it may include only paragraph [10], on the content of expletive justice. Either way Grotius does not intend to suggest that the natural law can be known *in full* irrespective of God's existence, because he now goes on to insist that assignative justice must also include the religious duty of obeying God. Once the point is

56. Cf. *IBP* 2.1.9.1: *ius naturae, quatenus legem significat, non ea tantum respicit, quae dictat iustitia, quam expletricem diximus, sed aliarum quoque virtutum, temperantiae, fortitudinis, prudentiae actus in se continet, ut in certis circumstantiis, non honestos tantum sed et debitos.*

57. The second is manifestly Ciceronian in inspiration (cf. *Laelius* 5.19), the third evangelical.

granted that whatever is possible to prudence may be necessary to justice, that metaphysical prudence which leads us to recognize God's existence and the demands he makes upon us necessarily becomes a matter of justice, too. When he first explored *iustitia assignatrix,* he took as a paradigm the justice of God's dealings towards us now he makes the paradigm the duties that we owe to God.

This duty is no mere *hypothetical* element of assignative justice, predicated on the contingent fact of divine revelation. Certainly (so the argument continues) there will be such contingent elements of justice which Christians alone, by virtue of their access to revelation, will recognize. But obedience to God is itself a duty of natural right, since natural reason and universal tradition are together quite sufficient to convince anyone that God exists and is good to us. In the same vein Grotius will later admit crimes against natural religion as a ground of just war, but not crimes against revealed religion.[58] We should hardly be surprised to find the author of the *De Veritate Christianae Religionis* arguing for a natural and universal duty of religion.[59]

If there is an innovation here, it does not lie where it has been supposed to, in a natural right free of obligation to God; it lies in the *location* of our duties to God. For Augustine the duty of true religion was proved by reference to the *suum cuique*: giving each his own implied giving God his own.[60] For Grotius, on the other hand, it is part of that justice that takes us beyond the *suum cuique*. Perhaps he is wary of a conception of divinity to whom one could speak of "mine" and "thine," as though between equals. His argument, at any rate, takes a different route, placing the duty to God among the duties of prudence-as-assignment. It turns on the fact that God is the supreme good of mankind, and that seeking the highest good of mankind is also a demand of justice.[61]

V

Two interpretative questions arise out of our survey up to this point. The first is why Grotius was dissatisfied with Aristotle's notion that *distribution* was the

58. 2.20.44-51.

59. Cf. also *De Imperio* 1.9: it is a "manifest pronouncement of that right reason common to the human race" that "the service of religion" is the chief business of the state. Also 3.3: *illum ipsum coli debere iuris naturalis est.*

60. *De civitate Dei* 19.21.1. *Iustitia porro ea virtus est quae sua cuique distribuit. quae igitur iustitia est hominis, quae ipsum hominem Deo vero tollit et inmundis daemonibus subdit?*

61. The importance of this theme for Grotius has been confirmed by our knowledge of *Meletius,* which begins from the idea of God as the *finis optimus* and *summum bonum* of mankind (2.13).

surplus of justice. The second is why he preferred to introduce a wider account of *ius* by way of Aristotle's second distinction, rather than achieve what he wanted with the help of the first distinction through the category of "general" justice.

Our answer to the first of these questions can be summarized and then elaborated under three heads: — (i) *Iustitia assignatrix* rejects uniform criteria which will justify preferences for all purposes; (ii) it severs the link between justice and ownership; (iii) it abandons the Aristotelian thought of proportion as an equality relative to four terms.

(i) In making just distributions, according to Aristotle's idea, one was bound to preserve an existing balance of dignity and worth, giving more to the more worthy, less to the less. There may be disagreement over what the balance of dignity is, so that someone who distributes things justly may nevertheless surprise us by unexpected judgments about how a claimant's worth is assessed; but in principle it is a unitary balance, good for all just purposes, needing only to be discerned. The restrictive implications of this are evident. Whether we cling to an egalitarian concept of equal worth, or whether we qualify it by one or another doctrine of social usefulness, favoring party members, aristocrats, the educated, or whomever, our conception of relative worth affects everything we do, appropriately or inappropriately. So egalitarianism prevents bright children from getting the extra educational stimulus they need, socialist party discipline prevents sick people from getting hospital beds earmarked for officials, aristocratic hierarchies prevent able but unconnected persons from being appointed to posts, and so on. With *iustitia assignatrix*, on the other hand, Grotius argues that there are different criteria of preference appropriate for different undertakings.

This incorporation of prudence into justice differs from that which two centuries later will be associated with the utilitarians. For Grotius the various social undertakings and the criteria appropriate to them are not to be conceived as means towards a single uniform goal. In seeing, for example, that educating children will benefit society, we are not conceiving first of a social good, happiness, and then positing education as a means to achieve it. The role of prudence in this case is precisely to discern the *good of education*. An agent embarked upon the task of education learns to respect the inherent logic of education and the criteria relevant to it, not to subordinate them to some abstract overriding goal of maximized happiness. For there is no one goal which serves as a principle of commensuration to tell us which of the many things we may do justly it would be most just that we should do. Grotius's linkage between prudence and justice is obligated to the structures of reality, and it leaves scope for the exercise of discretion.

(ii) Distributive justice was thought by Christian Aristotelians to be included within the general Roman legal characterization of justice as ownership, *suum cuique tribuere*.[62] To this extent the idea of distribution does not challenge the proprietorial conception which dominates rectificatory justice. The curiously abstract thought of unowned resources in search of the right owners is simply the shadow of a proprietorial idea in which everything susceptible to just treatment is owned already. Distributive justice was an idea which arose from a dominant feature of the Greek political experience, colonization, in which societies with already formed hierarchies of honor were suddenly transplanted into new and empty lands. It was the answer to the question: how can we preserve the existing shape of society in the face of a materially new beginning? The new assignment must faithfully preserve the relative proportions of strength in which the members already stood towards one another.

The disruptive effect of the distributive idea in the context of a more continuous political experience is obvious. On the one hand, the hint of a new beginning carries a revolutionary charge. The idea of unowned resources waiting for distribution has served as a kind of "state of nature" lurking in the wings ready to challenge and unsettle any actual historical moment in a society's communication of wealth. On the other hand, the importance it sets on preserving the existing balance of merit has encouraged the notion of an "economic justice" that preserves the balance, distinct from the various ways there are of spending public resources creatively: educating children, caring for the sick, fostering the arts, and so on. And that is true even, or particularly, when the balance of merit is interpreted not in an aristocratic but an egalitarian spirit, in which case an operative similarity of distributive to rectificatory justice is very obvious. Suppose the balance of merit to be *equality*: economic justice, in preserving this balance, posits a scale (running from "well off" to "badly off") on which every condition of welfare or deprival is commensurated, and it sets itself the single task of ensuring that the well off and the badly off are kept as equal as possible. But this ignores the incommensurable differences between ways of being well or badly off: being rich, being well-educated, being able to appreciate beauty, being securely situated in a functional community, having productive work to do, living with those one loves, adoring God, and so on. The imperatives of "distribution," i.e., the correction of disparity by transferring wealth from one private owner to another, become a serious rival to almost any *public* undertaking which seeks to disseminate these worthwhile but incommensurable goods appropriately: education, job creation or whatever. In this

---

62. Cf. Thomas Aquinas, *ST* 61.1 ad 2: *cum ex bonis communibus aliquid in singulos distribuitur, quilibet aliquo modo recipit quod suum est.*

respect the neo-liberal turn, exalting the market and making exchange the measure of everything, merely made the logic of the existing rhetoric of economic justice painfully clear.

(iii) "Distributing" is not an act anyone can intelligibly undertake in abstraction. It is an operation performed in the course of doing something else, whether private (e.g., making a will) or public (e.g., funding education). These other acts are the ones that make the distributive operation intelligible and provide relevant criteria for it in any case. But these criteria do not apply to the distributive operation alone; they apply just as well when there is no distribution to be done. Here we appreciate the force of Grotius's example about the appointment of a single applicant to a single post: the justice criteria for appointment are precisely the same, whether there is one or many applicants. Justice does not lie in how we balance our treatment of one candidate against our treatment of another. It has simply to do with assuring the appropriate correspondence between aptitude and attribution. On the one hand there is the moral qualification of the person, *open to* our acting towards it in a certain way; on the other there is the action *corresponding to* the moral qualification of the person. Treating one person like another, the idea that governed Aristotle's rendering of justice as equality, is secondary: it derives from the need for consistency in our response to the situations we confront. Because we understand a person's aptitude generically, i.e., as of a certain *kind*, we can respond to it adequately only by an act of a kind that befits that kind of aptitude. Similar kinds of aptitude merit similar kinds of attribution.

We will need to go further than Grotius will take us to suggest that justice so conceived does not require a *specific* moral quality of a *particular* person to correspond to. That is to say, not only does the fitness of a given candidate justify appointment to a post, but the *lack* of a fit candidate justifies *no* appointment to a post. In the one case as in the other, there is a just correspondence between act and fitness. One might say simply that acting justly *gives apt expression to the moral quality of the situation.* But there we have an account of just action that wholly fits the theological conception of justice as judgment. It is the nature of an act of judgment to express the moral truth of a situation effectively in a new action.

VI

Our second question takes us back to the definitions of *ius* in 1.1, for it was there that Grotius might very easily have, had he wished, taken up the category of general justice and used it to say what he thought was lacking in *iustitia expletrix.* To understand why he did not do so is to penetrate a little further than is usually done into his treatment of subjective right. The decisive study of Grotius's use of the term *ius* has yet to be made, and here we can only make a very limited contribution to it.

Villey's influential claim, echoed by Tuck, to have found in this text a decisive innovation in the definition of subjective right has attracted criticism. The *subjective conception* of a right has been traced back to thirteenth-century canon lawyers, while the *subjective definition* of a right in terms of a *facultas* goes back at least to Gerson, writing two hundred years before Grotius.[63] On the other hand, we may observe that Grotius is not yet in possession of a concept of *subjective rights*. The reader will turn over many pages of Grotius without finding the plural of the noun *ius;* and when that form does occur, it will mean not "rights," but "laws." (English translations are wholly unreliable on this point.) This is the more striking in the light of the unproblematic acceptance of the plural concept in the later school of what are called, appropriately, "natural rights theorists." An expression such as we meet without surprise in Samuel Pufendorf, "the reason for allowing war is to protect our rights *(iura)* or to assert them," is alien to Grotius's Latinity.[64] The plural of *ius,* "a right," seems to be supplied by *Ius,* "Right," the abstract noun. A glance at the collotypes of the manuscript of *De Indis* shows up many instances of the initial capital "I." Are we dealing here only with the scruple of a polished classical stylist, or does it also afford an important insight into his conceptuality: the particular right that a subject may possess is not an atomic unit that can be multiplied and added up, but a moment emerging out of a larger whole, *Ius* as an undivided garment?[65]

Now we return to the definitions in *IBP* 1.1. and examine the framework within which the Aristotelian distinction was placed. Grotius identifies three senses in which the word *ius* may be used, and is used in his book.

> [3] The title of this work, *On the Right of War and Peace,* should be understood in the first place in terms of the questions I have begun by raising: Is there such a thing as a just war? and What is just conduct in war? "Right" in this context means simply, *what is just* — "just" being understood in a neg-

---

63. See Brian Tierney, *The Idea of Natural Rights* (Atlanta: Scholars Press, 1997) on the canonists' development of the concept. Gerson's famous definition is at *De potestate ecclesiae* 13: *ius est facultas seu potestas propinqua conveniens alicui secundum dictamen primae iustitiae.*

64. *De iure naturae et gentium* (1660) 8.7.2.

65. It appears that the same observation will hold for Grotius's Dutch in *The Jurisprudence of Holland.,* ed. and trans. R. W. Lee (Oxford: Clarendon, 1926). The Dutch terms translated "real rights" and "personal rights" by Lee are singular nouns: *behering* and *inschuld,* not even compounds of *recht.*

ative rather than a positive sense, to mean "what is not unjust." "Unjust," in turn, means what is inconsistent with the nature of a society of rational beings. . . .

[4] There is a second distinct sense of "right" deriving from the first, which is attributed to a subject. A right is a *moral quality attaching to a subject enabling the subject to have something or do something justly.* A right, in this sense, attaches to the subject even though it is sometimes associated with a thing. An example: the ownership of an estate carries with it the right to certain services. These are called "real rights" in contrast to "purely personal rights." It is not that real rights do not also attach to persons; they simply attach to the person who has the thing. A moral quality may be said to be "perfect" . . . *etc. etc.*

[9] There is a third sense of the term "Right," which means the same as "law," understanding "law" in a broad sense as *a rule of moral action obliging us to do what is correct.*[66]

A search for antecedents to this passage yields some striking discoveries. There is no such attempt to marshal the various meanings of *ius* in the humanists who wrote on war in the sixteenth century, Pierino Belli, Balthazar Ayala, and Alberico Gentili; there is no such attempt in the *Controversiae* of Fernando Vázquez; and there is nothing comparable to it in Grotius's own *De Indis.* On the other hand, all the scholastics who had written on justice around the turn of the seventeenth century had passages closely comparable to this, identifying two or three senses of *ius* which turn out to be parallel to Grotius's three or four, and identifying one sense as "strict." At this point we cannot seriously doubt a literary influence.[67]

Behind these scholastic passages lie two major concerns. The first, arising

66. *De iure belli cum inscribimus hanc tractationem, primum hoc ipsum intelligimus, quod dictum iam est, sitne bellum aliquod iustum, et deinde quid in bello iustum sit? Nam ius hic nihil aliud quam quod iustum est significat, idque negante magis sensu quam aiente, ut ius sit quod iniustum non est. Est autem iniustum, quod naturae societatis ratione utentium repugnat.* . . . *Ab hac iuris significatione diversa est altera, sed ab hac ipsa veniens, quae ad personam refertur: quo sensu ius est qualitas moralis personae competens ad aliquid iuste habendum vel agendum. Personae competit hoc ius, etiamsi rem interdum sequatur, ut servitutes praediorum, quae iura realia dicuntur, comparatione facta ad alia mere personalia; non quia non ipsa quoque personae competant, sed quia non alii competunt, quam qui rem certam habeat. Qualitas autem moralis perfecta* . . . *etc. Est et tertia iuris significatio, quae idem valet quod lex, quoties vox legis largissime sumitur, ut sit regula actuum moralium obligans ad id quod rectum est.* Translation from *IG*, pp. 797-99.

67. For what follows, cf. L. Molina, *De iustitia et iure* (1602) 1.2; L. Lessius, *De iustitia et iure caeterisque virtutibus cardinalibus* (1605) 2.1; F. Suárez, *De legibus ac Deo Legislatore* (1613) 1.2.

from commentary on question 57 of the *Secunda Secundae,* is to sustain and develop the tradition of Thomas's doctrine that *ius* is the object of *iustitia,* in response to the fourteenth-century objections of Jean Buridan. In the seventeenth century this defence retains more or less the same shape as it had in Soto half a century earlier.[68] Buridan had argued that Thomas's definition was mistaken: *ius* could not be defined in terms of *iustitia;* derived philologically from *iubere,* to command, a *ius* was simply "a law." The scholastics replied to this in two steps: invoking the distinction between general and particular justice, they defended Thomas's definition for particular justice, but not for general justice, the sum of all the virtues; they then allowed Buridan's definition as a secondary sense of the word. This gave them, effectively, three senses of *ius:* (1) right in general; (2) right in particular, the "strict" sense of right, the object of justice; and (3) a law.

The other concern, peculiar to the early-seventeenth-century scholastics, is to incorporate the subjective sense of *ius* as *facultas* together with the Thomist sense in a single definitional framework. The earlier writers had introduced the subjective sense, mediated from Gerson by Conrad Summenhart, as part of an excursus on *dominium* that grew up around commentary on question 62.[69] Clearly it was unsatisfactory to have a different sense of *ius* in play at this point from that which had been generally defined, and the facultative right which was acknowledged as a feature of property had somehow to be included in the threefold (or twofold, subdivided) definitional framework. The seventeenth-century scholastics were not of one mind on how this was to be done: Lessius kept it as a distinct sense, though listing it together with the others; Molina and Suárez were clear that it belonged with the "strict" sense, right as the object of justice. "In accordance with the latter, narrower sense of *ius* we often hear *ius* described as a 'moral faculty', which one may have either over one's property or over something owed."[70]

This threefold exposition of *ius* bears eloquent testimony to the difficulty which Thomas's commentators had with Thomas's legacy on this subject. Not only had Thomas denied that *ius* could mean the same as *lex,* a point too contrary to common speech to sustain, but he had, with remarkable freedom,

68. D. di Soto, *De iustitia et iure* 3.1, 4.1.

69. The ancestry is made clear in Vitoria, *Commentarius de iustitia* q. 62.5. On the relation of this excursus in Vitoria and Soto to the legacy of Scotist commentary on *Sentences* 4.15, see Annabel S. Brett, *Liberty, Right and Nature* (Cambridge: Cambridge University Press, 1997), pp. 123-64.

70. Suárez, *De legibus* 1.2.5: *Et iuxta posteriorem et strictam iuris significationem solet proprie ius vocari facultas quaedam moralis, quam unusquisque habet vel circa rem suam, vel ad rem sibi debitam.*

turned the Aristotelian way of distinguishing general from special justice on its head. Justice, he wrote, was *always* a special virtue, the virtue concerned with the relation of *aequalitas* to other people. "General justice" was not the totality of all virtues, but a special case of this special virtue practiced with an eye to the common good rather than to the particular claimant. This, again, was too much for his seventeenth-century admirers to swallow whole. So Suárez, like Soto before him, provides a definition of the first sense of *ius* closer to Aristotle's than to Thomas's idea of general justice: "it means the whole of virtue, since every virtue contributes and achieves equity in some way or other"; while his definition of the second sense reflects not Aristotle's but Thomas's conception of particular virtue: "the equity due in justice to each individual." With these two ill-matched definitions the notion of the common good falls between the two stools. No longer, as in Thomas, does it determine the first sense of *ius,* nor, as in Aristotle, is it an aspect of the second sense. There is no just order to mediate between a general virtue on the one hand and a series of particular demands on the other.

This is precisely the position that lies behind Grotius's occasional suggestions about the meaning of right in the *De Imperio* (1618).[71] But before attending to Grotius's revision of the threefold scheme in *IBP,* we should consider a preliminary sketch for it that we find in the opening chapters of the *Jurisprudence of Holland:*

[1.1.3] Just is what corresponds with right.

[4] Right is understood widely or narrowly.

[5] Right widely understood is the correspondence of the act of a reasonable being with reason, in so far as another person is interested in such act.

[6] Right narrowly understood is the relation which exists between a reasonable being and something appropriate to him by merit or property.

[7] Merit is the fitness of a reasonable being for any object of desire.

[8] Property means that something is called ours: it consists, as will be seen, in real rights and personal rights.

[9] The justice which has regard to right widely understood is termed by learned men either "universal justice" (because it comprises virtuous acts of every kind, but in a particular aspect, namely so far as the same serve to maintain any society of men) or "legal justice" (because its extent is coincident with law, and it takes from the laws its measure and norm).

[10] Of the justice which has regard to right narrowly understood the

---

71. 5.11: *Ius hic vocamus facultatem moralem quam iustitia specialis considerat.*

kind which takes account of merit is called distributive justice; the other kind which gives heed to property is called "commutative justice": the first commonly employs the rule of proportion, the second the rule of simple equality. . . .

[1.2.1] Law (which is also sometimes called Right because it determines what is right) is a product of reason ordaining for the common good what is honourable, established and published by one who has authority over a community of men.[72]

The threefold scholastic definition has been adopted in a comprehensive way: (1) the wider sense, (2) the narrower sense, and (3) right as law. The difference between (1) and (2) is explained in terms of Aristotle's first distinction, with a classically scholastic account of general justice in terms of the virtues. The designation "strict" still serves to differentiate (2) from (1). But Grotius has innovated by subdividing (2) with the aid of Aristotle's second distinction, as he will again in *IBP.* That distinction has not yet been stripped of a version of Aristotle's doctrine of proportion, but it has shed its scholastic elaboration in terms of political agents. In order to incorporate this distinction into the scholastic definition, Grotius has devised the term "merit" (*waerdigheid,* corresponding to ἀξία, the later *aptitudo*) in parallel to "property" (*toebehoren*). Steps have thus been taken to overcome the problem of an unfilled gap between general right and proprietorial subjective right. But when we turn to the *IBP* itself, we find that more has been done.

The disappearance of the whole complex of ideas surrounding the first Aristotelian distinction is the most striking feature in his new formulation. The distinction of general and particular, the reference to all the virtues converging on the common good, are gone. Grotius has reached the decision that duties relating to other virtues than justice itself are not justiciable, and so have no place in a definition of *ius.* In the only passage of *IBP* that touches the problematic of general justice he tells us that "if anyone has a duty that springs from some other virtue than proper (i.e., particular) justice, e.g., liberality, kindness, mercy, affection, it can no more be insisted on by armed force than it can be exacted in the lawcourt."[73] So Grotius's version of (1) heads off, after the familiar initial assertion that *ius* is *quod est iustum,* in a new direction, with a striking

---

72. Trans. R. W. Lee. The work was written during Grotius's capitivity in 1620, but the version we now know was authorized by him in 1631, and we cannot be quite sure how exactly it corresponds to the original. Latin terms inserted in the margin appear to be the editor's work, and display the conventional forms, *distributiva* and *commutativa.*

73. 2.22.16: *Si quis quid debet, non ex iustitia propria, sed ex virtute alia, puta liberalitate, gratia, misericordia, dilectione, id sicut in foro exigi non potest, ita nec armis deposci.*

double negative: "'just' being understood in a negative rather than a positive sense, to mean 'what is not unjust'. 'Unjust', in turn, means what is inconsistent with the nature of a society of rational beings. . . ." To compare this with the corresponding definition in *Jurisprudence* is to see how Grotius has strengthened the mediation of virtue into law. In place of "the correspondence of the act of a reasonable being with reason in so far as another person is interested in such act" we encounter Right as *the negation of the negation of sociality.* This new formulation is, it should be observed, decisively Protestant. Right relates to sociality as the correction of its failure, not as a goal of its fulfillment. Sin, rather than sociality itself, is the reason for turning good into objective right, and so into subjective right. Yet equally decisively, sociality, not individual virtue, is the ground on which right rests; on that crucial point Grotius is with the scholastics, not the humanists.

Sense (1), Grotius insists, is the original from which the other two senses flow. This is no longer merely a list of the meanings of the term in relation to its proposed etymologies, as in Suárez. It is, as always with Grotius, an attempt to expound the whole subject matter of jurisprudence from fundamental principles. But the fundamental principle is now sociality, mediated by the double negation into objective right. The marginalization from which the common good suffered in the scholastic account, pushed aside by a "strict" special Right that was dominated in its turn by subjective right, is now reversed. The new account establishes "what is just" as the real source of the second and the third senses, not a preliminary concession later to be sidelined. The title of the book, *On the Right of War and Peace,* he tells us, is meant in the *first* place to pose the questions, "Is war just?" and "What is just in war?" Not, e.g., "Who has rights in war?" for though such questions are discussed in the book, they are secondary. This strictly consequential ordering is reinforced by the fact that sense (2) is no longer designated as "strict" in relation to (1); that designation is reserved for the contrast between (2a) and (2b). Subjective right is not more "strictly" right in comparison with general right; it is merely that expletive right is more "strictly" *subjective* right in comparison with assignative right. The effect of the relocation of the epithet is to establish objective right, the negation of the negation of sociality, as the foundational concept from which its secondary (subjective) and tertiary (legal) applications then follow.

Grotius's second major change to the scholastic pattern, which brings us back to the general concern of this essay, is the use of the second Aristotelian distinction to divide sense (2) into a more narrowly and a more widely conceived subjective right. The scholastics had never thought to introduce the second distinction at this point; for although the distinction between commutative and distributive was understood to be a division of *iustitia particularis,* it was not invoked in the definition of *ius*. Their order of discussion had followed the sequence of questions in *Secunda Secundae,* where *ius* is discussed in question 57, but the commutative-distributive distinction is introduced only in question 61. So the effect of Grotius's two changes taken together is to introduce the second of Aristotle's distinctions into the definition of *ius* precisely while excluding the traditional use of the first. This involves further consequential adaptations: since the Gersonian term *facultas* is required for the "strict" subjective right (2a), two new terms have to be found, *qualitas* for the overall definition and *aptitudo* for the looser right (2b). Grotius's (2a), which has a strongly proprietorial cast, corresponds closely to Suárez's (2); but his (2b) does not correspond to anything in the scholastic model. Tuck's final verdict on *iustitia assignatrix* is that it amounts to "claims upon other people for their assistance which . . . was not really part of the system of natural right." That is to say, the intention in locating the wider sense of right alongside the strict sense was simply to make it disappear. "There could be no true distributive justice."[74] We have now found reason to judge that this cannot be so. It was Grotius's own innovative decision to introduce Aristotle's second distinction into the tradition at this point.

Grotius understood primary objective right as constituted by the prohibition of wrong; it was the negation of injustice. Within the framework created by that prohibition there lay a range of permitted activities which could be called "right" *reductive,* by inference.[75] That is to say, any one of these activities would be "right" in general terms, simply by virtue of not falling under the prohibition of primary right; but that was not the same as saying that it was *the* right thing to do, i.e., the one thing that at a given time in given circumstances ought to be done. The idea of "the right thing to do" comes into view only with secondary right. This gives us the answer to the question of why Grotius introduces his wider sense at this point in his analysis, and not earlier. We may find an action demanded of us as "the right thing to do" *not only* as we are presented with a fully made out proprietorial claim demanding simple implementation, but as we encounter a situation marked by fitnesses, where something is required to be done, but demands the exercise of prudence in order to be done. What Grotius intends to establish, in other words, is the place of *judgment* in the positive enacting of right.[76] The field of right is not divided into a series of permissions, on the one hand, right in the minimal sense that the activities are

74. *Rights,* p. 98; *Natural Rights,* p. 75. This is another point at which Tuck joins hands with a tradition of Whig interpretation. William Whewell's note on the passage (Cambridge: Cambridge University Press, 1853) makes the same claim.

75. *IBP* 1.1.10.3.

76. For the importance Grotius assigns to *iudicium* cf. *De Imperio* 5.1-7.

not prohibited as such, and a series of concrete expletive claims of a proprietorial sort on the other. Our concrete obligations are not divided between the negative duty of not flouting prohibitions, on the one hand, and the mere enactment of moral *faits accomplis* on the other. We have a duty of responsibility which outruns subjective rights. The qualified candidate who has no right to assert (not even a "benefit right" that someone else could assert for him) nevertheless constitutes a positive obligation. The right that confronts us, we may say, is not *his* right, but the right *of his situation*.

This prepares the way, finally, for the third sense of right, that of "law," which is rendered in Thomistic terms as a rule of action. It follows in the same consequential order from what has gone before, since the formulation of a binding law or rule derives from the recognition of the particular claims of rightholders on one hand and fitnesses on the other. Law can be seen as the objectification of specified obligation. This sense of right, too, is important to Grotius's discussion, since his project has in view treating the *right* of war quite seriously as a *law* of war, formed by custom and convention in international practice. An adequate law of war could not be framed on the basis of expletive claims alone. It must take account of subjective rights; but the concept of subjective right requires the concept "expletive justice" to explain it, and "expletive justice" requires "assignative justice" to complement it. Aristotle's insight that there is more to justice than fair exchange corresponds to Grotius's double contention that there is more to justice than strict proprietorial right and more to the right of war than enforcing strict right-claims; and both these two contentions enter into the determination of what is and may be considered to be law. Without Aristotle's second distinction the full scope of *ius* as law cannot be unfolded.

In conclusion, it is hardly wonderful that Grotius entertained a subjective sense of right. Given the discussions in law and jurisprudence which he inherited, its presence was to be assumed; not only humanist influences but late scholastic influences ensured a central place for the idea. The question of interest is whether he anticipated later seventeenth-century thinkers in making subjective right foundational. The indications we have found suggest that Grotius's leading concern was in the opposite direction, to qualify the dominance of subjective right. From the late scholastics Grotius also inherited a structural concern to integrate subjective right into an objective conception, and his efforts in this regard did more than theirs to guard the subjective notion against totalization. He articulated a stronger and more decisive conception of objective primary right as a foundation, and broadened the idea of subjective right itself, stretching it beyond its paradigm connection with entitlement and ownership to delineate a kind of social justice. This was to look in the opposite direction from later theorists, such as Locke and Pufendorf, who attempted to derive the whole nature of a society of rational beings from the original right of the individual, the *dominium sui*. It brought forward the notion of a non-entitling "fitness," a correspondence of actor to social role, that must be prudently discerned in assigning benefits and burdens, and this belonged every bit as much to the justice required of law as proprietory right itself did. With assignative justice Grotius lifted the law of war out of the marketplace of private claims.

PART 2

Contemporary Themes:
Liberal Democracy, the Nation-State,
Localities, and Internationalism

a proper acknowledgement that, for most of us at least, the Enlightenment and its aftermath has happened, and theology has to live with that also. Rather, it would seem, beneath every hermeneutical gesture which acknowledges difference and multiplicity lurks a form of violence 'upon narratives that make claims in excess of the proportions of polite restraint' (p. 424).

It is precisely that which is missing from this work—a polite restraint, and therefore a beauty, not least in language, and a preparedness to listen that would give the claims of the book more legitimacy. This is a book of huge and often profound learning that, by its attitude and rhetoric ultimately does no good to the very theology and claims that it seeks to celebrate.

doi:10.1093/jts/fli070

DAVID JASPER
University of Glasgow

Bonds of Imperfection: Christian Politics, Past and Present. By OLIVER O'DONOVAN and JOAN LOCKWOOD O'DONOVAN. Pp. vi + 324. Grand Rapids, MI: William B. Eerdmans, 2004. ISBN 0 8028 4975 X. Paper $35/£24.99.

TO get at the heart of this outstanding book, stemming from lectures and articles, the reader needs not only the authors' *From Irenaeus to Grotius: A Source Book in Christian Political Thought* but a good knowledge of the 'classics' of the subject from Plato to Nato! We range here through theology, ethics, and political theory to the controversies facing the prevailing liberal–democratic institutions of the West, where many have lost what Oliver O'Donovan calls 'a sense of place'. The commonplaces of modern politics and human rights may not be thought normative, by what Roger Scruton calls 'the Rest', in a strangely apocalyptic world.

The historian may ask different questions about both the past and the present, so I raise matters which some of the chapters have stimulated, knowing that there is much more to be said. First the Book of Revelation. Oliver O'Donovan writes of 'God's decision to constitute history', meaning that 'written history should make God known ... at the heart of politics is true speech, divine speech entering into conflict with the false orders of human society, the guarantor of the only true order that the universe can ever attain' (p. 47). But what can the politician make of apocalypse, when it is so often the breeding ground of pre-millennial fanaticism, as well as the hope and New Creation which Christopher Rowland and Richard Baukham rightly stress? Was Sir Herbert Butterfield's Augustinian stance more realistic? We face the judgement of God's 'formidable non-intervention'.

We move to Augustine's *City of God*, which has so dominated Western Christian thought, protestant as well as Roman Catholic. Can we still speak of what A. D. Lindsay called 'the realm of grace' and 'the realm of my station and its duties'? Remove *justitia* and what are governments still but gangs of criminals on a large scale—the Saddam Husseins and Mugabes of our world? Is the Lutheran style of the 'two kingdoms' to be entirely dismissed? O'Donovan makes no mention of Cargill Thompson's sophisticated attempt to rehabilitate it. In the end are Christian leaders wise to disguise their advice on political matters as common sense—Gregory VII can hardly rise again, but can there be an equivalent of Oliver Cromwell's 'I beseech you in the bowels of Christ, think it possible you may be mistaken'? The late medieval and early modern thinkers from Gerson to Grotius still have their relevance. Wyclif reminds us of the danger of clerical power, shown later at the Council of Constance which burned Hus. Medieval views on wealth and usury reminded me of John Wesley's desire for a 'community of goods'—I fear his followers preferred 'possessive individualism' (p. 74). What can this say now to a community of borrowers?

Then Erasmus, the Flying Dutchman, appears. He rejected the just war theory, since no one says: 'My war is unjust' and there is no impartial umpire. Clearly the churches need to look again at the concept of just war. Much thinking still echoes the 'cold war'—Paul Ramsey is still relevant here. On many matters it is fascinating to compare the O'Donovans' approach to the Western Latin tradition with that of the Anglican monk–historian John Neville Figgis, who explored much of the same ground with prophetic acumen a century ago.

What now? Joan O'Donovan explores the relevance of Catholic social thinking from *Rerum Novarum* (1891) to the present Pope. How does that modern Thomism (Jacques Maritain reappears) apply to the concept of 'subsidiarity' so important in the European community, which is in danger of being pushed into secularism by fear of Catholic power and Islam? This is a positive contribution, replacing the older views of the state stemming from idealism, utilitarianism, and Marxism.

Much of what many of us have written on church, state,
and society seems feeble compared with the quality of this
book. It deserves a wide readership but I wonder how many
polititians will take it on and consider late medieval thought
as part of their agenda?

doi:10.1093/jts/fli071   JOHN MUNSEY TURNER
                                                Bolton, Lancashire

God and Realism. By PETER BYRNE. Pp. xii + 187. (Ashgate
Philosophy of Religion Series.) Aldershot: Ashgate, 2003.
ISBN 0 7546 1461 1 and 1467 0. Hardback £45; paper
£16.99.

THERE is no denying that some realities depend on human
practices and institutions. Money, for example. A British pound
coin *is* a pound coin because of certain laws and customs
prevailing in the United Kingdom. Most people, however, would
suppose that the metal of which the coin is made did not
depend on any human practice or institution, but existed quite
independently of us. Nevertheless, some thinkers in recent years
seem quite genuinely to deny this. An extreme form of what
Byrne calls 'anti-realism' (which may not actually be held by
anybody) would hold that the world is created entirely by our
representations of and speech about it; a less extreme (which
certainly has been held), that although there is some reality
independent of us, its features, such as objects and qualities,
are our constructions. And of course if objects and qualities
have no reality apart from us, then presumably the same
applies to God. Moreover, we have seen the odd spectacle of
people, including not just philosophers but parish clergy, who
would not necessarily hold this view as regards the world
in general, but who do hold it where God is concerned. They
avow a Christianity which lets them disbelieve in God, or rather
(they would say) to affirm his existence in a purely non-realistic
sense.

    The first part of Byrne's book (after he has made a number
of distinctions and definitions for clarity's sake) is devoted to
discussing the more general thesis and defending, by contrast,
what he calls (after Susan Haack) 'innocent realism', the doctrine
that 'for the most part, the world exists independently of us
and of our representations of it'. This takes up more than half
the book, because there are a number of different justifications

for anti-realism, each of which needs to be dealt with separately. There is, for example, the relativism of Joseph Runzo. According to this, there are different world-views or 'conceptual schemas'; each is in itself valid, and no two delimit the same world. All truth is relative to our conceptual schemas.

As Byrne points out, this is really a distortion of an undoubted fact, that the meaning of statements ('truth-bearers') depends in part on the concepts we use to frame them. Runzo is going further, and asserting that this also holds for the facts these statements are about (the 'truth-makers')—which does not follow—and concluding that apparently contradictory beliefs can each be true relative to the conceptual schema of the believer. There is what Byrne rightly calls 'a slide from sensible, arguable positions into...absurdity'. People interpret the world differently; therefore they experience it differently; therefore they live in different experienced worlds, therefore there is no objective world for them to experience. Where religion is concerned, Runzo does allow a noumenal Reality behind our religious worlds; but are we really allowed to say even this much about something that is purely noumenal?

Next, Byrne tackles elements surviving from logical positivism (not necessarily the same elements) in Robin Le Poidevin, Michael Scott, and Michael Dummett. Much of this is going over fairly familiar ground, but Byrne does it very effectively. Scott confuses the need for rules for the use of a term (such as 'God') and rules for collecting evidence to show whether there is anything the term refers to. Le Poidevin in effect rules out a real God in advance by treating 'existence' as the same as 'having spatio-temporal location'. And Dummett, in some ways resembling Scott, by advocating a verificationist theory of meaning, makes it unnecessary to hold also a verificationist theory of truth (which is what the non-realist needs).

Lastly (in this first section) Byrne tackles the 'postmodernists', whom he regards as indulging in 'magical' modes of thought: what we do with our symbols controls reality. The later Don Cupitt and certain feminists are his main targets here; I think perhaps he gives the impression that *all* feminists are postmodernists, which is not really fair. But his demolition of those who are (and of Cupitt) is devastating. Or at least it would be, if it did not depend on a rationality which they would probably reject with scorn. Byrne now moves on to deal with 'contrastive' anti-realism, which agrees that there is an independently existing world, but not an independently existing God. He sees the roots of this in Feuerbach, and its appeared in 1977, the last in 2004, and this is a long enough space to shake their determination that each article shall be up-to-date with modern research, especially when they determined on such excellent bibliographies. We are still promised an index volume to the whole. They have created an essential tool for Reformation studies and also, for patristic. It is pleasing that this volume begins with a full article on Wigand, the first of modern church historians, and later has thoughtful considerations of *Zeitgeschichte, Kirchliche*. As usual the German biblical critics of the nineteenth century are well represented, here Wrede the most impressive. Z is an important letter, with Zwingli and then Zürich at the top, and with our Cs, like Censorship and Celibacy (important) and the Centre Party (not very full); and studies of the complexities of tithe and rates of interest, and Jehovah's Witnesses and Glossolalia (*Zungenrede*) and Cyprus. Wyclif has an unusually long article. Württemberg is given the length it deserves. They always illuminate the history of universities – here Wittenberg and Würzburg and Yale.

SELWYN COLLEGE,   OWEN CHADWICK
CAMBRIDGE

Reviewed by
me in JTS April 2005.

Bonds of imperfection. Christian politics, past and present. By Oliver O'Donovan and Joan Lockwood O'Donovan. Pp. vi+324. Grand Rapids, MI–Cambridge: Eerdmans, 2004. £24.99 ($35) (paper). 0 8028 4975 X
JEH (56) 2005; doi:10.1017/S0022046905234383

Bonds of imperfection forms a companion piece to the authors' previous work, *From Irenaeus to Grotius: a sourcebook in Christian political thought*. The latter is an overview of the history of Christian political thought from the years to 1625, and is comprised of primary source texts with brief introductions and commentaries. The former provides a sustained analysis and application of significant figures, themes and developments from within this history. The work is mostly composed of previously published essays spanning nearly two decades, and is divided into two parts with part I treating 'moments' in the theological-political tradition and part II addressing contemporary themes. Part I covers a wide range of topics, including a rich study of the Book of Revelation and John's vision of the political; a probing survey of medieval usury theory; a fresh analysis of Erasmus' ethical poetics and its contribution to Christian social and political thought; and an exploration of jurist-theologian Hugo Grotius' understanding of distributive justice as it comes to him through its Aristotelian and Thomistic legacy. A particularly interesting essay is Joan Lockwood O'Donovan's 'The challenge and the promise of proto-modern Christian political thought'. O'Donovan challenges modern democracy's emphasis on populist and egalitarian elaborations of rights and self-government with the late medieval and early modern notions of 'God's continuing sovereignty over civil polity, the juridical task of civil government, and the waywardness of the multitude' (p. 165). This highlights a common theme throughout part I and indeed the book, namely, that the history of Christian political thought is marked by 'the sphere of judgment, divine and human, that gives order to the human community in history' (p. 2). Part II continues this theme by way of a discussion of Catholic social thought and subsidiarity; a comparison of Karl Barth's and Paul Ramsey's understanding of political power and force; and an evaluation of the modern notion of the nation state in the light of a theological understanding of 'the nation'. An important essay is Oliver O'Donovan's 'Government as judgment'. O'Donovan contends that the modern period locates political authority, especially legislative and judicial acts, in 'the people', as opposed to the late medieval and early modern periods when political life was rooted in natural and revealed divine law. Consequently, modern democracy is not capable of true judgement and therefore must assert its authority by way of legislation, resulting in a 'tyranny of legislative rationality' (p. 14). In the end, students of western and Christian political history will find something of interest among the essays of part I, and those interested in how the Christian tradition bears on contemporary political issues and problems will find ample resources for further thought and challenge in part II. With this collection of essays, there can be no doubt that Joan and Oliver O'Donovan have established themselves as leading thinkers in the growing field of both historical and contemporary political theology.

PRINCETON THEOLOGICAL SEMINARY   TODD V. CIOFFI

Religious identity and the problem of historical foundation. The foundational character of authoritative sources in the history of Christianity and Judaism. Edited by Judith Frishman, Willemien Otten and Gerard Rouwhorst. (Jewish and Christian Perspectives, 8.) Pp. x + 589. Leiden–Boston: Brill, 2004. €139. 90 04 13021 7; 1388 2074
JEH (56) 2005; doi:10.1017/S002204690524438X

This large book reproduces the papers read at a conference organised recently by church historians at the University of Utrecht and the Catholic Theological University of Utrecht. It treats of the question how sources have been used to establish and maintain the distinctive identity of Jewish and Christian groups. Rather surprisingly, no indication is given of the nationality, religious affiliation or academic position of the contributors, but it seems clear that they mostly hail from the Low Countries, and that is to some extent reflected in the subject matter of the papers. For example, there is a long chapter on university education as a mark of ministerial identity in nineteenth-century Dutch Protestantism, another on notions of identity in the nineteenth-century Dutch Reformed Church and a third on the theological formation of Roman Catholic clergy in eighteenth- and nineteenth-century Holland. Nevertheless, the scope of the contributions is wide, and the book works back from opening chapters concerned with questions about religion and modernity, through discussions of Reformation and medieval topics, to closing chapters dealing with the use made of biblical and patristic authority in the early Church. The papers vary considerably in their breadth of treatment and they are not informed by any common thesis. The title of the book seems more central to some of the contributions than to others. In a short review it is not possible to comment on all the twenty-eight contributions individually, and if a few are chosen for mention the choice will no doubt reflect the interests of the reviewer rather than the relative excellence of the papers themselves. No. 19 is an interesting treatment of authority and interpretation in scholastic theology, which reveals, for example, how Peter Lombard challenged Paul's teaching on celibacy, and dealt with the problem in a strikingly modern way. No. 18 casts a good deal of light on immediately pre-scholastic theology, while no. 25 opens up a discussion of how

Government as Judgment

OLIVER O'DONOVAN

The democracies that emerged victorious from the Second World War, in undertaking to entrench human rights against the cruel politics of power, left
themselves with a major problem of self-understanding, a cleft running deep
through the heart of democratic theory. The terms "democracy" and "human
rights" do not mean the same thing, and they do not refer to the same thing.
Whether democracy is compatible with human rights depends on two contingent factors: how the democratic societies conduct themselves, and what rights
human beings assert. One cannot champion "democracy and human rights"
without quite quickly having to decide which takes precedence between them, a
question to which there is no formally and universally correct answer; since either of those terms, and not just one of them, may from time to time be used as
a cloak for self-interest and tyranny, there is no universally correct answer. That
is the underlying problem of coherence in contemporary Western ideology.

My interest here, however, lies not with that problem, but with one deriving from it, a constitutional problem about the judicial review of legislation:
"legislation by courts" as it is often alleged to be, which in the service of human
or civil rights deprives lawmaking of democratic accountability. This problem
has often been addressed as a question for U.S. constitutional theory, in terms
of a shift in the traditional relation between the legislative and judicial branches
of government. But this is not the only possible constitutional form that the
problem may take. Similar difficulties confront European societies with other
constitutional traditions. The constitution of the Republic of Ireland, for example, has acquired the shape of a baggy Aran sweater, full of detailed amend-

---

Originally delivered as the 1998 Erasmus Lecture at the Institute on Religion and Public
Life, New York, and published in *First Things* 92 (1999): 36-44.

ments that would never belong in such a document had not the Supreme Court at some point in time maintained the opposite. Even the constitution of the United Kingdom, boasting a radical centralization of authority in parliament, meets the same problem through its adherence to the European Convention of Human Rights, with its attendant Commission and Court.[1]

It is natural to suppose that the solution lies in recovering early-modern doctrines about the separation of three powers of government. These doctrines derive originally from the fourteenth-century Italian thinker, Marsiglio of Padua, who distinguished the "legislator," the people itself or its representatives, from those who implemented the laws, in domestic adjudication on the one hand and against external threats on the other. Yet there is a difficulty with this approach: on the all-important question early-modern thinkers achieved no stable consensus to which we may appeal. We may compare two forms in which the separation of powers was argued, with contradictory emphases, within a fifty-year period at the turn of the eighteenth century. Locke and Montesquieu both claimed to base their observations on the best English practice; both affirmed three distinct powers of government (though only Montesquieu used their modern names, and only Locke used the word "separate"); and yet they are very different. In Locke's theory the greatest point of 'separation' is still between the originating legislature and the two consequential branches of government. The consequential branches are not so distinct from one another, since they must, Locke thought, rest in the same hands — so saving the face of the British monarchy.[2] But Montesquieu articulated something resembling the familiar three-leaved shamrock pattern, an equal distance separating each of the branches. He required also that the separation be concrete, with the different branches of government in the hands of different people. From these two perspectives, which provided matrices for later British and U.S. constitutional practice respectively, the causes of our current problem and its likely solution, appear quite different.

Moreover, Christian thinkers have their own reasons for not being content with a return to early-modern sources, for they have a long theological tradition in which judicial and legislative activities are related quite differently. This should raise the question, at least, whether the root of the problem lies not in recent neglect of early-modern theory, but in early-modern neglect of the yet earlier Christian understanding. What the Christian tradition maintained, and

1. The European Convention on Human Rights and its Five Protocols, in I. Brownlie, ed., *Basic Documents on Human Rights*, 2nd ed. (Oxford: Oxford University Press, 1981), pp. 242-65.

2. *Two Treatises* 2.13.151. Having "a share in the legislative," the executive was "in a very tolerable sense . . . supreme."

the early-modern thinkers denied, was the *primacy of the act of judgment.* And this primacy entailed a distinctive understanding of the task of legislation, which explains more satisfactorily the nature and scope of the legislator's authority over courts. In what follows, I shall first sketch the history of pre-modern Christian thought on the subject; second, suggest how it supports a superior account of the branches of government, and finally, return briefly to our problem, the right and limits of judicial review of legislation.

I

Jesus has ascended in triumph to God's right hand; yet the subdued "authorities" of this age, St. Paul maintained, "persist."[3] This, he said, was to approve good conduct and "to execute God's wrath on the wrongdoer." The reign of Christ in heaven has left *judgment* as the single remaining political need. We should remark that this was an unprecedentedly lean doctrine of civil government. Judgment alone never comprised the whole of what ancient peoples, least of all the Jews, thought government was about. Paul's conception stripped government of its representative, identity-conferring functions, and said nothing about law. He conceded, as it were, the least possible function that would account for its place within God's plan. The secular princes of this earth, shorn of pretensions to our loyalty and worship, are left with the sole function of judging between innocent and guilty.

1. In later centuries it was Latin speaking Western Christendom that adhered most fully to Paul's conception. "Jurisdiction" was the term that came to define that ever-fascinating and difficult relation between church and state. Courts were the central locus of government, for church as for kingdom. Human government was understood to differ from that of God, notably (for our purposes) in that God is a legislator as well as judge. His law provides human judges with a sufficient basis for their judgments; and the Latin Church Fathers were frankly suspicious of human attempts to add to it. "The term 'rights'," says Augustine, "cannot be applied to the inequitable constitutions of men."[4] What rulers do when they act obediently to their vocation is to apply divine law to the infinite possibilities of human wrongdoing. Still in the later Middle Ages, an Augustinian idealist, John Wyclif, harked back to this suspicion, representing

3. Rom. 13:6: εἰς αὐτὸ τοῦτο προσκαρτεροῦντες, "persisting for this very purpose," or perhaps, "to this very day," not, as contemporary translators prefer, "attending to this very thing" (RSV). See also pp. 227, 288-89.

4. *City of God* 19.21. Cf. also Ambrose's words to the Emperor Valentinian: "The law of God has taught us what to follow; human laws cannot teach us this" (*Ep.* 75.10).

the ideal judge in his court with "no law but natural law. . . . It would be the best form of government for a people to be ruled solely through the law of God by judges."[5]

In Eastern Christendom a difference of emphasis is noticeable. Here the way was beaten for the church by the greatest Jewish thinker of the classical world, Philo of Alexandria (ca. 20 B.C.–A.D. 50). Philo conceived Jewish social existence partly in contrast with, partly in correspondence to, the political experience of a Greek city-state, constituted by the work of a "legislator" (nomothetēs). Lawgiving in the Hellenistic world was thought of as foundation, the creation of a polis by the creation of a distinctive corpus of law. As Lycurgus was to Sparta and Solon to Athens, so, according to Philo, was Moses to the Jewish politeia, though he was unique in that he was directly inspired by the Logos or Reason of God. Also taken over from a Hellenistic commonplace about government was the conception that Moses was empsuchos nomos, a "living law."[6] The Christian Clement, a fellow-citizen of Alexandria, followed Philo's lead gladly. Now the lawgiver was Christ, the Logos himself, whom Moses had uniquely anticipated and represented.[7]

Yet this did not really lead Greek-speaking Christians in a different direction from the Latin-speaking West. The tendency of Hellenistic Christendom to allow a direct analogy between Christ the Logos and earthly rulers is notorious. But even when that analogy was most developed, as in Eusebius's panegyric on Constantine, there was no hint that Christ's role as lawgiver could be transferred to the earthly ruler. Law was a feature of all earthly government, but law-keeping rather than lawmaking was its characteristic activity; there was simply "lawful government."[8] In the East, too, the subject of human law-making is still passed over in silence. The term nomothetēs and its cognates is hardly ever applied to the emperor by theologians, though in secular writing it was common. And in 530 when Justinian acceded to the imperial throne in Byzantium, a work of exhortation addressed to him by a theologian insisted, among other things, on his being subject to law, but contained virtually no acknowledgment that the task of this most famous imperial jurist would include making law.[9]

2. That this is not at all the situation among the thinkers of the high Middle Ages is due to two influences, of whom Justinian himself, at a remove, was one. Through the growth of Western jurisprudence out of the legacy of his Corpus of Civil Law, Justinian came to be regarded as a model for the Christian law-

5. Civil Dominion 1.27 (62d).

6. Life of Moses 2.1.3f.

7. Stromateis 1.24-7. IG, pp. 30-38.

8. Speech on the Anniversary of Constantine's Accession 4. IG, pp. 56-65.

9. Agapetos, Heads of Advice. IG, pp. 180-88.

maker, and the description of human government came to include lawmaking as a dimension. But lawmaking was not understood simply as legal innovation. Justinian's influence served to dignify, above all, the task of codification; and the term *legis lator,* when it appears in the twelfth century, refers primarily to the early jurists who ordered and systematized the Roman law. The other influence was that of Aristotle, with whom the classical conception of legal foundation reenters the stream of Western thought. In the *Politics* and *Ethics* the term *nomothetēs* is applied not only to the legal founders of city-states, Lycurgus and Solon, but also to political theorists who advanced overarching proposals for social organization. Plato is one of Aristotle's *nomothetai,* and democracy and oligarchy are among his instances of *nomothesia.*

The Justinianic conception can be seen at its most persuasive in St. Thomas's great treatise on law in the *Summa Theologiae.*[10] The structuring of a social order requires, Thomas thinks, not merely the *application* of divine law, natural or revealed, but a *lex humana,* a "positive law" which is to *determine* matters otherwise left unresolved. The *ius ponendi leges,* the "right of making law," was the mark of a sovereign prince. Still, the authority of human lawmakers reposes on divine law, to which human law may never stand in contradiction. So the positive aspect of human lawmaking is safeguarded by a negative proposition: that a law defying natural or revealed law has no standing at all.[11] The influence of Aristotle, however, is particularly strong in another work attributed to Thomas (falsely, I am inclined to think), the variously named *On Kingship, to the King of Cyprus* or *On Princely Rule.* "We must first and principally expound the king's duty," the author tells us, "from the institution of the state or kingdom. . . . The name of Romulus would be unknown today, had he not founded Rome."[12] Those words, startling to ears attuned to early medieval political reflections, announce the reappearance of legislation as foundation, the concept which the early church had in effect neutralized by confining legislation to Moses and Christ. They attest a situation in which there is interest in how new political communities may be brought into being. At this point, the line between the Aristotelian revival and the early Renaissance seems very thin.

This is the context in which the modern theory of popular sovereignty first saw the light of day. The role of Marsiglio of Padua's *Defensor pacis* (1325) in articulating the new departure is commonly acknowledged, as is the fact that he drew both on Aristotle and Roman law in articulating it. Less commented on

10. *ST* 1a2ae. 90-108. For what follows cf. especially questions 95-96. *IG,* pp. 342-54.

11. This proposition has been vigorously reasserted by Pope John Paul II, *Evangelium Vitae,* pp. 68-74.

12. *De regno* 2.1 (alternatively, 2.5). *IG,* pp. 330-41.

is Marsiglio's startling use of the *term* "legislator," applying it to the people as a whole in the sense of "founding lawgiver." As originating legislator the populace is the primary authorization for any subsequent form or act of government. Legislation is not one of the things that government does; it is the constitutive act that lies behind all government. Even so conceived, however, legislation is ventured only *under God,* who is the author and vindicator of all law. The tradition of "constitutionalism" which arose from Marsiglio's new departure understood the founding legislative act as a response to a divinely given law of nature defining the possibilities of political society. It can arise only as it is authorized by what Wyclif called the *primum ius,* the First Right, i.e., God's. So what now comes to be said about legislation as constitutional foundation is formally parallel to what is said about judgment: as we may judge subject to God's judgment, so we may found lawful societies under God's law.

3. A decisive shift of perspective occurred in the seventeenth century. This was not the result of atheism, for atheism, by and large, came later. But its effect was to make divine law irrelevant to the foundations of political order. The nature and causes of this shift can be described in many ways. It is enough for our purposes to say that the *primum ius* vanished from consideration, so that the act of human foundation ceased to depend on divine foundation, and began to look like a repetition of it. The sovereign arbitrariness of God's creative decree was taken into the human act of founding a society, so that it appeared rather like a creation *ex nihilo,* presupposing no prior law, no preexisting social rationality, a new beginning not merely relatively and politically but absolutely and metaphysically. Legislation thereby became the *foundation of a social rationality.*

In setting out to radicalize the act of human foundation, this change actually destroyed it. The contractarians attempted to answer, without invoking God, the constitutionalists' question about how a civil society could begin. But they could not for long conceal a guilty secret: in reproducing the divine legislative act they had abolished the moment of beginning altogether. Since it seemed *possible* for human society to replicate the original *fiat lux* of God in constituting itself as a sphere of order, it was *necessary* for it to do so; and if it was necessary once, it was necessary again and again. The "beginning" was constantly reenacted, the drama of bringing order out of chaos was the perpetual law of every society's being; and the language of a primitive social contract was unveiled as what on contractarian terms it always had to be, a mere thought experiment to show how society works. With the progress of the early-modern era we see a waning of the Renaissance interest in genuinely new foundations (the North Americans were the last people, perhaps, in a position to draw on that legacy); in its place we find an interest in the possibilities of dissolution and reconstruction within existing societies, an interest in *revolution,* a word that enters the common currency of the West with the events of 1688 in Britain.

This explains the quite innovative place accorded to the legislators by early-modern constitutional theories. As in the Renaissance, legislation is foundational; but foundation is no longer *origin,* but a continuous spring of rationality that sustains the political society in being. In place of the originating assembly that first constituted the political society, the legislature is now a standing branch of government that lays claim to the sovereignty hitherto held by the Head of Government. In this way early-modern theory fulfills the aspirations of ancient democracy; but it does so only indirectly and covertly, since the whole point is (as it never ceases to insist), not the rule of the people but the rule of law. Political society is a lived rationality, of which lawmaking is the source and spring. And as, when government was seen as judgment, God, the supreme judge, was known to be "angry every day," i.e., to hold daily assizes;[13] so now the legislative branch, standing in for the rationality of divine providence, had better not slumber or sleep. An incessant stream of lawmaking is the fundamental proof of political viability.

Against this background we understand our own late-modern crisis. It is, first of all, born of a reaction against this notion of positively legislated rationality, of a desire for freedom to assert right prior to and independent of the "unequal constitutions of men." It responds to a Judeo-Christian impulse. In the postwar documents that express the late-modern faith in human rights, the use of quasi-religious concepts is decisive, as in the UN Declaration of Human Rights, which speaks in its preamble of the "recognition of the inherent dignity and of the equal and inalienable rights of all members of the human family."[14] That the problem of autonomous courts should have come to the fore in *this* period, and in the nations most involved with *those* documents, attests the twentieth-century search for a prepolitical moral ground of law. The distinctive features of the U.S. Constitution merely served as a channel for an anti-positivist reaction common to our civilization. It is, of course, profoundly disappointing that no better alternative should have been found than the fragmented and antisocial notion of "human rights"; but the impulse deserves, for all that, its due recognition and acknowledgment. Our crisis, however, also attests that we have *not* in fact succeeded in breaking with the early-modern concept of positively legislated government. Neither we nor our courts have proved capable of forming a clear idea of what it is to recognize a claim of natural right

---

13. Psalm 7:11.

14. I. Brownlie, ed., *Basic Documents in International Law* (Oxford: Clarendon, 1983), p. 250. On the UN Declaration, see also pp. 280-81, 291-93 below.

without erecting the courts as counter-legislature, an equal and opposite imitation, and so precipitating the crisis over sovereignty.

II

Let us attempt, then, to reconstruct, starting from the Pauline premise that the defining role of secular government is to exercise judgment. In this case, the *court* is the central paradigm of government *in all its branches*.

1. In the simplest model, such as we find in the political pedagogic of Ancient Israel, in the narratives of David and Solomon, and in the Psalms, the monarch is a judge who sits in court. "Morning by morning I will destroy all the wicked in the land," he declares in what is probably a kind of oath of office.[15] Daily assizes are the proof of a just king. Ancient Israel also knew, however, that the task of judgment required not only that the monarch sit in court, but that he also found courts. Three separate Pentateuchal narratives, each with a slightly differing emphasis, explore the logic of this move in relation to Moses. In Exodus 18, the first of these narratives in order of canonical appearance (I imply no conclusions about historical sources), Jethro persuades Moses of the simple fact that the business pressing on any court is far too great for only one judge to deal with. A unified system of justice, then, requires a tiered system of courts in which the ruler hears a case only as the last resort. In the second narrative (Numbers 11) it is recognized that the community possesses a variety of local, family and tribal loyalties which need to be harnessed to the task of judgment, since without their cooperation the ruler cannot achieve his purpose. The third, combining elements of these two, stands in a programmatic place at the opening of that highly programmatic book, Deuteronomy, and employs the concept of law to conflate the monarchical emphasis of the one with the tribal emphasis of the other. The various courts based on tribal identities are held together by the authority of one law, authenticated by the monarch.

Looked at from one angle, this development logically presages the exclusion of the monarch from the judiciary; for as the court of last resort, the monarch should never sit, but rather so act through ministers as to retain one last throw, should it be needed. Yet it also presages a sphere of administrative government in which the monarch *still* exercises judgment, though not in court. For to provide a court in which a judge sits is no less an act of judgment than to sit in court himself. The monarch considers the situation in which those who are wronged lack access to public interest and vindication, finds it wanting, and

15. Ps. 101:8.

redresses it by inaugurating courts. The monarch does not found the judiciary *from outside*, as it were, like a businessman founding a University Chair without himself being a man of learning. The founding of the judiciary is precisely the founding judicial act; it gives judgment in favor of the oppressed. Not in favor of one particular oppressed person in this case, but in favor of the oppressed as a class; yet not a universal class (for the ruler does not undertake to remedy the wrongs of all oppressed people everywhere in every age), but a concrete histori-cal class, the oppressed of *this* kingdom at *this* juncture of history. What can be said about the foundation of courts applies equally to the *maintenance* of courts: the monarch's duty is to keep the courts open. To let "judgment flow like a torrent and vindication like a river in flood," as Amos picturesquely put it,[16] is quite simply a responsibility to exercise conscientious judgment.

What early-modern theorists speak of as "the separation of executive and judiciary" is a distinction *within the single task* of giving judgment, between the originating judgment that founds courts and the dependent judgments that take place in the courts. If we are to express this in other than a monarchical context, we shall need to find some other term than "executive." I shall employ "the Head of Government" to refer to that locus of government to which re-sponsibility for maintaining justice ultimately reverts. For "executive" has built into it the suggestion of a role that is both dependent and non-judicial. When we think in such ways, we run into the troubling modern cleavage between gov-ernment and justice, the idea that there are excellences attainable in govern-ment which are only contingently related to justice. The amoralism of this con-ception of the executive generates an equal and opposite moralism about the judicial task. A justice pursued by courts without prudence is purely formal, and no more satisfying than prudence pursued by executives without justice. Prudence, the provision of what people need, integrally belongs to justice, as justice belongs to prudence.

At the same time, however, as we stress the juridical matrix of all govern-ment, the differentiation of roles must be allowed due space. And not only for the practical reasons that Jethro gave Moses, but because any given instance of wrong may be examined in more than one perspective, more broadly or more narrowly. Faced with a social crisis over drug abuse, for example, we must at-tend practically to the pressing problem of protecting young people against the influence of drug dealers; but we must also attend with impartial minds to the charges of drug dealing brought against *this* person at *this* time and place. We cannot attend to the second, more focused matter if we are preoccupied by the first. ("If this man is acquitted, what sort of message will it send out to drug

16. Amos 5:24.

dealers everywhere?") *Both* ways of practically attending are acts of judgment: *both* are particular, i.e., belonging to a definite time and place and situation; but the second way is more limited in scope, because injustice may be committed on a narrow front when we try to do justice on a broad front. The public interest in justice is an interest in both levels of judgment being pursued, each on its own proper terms. So the government confines itself to policy making, the court excludes policy making. The *sub judice* rule, which is the essential element of truth in the differentiation, protects the examination of narrow questions about individual cases.

But the policy which is the Head of Government's business is not other than *judicial* policy. We depend on rulers keeping an eye on courts, just as we depend on their keeping their hands off cases. If over a significant period courts prove incapable of convicting terrorist offenders, they, or the law they administer, must be reformed. The Head of Government must ensure not only that courts exist, but that they function, those two responsibilities being in fact one and the same. Reasonable expedition of legal process, reasonable restraint of legal fees, reasonable rules of procedure over such matters as the admissibility of evidence, use of juries, and so on — all these are the proper concerns of the Head of Government, who is charged with ensuring that justice, not arbitrary whim, prevails in social relations. Legislation is one form that the discharge of this responsibility takes.

2. In the unfolding of the different moments of human government, the judicial moment comes first, the administrative moment second, and the legislative third. The mistake in the modern tradition was to place legislation first, following the Hellenistic association of legislation and founding. This supposed that law and legislation, *nomos* and *nomothesia*, were coextensive; that without the framework of founding legislation there was no law. The Christian assertion, on the contrary, was that no human creation was ever prior to law, that lawful government never depended upon prior legislation as a precondition. "If 'laws are silent among arms,'" says Hugo Grotius, "it is the *civil* laws that are so . . . not those other laws that are perpetually in force and appropriate for each and every season."[17]

In Hebrew the most general word for law, *tôrah*, meant simply "a decision." It referred to the "ruling" that a priest would give when consulted.[18] In the same way we say that the judge "declares the law" in relation to a case, meaning not that he quotes from lawbooks, but that he announces a decision. "The law of the case" is simply the generic principle applied in the particular judgment. But since judgment is not merely a series of separate and discrete de-

17. *The Right of War and Peace,* Proleg. 26. Translation from *IG,* p. 797.
18. Ex. 18:16, 20; Deut. 17:11.

cisions but a continuous activity, the law of each case is discerned in relation to the law of preceding cases; if it is to be justly proportioned, it cannot be wildly out of line with previous decisions. No act of judgment, then, simply invents law *de novo;* for that would defeat one of the purposes of judging, which is to determine what is proportionate. Each judgment depends on a law derived from many cases, a law of precedent that stands over and behind the present decision and can be appealed to in support or in criticism of it. But a law of precedent requires no distinct human legislator. Divine law, natural or revealed, when mediated through traditions of right innate in the society, is sufficient to allow courts to develop a law by way of their own judgments, a conception which our shared English legal tradition names the "common law."

But when the authority of courts is undermined because they operate on principles repugnant to the community's conscience or because their orders are impossible to implement, the responsibility for correcting their law lies with the Head of Government. The legal tradition needs correction. The obligation of the courts to maintain self-consistency makes them reluctant to innovate. But innovation may sometimes be required, and that for two causes: first, where tradition has deviated from natural right; secondly, where it is ill-adapted to the practical possibilities within society. These two concerns are often confused, but they are in principle quite different, moving, as it were, in opposite directions, the one bringing law closer to the moral norm, the other removing it further from it. There are idealistic reforms, attempting to correct our vices; there are compromise reforms, making some kind of settlement with them. Either kind of reform may be necessary at one or another juncture, since acts of judgment have to be at once truthful and effective. Every change in law aims to squeeze out, as it were, the maximum yield of public truthfulness available within the practical constraints of the times. Sometimes it does this by attempting more, sometimes by attempting less.

The Christian legal tradition took over, gingerly enough, the Hellenistic commonplace which saw the ruler as the *empsuchos nomos,* the "living law." Whereas this had meant originally to identify the ruler as the source of law, in Christian use it was combined with the assertion that the ruler was under the law, charged, like anyone else, with keeping it. But the *way* in which the ruler 'keeps' the law is different from others: he keeps it by ensuring that it is applied and upheld in courts. Furthermore, when the fluid character of the practice of law is recognized, its tendency to fall into disuse and neglect, it is added that the ruler 'keeps' it by intervening, where necessary, into the legal tradition, safeguarding it from degeneration.

The paradigm instance in the traditions common to the U.S. and Great Britain was the invention of the Court of Chancery in fifteenth-century England and Wales. The common-law courts being widely perceived to have become ineffective on many fronts, the government responded by developing a new court, derived from royal council and under the supervision of the Lord Chancellor, a minister who to that date had had no special connection with the operation of law. Chancery devised rules for its own operation superior to those prevailing in the common-law courts, and took over areas of litigation where those courts had seemed peculiarly incompetent. This illustrates on a large scale what happens in fact in any act of legislation: some element in the existing tradition of the court's law is corrected or adjusted from the source of government. But it also illustrates a precise danger, which required further correction at a later stage: the setting up of conflicting jurisdictions within a single system. This has a bearing on our contemporary problem, as we shall see.

Yet one more dialectical distinction arises between this act of government and other acts. Legislation is *generic,* which is what distinguishes it from acts that concern bare particulars. When the Head of Government appoints a chief justice or supplies a sum of money to create new courts, he decides only who is to be the Lord Chief Justice *next,* or where the money is to come from *now.* When a law is passed, on the other hand, it concerns what is *always* to be done in such cases as it specifies. Imagine two supposed miscarriages of justice, both uncorrected by the courts themselves, which provoke public anxiety and demands for government action. In the one case there is public doubt about the evidence for identification on which a conviction was secured. In the other case there is a judicial ruling that evidence important to the defense is technically inadmissible. Both are assumed miscarriages, but for different reasons. The first related to a particular, "*This* is the man who was observed at the scene of the crime"; the second related to a generic principle, "*This kind* of evidence is not admissible in defense." The two miscarriages must be addressed quite differently. In the one case the Home Secretary reviews the case, and if it seems warranted, instructs the Court of Appeal to look at it again. In the second case the Lord Chancellor prepares new legislation to amend the law of evidence.

Now, these two different kinds of corrective action require a different measure of public support. If the Home Secretary refers the first case back, or simply issues a pardon, not much is needed by way of public consent. We understand that the minister has these powers, and we require only that he use them reasonably. It is not possible to settle the validity of any verdict by public consensus. Nor does it matter to the public very much in the long run if the minister actually reaches the wrong answer, provided that he is seen to reach it reasonably, conscientiously, and without prejudice. In the second case, though, where legislation is in question, it is a far different matter. Hundreds of cases yet undreamed of will be affected. So something more than bare consent is needed to validate a legislative act. There must be a positive *assent* to the principles on which reform is proposed. No deep cleavage can be allowed to develop between the general sense of what is right and what the law exacts. So the two kinds of governmental act proceed in quite different ways. Proposals for legislation need examination, both to explore unforeseen implications and to test them against the moral attitudes and convictions of those who will be governed by them and may ultimately be tempted to find them tyrannous.

Hence the British constitutional doctrine, maintained by Locke despite his advocacy of 'separation', that the legislature in a government is *the monarch in parliament.* That is to say: not some *other* agent than the Head of Government, but the Head of Government as engaged in a process of consultation. But what is the status of parliament as a consultation partner? Among the radical constitutionalists of the later sixteenth century, Parliament (or, in other European traditions, the Estates or the Diets) underwent a change of status, from a body that existed to represent popular concerns to government, to become a *branch* of government. It drew to itself the role of the founding people covenanting with God and monarch to establish government, but also, in Reformed thought especially, the role of a distinct magistracy charged with protecting the state against abuses practiced by the sovereign. In this development its true significance was lost sight of. In England parliament began life as a *court of common pleas,* a means by which the governed spoke to government about their frustrations, an organic line of communication between the two that served to legitimate government as pursuit of the common good. The extension of parliament's role to that of a deliberative forum, first for the authorizing of taxation and then for the formation of legislation, recognized the need for government to listen to the *vox populi,* to respect its deeply held convictions, and to take stock of its anxieties.

In this context we may see a point in Montesquieu's anxiety: "When the legislative and executive powers are united in the same person, or in the same body of magistrates, there can be no liberty; because apprehensions may arise, lest the same monarch or senate should enact tyrannical laws, to execute them in a tyrannical manner."[19] It is at first sight puzzlingly expressed. What other than tyrannical manner could there be, we might ask, of enacting tyrannical laws? And given the lamentable hypothesis that a legislature will legislate tyrannically, does not the separation of powers merely entrench the legislature against correction? We can understand the point of the remark, however, as being that when a certain *dialogue* fails to accompany the formation of a law,

---

19. *The Spirit of the Laws* 11.6, trans. Thomas Nugent (New York: Hafner, 1949), p. 151.

its enactment simply becomes another form of executive action. It loses its distinctive law-like character. But Montesquieu mislocated the dialogue required, and so underestimated it. What is needed is not simply a dialogue between departments of government, but a dialogue between government and people.

By converting parliament into a branch of government, modern constitutional theory lost a vital sense of the dialogue between government and governed as the heart of the legislative process. This, I believe, lies at the root of the perceived problems of the British constitution in our century. Many contemporary critics have identified the difficulty simply in terms of the excessive power of the executive. But this analysis is one-sided, since the source of the current imbalance was parliament's absorbing, one by one, all the powers of sovereignty that used to belong to the monarch's ministers. The sheer success of parliament in taming the willfulness of monarchy led to an implosion of government and parliament upon each other, leaving unhealthy mutual dependence. Parliament (in effect, one chamber of Parliament) wrested effective control over ministerial appointments, so that ministers depended on it for continuance in office. Ministers forced parliament to agree to their legislative proposals with the threats of resignation or dissolution, for which Members of Parliament would have to answer at the polls. The sense of dialogue was lost. Ministers and Parliament gained, and still have, too much power *over each other,* too little authority on their own ground. The stranglehold exercised by the party system, effectively controlling the terms of all political debate, is the worst symptom of the stasis. But the long-term cost of co-opting parliament into government has been a loss of belief in the capacity of 'politicians' — the term is an expressive one, bundling ministers and popular representatives together in one homogeneous class — to respond to what actually moves the people. 'Politicians' argue energetically with one another about 'the issues'. But what the issues are to be, they have settled among themselves.

III

We return at last to judicial review of legislation, which we may understand as a reaction against the paradoxical dominance of parliamentary government and the positivism of legislative supremacy. The turn to the courts expresses frustration with legislative parliaments that claim to be the sovereign government and fail in any meaningful sense to be a court of common pleas.

We have said that there is nothing impossible in the idea that law may be made by courts. Indeed, if we understand the work of courts correctly, the making of law is an essential part of it: they must declare the principles on which they have decided cases, and those principles must in some measure be a law for subsequent courts. The question, then, is not whether courts shall make law, but how. Are they to be autonomous, or under correction from some other locus than a higher court? When we contemplate the sight of military leaders ruling by decree, we may wish to concede that there can be worse forms of autocratic rule than that which judges exercise. Nevertheless, there are reasons, which I will not now explore, why autocratic government is not good government; and there are also, as I have tried to show, three good reasons why good government requires courts to be subject to external correction: (a) good court practice requires concentration on the particular case, but good lawmaking requires attention to general policy (the *sub judice* principle); (b) good court practice requires insulation from pressures of public concern, but good law making requires exposure through consultation to public concern (the democratic principle); (c) good court practice requires a conservative approach to legal tradition, but good lawmaking needs a measure of critical distance on tradition (the natural law principle).

As I have reflected on this problem, I have come to the conclusion that the root of the matter lies in the faulty early-modern articulation, which, lacking a sense of the judicial character of all branches of government, allowed separation to create *competing jurisdictions.* This is a situation which political authority cannot endure. The multiple variation of functions within a complex government allows for an extensive plurality of function and decision, but the plurality rests on the hypothesis of a *summa potestas,* a source of governmental authority, to which in the last analysis the resolution of conflicts must return. That is the heart of the matter.

There is an alternative analysis of the problem, frequently argued in Canada at the time of the introduction of the Bill of Rights in 1982, and often urged by British opponents of a Bill of Rights: that the root of the problem lies in assigning legal status to a *philosophical document,* whether a Bill of Rights or a *Grundrecht* or whatever else it may be, that is *too underdetermined* in legal terms, and so undercuts the concrete determinations of ordinary legislation. This is not the root of the problem, because if an underdetermined document has the status of law, it is easy enough in principle to provide it with determinations. A problem arises only when there is competition between *rival* determinations.

This is illustrated by a famous controversy between the European Court of Human Rights and the British government, which turned precisely on such an underdetermined expression, and led to Great Britain's only derogation from the Convention. Article 5(3) of the European Convention on Human

Rights requires that an arrested person must be "brought promptly before a judge."[20] In British anti-terrorist legislation the time lapse between arrest and appearance in court was, in exceptional circumstances, allowed to be as long as seven days; the Court of Human Rights insisted on a limit of three days. Now, either three days or seven days will plausibly serve as a determination of the word "promptly." Which is the *better* determination will depend on the circumstances in which one has to be prompt, which is why alternative determinations for differing circumstances are conceivable, even desirable. The controversy, then, did not follow from the bare possibility of differing determinations, nor from the fact that the phrase was, as it stood, underdetermined. It was simply born of a failure to achieve a workable conception of the way in which the jurisdiction of the court related to that of the government of the United Kingdom.

Unlike most other signatory countries, Britain regarded the Convention simply as a treaty, without any direct force in domestic law. The Strasbourg court thought it had no reason to attribute to the British courts and legislation the intention of enforcing the Convention and applying it appropriately. In relation to Great Britain it seemed to enjoy a monopoly on interpreting human rights, standing over against a civil society in which both legislature and courts apparently ignored them. This was not *concretely* the case, of course; but *formally* the matter so appeared. One can hardly blame the European court for acting out a legally subversive role. But that role was simply the result of allowing competition to arise between jurisdictions: on the one side, a court with a document all of its own; on the other side, national government and courts, obliged to respect the document but with no share in interpreting it.

It was understandable, therefore, that the British Government should recently have incorporated the European Convention of Human Rights within English and Scottish law, in a way that, it was hoped, would overcome the existing liability to generate conflicts, while also protecting the legislative supremacy of the Queen in Parliament. The Human Rights Act allows the Convention to be interpreted as British law in British Courts, and so allows British statute law to be applied within the interpretative context of the Convention. It will have the effect of presenting the Strasbourg Court with interpretative decisions on the Convention reached under British law by British courts, and so do something to reconcile the jurisdictions. While stopping short of according Strasbourg rulings *ipso facto* force in British law, it requires British courts to take those rulings into account, thereby allowing a serious contribution to the interpretation of British law from outside Great Britain. But by depriving the

20. Brownlie, *Basic Documents,* p. 323.

Strasbourg court of its interpretative monopoly, it ensures that the interpretation of the Convention begins to reflect British legal realities.[21]

One might say that this measure attempts to do *institutionally* what still remains to be done *conceptually,* which is to reintegrate the falsely polarized conceptions of positive law and human rights, the one supposedly enjoying immunity from moral criteria, the other supposedly enjoying natural-law supremacy over positive law. The truth of the natural-law principle, that for law to be valid it must be morally tolerable, must apply across the whole range of legislative endeavor, not merely to claims of individuals against governments. The truth of the principle behind positive law, on the other hand, must also be maintained: the rights of individuals cannot be given proper effect simply by letting them cut across legal traditions, invading, as it were, by sudden irruptions of court judgment at unpredictable moments; they must be an essential aspect of the spirit of a well-tempered law, a "Right" in the singular, which government takes responsibility for sustaining and correcting.

We return to the respective roles of courts and legislators. The essence of the courts' task, in the first place, is to apply statute law intelligently in the light of natural law; to make good moral and social sense of a body of legislation that may sometimes have been incoherently or inconsiderately compiled. In handling this body of law we should not require that the courts be slavish. There should be no prejudice in favor of 'strict construction', except where that has become the only acknowledged alternative to sheer willfulness. What we should require of courts is a due acknowledgment of the authority of government in providing law, and a commitment to giving it the best interpretation to which it is susceptible, according to the most consistent interpretative principles (not necessarily the most literalistic) that can be developed. The possibility of absolutely rejecting some legal provision as inconsistent with divine and natural right cannot be ruled out *a priori,* since we cannot *a priori* exclude the possibility of tyrannous law, which requires the performance of wicked actions or forbids the performance of obligations. Such an event, however, needs to be seen as a last resort, implying the invocation of an emergency procedure — our new British legislation envisages a formal declaration — which will bring the legislators urgently to the point, and cause bad statutes to be remade, but by parliament, not by the courts. The procedure of "striking down" was rejected by the

---

21. The tackling of the problem of monopoly may be the key to the very different constitutional context of the U.S., as one recent contribution to the debate suggested: "The Founders never intended to give the federal courts a monopoly over the interpretation of the Constitution. . . . Courts must apply the Constitution . . . other branches must do the same according to their own best lights." Robert George and Ramesh Ponnuru, "Courting Trouble" in *National Review,* August 1998.

British Government, and rightly, since it is precisely that procedure that produces the situation in which legislative responsibility slips away from parliament.

But here we must recall the main point of our analysis: that the problem arose in the first place because populist constitutional doctrine asserted an idolatrously inflated conception of legislative power. The aggrandizement of positive legislation has resulted in a cheapening of law and a general contempt for legislative process: too much law made too fast and too carelessly. Law, as Montesquieu feared, has turned into a form of executive action, as parties compete at elections with their rival legislative programs, which they promise to ram through within one parliamentary term (or, even worse, within the first hundred days). In this ethos the shifting of real responsibility to the courts by no means occurred without the collusion of politicians. It enabled them to sustain a flurry of lawmaking without being ultimately answerable for its consequences. (I recall, with a shudder of despair, one Premier of Ontario, who, promoting a controversial and wide-ranging amendment to the Province's Bill of Rights, answered all questions about what it would mean with the simple formula: "We don't know. The courts will decide!") In consequence, the forms for sanctioning legislation came to be seen as merely provisional, and in some places new law was hardly thought authoritative until it had been challenged at least once through the court system.

No solution of the problem can be imagined which does not involve an address to the process of legislation. What our democracies most need is not judicial review of law after the event, but a high standard of preparatory scrutiny before laws are entered in the statute book. One of the most positive aspects of the new British law is that new legislation must come before Parliament accompanied by a statement assuring its compatibility with the provisions of the Convention. The courts are not bound to agree with the statement, of course, should it be challenged. But the practice requires legislators to respect the Convention in their legislative endeavors, and to heed the advice of jurists on the matter *ab initio*. Yet something will be required of the courts in turn: to recognize the implications of this legislative process, to acknowledge the intent of a law to insert itself into a natural-law-governed practice, and to interpret it in good faith. In this way real understanding between lawmakers and courts may be developed, and the burden against impugning a law which has had a clean bill of health will be a greater one. Self-discipline in legislative quarters and self-discipline in judicial quarters must go hand in hand.

Subsidiarity and Political Authority
in Theological Perspective

JOAN LOCKWOOD O'DONOVAN

It is in the nature of fashionable social concepts to be of amazing plasticity and versatility; the concept of 'subsidiarity' is no exception. In the seemingly interminable debate over the evolving form of the European Community and Britain's participation in it,[1] subsidiarity has been on the lips of Euro-skeptics as well as Euro-enthusiasts, and proved serviceable to quite antagonistic visions of European political organization — from federalism to associative confederalism to anti-integrationist nationalism. If there is any concurrence on the term's meaning, it is concurrence on the merely formal principle that decisions should be taken at the lowest level of political authority competent to take them.[2]

Such a working interpretation of subsidiarity presents a considerably attenuated understanding of the principle that Roman Catholic social thought has continuously elaborated over the past century. Even in its formal statement the Roman Catholic principle is a more complex proposition: it proposes that

1. The Maastricht Treaty (agreed in 1991, enacted in 1993), which legally established the European Union, was erected on a foundation of previous economic communities formed in the 1950s, the most important of which was the European Economic Community ('Treaty of Rome', 1957), later amended by the European Single Act (1986) and renamed the European Community. Until 1980 the EEC/EC was comprised of nine states (initially Germany, France, Italy, Belgium, Netherlands, and Luxembourg, with Denmark, Ireland, and Great Britain entering in 1973), but has since grown to fifteen members, with the admission of Greece, Spain, and Portugal in the 1980s, and Austria, Sweden and Finland in the 1990s.

2. For example, in the preamble to the Maastricht Treaty on European Union, the principle of subsidiarity is understood as requiring that public decisions be "taken as closely as possible to the citizen."

An earlier form of this paper was presented to the Society for the Study of Christian Ethics (Oxford, 1992) and subsequently published in *Studies in Christian Ethics* 6:1 (1993): 16-33.

in a well-ordered social body all the members or parts (whether they be individuals, groups, or institutions) assist one another (the Latin root of "subsidiarity" being *subsidium* meaning "aid") in making their particular and proper contributions to the perfection of the whole; and further, that the larger, more powerful, and self-sufficient parts are especially obliged to support and provide for the smaller, weaker, and less self-sufficient parts, but always so as to preserve the latter's freedom and integrity of action — hence, the popularly perceived bias of the principle in favor of individual, institutional, and even national freedom of action. The formal principle does not, of course, specify what the parts of the social body are, nor in what its perfection consists, nor the precise assistance that each part owes to every other, and particularly the more self-sufficient to the less self-sufficient. Moreover, it only vaguely bears on the central questions of political theory concerning the basis, purpose, form, and limitations of political rule.

To answer these questions of theoretical substance we must have recourse to three fundamental structuring concepts of Catholic social thought, all of Thomistic provenance: namely, natural law, public society or body politic, and the common good. By means of these concepts, the principle of subsidiarity, together with the nature and task of political rule, has been progressively articulated: in papal encyclicals and other official church statements, in the unofficial writings of Catholic social thinkers, and in the platforms of Christian Democratic Parties, for which the original and continuing intellectual inspiration has been predominantly Roman Catholic. This progressive articulation reveals an evolution undergone by Catholic social theory over the last century, from a more traditional political Thomism to a thoroughly modernized political Thomism.

My first theoretical concern is with this evolution; and in regard to it I shall develop the following thesis: namely, that it is certain Aristotelian features of Thomas Aquinas's political synthesis which have permitted an easy incorporation of modern liberal democratic tenets, and conversely, it is his dependence on the earlier Christian tradition (scriptural, patristic, and medieval) that has theologically contained and moderated these tenets. The modernizing of the Thomistic political framework has reinforced its Aristotelian character at the expense of its traditional Christian aspects. My second theoretical concern is with the question of whether modernized Thomistic theory affords an adequate Christian perspective on the *political* issues posed by European integration. It is no exaggeration to propose that all the best aspects of European Community ideals and practices conform to the modern Catholic social vision, and have, to a considerable degree, been shaped by it. I shall, however, raise grounds for doubting that the contemporary Catholic synthesis of Thomistic and liberal democratic concepts can satisfactorily illuminate and resolve the more problematic aspects of Europe's political future.

Subsidiarity and the Evolution of Catholic Social Thought

In charting the evolving theoretical articulation of the subsidiarity principle in Catholic social thinking, I am concentrating on official papal teaching as presented in four encyclicals: *Rerum Novarum* published by Leo XIII in 1891, *Quadragesimo Anno* published by Pius XI in 1931, *Pacem in Terris* published by John XXIII in 1962, and *Centesimus Annus* published by John Paul II in 1991. The first three are programmatic markers of the transition from traditional to modernized political Thomism, the fourth casts a somewhat revisionist eye over this development. I am supplementing the encyclicals with the mature political treatise of Jacques Maritain entitled *Man and the State* as illustrative of the powerful modernising impetus emanating from the defeat of Nazism and Fascism in Europe.

As I have indicated, we cannot understand the modernizing of Thomistic social theory without grasping the original tension in St. Thomas's synthesis between its traditional theological and Aristotelian orientations. Briefly, this is the tension between two accounts of political authority: an account of political authority as primarily juridical and an account of it as primarily directive and administrative.[3] Taking as its cornerstone St. Paul's political injunctions in Romans 13:1-7, the Western patristic tradition, systematized above all by St. Augustine, taught that political rule was established by God for the purpose of restraining human evildoing and encouraging virtuous conduct. By rendering binding public judgment concerning matters of right and wrong, vindicating right and punishing wrongdoing, the ruler manifested, on the one hand, God's righteous wrath against human sin and, on the other, his merciful will to protect the goods of human life from the assault of blind and wayward passions, by providing a limited judgment and punishment of human wrongdoing, in lieu of the limitlessness of both divine judgment and the sinful human passion for vengeance.[4] In the older Christian political tradition, the ruler's authoritative acts interpreted not only divine law (in an admittedly imperfect and incomplete way) but also human law, customary and statute, that embodied the common judgment of the whole community. The social right that political authority was instituted to defend and vindicate was given, first and foremost, by

---

3. The issues arising between these accounts are discussed on pp. 207-24 above.
4. See also p. 209 above, and pp. 288-89 below.

God's revealed Word of Scripture, and included religious and moral obligations beyond those of respecting and protecting personal life, liberty, and property.

In Thomas's political thought this older tradition is still a presence, but receding before the tide of Aristotelian influence. Aristotle's *Politics* presented Thomas with a conception of political authority as more directive and administrative than the prevailing Augustinian conception. Aristotle attributes to the ruling part of the body politic a more creative and comprehensive role in establishing the common good, and in organizing the community to pursue it. Chiefly through the activity of lawmaking, Aristotle's rulers direct the ruled toward an order of public and private benefits in which all citizens, to some degree, participate. Here, the essential purpose of government is less the adjudication of right and wrong on the basis of received communal understandings of divine and natural law, than the active orienting of the political whole to the order of right defined by positive law. Consequently, in Aristotle, the political regime, in principle and in practice, for better or worse, determines the material and spiritual welfare of the society and its members, and subordinates the individual to the common good.

Turning now to Pope Leo XIII's *Rerum Novarum*,[5] let us consider how his traditional Thomistic articulation of the concept of subsidiarity exhibits the tension between the juridical and the directive (regulative and integrative) conceptions of political authority. Pope Leo XIII used the occasion of expressing pastoral concern about "the condition of labor" under industrial capitalism to undertake a sophisticated diagnostic analysis of the spiritual and institutional disorders of liberal, laissez-faire society. He regarded the industrial degradation of the laboring class as symptomatic of the deeper social malaise of atomistic individualism, with its emancipation of the baser passions for profit and power. Anxious about the seductive appeal for the downtrodden of the socialist critique and program, he determined to hold out an alternative vision for society and an alternative campaign of action. Consequently, in opposition to the socialist vision of a classless society of free and equal persons engineered by an omnipotent state on the basis of contempt for private property and the traditional family, Leo XIII pitted the Catholic vision of an organically pluralistic society of hierarchically ordered communities, knit together by Christian friendship on the basis of the natural inviolability of the family and private property. This harmonious future society would be effected, not chiefly by the state, but by the free initiative of independent social groups and institutions. In the context of industrial class conflict, the enterprise of social reunification called for the formation of a network of associations

5. All quotations from the encyclicals of Leo XIII, Pius XI and John XXIII are from English translations in *Seven Great Encyclicals* (Glen Rock, N.J.: Paulist Press, 1939, 1963).

to promote the material and spiritual well-being of the laboring class, and the mutually sympathetic cooperation of employers and employees.

With a high degree of fidelity to Thomas and to his neo-scholastic disciples, Pope Leo XIII's vision incorporated the concepts of natural law, the public society, and the common good. Natural law is the lynchpin of the papal conception, for it comprises the fundamental, unchanging principles of human individual and social being. These are the teleological and moral principles, accessible to unassisted reason, that give structure and direction to human action and relationships. They give intellectual expression to the entelechy of human powers that actualize themselves in the social hierarchy of communities, associations, and institutions: the family, the firm; the industrial, agricultural, or professional guild; the parish, village, town, province, rising to the whole body politic.

In the political realm these principles are articulated as natural rights belonging to individuals and groups (following the late scholastic development of Thomas's thought): chiefly, the right of the individual to private ownership of property, and the right of the family to independent fulfillment of its natural purpose of mutual love and provision. In Leo XIII's teaching, the family right takes priority over other natural rights, as the family group has a primacy of status over other natural groups. The family, we are told, is a "true society anterior to every kind of state or nation," and "governed by a power within itself, that is to say, by the father" (§§9-10).

The institutional authority of the familial society is rivaled only by that of the "public society," which is the totality of individuals, groups, and institutions in their political unity and intentionality. It is the *societas perfecta* in two Aristotelian senses: in the sense of self-sufficiency, of possessing all that is necessary for "living and living well," and in the sense of inclusion, of comprehending all other "particular" communities and their "private" goods.[6] Only the self-sufficient and inclusive society is, in its political intentionality, the common will with full authority to define and realize the common good, understood as both the collective good of the social whole and the aggregated goods of its parts. Leo XIII follows a propensity of Thomas, that subsequent Catholic theorists will sharply repudiate, to identify the public society with the state, as when he says that private societies are "formed in the bosom of the state," "exist within the state, and are each a part of the state" (§§37, 38).

This identification suggests what the Pope's general remarks appear to confirm: that he subscribes to the Aristotelian concept of political rule as directive and creatively administrative. The ruler's "first duty," he proposes, is to ensure "that the laws and institutions, the general character and administration of

---

6. For Aristotle's concept of political self-sufficiency, see *Politics* 1252b 29.

the commonwealth, shall be such as to produce of themselves public well-being and private prosperity" (§26). Since public well-being is comprised of such diverse communal goods as "well-regulated family life," "respect for religion and justice," "progress in the arts and trades," and "the abundant yield of the land" (§26), all social orders are, in fact, the proper objects of governmental concern and "benefits." It would seem that the government, consulting the public good, positively aids every part of society to fulfill its telos and contribute to the welfare of the whole.

However, Leo XIII's subsequent exposition of the precise modes of governmental action conforms more to the juridical conception of political authority as engaged in judging and punishing wrongdoing and rectifying its effects, for the sake of protecting rights and just order in society. So that, for instance, he sanctions governmental intervention to terminate strikes that threaten "the public peace," or to restore to industrial workers "the time and opportunity" to practice religion, or to release them from unjust employment burdens and degrading work conditions. Furthermore, he strictly limits governmental interference to that "required for the remedy of the evil or the removal of the danger" (§29). Most significantly, it is in the context of juridically qualifying state intervention that he lays down the principle that will be developed as "subsidiarity": namely, "that the state must not absorb the individual or the family," but rather permit them "free and untrammeled action as far as is consistent with the common good and the interest of others" (§28). Here, the freedom of society's members to pursue their proper goods appears dependent on the traditional Christian conception of the state as judge, punisher, and rectifier of social evil.

It is important to notice that the principle of subsidiarity encompasses only 'natural' and 'temporal' social and political relationships, and not the supernatural and spiritual realm of the church. As his earlier encyclical *Immortale Dei* (1885) made clear, Pope Leo XIII strictly adheres to the medieval (Gelasian) dualist theory of ecclesiastical and civil rule as comprising the two earthly governments set by God over divine and human things respectively, each possessing supremacy within its fixed sphere. The church's authority over all things pertaining to humankind's eternal salvation does, however, make her the highest instructor of human thought and action in every sphere with respect to its religious and moral obligations. Therefore, the church is entitled and obliged to bring its divine wisdom to bear on all political and social issues, and to require the state to respect and defend its authority and judgments. While the church and state should mutually assist one another in that harmonious collaboration which the principle of subsidiarity makes the social norm, they do so as two supreme authorities belonging to different orders, and not as two parts of the social whole.

When we approach Pope Pius XI's letter *Quadragesimo Anno* by way of *Rerum Novarum* we are struck by the similarity of perspective in the two encyclicals, including the characteristic ambiguity over the role of political authority. However, in this regard, the theoretical tension is less marked, owing to a weakening of the juridical orientation. It is noticeable that the Pope's explicit formulation of the subsidiarity principle is detached from any juridical circumscription of governmental action. Rather, subsidiarity appears to be simply the negative statement of Pius XI's social ideal of organic corporatism: that is, of an organic social hierarchy of functionally-specific, self-regulating, yet interdependent groups, within which the dignity and freedom of individuals are realized. Such a hierarchy is protected by the twofold proscription of the subsidiarity principle: namely, "that one should not withdraw from individuals and commit to the community what they can accomplish by their own enterprise and industry" nor "transfer to the larger and higher collectivity functions which can be performed and provided for by lesser and subordinate bodies" (§79).

Undoubtedly, in the Pope's corporatist society the 'lesser bodies' would relieve the state of many of its present responsibilities and encumbrances. In the economic sphere, for instance, he envisages free corporations assuming the management of industry and commerce, in bold defiance of Mussolini's scheme of state-run corporations.[7] At the same time, the government's role in "directing, supervising, and encouraging," as well as "restraining," economic activity (§80) is still prominent, partly owing to the magnitude of the "reconstruction" required to orient economic life by norms of justice and benefit. The government alone has the public authority and power to advance the rights of labor and its cooperation with "capital," and even more, to subjugate the "despotic economic domination" of large investment corporations, enhancing corporate accountability, punishing corporate fraud and speculation, and reducing corporate control of credit supply and allocation (§§105-108, 132). Moreover, it has the continuous responsibility "to define in detail . . . when the need occurs" the lawful economic uses of private property, in view of its social character (§49).

While, on the economic front, Pius XI seems to pass easily between the directive, regulative, and juridical roles of government, this is not so on other fronts. Most notably, in respect to the education of youth, addressed by his en-

---

7. In Mussolini's scheme of state corporatism the activities of legal syndicates were coordinated and directed by state-run corporations. Pope Pius voices contemporary anxieties about the "excessively bureaucratic and political character" of Mussolini's "new syndical and corporative order," about the state "substituting itself in the place of private initiative" (§95).

cyclical *Divini Illius Magistri*,[8] he more sharply restricts governmental involvement to that of providing necessary material assistance and of protecting basic justice, placing forceful emphasis on the primary, independent rights and responsibilities of family and church. The primary responsibility for educating youth, he counsels, falls to the natural society of the family "instituted directly by God for . . . the generation and formation of offspring" and to the supernatural society of the church, established for the "eternal salvation of mankind" and divinely endowed with supreme teaching authority and the power to "generate," "nurture," and "educate" souls in the "life of grace." As Christian education gives spiritual unity and direction to all knowledge, culture, and practical art, the church has the clear prerogative in "founding and maintaining schools and institutions"; the state's responsibility in the educational sphere being to "protect and foster" the prior rights of family and church. And whereas the state lends support to the family as a subordinate, dependent, and imperfect society, deficient in self-sufficiency, it lends support to the church as a superior, perfect society, divinely equipped with "all the means required for its own end. . . ."

The triumph and defeat of political barbarism and tyranny in Europe brought into prominence in Catholic intellectual circles a fully modernized Thomism, equipped with the liberal democratic devices for constructing a more stable, just, and universal political order. One architect of this post-war Thomism was Jacques Maritain, whose political writings of the 1940s and early 50s powerfully shaped Roman Catholic political theory and organization, at least in the post-war Christian Democratic Parties.[9] Maritain's *Man and the State* (1948) presents in a systematic and persuasive form the type of integration of Thomistic-Aristotelian and modern liberal-democratic ideas that has fed the impetus for European union over forty years, and is reflected in the existing formal basis for the European Community.

This treatise demonstrates how the modernizing of Catholic social theory has affected the principle of subsidiarity by modifying its interpretative conceptual framework. The structural concepts of natural law, the public society and the common good have all been substantively refocused by means of a pervasive shift in historical-political perspective. For, whereas pre-war Catholic social thought was largely controlled by the aspiration of restoring a past hierar-

---

8. Numerical divisions are absent from the English translation of this encyclical. The following quotations are from *Seven Great Encyclicals*, pp. 40-41.

9. For a comprehensive presentation of Christian Democratic Party theory and practice, see M. P. Fogarty, *Christian Democracy in Western Europe, 1820-1953* (London: Routledge & Kegan Paul, 1957); also R. E. Irving, *The Christian Democratic Parties in Western Europe* (London: Allen & Unwin, 1979), pp. 29-57.

chy of spiritual and temporal authorities, and of organic social institutions, post-war thought has been controlled by the aspiration of fulfilling the evolutionary potential of an idealized present. In other words, post-war Catholic thought has accepted the historical progressivism of the majoritarian creed of European society, which regards modern liberal democracy as the outcome of Western political maturation. For modernist Thomists like Maritain and Gilson, however, this outcome falls short of the full realization of Western political maturity; for the latter requires the re-spiritualization of liberal democracy by the Christian political leaven, to produce a democratic society that is at once 'personalist', 'pluralist', and 'communal'. While such a description is evocative of traditional papal teaching, the evocation is belied by the novel centrality in the modern Catholic vision of such concepts as natural rights, democratic culture, and individual freedom of choice. It is these concepts which comprise the altered substance of the traditional Thomistic concepts of natural law, public society, and the common good. Let us show how this is the case with respect to Maritain's post-war political thought.

In keeping with the tradition, Maritain understands natural law as comprehending the fundamental regulative principles of human action and relationships that make possible a consensus of rational inclination within and among societies. However, with characteristically modern historical optimism, he discerns a progress in this civilizational moral consensus toward an extension of natural moral knowledge. This extension consists in the widespread public recognition that not only human obligations, but human rights, are implied in natural law. These rights include, beside the longer-standing human, civil and religious rights (to life, personal liberty, pursuit of perfection, property, freedom of association, speech, religious belief and practice, and equality before the law), the 'civic' right of full political participation, and the extensive catalogue of social rights that we now take for granted (e.g., to humane employment, material security, medical care, suitable education, and cultural involvement).[8]

For Maritain the natural rights of persons express in the public-legal realm the unifying good and common task of the public society or 'body politic', namely, the perfecting of individual, personal life. It is to this good that the activities of all inferior communities, groups, and institutions are finally ordered, and in terms of which their autonomous welfare is finally justified. One theoretical result is that the subsidiarity principle (which Maritain prefers to

---

10. *Man and the State* (Chicago: Chicago University Press, 1951), pp. 95-107. See my criticism of Maritain's presentation of universally recognized rights as the *"ius gentium,"* p. 293 below.

call "the pluralist principle") becomes a derivative, secondary principle, less politically fundamental than the supreme good of the person publicly articulated in the body of subjective natural rights.[11]

Another theoretical result is that the political society that has the responsibility of defining, as well as promoting, natural rights, assumes increased moral-social importance, prestige, and authority. It is itself the subject of inalienable natural rights, the foremost being the constitutive political right to self-government. According to Maritain, this inalienable right finds most adequate political expression in the institutions of democratic, representative government — election, continuing public accountability and separation of powers — which, in modern society, comprise an essential part of the common good.

The preeminence accorded by Maritain to the political common good and the body politic is most fully disclosed in his concept of democracy as both the unifying culture and the 'common faith' of a religiously, culturally, and socially diverse society. For the body politic to achieve the common good under the conditions of modern pluralism, it must be integrated through the purely "civic or secular faith" of "the democratic charter," which enshrines the rights and corresponding duties of the political society and its members, including its highest and most powerful institutional member, the state. Of necessity, the civic faith takes precedence in the universal public order over the particular religious faiths present in society, although the latter may inspire, deepen, extend, and rationally reinforce the former. This precedence is especially reflected in the educational system, wherein the "democratic charter" must be "taught in a comprehensive, far-reaching, and vitally convincing manner," but in sufficiently "pluralistic patterns" as to enable "teachers to put their entire convictions and most personal inspiration in their teaching. . . ."[12] In other words, the civic faith can publicly accommodate diverse religious perspectives, but is not in the service of any one of them.[13]

While Maritain shares the concern of Popes Leo XIII and Pius XI to place limitations on governmental authority, he conceives these limitations less in the

11. Maritain defines "the pluralist principle" as follows: that "everything in the body politic which can be brought about by particular organs or societies inferior in degree to the state and born out of the free initiative of the people *should* be brought about by those particular organs or societies." *Man and the State*, p. 67.

12. Maritain, *Man and the State*, p. 122.

13. Contrary to the papal advocacy of state subsidization of denominational schools, Maritain maintains the "general principle" that: "Either the various religious inspirations traditional in the nation are integrated in the public schools system, or they give rise to merely private schools." *Man and the State*, pp. 124-25, note 8.

light of the traditional distinctions, e.g., between the state and the church, or the state and the family, as in the light of the distinction between the state and the body politic. In opposition to all theories of sovereignty that describe the state as an ontological subject of supreme right and power, superimposed on the body politic, or absorbing it, Maritain is at pains to describe it as merely the highest part of the body politic that is "instrumental" for accomplishing its "common task."[14] However, the broad social scope of personal rights means that the state's instrumentality covers an ever-expanding field of action, inclusive of all the directive, regulative, and organizational functions characterizing the liberal welfare society. And inasmuch as personal rights take precedence over the rights of particular communities, groups, and institutions, the latter are especially vulnerable to state interference with their authority or responsibilities.

This is most evident in the diminution of the public rights and responsibilities of the church in Maritain's pluralistic polity. Here, the Gelasian "two spheres" doctrine is made to underwrite the radical autonomy of the temporal from the spiritual order. The church as a universal, supernatural *societas perfecta* makes no institutional, communal claims on the body politic. Rather, her claims are mediated entirely through the conscience of the Catholic individual, and her rights are the natural political rights of the Catholic believer qua citizen. At the same time, the church as a social institution is an integrated part of the body politic, enjoying the same kind of public, official, and juridical recognition as is accorded to all other voluntary associations and corporations deemed to be a major asset to the common welfare. Under the "Democratic Charter," the decisive principle determining the public status of the Catholic church among other religious organizations must be the equal right of individuals to practice the religion of their choice. Otherwise, warns Maritain: ". . . the fact of inserting into the body politic a particular or partial common good, the temporal common good of the faithful of one religion (even though it were the true religion), and of claiming for them, accordingly, a privileged juridical position in the body politic, would be inserting into the latter a divisive principle and, to that extent, interfering with the temporal common good."[15]

---

14. *Man and the State*, pp. 12-13. See my discussion of Maritain's criticism of the theological tradition of Christian kingship, pp. 287-91 below.

15. *Man and the State*, pp. 175-76. Maritain may justifiably be accused of wanting to "have his cake and eat it" when he suggests that a "Christian political society" that refuses legal privilege for one church could, nevertheless, "recognize the juridical personality of the Church as well as her spiritual authority in ruling her members . . . and [could] deal with her as a perfect and perfectly independent society, with which it would conclude agreements and with the supreme authority of which it would maintain diplomatic relations" (p. 175).

Such is Maritain's synthesis of Thomistic and liberal-democratic theory. It draws on the leading Aristotelian concepts of St. Thomas's thought: those of *societas perfecta,* the self-sufficient polity built up of subordinate functional units; natural law as the permanent totality of principles of moral good and order; directive rule that legislates and administers the common good and orients the political whole and its parts toward it. Infusing these concepts with the tenets of liberal democracy produces a conception of the inclusive body politic, unified by a single democratic political creed that articulates the common good as a body of universal, natural political and social rights and obligations (principally of individuals), for which the government is authorized by the body politic to make provision.[16]

It is essentially this conception of political society that Pope John XXIII internationalized in his 1962 encyclical *Pacem in Terris,* which has enjoyed something of a revival in recent years on account of its elevation of subsidiarity into a principle of global political organization. Moreover, the logic of the Pope's argument for world government is basically that developed in Maritain's last chapter. It is that the "progress of science and technology" has brought about closer social ties among the members of "different political communities," greater "interdependence of national economies" to the extent that they are "integral parts of the one world economy," and a potentially catastrophic nuclear threat to world peace, with the result that "the public authorities of the different political communities" are no longer able "to provide for the universal common good, either through normal diplomatic channels or through top-level meetings, by making use of juridical instruments such as conventions and treaties . . . suggested by the natural law and regulated by the law of nations and international law" (§§130, 133-134). In that "the universal common good poses problems of world-wide dimensions," it requires "public authorities endowed with a wideness of powers, structure and means of the same proportions . . ." (§137). Such a worldwide public authority, "set up by common accord and not imposed by force," would "have as its fundamental objective the recognition, respect, safeguarding and promotion of the rights of the human person" (§§138-139). This objective can be effectively pursued only by having regard to the equal rights of individual political communities, and by allowing the prin-

16. It is true that Maritain's mature synthesis exhibits certain emphases suggesting his intellectual debt to American political culture (and possibly the closeness of the American and the French political cultures): e.g., the strongly individualistic bias of the democratic charter, its social pervasiveness as civil religion, and the strict separation of church and state. Nevertheless, its central features, shared by various Catholic political contemporaries, are those that have dominated the European Catholic political mainstream over the last fifty years, and have contributed to the formation of a political will for European integration.

ciple of subsidiarity to regulate their relationship with the world public authority. Accordingly, the latter would not "intend to limit the sphere of action of the public authority of the individual political community, much less to take its place," but rather "to create, on a world basis, an environment in which the public authorities of each political community, its citizens and intermediate associations, can carry out their tasks, fulfil their duties and exercise their rights with greater security" (§141).

Implied in Pope John XXIII's argument are two axioms to which Maritain, in his apology for world government, attaches vital theoretical importance. The first is that, given the economic and technological interdependence of modern political societies, no one of them can claim the natural rights to self-government belonging to a self-sufficient polity, a *societas perfecta*. Rather is each an imperfect political society that can achieve its proper end only as part of a truly perfect society, a universal world polity, which alone can lay claim to political autonomy. The second is that, since government is merely an instrument of the body politic for realizing the common good, world government must function as the agent of an international body politic, unified by a common world political culture. Pope John XXIII makes no secret of his hope that the United Nations may develop the "structures" and "means" equal to the task of world government, and that its *Universal Declaration of Human Rights* (1948) may become the backbone of a global body politic (§§142-145).

Pacem in Terris, we would propose, provides the theoretical terminus of the substantive development of the concept of subsidiarity that has shaped European political aspirations in the post-war period. With Pope John Paul II's re-reading of *Rerum Novarum* on its centenary in 1991 *(Centesimus Annus)* we detect a different theoretical synthesis taking form. The collapse of Communism in Central and Eastern Europe, which (so to speak) closed the historical circle on a century of papal social teaching, furnished Pope John Paul with a unique occasion for launching a distinctive configuration of the modern Catholic tradition.

Displaying the balanced judgment of its predecessor, *Centesimus Annus* both celebrates the liberation of European peoples from spiritual and material bondage and exposes the hollow triumphalism of liberal capitalism. In addressing yet again the 'social question', the Pope sets forth a moral economy in which market freedom is wedded to social responsibility so that the production and exchange of goods benefit all parties equitably and serve authentic personal and communal needs. Enlarging upon Leo XIII's concern for the nature and conditions of wage-labor, John Paul II makes the common activity of disciplined and meaningful work central to the vocation of persons and to, what he terms, the "subjectivity of society." By "subjectivity of society," the pope intends all the types and structures of social-moral relationship, covered by the generic term "solidarity" — relationships of "friendship," "collaboration" and "cooperation," "charity," "sharing," and "communion." Institutionally considered, these comprise the various, independent, "natural" groups (familial, economic, social, political, and cultural) through which persons fulfill their social human nature (§13).

It is the controlling place occupied in this encyclical (as in earlier and later encyclicals of John Paul II) by the twin concepts of "solidarity" and the "subjectivity of society" that accounts in large part for its distinctive gloss on the papal social tradition. Together, they are coextensive with "the common good," with the fabric of communities, associations, and institutions knit together by "natural laws." While John Paul II retains the language of natural rights for articulating "the common good" of civil society, it is not the primary moral language that it was for his post-war predecessors; indeed, it sometimes appears to be more of a strategic political language. Likewise, the concepts of "public society" and "body politic," designating a moral-juridical totality, whether identified with or distinguished from the state, are not prominent in his theortical perspective; while the notion of a civil *societas perfecta* has slipped away. He not only vigorously resists the identification of the social totality with the state, he is more reluctant than his predecessors to promote a political articulation of it. His view of society resonates most with Pius XI's organic corporatism, but is in subtle ways less political. As for Pius, however, the principle of subsidiarity is for John Paul II the negative statement of the principle of solidarity, that counters the state's totalitarian aspirations without effectively curbing its range of interventions. For the state remains the 'instrument' of a democracy of rights-bearing individuals and groups, and has responsibility for directing and furthering as well as defending and vindicating the exercise of human rights (§§47-48).

To penetrate the core of John Paul II's social theology, we must realize that solidarity is "ultimately" a "Christian virtue." "In the light of faith," says the Pope in his encyclical *Sollicitudo Rei Socialis* (1987), "solidarity seeks to go beyond itself, to take on the *specifically Christian* dimension of total gratuity, forgiveness and reconciliation. One's neighbour is then not only a human being with his or her rights and a fundamental equality with everyone else, but becomes the *living image* of God the Father, redeemed by the blood of Jesus Christ and placed under the permanent action of the Holy Spirit" (§40). The wellspring of Christian solidarity is "the new model of the unity of the human race" discerned by faith, that of personal communion which reflects the inner trinitarian life of God and is "the soul of the Church's vocation to be a 'sacrament'" (§40). The unity of every society (community, structure of solidarity), therefore, is to be found in the Church's communion. As Russell Hittinger perceptively suggests, John Paul II's postmodern revision of the modern papal tradition returns to "a rather old-fashioned doctrine of the incorporation of society into the life of the Church."[17]

Subsidiarity: An Evaluation in View of European Integration

To return to the issue of European political integration, which is responsible for the recent vogue of intellectual fascination with the principle of subsidiarity, it should be evident from the preceding that the substantive principle is no more and no less adequate for tackling problems of international political society than national political society. The issues of political order and authority do not decisively alter with the level of political community under consideration: the strengths and weaknesses of a concept or theory at one level will merely be duplicated at another. In our judgment, the strengths and weaknesses of the subsidiarity principle are those of its Thomistic-Aristotelian conceptual framework in its original and modernized versions. The moment has arrived for us to formulate some criticisms of this framework from the older Christian political perspective, while not neglecting the revisions of John Paul II, indicating its inadequacies for resolving the most pressing political issues of the European Community. Let us then review the concepts of natural law, the public society, and the common good.

Natural Law

The concept of natural law as the permanent moral order within which God intends human life in its personal and social aspects to be lived is a fundamental theological concept, common to biblical, patristic, and early medieval, as well as late-medieval and Reformation Christian thought. From the beginning, the Christian concept exhibited internal complexity and dialectical tensions, the chief of which lay between the structures of created nature and fallen nature. For many Church Fathers and their medieval successors, the prelapsarian and postlapsarian social orders bore dramatic differences. The former, for which the institutions of marriage and the family were paradigmatic,[18] were thought to

---

17. "The Church and the De-Sacralized State: An Analysis of *Centesimus Annus* on the Occasion of Its Fifth Anniversary," delivered to the Union League Club, New York City, 1997, p. 34.

18. For Augustine's view of the Christian household, see pp. 67-68 above.

embody more fully God's original law of creaturely love than the latter, which intrinsically manifested the fact of human sin and God's response to it. Such postlapsarian institutions as political rule, private property, and slavery were viewed as simultaneously accommodating, restraining, and punishing wayward human passion, and so as forming an order of justice connected with, but also removed from, God's law in creation. Thus, while the inequality between ruler and ruled was viewed as a necessity of sinful human nature, it was not considered 'natural' in the sense of being intrinsic to created nature.

The novelty of St. Thomas's Aristotelian handling of natural law was its minimizing of the acknowledged divisions between the pre- and postlapsarian social orders. His admission of private property and political rule (without its coercive aspect) onto the moral plane of created human nature[19] enabled him to weave social life into a unified moral texture. Whereas the older Augustinian tradition viewed sinful society as an inherently disjunctive organization of communities with disparate ends (e.g., familial care versus civil judgment), Thomas viewed sinful society as retaining the inherent harmony of a hierarchy of natural ends, of natural functions, in which each part had its appointed place, and all parts together constituted a real social totality, a common will directed toward a common good. It is doubtful, however, that this vision of hierarchical harmony and functional integration does justice to the disparate and divisive character of social goods under the conditions of human sin. It would seem logical that the more disparate the purposes and laws of separate communities and institutions, the greater their requirement of functional autonomy, and the less easy a coordination of their activities within a system of social ends, or an incorporation of their good within a larger social aim. Moreover, with less truthfulness can their incommensurable goods be articulated within a single public language.

Modern liberal-democratic society is marked by a failure to differentiate communal goods and laws: contrary to its self-profession, it is insufficiently

---

19. Admittedly, Thomas's presentation of the relationship of private property to prelapsarian community is somewhat ambiguous. While in *ST* 1a. 98.1 ad 3 he gives passing assent to the traditional view that community of goods (as distinct from private possession) is fitting to the state of innocence, his more considered statement of *ST* 2a2ae. 66.2 ad 1 presents private ownership as a rational extension of, rather than a derogation from, the original community of goods. Argues Thomas: "Community of goods is said to be part of the natural law not because it requires everything to be held in common and nothing to be appropriated to individual possession, but because the distribution of property is a matter not for natural law but, rather, human agreement, which is what positive law is about . . ." (ed. and trans. M. Lefébure [London: Blackfriars, 1975], p. 69). Moreover, while his Aristotelian justifications of private possession over common possession do actually presuppose sinful human dispositions, Thomas makes no explicit admission of this significant point.

pluralistic on the moral and spiritual plane. The public realm suffers from moral monism, being enslaved to one universally acclaimed good, that of individual self-determination. The public hegemony of this good is both disclosed and maintained in the public hegemony of the language of subjective rights. Increasingly in liberal-democratic polities, communal and institutional aspirations and claims must be articulated in this individualistic and voluntaristic language in order to be heard. (The language remains individualistic even when rights are predicated of communities, in that community membership is most often construed as a matter of the individual's free choice and free self-identification.) But this language is unsuited to express the purposes and structural laws of diverse communities. It is equally unsuited to express the goods and the law of marriage (personal communion and sexual fidelity), the bond and duties of family life (parental care and filial obedience), or the purpose and normative structure of economic activity (production and exchange to fill material needs and stewardship of material resources) or of education (the communication of truth under conditions of openness and sincerity). Granted that all these communal undertakings contribute to and are sustained by the mature moral and spiritual freedom of persons, their specific norms are, nevertheless, not properly articulated by the language of moral individualism. The contemporary language of solidarity is more generically appropriate in conveying the participatory and communicative aspects of moral-social bonds, but is muddied by being joined to the political agenda of defending and procuring rights. Moreover, the theoretical intention of such an encompassing term is unclear and its populist appeal all too apparent. Its danger is to suggest evocatively a spiritual unity of the social totality that does not exist in the fallen condition of mankind.

The threat to communal pluralism posed by public moral monism and the hegemony of the language of rights is exacerbated when the polity is an international one in which those authorized to take public action are further removed from the historical-cultural particularities of the communities affected by their action. The consequences of public action based on ignorance or want of sympathy are bound to be more detrimental in an international than in a national setting, where the ignorance is unlikely to be so acute and where corrective pressures are closer to hand. Thus far, the agreements and legislation forming the political and social basis of European integration demonstrate the hegemony of the language of individual rights.[20] This basis has been endorsed

20. See the European Convention on Human Rights (1950) and its Five Protocols, the European Social Charter (1961), the Final Act of the Helsinki Conference (1975), and the Single European Act (1986). The Maastricht Treaty on European Union (1991) assumes the previous state-

by many supporters of social pluralism who do not understand its monistic moral implications. To the extent that European Catholicism has offered an uncritical endorsement, it has weakened the defense of communal autonomy intended by the subsidiarity principle, but has also revealed the longstanding weakness of the Thomistic natural law conception of the social totality.

The Public Society and the Common Good

These two concepts have had a long history of interdependence in Christian political thought. Their usage in the patristic age was shaped by the definition of *res publica* quoted in Cicero's *Republic:* namely, "an association united by a common sense of right and a community of interest."[21] The *res publica* or common weal was always susceptible of a double reference — to the human association and to the interest uniting it. For St. Augustine as for Cicero, the common interest was inseparable from the "common sense of right," of justice; but as justice was constituted by the seminal virtues of piety and equity, by the love of God and the love of neighbor, the *res publica* could truly exist only as the community of true faith, wherein "the highest and truest common good, namely, God, is loved by all, and men love each other in Him without dissimulation . . ."[22] Thus, the *societas perfecta* could have only one meaning for Augustine: the community of total and sufficient right, united by divine commandment and the realization of the absolute common good; and likewise, there could be only one association worthy of the title: the communion of saints, imperfectly present in the church militant on earth.

Of course, Augustine recognized another political society, that of the "earthly city," deficient in right and in its common good. According to *City of God,* Book 19, its unity resided in "a consensus of human wills" and concerned the temporal common good of "resources for this mortal life."[23] The purpose of the ruler was to establish and maintain, by promulgation and enforcement of law, an acceptable and stable arrangement of those provisions that would pre-

---

ments of rights and asserts its conformity with them in various places: e.g., Common Provisions, Articles B and F2. It should be noted that not all signatories to these pre-Maastricht documents were members or full members of the European Community. See note 1.

21. Cicero, *De republica* 1.25.39; quoted by Augustine, *City of God* 2.21; trans. H. Bettenson (Harmondsworth, Middlesex: Penguin Books, 1972), p. 73.

22. Letter 137, 5.7; trans. J. G. Cunningham, *Nicene and Post-Nicene Fathers,* 1st series (Grand Rapids: Eerdmans, 1974), 1:480.

23. *City of God* 19.17; *IG,* p. 159. See the fuller discussion of the "earthly city," pp. 48-72 above.

serve communal peace. Not surprisingly, the mainstream of late patristic and medieval political theology disregarded the minimalist overtones of this most tendentious of Augustine's formulations of the common weal, and rooted civil order and justice firmly in the dictates of natural and divine law, emphasizing the godliness and wisdom required of the Christian ruler. They gave weight to his role in promoting public virtue and true religion, but nonetheless retained the juridical focus of his action. His chief duty remained the restraining of sinful passions in society by the judgment and punishment of wrongdoing. His commission was to vindicate God's righteous order embodied in the laws of nature and Scripture, and reflected in the universal customs of nations and the laws of kingdoms, discriminating and punishing violations of it.

Thomas's adoption of Aristotle's concept of the political community as a *societas perfecta* represented a departure from the older Christian political tradition. Now, not only must the body politic be self-sufficient in all things requisite for the 'good life' of its members, but on this self-sufficiency rested its moral claim to be self-ruling; whereas previously this claim had rested on the capacity of a community's rulers to maintain a stable and relatively just social peace. Accordingly, entrusted with responsibility for communal self-sufficiency, civil rulers assumed a directive and administrative role with respect to the whole range of 'natural' public interests, economic and social, as well as juridical and military.

For adherents to the older theological tradition, a highly problematic feature of Aristotle's conception of the self-sufficient polity was his correct perception that its ruling regime would shape the spiritual disposition of its members. He perceived that the love of the regime for virtue, glory, wealth, or power, would foster that same disposition in the ruled. But Augustine saw clearly that the very striving for a self-sufficient polity would ensure that the outcome would not be a harmony of natural virtues, but an arrangement of "splendid vices" with an ultimately demonic telos. For Christians should be formed, above all, by the evangelical law of Christ, the law of faith, hope, and charity, which was distinct from, superior to, and in tension with, the laws and structures of sinful human nature. The evangelical law was held to constitute a higher and better regime, polity, type of authority, and common good than the laws of the civil commonwealth. It was in accepting the partial and deficient nature of the civil common weal that the godly prince witnessed its openness to the life of Christian virtue. Thus, to enlarge the scope of the civil common weal to social self-sufficiency was a threat to the community of faith that could be countered only by strengthening the economic, social, and political autonomy of the institutional church, and by surrounding its sphere of action with elaborate legal safeguards. In fact, the absorption of Aristotle in the thirteenth century did much to produce the theoretical standoff of royal and papal imperialism in the fourteenth century, from which the Roman Church has never entirely recovered. Right up to the post-war years of the twentieth century, European Catholicism has been continually embroiled in a battle between a sovereign, self-sufficient ecclesiastical polity and a sovereign, self-sufficient secular polity, despite the theoretical and practical possibilities for cooperation and compromise. Only with the official incorporation of modern liberal-democratic content into the traditional Thomistic political framework has the Roman Church decisively fallen back on a rearguard action.

Whatever criticisms may be brought against pre–Vatican II Roman ecclesiology, and whatever political benefits may have issued from the Catholic Church's acceptance of liberal-democratic principles, her political conversion may, nevertheless, be considered as a milestone on the road to the imperialism of the liberal-democratic polity. For this is the universal and homogeneous polity integrated by a civil creed that is inimical to communal pluralism, regardless of its professed support for it. The independent well-being of the most important communities and institutions in society is sustainable only if it is widely believed that they embody transcendently given and permanently binding constraints on human action; that they have purposes and structures which are not entirely subject to historical and cultural arbitrariness, are not manipulable by the will of individuals and groups. But this is denied by the civil faith of universal subjective rights, the motor of which is belief in the indefinite enhancement of individual and group freedoms and benefits through the technological mastery of nature.[24] In the prevailing civil cult of European polities today, the final public good, which is the measure of all others, is the self-determination of the subject (individual or collective), who, acting in an arena of increasingly open-ended choice, regards human and non-human nature as the mere stuff of technological manipulation. The growing boredom with consumption and anxiety about environmental deterioration have as yet only taken the edge off the communal will to freedom through management.

It is everywhere daily apparent that the universal aspiration to overcome natural constraints on human freedom such as poverty, ignorance, sickness, immobility, and climatic adversity, not to mention sex, gender, and aging, requires the coordinated development and application of innumerable technologies. And this in turn requires highly complex and centralized administration, with vast planning and regulative powers. All government, as the primary instrument of communities of rights to accomplish their well-being, has become a vast bureaucratic locus of technological expertise: in fiscal and monetary

24. See my interpretation of liberal democracy, pp. 139-41 above.

strategy, trading and labor law, employment and education policy, and natural resource allocation and preservation. As such, government action cannot help but diminish the initiative and independence of other social institutions and communities.

For over a century papal social teaching, in setting forth the principle of subsidiarity, has forcefully affirmed the transcendent basis of social pluralism. But this affirmation has been blunted by its embracing of the civil creed of rights, which is the modern version of the secular *societas perfecta*. Perhaps no pope of this century has achieved such detachment from the liberal-democratic ideology of modernized Thomism as John Paul II, and yet his 'rereading' of the tradition still falls short of what is needed. While he places unrivalled emphasis on the primacy, dignity, and independence from political authority of *social* bonds, he is less theologically clear about the nature and dignity of political authority and the communal bonds of law, justice, and political judgment.

The strongest impetus for European integration in the last two decades has come from the drive of its member communities for economic and technological self-sufficiency, for the sake of which, with impeccable Thomistic logic, some governments and some citizens are prepared to cede some political power to a polity more closely approximating the Aristotelian ideal. In this situation, the crucial political questions concern not whether a European political administration is the right route to economic and technological self-sufficiency, but whether such self-sufficiency is a right public aspiration and the chief business of government. On these questions the concept of subsidiarity can give sufficient guidance only as it draws on the older, and, historically considered, majoritarian, tradition of Christian political thought.

[handwritten note: I am not convinced that Maritain is a fool much for that but there is much for it Papal statement which Protestant to will look at carefully]

Karl Barth and Paul Ramsey's
"Uses of Power"

OLIVER O'DONOVAN

Paul Ramsey conceived his essay "The Uses of Power" as a quick response to the foreign policy debates of the 1964 U.S. Presidential election campaign, and published it before the end of the same year. Yet by placing it at the head of *The Just War* four years later he suggested that he saw more in it than an occasional commentary on current events.[1] Furthermore, at the same time as the compilation of *The Just War* he reused the material of "The Uses of Power" for a lengthy paper surveying the issues of the 1968 Presidential electoral campaign that was just beginning. This paper develops, and in some ways corrects, the analysis offered in the earlier article; but since it never found its way to a publisher's office, "The Uses of Power" remains Ramsey's nearest approach in print to a theory of political agency.[2] In it he contests the view, which he denominates with some

1. *The Just War* (New York: Scribner, 1964), pp. 3-18.

2. The unpublished paper, "War and Peace as a Religious Issue: On Extricating the Church from Liberal Disillusionment," was drawn to my notice by Dr. David Attwood, to whom I owe my thanks, as I do to the William R. Perkins Library at Duke University for permission to consult and quote from it. It contains 65 typescript quarto pages with manuscript corrections and additions. Internal references date it to the summer of 1968, and its composition must be supposed to be subsequent to the collection of material for *The Just War*. Did Ramsey perhaps

This article was originally published in the Special Focus issue of the *Journal of Religious Ethics* 19.2 (1991): 1-30, devoted to the ethics of Paul Ramsey (who had died in 1988), edited by James T. Johnson. It was written, as was stated in the original version, "in grateful admiration for both these major Christian thinkers and as a personal tribute to Paul Ramsey, whose kindnesses and intellectual stimulus leave me with a debt that defies account." It is here reproduced with only minor revisions, and there has been no attempt to change time references — "now," "hitherto," "not yet," etc. — which belong to the period of composition.

reluctance "liberal," "that there can be no positive use of force . . . for political ends," and identifies as one source for the dissemination of this view among theologians "Karl Barth's Christological view of the *normal* functions of political authority."[3] The respect in which Ramsey held Barth as a theologian and moralist can hardly be in doubt.[4] Yet it is interesting that another important formal essay, "The Case of the Curious Exception," also identified Barth as the progenitor of views which Ramsey had to combat.[5] The extent of the difference between Barth's notion of exceptional moral cases and that of the casuistic tradition with which Ramsey associated himself has been explored by others.[6] In this contribution I hope to explore the disagreement on the nature of political action.

This is the right moment to explore their disagreement, since we have had important posthumous works from the pen of both Ramsey and Barth recently put before us, permitting us to speak more definitely about the shape of their respective political ideas. Paul Ramsey's *Speak Up for Just War or Pacifism* carries his lifelong wrestle with pacifism onto an explicitly theological plane. From it we learn of his belief that "the crux at which Christian pacifists and justifiable-war Christians part company is our respective accounts of the person and work of Jesus Christ."[7] We learn how he understood the divergence to

---

plan this extended version of "The Uses of Power" for that volume? If so, it is not difficult to imagine why he finally judged it unsuitable: its sometimes polemical tone and its extended references to the politics of 1968, as well as its extended discussions of economic foreign policy and aid to developing nations. Alternatively, perhaps he planned it as a contribution to the election campaign, but decided that its publication would be inconsistent with the incorporation of "The Uses of Power" as a theoretical introduction to *The Just War.* However that may be, this paper contains some fine Ramsey on some unaccustomed topics. Most striking is a fierce defense of President Lyndon Johnson, who had been "driven from office for . . . practicing the art of the politically possible at home. . . . and for trying to practice the art of the politically purposeful abroad." Also memorable is his excoriation of American isolationism for its abandonment of development aid. On its analysis of liberalism I comment further below.

3. *Just War,* pp. 3, 5.

4. Cf. the use made of Barth in *Christian Ethics and the Sit-in* (New York: Association Press, 1961), p. 22, and the constant references in *Deeds and Rules in Christian Ethics* (New York: Scribner, 1967).

5. *Norm and Context in Christian Ethics,* ed. Paul Ramsey and Gene H. Outka (New York: Scribner and London: S.C.M., 1969), p. 69.

6. Nigel Biggar, *The Hastening That Waits: Karl Barth's Ethics* (Oxford: Oxford University Press, 1993), pp. 7-45. To the obligations I have acknowledged in note 2 above I must add an expression of gratitude to Professor Biggar for his help in my reading of Barth. However, *labia nostra a nobis sunt* (Ps. 11:5, Vulg.)

7. *Speak Up for Just War or Pacifism* (University Park, Pa.: Pennsylvania State University Press, 1988), p. 111.

be reflected in accounts of creation, eschatology, and the church. At the end of his life, drawn on by an unappeasable enthusiasm for Jonathan Edwards, Ramsey turned his mind consistently to questions of dogmatic theology; and this is what makes his last book on deterrence so much more than an apologia for positions already taken. Yet the pacifism that Ramsey addressed in these theological terms was the confessional pacifism of John Howard Yoder and Stanley Hauerwas, and *Speak Up* contains no theological analysis of that "liberalism" with which he came briefly to grips in "The Uses of Power," and brushed up against constantly besides. Ramsey had his own reasons for turning the discussion towards debating partners who were not only worthy of attention in their own right but spoke with the voice of his own erstwhile student pacifism; yet the Methodist bishops who provided him with his point of departure were not pacifists, but liberals. And although he knew that liberalism was a much wider phenomenon than was envisaged in Reinhold Niebuhr's equation of "liberal" and "idealist," he never subjected the moral habits of Western liberalism to a distinct theological scrutiny.

The late appearance of Karl Barth's 1931 *Ethics* in the last decade has yet to receive the notice that it deserves.[8] For the specialist student of Barth's writings it is more "early Barth," another paving-stone on the master's road to the mature convictions of the *Church Dogmatics*. For the moralist it is something of rather greater importance. Until recently we have not had a complete Barth ethics which permitted us to see how he might dispose of the material of the subject as a whole. In the *Dogmatics* there exist only two out of four projected parts complete: the Ethics of the Divine Command (II/2) and the Ethics of Creation (III/4). The fragment of IV/4 published posthumously as *The Christian Life* contains the beginnings of a third part, the Ethics of Reconciliation.[9] But in the *Ethics* we have an extensive third part, including material on the state, and a small but scintillating fourth part, the Ethics of Redemption, as well. This is not to say, of course, that the *Ethics* tells us what Barth would have written in the missing sections of the *Dogmatics*. There are points on which he changed his mind; in addition to which, there are signs that as he neared the end of his course, he followed the original architectural plan rather more loosely. But it does show us how he originally conceived the plan which came to govern the *Dogmatics*.[10]

8. Ed. Dietrich Braun, trans. G. W. Bromiley (Edinburgh: T&T Clark, 1981).

9. *The Christian Life* (Church Dogmatics IV/4, Lecture Fragments), ed. H.-A. Drewes and E. Jüngel, trans. G. W. Bromiley (Grand Rapids: Eerdmans, 1981).

10. The editors of *Ethics* draw attention to the appearance of a notion of "creation orders" (215 and vii), which was rejected in the *Dogmatics* (*Church Dogmatics III: The Doctrine of Creation*, vol. 4, various translators [Edinburgh: T&T Clark, repr. 1961 (orig. 1951)], pp. 36-38). Of

The earlier book is of special importance for interpreting Barth's views on the state. Ramsey based himself on some remarks in *Dogmatics* III/3 which are by way of *obiter dicta* in the discussion of "The Protection of Life." Barth's formal treatment of the state was to follow in IV/4.[11] We are now in a position to see that these remarks, anticipated in 1931, represent a constant element in Barth's thinking on the subject, and to reject the temptation presented by his wartime writings to regard them as a later development. But the question of consistency and change in Barth's political views is a matter so specialized and extensive that it requires another context than this to deal with it, and another author than myself. I shall excuse myself with a simple statement of what I presume: (a) There is a central stream in Barth's thinking about the state that is represented in his writings from about 1930 onwards, encompassing on the right hand the possibility of the state's use of force and on the left the abnormality of it. (b) In relation to this stream the nearly anarchist positions of *Römerbrief* may be discounted as a backwater. (c) In the wartime writings and those which shortly preceded and followed the war the stream flowed nearer its right-hand bank, and in the later post war writings veered towards its left-hand. (d) This vacillation, if so it may be called, arises from pressures within Barth's thought rather than from pressures outside it. That is to say, the dialectic between the normal, central functions of the state and its marginal, occasional function exercises a control over these shifts of emphasis. (e) But the controlling dialectic itself is obscured by a kind of *disciplina arcani*, springing from Barth's unwillingness to appear to toy with the alternatives of a peace-state and a war-state, as though we could at any time include these two contrasting possibilities within a theoretical synthesis, whereas the claim of each, at the point where we genuinely encounter it, is absolute for us. In *Dogmatics* III/4, however, it is given some formal expression with

---

even greater interest, perhaps, is the fact that Barth once thought he could confine the concept of neighborhood to the christological section of ethics, where it is associated with the reconciling work of law, and exclude it altogether from the ethics of creation. In the *Dogmatics* the neighbor is an aspect of creation; and this change may have contributed to the great difficulty Barth had in his search for a new master concept for the ethics of reconciliation, a search which ended with "invocation" (*Christian Life*, pp. 37-46 and x, xi). However, there is much that is ambiguous about the relation of *Christian Life* to the plan with which Barth began. At seventy-five he was still restless to find new approaches, and his treatment of political questions there started on fresh ground, yielding what has been called "one of the few significant treatments of revolt in recent theological literature." But he never made the connection with the question of government, and the section where this might have happened can reasonably be called "a little tired, a little less taut" (John Webster, "The Christian in Revolt: Some Reflections on *The Christian Life*" in Nigel Biggar, ed., *Reckoning with Barth* [London: Mowbray, 1988], pp. 136, 138. For the wider question cf. John Webster, *Barth's Ethics of Reconciliation* [Cambridge: Cambridge University Press, 1995]).

11. *CD* III/4, p. 303.

the aid of Barth's conception of the *Grenzfall,* or "exceptional case"; so that the two matters on which Ramsey set himself in public opposition to Barth turn out to have an inner connction.[12]

Should we add: (f) At the end of Barth's life the stream swung back to the right-hand bank again? There is a single sentence about the state in *The Christian Life* which would appear to justify the claim that "Government is not just the establishment and exercise of right among men but also, for the sake of this, the establishment of sovereignty and dominion and the exercise of power and force by man over man."[13] We may agree with Williams's observation on the "shifting and unfinished character" of Barth's reflections on the state, and take note of his warning: "The powerful underlying consistency of his thought can best be seen as the consistency of a lifelong process of reworking and purifying what was last said, and it is no tribute to him to exploit only one 'moment' of his exploration."[14]

II

Ramsey states his chief contention in "The Uses of Power" in two corresponding claims: "The use of power, and possibly the use of force, is of the *esse* of pol-

12. On *Römerbrief* and the difference between the two editions, see Rowan Williams, "Barth, War and the State," in Biggar, ed., *Reckoning,* pp. 170-90, with which I disagree only in emphasis. In *Ethics* Barth makes only occasional mention of the state's use of force, and presents a formal description of its role with a single passing allusion to force (pp. 445-49). But at the end of the 1930s he would write: "Because the State 'beareth the sword', it is clear that it participates in the murderous nature of the present age. . . . Human law needs the guarantee of human force. Man would not be a sinner in need of justification if it were otherwise. The State which is threatened from within or without by force needs to be prepared to meet force by force if it is to continue to be a state" (*Church and State,* trans. by G. W. Howe from *Rechtfertigung und Recht,* [London: SCM, repr. 1939 (orig. 1938)], p. 75). And both during and after the war Barth affirms the fifth thesis from the Barmen Declaration: "Scripture tells us that by divine appointment the State, in this still unredeemed world in which also the Church is situated, has the task of maintaining justice and peace, so far as human discernment and human ability make this possible, by means of the threat and use of force." (Cf. *Church Dogmatics II: The Doctrine of God,* vol. 2, various translators [Edinburgh: T&T Clark, repr. 1957 (orig. 1942)], p. 722; "The Christian Community and the Civil Community," in *Against the Stream,* trans. R. Gregor Smith [London: SCM, repr. 1954 (original 1946)], pp. 21, 50.) In 1951, as we shall see, Barth put a question mark not only against force but against power, making no use of the distinction between *potestas* and *potentia* of which he had availed himself five years before.

13. *Christian Life,* p. 219. This is accompanied by a promise, never honored, of a fuller treatment "in the last subsection."

14. Biggar, ed., *Reckoning,* p. 173.

itics"; and "The use of power, and possibly the use of force, is inseparable from the *bene esse* of politics."[15] Both these propositions, we are told, are denied by "liberals," the more profound of whom base themselves on Barth's christological view of the normal functions of political authority. Ramsey then renders Barth's view in three statements, two in his own words and the third in Barth's: (1) "It is the *polis* that is destined for perfection in the Kingdom of God, while the church shall wither away."[16] (2) "Meantime . . . the state derives its meaning from the fact that Jesus Christ has already assumed the human reality which magistrates govern."[17] Consequently, (3) "War should not on any account be recognized as a normal, fixed, and in some sense necessary part of . . . the just state."[18] But statement (3), Ramsey points out, is susceptible of two readings: (a) an uncontroversial surface-reading, with which we must all agree; and (b) a controversial reading, with which we should take issue. The first of these (3a) makes it the state's task (again in Barth's words) "to fashion peace in such a way that life is served and war is kept at bay." However, taking (3) in conjunction with (1), it becomes clear that Barth meant not merely to abnormalize war, but to abnormalize power itself, and this is proved by Barth's own commentary: "It is no primary task of Christian Ethics to . . . maintain that the exercise of power constitutes the essence of the state, i.e., its *opus proprium*, or even a part of it. What Christian Ethics must insist is that it is an *opus alienum* for the state to have to exercise power."

It is not immediately clear that (1) and (2) form an adequate statement of what Barth means by grounding the state in Christ, nor that Ramsey is correct to derive (3) from that premise. The christological root of the state, as Barth understands it, has to do with the proper location of the political order within the covenant of reconciliation between God and man. This covenant is the christological covenant; for although Barth's doctrine of the Trinity does not allow him to assign God's works of creation, reconciliation, and redemption exclusively each to one person of the Godhead, nevertheless the *proprium* of each person is displayed within the triad of these three works, so that the doctrine of reconciliation is the place where the central subject-matter of the Incarnation, Passion, and Exaltation of the Son of God is handled.[19] In that section the doc-

---

15. *Just War*, p. 5.

16. Cf. Barth, *Church and State*, p. 41.

17. For this I can find no source in Barth, and notice elements that seem un-Barthian: the "already," which expresses Ramsey's belief in Barth's realized eschatology; the derivation of the state from Christ's assumption of humanity rather than from the election of humanity in Christ; the concentration on the humanity of the governed rather than that of the governors.

18. Quoted from *CD* III/4, p. 456.

19. Cf. *Christian Life*, p. 7.

trine of the state also belongs: "In this authority we are dealing indirectly but really with the authority of Jesus Christ."[20] According to the *Ethics*, the command of God the Reconciler comes to us as "the necessity of law," which we know through the authority of the divinely commissioned fellow-man, who requires of us the subjection of humility as we acknowledge that we deserve to be contradicted and that contradiction is good for us; and this yields as its fulfillment the love which we owe to God and neighbor.[21] The divinely commissioned fellow-man, who is Jesus Christ, is represented to us in different ways both by the state and the church, but by the church more inclusively since it "contains the state in itself."[22]

Central to Barth's conception here is the collapse into one theological moment of the traditionally differentiated ages of God's preserving providence and saving atonement, the collapse of BC into AD. The state "is not an order of creation . . . nor is it an order of eternal life. It is an order of the sustaining patience of God which is necessary and good because *even those who have been blessed in Christ* are wholly and utterly sinners."[23] There is no justification here, or elsewhere so far as I can see, for Ramsey's talk of "Barth's post-evil, Christ-formed man."[24] Moses is Christ's witness *within* Christ's church.[25] The effect of the collapse of BC into AD and of the refusal to treat of the state outside Christ, is to characterize both the state and the kingdom of Christ in terms of each other. The state, on the one hand, is interpreted in terms of its end: all human authority is understood in the light of the supreme authority which completes it. But the kingdom of Christ is allowed to include all authority and to be seen within all authority, not excepting that of Pontius Pilate.[26]

So far from providing a reason, then, for the denial of power to the state, Barth's rooting of the state in the kingdom of Christ acts as a reason to *affirm* the power of the state. There is no question of a transformation, whereby a state formerly rooted in natural power comes later to be rooted in Christ. On the contrary, every power which any state at any time properly exercised over its citizens always was a reflection of the rule of Christ, at once the God who commands and the fellow-man through whom God commands a second time. Barth's mode of political theology could lead him towards something like the Christos Pantokrator model, though not quite to that, since the difference be-

20. *Church and State*, p. 36.
21. *Ethics*, pp. 56-61.
22. *Ethics*, pp. 332, 449.
23. *Ethics*, p. 445, emphasis added.
24. *Just War*, p. 7.
25. *Ethics*, p. 359.
26. *Church and State*, p. 17.

tween reconciliation and redemption acts as a guard against premature eschatological pretensions.[27] Nevertheless it affords no ground for *denying* anything to the state.

However, there is to be a further qualification. The solitary sentence in the *Ethics* in which Barth indicates the ground on which he will normally deny to the state the use of power, or at least of force, suggests a logic quite different from that envisaged by Ramsey: "The final weapon whereby the state defends itself against its members is the coercion with which it dares to forestall God's own claim to man."[28] Here Barth indicates a *reservation* within the state's authority as witness to God's authority. This claim is "God's own," i.e., not, or not normally, the claim of the witness. The source of this reservation is easily recognized: it is the sense, generally Augustinian in inspiration, of the ambiguity of political right, a sense which draws Barth much closer to Ramsey than either of them can come to idealist pacifism. Barth does not forget the reservation of the Barmen Declaration: "maintaining justice and peace, *so far as human discernment and human ability make this possible*, by means of the threat and use of force." Can we say, Barth asks, that "the last resort of the social order, the putting to death of those who oppose law, can have for us the appearance of true right? Can I understand the killing of others as . . . an act that serves their sanctification . . . and to that extent as an honouring of God?" That our justice falls short of true atonement, that it fails to sanctify and regenerate while it judges and destroys, that when it kills it cannot raise to life again, there is the tragic gap which separates the authority of Christ from the authority of the witness; there is the "indirect relation" between the God who alone does right and the right of the "earthly city of God."[29]

It is in his *response* to this gap between divine original and human reflection that Barth separates himself from the tradition of Augustinian realism that shaped Paul Ramsey. That tradition makes its home on the bleak and twilit terrain of sorrowful resignation, unforgettably mapped out in Augustine's sketch of the anguished judge.[30] Barth himself is not a total stranger to that terrain.[31] Yet his final response is to turn back from it, and to locate a different ground on which a 'normal' politics can function without having to incur the perpetual self-affliction of those who think they must put to death, but know that they cannot raise from the dead. He imposes a generally binding *ne plus ultra* on the state's witness to God's right, and so abnormalizes the use of coercive force.

27. Cf. *Christian Life*, p. 16.
28. *Ethics*, p. 447.
29. *Ethics*, pp. 388f.
30. *City of God* 19.6. See also "The Political Thought of *City of God* 19," chap. 2, above.
31. Cf. *Ethics*, p. 387.

Yet this limit is only *generally* binding, and the use of force is only abnormalised, not ruled out. At a moment of supreme emergency, the limits set upon the state's freedom may be set aside, and at that point the putting of the enemy to death takes on the purpose of defending authority against its overthrow and so becomes a sanctifying act which honors God. War is not the only means by which this may be done — in 1931, at least, Barth thought he knew of some necessary exercises of the death penalty[32] — but war is usually Barth's concern when he writes in these terms. The occasional writings of the war years, which, on the surface, conform closely to a classical Augustinian doctrine of the state, actually take their occasion from the assertion that the extraordinary moment of confrontation has come. In describing the war as a "police measure," to be sure, Barth shows that he is aware of the continuity between what the state must do now and what it normally must do, and he still insists that there are crucial differences between the war and "a crusade or . . . war of religion."[33] Yet this is a police measure carried on by other means and in exceptional times against "an active anarchism which has become a principle" and against "the Revolution of Nihilism as the ruling principle of conduct."[34] The war to which Barth lent his countenance was, he thought, "a very special war, that . . . bears a totally different character from . . . nearly all the wars of previous centuries."[35] Later he will describe the occasion of the "exceptional case" as "only at the very last hour in the darkest of days," in which the state finds "its very existence and autonomy are menaced and attacked."[36]

In general, then, we have to think that Ramsey misunderstood Barth's doctrine of the christological foundation of the state, assimilating it wrongly to the concepts he was more used to criticizing, those of a perfectibilist realized eschatology. Barth is innocent of the errors in eschatology which Ramsey lays at the door of all pacifists, and innocent of the separatist ecclesiology which he lays at the door of some. He is innocent above all of the *imitatio* Christology which Ramsey thought to be the crux at which pacifists parted company from just-war Christians. His positions, indeed, on all these questions are at the opposite pole, and that is what makes him so interesting as a "liberal" opponent of Ramsey's doctrine of power. But on one point Ramsey did not misunderstand Barth, and that is the principle that the being of the state was defined in terms of its end in the kingdom of God. The kingdom of God is eschatological, while the state, like the church, belongs to a "world not yet redeemed"; yet the king-

32. *Ethics*, p. 153.
33. *A Letter to Great Britain from Switzerland* (London: Sheldon Press, 1941), p. 21.
34. *Letter to Great Britain*, p. 7.
35. "First Letter to the French Protestants." Appendix to *Letter to Great Britain*, p. 32.
36. *CD* III/4, pp. 456, 461.

dom present in Christ is the "original and final pattern" of the state.[37] This is seen in the context of Barth's famous analogy between the church and the state, in which the church is the "inner circle" of witness to the kingdom of God, and the state the "outer circle," so that they "share a common centre."[38] This formally reverses the earlier statement that the church "contains the state in itself";[39] but the change in spatial imagery is not of great moment, for either way the initiative in witness rests with the church, which must "remind the state of those things of which it is unable to remind itself" and be its "model and prototype."[40] The state is "a kind of annex and outpost of the Christian community, erected in the world outside which thus, in a certain sense, is included in the ecclesiastical order as such."[41] One might say: since there is no state which is not within the kingdom of Christ, there is no state which is not, implicitly at least, within Christendom — though the overt concessions which Barth once made to Christendom conceptions of church-state relations are later qualified by the description of every state as "pagan."[42]

The definition of the state in terms of its end raises two interconnected questions: first about a universal substratum of political reality given in nature; second, about the possibility of a distinctly Christian interpretation of political responsibility, given in the gospel. I shall attempt to show that Ramsey affirms both of these, while Barth has some difficulty in affirming the second because he is unwilling to affirm the first. This is the matter for the next two sections of our discussion, after which I shall propose a different account of their disagreement, based on a general characterization of two contrasting strands in the Western liberal tradition.

III

"The use of power, and possibly the use of force," Ramsey tells us, "is of the *esse* of politics. . . . The use of power, and possibly the use of force, is inseparable from the *bene esse* of politics."[43] We may interpret this to mean: the use of power, *which implies the possible use* of force. Ramsey does not intend to treat the questions of the use of power and the use of force as distinguishable, nor

37. "Christian Community," pp. 31, 20.
38. "Christian Community," pp. 32f.
39. *Ethics*, p. 449.
40. "Christian Community," pp. 34, 48.
41. *Church and State*, p. 59.
42. *Ethics*, pp. 450f.; "Christian Community," pp. 25, 27f.
43. *Just War*, p. 5.

does he intend to make his affirmations about the use of force more tentative than his affirmations about the use of power. But he does, as we have seen, intend to accept the more modest reading of Barth's thesis about the abnormality of war. The different construction of the predicates in these two sentences is revealing: the use of power is "of" the *esse* of politics, but it is merely "inseparable from" its *bene esse,* for it has "a conditional value only," while it is *ordo* (the ordered disposition of power) which, together with law and justice, actually "comprise[s] the well-being . . . of political affairs."[44] But since, in this state of imperfection, the stability of any order depends on the expenditure of power, we may say that the use of power "is inseparable from" the good that politics aims at.

Inseparable, that is, not only as a necessary means but also as one feature of the *ordo* that co-constitutes its end; for a stable order must be one in which power, once expended, can be replaced for further occasions of need. In the kingdom of Christ, of course, a single decisive exercise of divine power, the judgment and resurrection of the world, will establish an eternal and unshakable order. For those, therefore, to whom it is sufficient to prepare the way for the coming of that kingdom, for saints, martyrs, evangelists, and for all Christians when attending to their final end, it would be impudent to include the recruitment or expenditure of power within their goals. But citizens and statesmen concerned to preserve a proximate order that is threatened with entropy too soon before that kingdom dawns, cannot regard the recruitment and exercise of power as a matter of indifference to their penultimate goals, though always subject to the interlocking purposes of politics, *lex, ordo* and *iustitia.*

Ramsey so repeatedly asserts that earthly politics belongs in *unfulfilled* salvation history ("this side the ploughshares") that it is too easy to lose sight of the obvious: politics construed in terms of *lex, ordo* and *iustitia* is a fruit of that *provisional fulfillment* which is given in the advent of Jesus Christ. Ramsey's own misleading remarks about Barth's "post-evil, Christ-formed man" reinforce an equally misleading impression of Ramsey's own point of reference in salvation history. It can appear that Barth situates politics, as it were, in the gospels, while Ramsey throws it back into the depths of the Old Testament, somewhere in the middle of the Yahwist's primal history: the expulsion from Eden, or the city of Cain, or the post-diluvian covenant, or the Tower of Babel.[45] But Ramsey's characteristic appeal to the mythical resonances of the Fall is authorized and necessitated by a more fundamental reference: "A Christian . . . will think politically in the light of Christ, and this leads him to espouse ideals and

44. *Just War,* p. 11.
45. Cf. *Just War,* p. xxi; *Speak Up,* pp. 184-86.

the longing of the whole human family for justice and peace. But he will not forget to think politically in the light of the revealing shadow thrown by the cross of Christ over our fallen existence. This darkness does not envelop that light. Neither does the light diminish, it rather throws the shadows."[46] It was on this basis that he contended against Hauerwas and Yoder that it was not christocentricity that divided them but the interpretation of it, against Gustafson that his own 'rigorist' principles sprang from "the role Christology plays in moral analysis and life," and against McCormick that the inviolability of human life is grounded in the impossibility of "killing Christ anew."[47]

But even if these explicit avowals of a christological center for ethics and politics were not to hand, we ought still to know better than to read Ramsey as though he were a "two-kingdoms" Lutheran. If we grasp the logic of his agapism we see that political ethics must submit to the commanding principle of Christ-like love, a love that authorizes or refutes what may from time to time be suggested by our natural sense of justice. Political ethics, too, is "in-principled love." Most striking in this connection is Ramsey's rejection of the natural law basis which the great Renaissance architects of just-war theory laid for their work, and his replacement of their appeal to the right of self-defense with what he saw as a more primitive tradition relying on charity alone.

Within "The Uses of Power" there are two points at which we find confirmation that the *bene esse* of politics, as he understands it, is a work of Christian love. At the beginning he tells us that the just-war theory was the "working politico-military doctrine" of "the empires and nations of Christendom." The *political* theory outlined in the article is intended to do no more than elaborate what was implicit in the just-war theory as a *military* ethics, which was always a political doctrine by implication. But the just-war theory, as we have said, is the work of Christian love within the military arena. The second point of confirmation comes at the end, where Ramsey laments the depoliticization of the modern world and attributes it to a loss of the sense of the transcendent, with a concomitant inability to distinguish the supernatural from the temporal good. Without a grasp of the transcendent we cannot conceive the political community as "the proximate solution" to "the ambiguity of historical sacrifice." We invest it with a false ultimacy that it cannot bear, and this inhibits us from the risk of political action for the defense of real but not ultimate goods that are properly invested in the political community. To Ramsey's mind the attempt to

46. "War and Peace as a Religious Issue," p. 19.
47. *Speak Up*, pp. 111f.; "A Letter to James Gustafson," *Journal of Religious Ethics* 13 (1985): 83; "Incommensurability and Indeterminacy in Moral Choice" in *Doing Evil to Achieve Good: Moral Choice in Conflict Situations*, ed. R. McCormick and P. Ramsey (Philadelphia: Loyola University Press, 1978), p. 93.

limit politics to a single international agent representing the world-community, as some would like to do with the United Nations, is a false ultimizing of the penultimate. Such a totalized global agent would not only fail to free us for risk in the service of subordinate communities, "proximate" communities in a different sense, i.e., communities of neighborhood, but would fail to free us for risk in its *own* service, since it could not justify to us the sacrifices we would be summoned to make on its behalf. Thus in our age the political pursuit of political objectives is ruled out, "spiritualized" into pure discourse of those who "are resolved to negotiate so that negotiation will never fail."[48] Behind this argument lies an appeal to Augustine's two cities. Worldly politics depends on a knowledge of the transcendent, a knowledge of what differentiates the heavenly from the earthly and of what provides the human person with a destiny beyond death. Only this knowledge can set us free to take the risk of sacrifice for the proximate goods of worldly community.[49]

Yet Ramsey presents us with a contrast between the *esse* and the *bene esse* of politics, between its being and its end, echoing the famous dictum from the beginning of Aristotle's *Politics* that the polis "is born that we may live, and continues that we may live well." About the *esse* of politics he has almost nothing to tell us, other than that power is "of" it. But its role in his thought is important: it is a safeguard against utopianism in our speculations on the *bene*

48. *Just War,* pp. 4, 17. In his revision Ramsey considerably expanded this section, and made it clear that he did not oppose the further development of international institutions of peace, but the utopian hopes placed in them. "If the leaders of religious opinion manage to repress their penchant for exercises in day-by-day political decision-making, our energies could then be devoted to *studies of the international system,* its nature and limitations, and to an investigation of the *structural improvements* of international practices and institutions which by manifold efforts of thought and action might become possible of achievement." "War and Peace as a Religious Issue," p. 54.

49. In an inverted form the argument reappears with memorable effect in a sermon prompted by President Reagan's controversial visit to the German war cemetery at Bitberg, West Germany in 1985. (This was distributed privately in typescript by the author.) Here Ramsey found an absolutizing of the proximate in the "icy mercilessness" of those who objected to any hint of softening on the part of the liberal West towards the troops who died for Nazi Germany, and was especially moved by Elie Wiesel's words: "The fear of forgetting remains the main obsession of those who have passed through the universe of the damned." "Transfixed by abysmal evil," he commented, "we must invent a substitute for Hell's retribution. . . . If only there was a Deity, who does not know that *anger* would be a quite proper emotion on his part, entirely 'fitting' the absolute evil we have seen in the twentieth century? Therefore we must invent anger in a universe that affords none." To this need of anger we find that memory is the key, which "not only holds fast the victims, but also holds in uninterrupted condemnation the evil done to them." But "the point Western religions have in common must be pressed: the inscrutability of the embrace of justice and mercy in God, without negotiation weakening either."

esse. Because the survival of a human community depends in the first instance on its capacity to use force if required, the flourishing of that community cannot be described without reference to the proper disposition of that capacity. "Living well" must be described in terms consistent with simply "living." *Ordo,* the disposition of power, must be preserved together with *lex* and *iustitia.*

Here, evidently enough, is a critical point of separation between Ramsey and Barth. There is no dialectic of *esse* and *bene esse* in Barth's view of politics. Though the state has no alternative but to think of itself and its task in terms of natural law, the church must never agree to think of it in those terms.[50] A natural substratum of politics is excluded, together with all other natural substrata, by the rejection of any purchasing-point for grace in nature. Yet it is the ontological and not the epistemological form of that rejection which has forced a parting of the ways. In speaking of an *esse* of politics Ramsey has not forsaken his principle of thinking politically "in the light of the revealing shadow thrown by the cross of Christ over our fallen existence." The *ordo cognoscendi* is not at issue between them; rather, the separation is forced by Barth's insistence that the *ordo essendi* must follow the *ordo cognoscendi* exactly.

Ramsey has taken his cue from the fact that it is a *shadow* that the cross has thrown, and not pure light. The cross is a contradiction, not only of what goes before it but of what comes after, so that Christian politics, too, stands subject to that contradiction. This is how he knows (in terms of a theological derivation of knowledge) that there is an *esse* to be reckoned with, as distinct from a *bene esse.* The *esse* is not brought in as an independent datum; rather, it is the hypothesis demanded by the shadow that the cross throws, together with its light, across the *bene esse.* In terms of salvation history the *esse* may have preceded the *bene esse,* but in the order of Christian knowledge we know the *bene esse* first and the *esse* through its lens. It is because we find even our best efforts of in-principled love still subject to the contradiction of the cross that we discern, within our political life, conditions that forbid it to be a true and unambiguous shining of the light of Christ's reign. What opens up to us at the point where that light and its shadow fall is a mode of communal action to "effect the largest possible area of incidence" among goods which must compete with one another in this age. Our goal is to make right appear in our midst *(iustitia);* to make it appear conformably to the safety of that organism of human relations which we inherit *(lex);* and to refound that organism securely upon the appearance of right by means of an appropriate disposition of power *(ordo).* The task of politics is to be a sign of the rule of Christ, disclosing right, preserving community and determining the basis of community in right; yet it must function within the penultimate sphere

50. "Christian Community," pp. 27-29.

of divine providence, subject to the contradiction of the final sphere of Christ's reign. It is not empowered by divine judgment and miracle, but by human insight and might. Human insight is not certain nor all-encompassing; and human might, when it has killed, does not raise to life again.

IV

Had Ramsey addressed directly Barth's refusal of a natural substratum of politics, he might have criticized it first of all for precisely the opposite failing to that which he did in fact identify. Far from abolishing power in the all-embracing "already" of the rule of Christ, Barth constrains it within a tight "not yet," which denies to the normal functions of the state a sufficient confidence to exercise judgment with the redemptive decisiveness that the use of force implies. Barth, that is, represents a more austere version of Ramsey's own program of constraining force within the canons of a justice that is fit for unperfected human beings to exercise. It is on this ground that they would both merit the appellation "liberal." Situated no less distantly from eschatological enthusiasm, Barth has apparently allowed less than Ramsey, if anything at all, for the provisional disclosure of Christ's rule which has brought politics under the transforming discipline of love. There is little space in Barth for the idea of a distinctly Christian political ethics. Of course, much in Barth bears a distinctly Christian stamp in fact; but his is a distinctly Christian idea of political ethics, not an idea of a distinctly Christian political ethics. It is the *esse* of politics that is in his view, not a Christian *bene esse* that would correspond to some *esse* that lies behind it.

We might elaborate a possible Ramseyan critique by saying that Barth's account of the Christ-event has left no room for Advent. The threefold organization of the divine economy as creation, reconciliation, and redemption finds its authority in the Christ-event, but is deficient. It is not enough to say that God's anointed has reconciled us by his death, has vindicated the order of our created being by rising from the dead, and has made us share in the power of God's rule by sitting at God's right hand. The gospels do not begin there, but with the prior assertion that he *has come*. The Messiah has presented himself to the recognition and welcome of faith. He has gathered around himself a company of human beings which has challenged all other social groupings. He has reached for the crown which will allow no rival crowns beside it. Because he has come, history has divided into two, its back broken on this outcrop of rock which it cannot negotiate. The time of waiting has given place to the time of fulfillment — and that without yet taking account of Easter.

It lies beyond our scope to test the claim comprehensively that Barth's

Christology lacked a sufficiently defined Advent moment, and I shall be content with three comments on section 34 of the *Church Dogmatics*, entitled "The Election of the Community." In the first place, the distinction between Israel and the church is there rooted christologically in the death and resurrection of Christ, his 'double election' to the wrath and favor of God, which is the ground for the articulation of the community into two. Thus Christ's own history is shaped entirely by the thesis-antithesis of the paschal mystery, according to which he is "the suffering inaugurator of the passing of the first human form of the community" and "the triumphant inaugurator of the gracious coming of the new form of man."[51] Secondly, the community's articulation tends to be de-historicized, so that instead of a simple succession of Israel followed by the church we have a permanent two-sided emblem of the paschal event: Israel is "the community of God in so far as this community has to exhibit also the un-willingness, incapacity and unworthiness of man with respect to the love of God directed to him," while the church is "the community of God in so far as this community has to set forth to sinful man the good-will, readiness and hon-our of God." Thirdly, inasmuch as this representative opposition of Israel and the church is, nevertheless, still the key to the *history* of election, it shows a his-tory of disjunction *within the community,* not in the works of God as such. His-tory displays successively on the human side what is always insusceptible of dis-tinction on the divine side.

Certainly, this allows more historical differentiation than the bald state-ment that "in Christ's church Moses is the neighbour."[52] Yet it retains a curi-ously ahistorical feel, and if it is a correction to Luther's Two Regiments of God, it is one that operates very much within the same framework. "Old" and "new" are designations for contrasting spheres that coexist; Barth's correction is sim ply to deny that this coexistence in difference extends to the being and works of God as such. We may helpfully contrast this approach with that of another leading exponent of the Reformed tradition, supremely authoritative for Ramsey, Jonathan Edwards, whose *History of the Work of Redemption* set out to display the articulation of redemption historically, as a history of the acts of God. Edwards continually notes new things that God did at different points in biblical history; yet there is about his presentation something that we may, per-haps, call naive historicism, in that every articulation has its rationale in the sheer successiveness of events itself, so that there is no qualitative deposit from the kaleidoscopic sequence, no difference which transcends those temporal dif-ferences. The result is a tendency to perpetual recurrence, such as besets every

51. *CD* II/2, p. 198.
52. *Ethics*, p. 359.

[handwritten margin note top: historicism / Needs careful / defining!]

radical historicism. This is seen in the charming but disconcerting way that events in Israel's deepest patriarchal or tribal past assume, by typological means, the character of a revival movement in a New England congregation.

Ramsey stands halfway between the historicism of Edwards and the ahistoricism of Barth. For him, as for Barth, the succession of BC and AD discloses and interprets the moral complexity of present reality. This emerges from a comparison of his treatment of the "coats of skins" which God made for Adam and Eve on their expulsion from Eden with that of Edwards. For Edwards these were "a lively figure of their being clothed with the righteousness of Christ."[53] For Ramsey they are "limiting" as well as "clothing garments"; they are "impersonal ways" of keeping fellow humanity from becoming man-against-man in the best of causes; they are the socio-political orders which "partake of the sin and injustice they repress."[54] The true significance of this event in the Genesis narrative is not prophetic but symbolic, an "old" which points to a continuing contrast of coexistents. Yet for Ramsey, as hardly for Barth, we can speak of something in the era AD that is not merely "new" in co-existent contrast with the "old," but decisively new. The law of love declares the old not "passing" but past, the new not "coming" but come.[55] A new situation has come to exist, marked not merely by a tension between old and new but by a decisive struggle for succession. This struggle must be a feature of any politics in the Christian era, until those forms of society that Christ has challenged reach, whether graciously or ungraciously, the end of their usefulness.

So is Ramsey among the theologians of struggle? Definitely so, although for him it is a struggle of reason — which is to say, of *practical* reason — to transform the recalcitrant institutions of human justice into obedience to the law of love. The word "transform" is, admittedly, ambiguously helpful; we can accept the suggestion that Ramsey abandoned earlier talk about "love transforming natural law" because it was unclear about the primacy of love and carried overtones of progressivism.[56] Yet Christian love is not simply a legitimizing reference-point. It is an energy that works to "overcome evil with good," engaging the sinfulness of humankind and the limitations of its fellowship on every front, searching both cautiously and boldly for the grips that will wrestle them to the ground. Ramsey's sense of struggle contrasts with some rather flat

53. *History of the Work of Redemption* (Works of Jonathan Edwards, vol. 9), ed. J. F. Wilson (New Haven: Yale University Press, 1989), p. 136.

54. *Christian Ethics and the Sit-in*, pp. 48-50.

55. Only the contrary pattern in Barth requires us to make the obvious point that for Ramsey the "old" is not identified specifically with Israel.

56. Cf. David Attwood, *Paul Ramsey's Political Ethics* (Lanham, MD: Rowman & Littlefield, 1992).

accounts of political responsibility that we find in Barth: the inventiveness which he counsels the church to show in the political realm is hardly fleshed out with any serious probing of the difficulties faced by practical reason in this area, and the analogy of church and state may suggest a church rather complacent in its political knowledge.

The absence of struggle was the feature which led Ramsey to his interpretative surmise about Barth's "post-evil, Christ-formed man." This, as I have argued, was mistaken. If Ramsey's struggle of love was based on a sense of being between the times, bounded by the Advent on the one hand and the Eschaton on the other, it is the former, not the latter, which has disappeared from Barth's thought, leaving the space of Christian history insufficiently defined. Yet Ramsey was not wrong to fear a tendency for political action to disintegrate in an explosive fission of old and new, a dissociation of the "passing" and the "coming" humanity of Christ generated by too exclusively paschal a Christology. The true being of Christian politics has to be rooted in God's acceptance of Christ's regnant new humanity; but for Barth that implies that it is rooted in God's rejection of the old humanity. And this has some alarming implications for the evaluation of political power.

These are already apparent at the level of normative political ethics in Barth's prohibition of such a generally beneficent institution as the professional army and his narrowing of the state's scope to education and lawmaking.[57] But it is his commentary on the actual exercise of force, past and present, that really shows the difficulties he is in. For here a chasm opens up between everything that Barth conceives as a truly political use of force and almost everything that has ever been done in that way. His remarks take on a shrill note of denunciation, from which even the attempt to understand the causes of failure is missing: "Much is already gained if only we do at last soberly admit that, whatever may be the purpose or possible justice of a war, it now means that, without disguise or shame, not only individuals or even armies, but whole nations as such, are out to destroy one another by every possible means. . . . To kill effectively . . . must not those who wage war steal, rob, commit arson, lie, deceive, slander, and unfortunately to a large extent fornicate . . . ?" "We have no good reason not to recognise that modern war is primarily and basically a struggle for coal, potash, ore, oil and rubber, for markets and communications, for more stable frontiers, and spheres of influence as bases from which to deploy power for the acquisition of more power, more particularly of an economic kind."[58] This list, closely shadowing a similar catalogue of twenty years earlier, naturally prompts the

57. *CD* III/4, p. 460; *Ethics*, pp. 447f. Cf. pp. 363-99.
58. *CD* III/4, pp. 452-54. Cf. *Ethics*, p. 159.

question: what did Barth think he had learned from his untiring exhortations in the intervening conflict about the possible reasons for which one might make war — apart from fornicating to a large extent? The answer seems to be, quite self-consciously, nothing. For that conflict was, even at the time not a part of the history of war as such, but more "a totally different character from . . . nearly all the wars of previous centuries."[59]

These descriptions of war are some of Barth's least successful pages. The history of the use of force appears, with fairly little qualification, as the history of sin, but not as the history of grace abounding yet more. In contrast to Ramsey, who can point to monuments of grace in the midst of human sinfulness, Barth can only advise Christians to manifest "a distinctive horror . . . and aloofness" and to make a "detached and delaying movement."[60] There is no gracious "You may!" in relation to the state's use of force, so that in Barth's political thought we miss that note of redemptive divine permission which is so unforgettable elsewhere in his work. Divine permission for *power* there certainly is; but even this is not addressed to the political community or its officers: "the power which man may and should will and use is always the power which God has given precisely to him as an individual."[61] The irony of this is that Barth ends up precisely in the place he had intended to bypass, in a politics that can only be viewed "soberly" and not with evangelical faith or hope. He leaves us with the gulf unbridged between an ideal, evangelical politics grounded in the reconciling covenant of God with man in Christ and actual political phenomena that we can only deplore and cannot interpret favorably. What is needed to sustain an evangelical interpretation of politics is some way of bridging this gulf, so that the *homo politicus* redeemed in Christ is recognizably the same *homo politicus* in need of redemption. This is what Ramsey offers us with his disjunction between the *esse* and the *bene esse*.

This disjunction can, in fact, be carried a long way towards Barth's principle that the being of the state should be defined by its end. Ramsey renders the term *bene esse* with a variety of English equivalents, "goal," "end," and "purpose" among them; but more than once he suggests that it means "the proper being of politics" or "the proper act of being politics."[62] His notion of an end, it appears, is entelechic; he is not speaking of an end of politics *beyond* politics, but of *true* political activity. So that in the "end" of politics we have the "true" being of politics, not merely as something presupposed, but as something fully

<hr>

59. "Letter to French Protestants," p. 32.
60. *CD* III/4, p. 456.
61. *CD* III/4, p. 393.
62. *Just War*, pp. 9f.

realized. There is an ontological concession implicit in the term, which has implications not only for the sections of Ramsey's discussion which treat of *lex, ordo,* and *iustitia,* but for those which defend the claim that world politics is pluralistically international rather than homogeneously international. This latter claim could easily be cast in Barthian terms by saying that politics-in-Christ must take the form of encounter with the neighbor. A single self-sufficient world state is as much a solipsistic dream as a single self-sufficient individual.[63]

Such a further approximation of Ramsey's thought to Barth's is not only satisfying in itself, but provides substantial assistance for some of Ramsey's own favorite claims. The just-war doctrine was a politico-military doctrine which tied strategy to political purposes, but these political purposes are themselves justified by the nature of politics, not imposed upon politics from outside it. Here is a familiar *Leitmotiv,* one which constantly surprises the half-attentive moralist who is alarmed to be told that this or that offense is 'unpolitical' when he had expected to be told that it was immoral. It has proved possible to misunderstand it as the expression of an amoralist political 'realism', whereas in fact it derives from a truer 'realism', an essentialist understanding of what political agents are and what politics is good for. Only such moral counsel as derives from the *being* of political agency can be relevant to decisions which statesmen and citizens must make. But if God's covenant in Christ shapes political decisions relevantly through the law of love, it must be because the being of political agency is included there.

So far, then, we may draw the strands of Ramsey's and Barth's thoughts together. Yet there is still a distance that refuses to be conjured away. Once we have understood what politics is good for, Ramsey invites us to say, we will also understand what that otherwise troubling phenomenon, political power, is good for. This need not necessarily imply a substantial political substratum of power politics; it need not imply everything that Brunner meant by his claim that "war belongs to the very nature of the state so long as it has no better protection of its rights," let alone all that Barth took him to mean.[64] Perhaps we ought not to say that power is of the *esse* of politics, but should use some other term that will point to the purely inchoate character of power, e.g., the *material* of politics. Yet in true politics power is taken up and given a role in the service of mankind; in true politics we can see its 'uses'. Retrospectively power has been justified for us, rather as that other problematic and sometimes destructive potency, the erotic, has been justified for us by the covenant of marriage. The gospel offers a fulfillment of political power, as well as a judgment on it. Only so

---

63. For criticiam of a self-sufficient world state, see pp. 236-37, 241-42 above.

64. Emil Brunner, *The Divine Imperative,* trans. Olive Wyon (Philadelphia: Westminster Press, undated repr. [orig. 1932]), p. 469. Cf. Barth's capricious comment, *CD* III/4, p. 458.

can the *homo politicus* that is redeemed be the same *homo politicus* that was in need of redemption. The best model for Ramsey's contention is found in the doctrine of the Incarnation: what he requires is a political analogue of the *homo assumptus.* But that is what Barth is not ready to grant, in the political realm at least. His anthropology contains more than a few moments of sympathy with Apollinaris, where we find an analogy to his separation of the ideal and the actual in the discussion of war: on the one hand there is the "real man," God's covenant-partner, on the other there is "humanity which runs amok. . . and plunges like a meteor into the abyss, into empty space."[65] However there is more than sufficient evidence that Barth resisted the temptations of Apollinarianism, and conceded a place in Christology to the *humanum.*[66] But in political theory there is no analogy to this. Our final question is why not, and this can usefully be answered by exploring the grounds on which his thought, and that of Ramsey, may be called "liberal."[67]

V

In 1964 Ramsey conceived that Barth supported a view which he uneasily called "liberal" to contrast it with another which he called, without apparent qualm, "conservative." To each of these positions he attributed one "piece of the truth," one error of its own, and a common error to unite them. This analysis, however, fell to pieces in his hands. To begin with the common error: "they both believe that peace, justice and freedom can be preserved by 'bluffing' . . . therefore they both avoid thinking through the actual *use* of power for positive purposes, and the political morality governing such use."[68] That is to say, they both "split politics and military doctrine apart."

65. These moments appear especially in his discussions of the first and last Adam passage in 1 Corinthians 15, where Barth could not bring himself to believe that Paul meant what he said in 15:46 about the order of the two: *Church Dogmatics III: The Doctrine of Creation,* vol. 2, various translators (Edinburgh: T&T Clark, repr. 1960 [orig. 1948]), p. 205; *Church Dogmatics IV: The Doctrine of Reconciliation,* vol. 1, trans. G. W. Bromiley (Edinburgh: T&T Clark, repr. 1956 [orig. 1953]), pp. 512f. This reverses his judgment in *The Resurrection of the Dead,* trans. H. J. Stenning (London: Hodder & Stoughton, repr. 1933 [orig. 1926]), pp. 209f.

66. *Church Dogmatics IV: The Doctrine of Reconciliation,* vol. 2, trans. G. W. Bromiley (Edinburgh: T&T Clark, repr. 1958 [orig. 1955]), pp. 45-50.

67. In speaking of Barth's "liberalism" I mean to express no view, negative or positive, on the question of his "socialism," which occupied German-language commentators a generation ago (See George Hunsinger, ed. and trans., *Karl Barth and Radical Politics* (Philadelphia: Westminster Press, 1976).

68. *Just War,* p. 4.

It is easy to specify how Ramsey thought that liberals made this error. Their piece of the truth was that "there can be no victory if the means of violence used are disproportionate to any possible political goals"; their error was to conclude from this "that there can be no positive use of force . . . for political ends," so that "force has at most the purpose that a show of it stimulates negotiation." But what of the conservatives? Their piece of the truth was the denial of the liberal error: "there must be a positive use of armed force in the political affairs of mankind." This is immediately disconcerting, since it appears to conflict with the common error. Perhaps Ramsey meant us to understand that conservatives believe in the positive use of force at lower levels, but are diverted by their confidence in bluff from delineating the upper limits to acceptable force. However that may be, their peculiar error is even more elusive than their peculiar truth. What they ought to believe erroneously, to preserve the formal balance, is the denial of the liberal truth: "there can be victory even if the means used are disproportionate." But Ramsey is unwilling to attribute this view to them; and anyway, if they truly believed that, they did not, after all, share the common error with the liberals. So he manages to attach to the conservatives no more than a *seeming* determination "to 'win' all the way up the scale of available violence." From which he ought probably to have concluded that there was only one erroneous view, and that was the liberal view, both in its supposedly peculiar and its supposedly common aspects. The appearance of a distinctly conservative position in the 1964 Presidential election was a mirage, and what Senator Goldwater actually offered the American people was a thoroughgoing application of the liberal doctrine of bluff ("force is to deter with") carried to such steely-nerved lengths that the more sensitive stomach of the liberal *moyen sensuel* turned sick at such a concentrated dose of his own medicine. It was a matter of degree: "a *show* of force at the lower levels" on the one side, "a *show* of force at the upper nuclear level" on the other side.

And perhaps Ramsey did conclude this, though he did not admit it at the time. In 1968 when he reworked the material of "The Uses of Power," the liberal-conservative analysis disappeared, and Ramsey undertook instead to describe the important disagreements in terms of a variety of liberalisms. This gave him one immediate advantage: he could classify the truth as liberal, too, under the name of "tempered liberalism." Again it had error both to the left and the right of it: an "illusioned liberalism" on the left, which thinks "there is no limit to the political attainment of freedom, justice, and equality," and on the right a "disillusioned liberalism" that shrinks from any exercise of policy for fear of the inherent risk of power corrupted in the service of self-interest.[69]

69. "War and Peace as a Religious Issue," 9. Ramsey consistently writes of illusioned or disillusioned "liberalism or idealism," thereby keeping contact with Reinhold Niebuhr's under-

Tempered liberalism in the middle understands both that there are moral gains to be achieved by policy and that those gains are limited in scope and not free from the risk of corruption.

On this occasion the errors are not those of the competing political parties. They are both perpetrated simultaneously by the American people as a whole, a nation of "illusioned liberals" in their domestic policy and of "disillusioned liberals" in foreign policy. Overconfident of political possibilities at home, Americans are vulnerable to "a kind of domestic fascism," in which even the extirpation of prejudice from the human heart is thought of as a realizable policy goal. Lacking confidence in the possibilities of policy abroad, they are determined to root out idealism in foreign affairs, which, they believe, always masks arrogance and self-aggrandizement; and in its place they erect a simplistic *laissez-faire* doctrine that each nation's pursuit of its own domestic interest is conducive to a better world.[70] As the subtitle of the paper suggests, "on extricating the church from liberal disillusionment," it was the foreign policy aspect of this isolationist posture that engaged Ramsey the more closely.

About this new analysis of American liberalism there are two questions that suggest themselves immediately, neither of which receives a direct answer. In the first place where are the "conservatives" of 1964, who turned out to be closet liberals with an advanced taste for daredevil stunts? With the mid-60s shift in foreign policy concerns from nuclear confrontation to involvement with southeast Asia, Ramsey lost interest in them, and we can only speculate on how he might have measured their views against his new grid. Was their position a looking-glass version of liberalism, full of illusory hopes abroad but cynical at home? Or would they fit the general characterization of "we Americans," their domestic conservatism one more species of idealism, their hawkish foreign policy, precisely because it was conceived on the negative principle of nuclear containment, one more species of self-interested disinvolvement? The second question is also concerned with the connection between Ramsey's first and second thoughts: how does this later analysis, framed in terms of oscillating confidence in the moral possibilities of political action, relate to the earlier analysis in terms of the divorce of politics and power?

We can reach an answer to both these questions by way of a third. The two strands of liberalism, reformist illusion and isolationist disillusion, belong together: why? Ramsey offers no account of their association. He clearly thinks that American liberalism is vitiated as a moral stance by its oscillating over-

---

standing of liberalism. Yet it is clear that the disillusioned idealist is an *ex*-idealist, now an *anti*-idealist. Indeed, it is Niebuhr himself in some moods.

70. "War and Peace as a Religious Issue," pp. 11-15.

confidence and under-confidence. Better, because more consistent, the pursuit of "a *measured* good to be attained at home and a measured *good* for which we are responsible abroad." Yet these oscillations yield a kind of coherence, not merely a series of inconsistencies. What is the element in American liberal thought that allows them?

The answer, I suggest, lies in the continuing influence of John Locke's version of social contract theory upon the liberalism of the anglophone West. The contractarian opposition of the state of nature and the state of civil society shapes the way in which some strands of the contemporary tradition differentiate foreign and domestic policy. For this Locke is to thank, who rescued Hobbes's "state of nature" from being an implausible etiological myth and gave it an actual reference in the relations of sovereign states: —

> It is often asked as a mighty objection where are, or ever were, there any men in such a state of Nature? To which it may suffice as an answer at present, that since all princes and rulers of "independent" governments all through the world are in a state of Nature, it is plain the world never was, nor never will be, without numbers of men in that state. I have named all governors of "independent" communities, whether they are, or are not, in league with others; for it is not every compact that puts an end to the state of Nature between men, but only this one of agreeing together mutually to enter into one community, and make one body politic; other promises and compacts men may make one with another, and yet still be in the state of Nature.[71]

Locke did not mean that all independent sovereigns were at war. He challenged Hobbes's equation of the state of nature and the state of war, and it may be here that we should locate the gulf between those whom our convention calls "conservatives" (regardless of what, if anything, they wish to conserve) and those designated "liberals" in opposition to them. On this account conservatives have given Locke's theory a turn back towards Hobbism, supposing that absence of civil association implies a latent warfare. But the difference between these two groups can only be a relative one, since they agree on the fundamental point: the moral possibilities of politics are confined to the internal relations of societies constituted by an act of political association. Within the terms of that association all politics, even the use of force, is based on consent; outside it all politics, even the securing of consent, is based on force. Thus the Lockean-liberal distaste for force drives one group away from foreign involvement in the hope of developing a politics of pure consent, while the Lockean-Hobbist belief

---

71. *Second Treatise of Civil Government*, 2.14.

in the inevitability of latent war outside the association drives the other group into a self-protective deterrent stance — in pursuit of the same end.

The term "liberal" is susceptible of different forms of accounting, narrow and broad. For the purposes of this discussion I assume a broad one, relating liberalism to a development in the notion of equity which became prominent in the sixteenth century, shaped by medieval dramaturgy on the gospel story of the woman taken in adultery, which stressed the inadequacy and the imperfection of every human attempt to render justice.[72] The concept of equity — the use of more or less rigorous judgment in response to the needs of the case — became associated with a humane humility of judgment, reminiscent of Augustine's judge in *City of God* 19.6, and with a scepticism at the pretensions of human judgment. From these flowed the characteristic liberal concern that the magistrate's power should be limited. *Summum ius summa iniuria:* Cicero's mocking reflection on lawyers was a favorite in the sixteenth century, as it was a favorite with Karl Barth. But its spirit is also captured in Ramsey's crenellated proposition that "not all of the *ought to be* ought to be by us done."[73] Within this general tradition we may see different strands of development. The liberal assessment of political power — suspect, but necessary — receives different interpretations from Ramsey and Barth. For Ramsey power is *always* suspect and *always* necessary, while Barth considers it *usually* suspect and *occasionally* necessary.

If there is one important thing that may be said about Ramsey's struggle with liberalism, it is that he challenged the Lockean hegemony of the Western liberal tradition — not in every respect, certainly, but at the point where it separated the politically normed sphere of domestic relations from the unnormed sphere of international politics. Ramsey's challenge runs in both directions. International relations, on the one hand, are governed by the same moral principles that are proper to all political agency, principles summed up in the triad *lex, ordo, iustitia.* The norms of domestic justice, on the other hand, must be seen to share the unsatisfactory power-dependence of international relations. The challenge was thrown out dramatically in Ramsey's first book on war: "What then is democracy but *justum bellum?* No Teacher in Galilee taught his disciples to resist evil by ballots."[74] The same challenge underlies a great deal that Ramsey wrote, and especially his lifelong insistence on the moral continuum that links violent with non-violent resistance. Almost every quarrel of po-

---

72. See John D. Cox, *Shakespeare and the Dramaturgy of Power* (Princeton: Princeton University Press, 1989).

73. *Just War,* p. 11; cf. "War and Peace as a Religious Issue," p. 25.

74. *War and the Christian Conscience* (Durham, NC: Duke University Press, 1962), p. 126.

litical principle that Ramsey picked with his contemporaries comes back to this at some point. The contractarians had overthrown an earlier and better understanding of international politics as the *extension* of domestic politico-moral principles beyond the limits of the constitutional state. The international sphere was a constitutional vacuum, but by no means a moral or political vacuum. This was the understanding of the Salamanca school of Thomists and of Hugo Grotius. It was also, Ramsey believed, the implicit theory of Augustine and Aquinas. It was the just war theory of Christendom.

The best insight, in some ways, into the tradition behind "War and Peace as a Religious Issue" may be gained from the Prolegomena to Grotius's most famous work, *On the Right of War and Peace.* There the author combats, under the guise of the ancient sceptic Carneades, views in which it is easy to recognize the nascent contractarianism of his own time with its scepticism about the possibility of right outside the constituted civility: "a sovereign, or a sovereign state, knows no injustice where utility is at stake"; "war is utterly remote from the norms of right"; "expediency, the virtual mother of justice and fairness"; "justice arose from fear of its opposite"; "all rights disappear in war." In response, Grotius proposes to identify precisely the elements of lawfulness which obtain in human affairs when the constituted civility is abstracted, "laws perpetually in force and appropriate for each and every season."[75] Like Ramsey, Grotius understands the Christian law of love as an innovative and transforming force, shaping a political ethics that belongs distinctively to Christendom; and alongside it he acknowledges universal perceptions of moral order that comport with, and are illumined by, the gospel law. Yet the place Grotius accords to a self-standing natural law is much larger than that envisaged by Ramsey; he does not share the epistemological christocentrism which Ramsey found attractive in Barth.

But how well does this illuminate Ramsey's disagreements with Barth? It must at first sight seem an unlikely speculation to line Karl Barth up alongside John Locke. Without, however, supposing a line of direct influence, we may make three observations which serve to illustrate Barth's general sympathy with a contractarian notion of the state. Social contract theory was a pan-European movement, which left deep imprints on the philosophical idealism of the German-speaking world. These can be seen in the political thought of Kant, and even in Hegel who denied the contractarian premise. It formed an intellectual matrix within which some of Barth's political thinking was done, and determined the principal points of divergence between him and the Grotian stream of Western liberal internationalism.

75. *De iure belli ac pacis*, Proleg., pp. 3, 16, 19, 25, 26; translation from *IG,* pp. 792-96. On this passage see also pp. 187-91 above.

(1) The formal distinction that Barth makes between normal and abnormal exercises of political authority suggests a differentiation within political practice by which consent-politics rules at the center, coercion rules at the margin. Now, as Ramsey sees, this normal-abnormal distinction is capable of an uncontroversial reading. No one will question the claim that the end of politics is just peace and peaceful justice, so that when its tasks are responsibly discharged, the risk of war and social conflict is reduced, the need for coercion made more remote. Yet according to Ramsey it is the perpetual *possibility* of the use of power which undergirds this normal state of affairs. As the use of power rests upon the possibility of the use of force, so the enjoyment of free political association rests upon the possibility of the use of power. To think of coercion, or even of power, as 'abnormal' in a *strong* sense is to withdraw the conditions on which it can become more infrequently necessary to invoke them.

Consider here the strange, even alarming, position that Barth takes up on capital punishment. It may be, he thinks, occasionally needed, but it must not be provided for "as a regular institution, for this will be a time of decisions and actions rather than rules. . . . The extreme and extraordinary character of the death penalty in such situations will be seen in the fact that extraordinary organs of authority will necessarily emerge and function."[76] These extraordinary organs of authority are not, it seems, organs of *law*, so that this exceptional measure looks bound to take on the character of an illegal act. Barth will concede, but only reluctantly, as the furthest possibility he will entertain, that there might be a legal provision framed to designate "this critical and exceptional situation"; but he prefers to think of justified executions as taking place at the very margin of the constitutionally constructed world, a space into which we are driven "at the very last hour and in the darkest of days."[77] It is, in effect, a measure only for constitutional emergencies, for the circumstances of a *coup d'état* or the collapse of lawful government, for resistance to tyranny, and for a state of war. We may doubt whether it is capital punishment that is being justified at all, in fact, rather than simple assassination. Ramsey contests the existence of such an empty pre-political space, contests the possibility of justified decisions generated outside and apart from the principles that govern lawful politics. All the space available for action is mapped out in general terms by the same norms that govern the direction of civil society.

(2) Barth is confident in our ability to determine *definite rules for the limits of normal politics.* These rules prohibit actions which take human life, since such actions are "lacking in humility" and exceed the humane scope that is allowed to

76. *CD* III/4, p. 447.
77. *CD* III/4, p. 456.

political order.[78] The focus of prohibition upon the taking of human life, rather than imprisonment, taxation, or any other oppression that government may impose upon the human subject, owes its tradition to a discussion among contractarian thinkers about the transference to the sovereign of the individual's original right to defend his own life.[79] It is a limit *on* politics, imposed as a condition for politics by the nature of individual existence. Ramsey's view of the prohibitions that limit human justice is that they define the intrinsic norms of political practice itself, the intention to effect justice. Thus they are not to be understood as limits set *on* politics, but as limits set *by* politics. There is no renunciation of justice in favour of humility; there is simply a point beyond which by failing to think humbly we would fail to think justly and politically. The rules are those generated by the political intention itself: on the one hand, the prohibition of direct attack on the innocent, on the other the demand for proportionately measured force. Humility must take on a political form in the realism with which the politician assesses the possibilities open to his action. Consequently Ramsey resists when invited to produce "definite action-rules" of political practice. Those who shared his commitment to the just war tradition were often enraged by his refusal even to deduce the categorical immorality of city bombing from the "exceptionless" rule against direct attack on the innocent.[80]

(3) Barth associates the move from the political center to the pre-political margin with the *threat to the existence of the state*. "The abolition of the lawful State" and the state's "very existence and autonomy" are the causes for which we may undertake the exceptionally permitted act against another's life.[81] This is because there "may well be bound up with the independent life of a nation responsibility for the whole physical, intellectual and spiritual life of the people comprising it, and therefore their relation to God." A comparison of these ex

---

78. *CD* III/4, p. 442.

79. Hobbes, *Leviathan*, II.21.10-17; Cesario de Beccaria, *Essay on Crimes and Punishments*, Eng. trans. (London, repr. 1785 [original 1764]), p. 102.

80. Nevertheless, Ramsey came to formulate the application of the double-effect principle in such a way that it is difficult to see how, if he had pursued the discussion, he could have avoided the conclusion reached from similar premises by Germain Grisez (*The Way of the Lord Jesus*, 1: *Christian Moral Principles* [Chicago: Franciscan Herald Press, 1983], p. 220), that the death penalty was categorically wrong. "Killing a human being must surely be classified . . . as something that Christians ought never to encompass with direct voluntariety" ("Incommensurability and Indeterminacy in Moral Choice," in *Doing Evil to Achieve Good: Moral Choice in Conflict Situations,* ed. Richard McCormick and Paul Ramsey [Philadelphia: Loyola University Press 1978], p. 93). Earlier, however, he had written that it was "perhaps for a good reason" that the later moral-theological tradition had confined the double-effect principle to the problem of killing an *innocent* person (*War and the Christian Conscience*, p. 57).

81. "Christian Community," p. 41; *CD* III/4, p. 461.

pressions with those of Ramsey's deeply-felt defense of the nation-state shows at once how much more modest are Ramsey's claims for the state than Barth's. It is a "proximate answer" (only) to "the ambiguity of historical sacrifice." In fact Ramsey has few illusions about the success of the nation-state system, either in the developing or in the developed world, and what his argument is really directed to is the importance of *tradition* in the identification of citizens with their communities and the *Ersatz* character of world governmental organs.[82] Ramsey could never have associated himself with the suggestion that the nation-state might "take responsibility for" a people's relation to God. That Barth, temperamentally so much more the cosmopolitan of the two, should have made such a concession to statism, is a measure of the strength of the underlying contractarian assumptions of his thought. On the one hand he shares the contractarian over-estimate of the state as the sole ground on which the social realization of spiritual values can be attempted; on the other hand he shares its anxiety over the fragility of this construct.

But was Barth driven by any theological necessity to stand in this position? Not at all. There was much in his thought that could and should have taken him the other way. The *humanum* of Christ, of the one Christ who represents both the passing and the coming humanity in himself, demonstrates that even the old humanity was never unnormed, but was claimed from the beginning — and in the event, decisively claimed — by the God of the covenant. And as the old humanity is within and not outside the covenant, so human relations even outside the state belong within and not outside the sphere of God's law. Indeed, these considerations *did* carry him the other way on occasions. His last discussion of politics was organized around the theme of Christian revolt against the demonic powers and the suppositious "lordlessness" of demonic authority.[83] All we can say is that because the historical definition of salvation tends in Barth to be submerged in emblematic representations, so the contractarian opposition of civil institutions and the normless state of nature commended itself as a possible and sometimes tempting political emblem for the antithetic poles of lordlessness and obedience which presented themselves to human choice.

For Ramsey this emblem could never be tempting. The just war doctrine, he claimed, "entailed an entire theory of statecraft, of political authority, political community, and political responsibility — or what Professor Quentin Quade calls the nature of the *political act*."[84] Perhaps it is not only the lack of a

---

82. *Just War,* pp. 14f.; "War and Peace as a Religious Issue," p. 53.
83. *Christian Life,* pp. 215f.
84. "War and Peace as a Religious Issue," p. 34.

final polish to the drafting that has left it ambiguous whether the phrase "political act" paraphrases the last item in this list or summarizes the whole of it. On the one hand there was a great deal to be said about political authority and political community which was not directly addressed by Ramsey's reflections on the political act; on the other hand there was nothing there that was not in principle illuminated from this central point. For Ramsey (and I do not think he misunderstood the sixteenth- and seventeenth-century just-war thinkers whose support he claimed) the form of the *act* was decisive for everything else in political theory. It bound together international and domestic, public and private, in one moral field; it laid the foundation for civil society and the authority of government; it drew justification from theologico-moral principle and in turn provided justification for a diverse range of political responses to diverse situations. At once flexible and comprehensive, it allowed of no exceptions, inhibited no properly political judgments, and by its very flexibility prevented the absolutizing of relative political values, however important. The political act was not bounded by institutions; at home in the city, it could extend itself into open spaces across the boundaries erected by civilized institution-building. It was impossible for Ramsey to conceive politics as an island kingdom, washed on all sides by the trackless ocean of a state of nature. The Lockean liberalism that conceived it that way had planted the abstract political institution at the core of political theory; but that was the place where political action belonged.

Nation, State, and Civil Society
in the Western Biblical Tradition

JOAN LOCKWOOD O'DONOVAN

Throughout the twentieth century, the idea of the nation-state has pervaded the conceptualization of political order. The idea has been endorsed or attacked, and frequently both endorsed and attacked, but ignored only with difficulty. For most of the century, it has played a strategic role in the formation of new political entities out of the old European and colonial empires: the Ottoman, Hapsburg, and Tsarist empires in Europe and the Middle East, and the European colonial possessions throughout Africa, Asia, and the Far East. In the course of imperial dismemberment exacerbated by war and of comprehensive decolonization, the idea of the nation-state has also been implicated in unprecedented state persecutions and territorial displacements of ethnic populations and the creation of 'stateless' peoples or official refugees. Thus, much ink has been spilt on the dramatic ambiguities of the concept for political morality.

That these moral ambiguities have continued to loom large in contemporary political and social analysis of the nation-state is primarily owing to two phenomena. The first is that of "ethnic cleansing," the horrific instances of which have attracted universal attention over the last decade — in the former Yugoslav republics, in African countries such as Rwanda, Burundi, the Sudan, and in Sri Lanka. To the extent that these assaults on civilian populations have

An earlier form of this essay was presented to the Scripture and Hermeneutics Seminar: 4th International Consultation (Cheltenham, 2001) under the title "A Timely Conversation with *Desire of the Nations* on Civil Society, Nation and State." For the revisions that I have subsequently made, I am especially indebted to Luke Bretherton's paper presented at the Bible Society/KCL Institute for Systematic Theology Seminar on Theology and Culture, Royal Holloway College, London, September 2002, "Valuing the Nation: Nationalism and Cosmopolitanism in Theological Perspective."

been carried out by militias with various degrees of governmental backing, they are perceived to manifest not merely tribal lawlessness in an anarchic atmosphere but perversions of the modern state. The second and intimately related phenomenon is the rising incidence of a belligerent form of political self-consciousness in which ethnic and religious identities are wedded. To the extent that the ethno-religious nationalisms that are currently generating widespread alarm are judged to be political distortions of the believing communities in question, they too direct our attention to the magnitude and global proliferation of political perversions in our century.

Over recent decades, the idea of the nation-state has also become a locus for a range of issues affecting liberal-democratic polities in the global era of mass communications technology, mass immigration, multinational corporations, and international finance and defense. The controlling question of these discussions concerns not so much the political morality as the political efficacy of the nation-state, whether it continues to be a viable and useful form of political organization in the contemporary world. However, the inescapable need of conceptualizing "the nation" in these discussions ensures that moral considerations are never far away.[1] For to conceptualize the nation is to conceive a community whose members are united by their common participation in certain social realities — material, institutional and spiritual, including the community's self-representing or self-imaging. And the permanent, overriding issue posed by the nation-state concerns the relation of this lived and represented community to political society and political order, to government and the practice of political justice.

The concepts of the nation that have dominated historical, social, and political analysis for a century all address these issues of political morality and political efficacy at one or another level. The widely diverse stances presented by the "romantic," the "civic," and the "functional" concepts of the nation reflect serious differences of philosophical understanding and historical interpretation: different accounts of what the nation is and of its historical genesis. At the same time, the concepts exhibit an underlying likeness as distinctively modern, their modernity residing in the idea of the nation as a totality distinguishable from the state, to which the state is instrumental. Not the reality of this totality but its nature is disputed in political and scholarly circles, and in the latter with infinite scholastic variations, concerning whether the nation is perennial or re-

---

1. It is interesting to observe that the various socio-historical interpretations of "the nation" as an ideological and/or functional requisite of modern industrial capitalism (including, of course, neo-Hegelian and Marxist-inspired interpretations) combine criticism of industrial capitalism and its ideological offshoot with a conviction of their supercession.

curring, natural or historical, biological or cultural, ethnic or ethno-religious, purely ideological or actually lived etc., etc.[2]

My intention in this essay is both critical-analytical and constructive. Firstly, I intend to explicate the prevailing concepts of the nation as they have interacted in the thought of the last century, raising doubts along the way about their adequacy to address the pressing issues of political morality and efficacy. Secondly, I shall propose that the most adequate concept of the nation, both historically and theoretically, is a Christian theological one that lays hold of the resources of Scripture and the exegetical and theological traditions of the past. For, I shall argue, in the revelation of God's historical dealings with Israel fulfilled in the coming of Jesus Christ and the gathering of his kingdom is given the reality of political authority and of political community, and therein the proper meaning of nation, state, and civil polity in their interrelationship. Thus, my constructive task is to lay out the biblical points of reference for a theological concept of nation and to indicate their historical outworking in the formation of Western Christian nations.

The "Romantic," the "Civic," and the "Functional" Nation

Intrinsic to contemporary usage of the term "nation" is a conceptual ambiguity of decisive importance. On the one hand, the double-pronged noun "nation-state" implies that the nation is a reality distinct not only from the mechanism of government (one meaning of "state") but also from the political community (another meaning of "state"). On the other hand, "nation" is frequently employed as a synonym for "state" in its second meaning, most famously in the rubric of the United Nations. In this duality of meaning lurk significant and long-standing issues concerning which referent has historical and moral priority so as to justify and determine the reality of the other.

The answer of *romantic nationalism* is that the nation as a unique communal totality, at once natural and historical, gives rise to and morally justifies the sovereign state. Constitutive of this prior totality, on the romantic view, are such features as a common language and ethnic inheritance — shared sentiments, mores, spiritual capacities, and historical memories — and a continuous relation to a particular soil. When such an organic social-cultural reality becomes self-conscious (through the educating and mobilizing activities of

2. For those who are interested in these disputes, the best review of the scholarly literature is A. D. Smith, *Nationalism and Modernism: A Critical Survey of Recent Theories of Nations and Nationalism* (London: Routledge, 1998).

cultural, social, and political elites), it seeks to express its subjectivity in the realms of power and law. In assuming statehood it becomes self-determining: it takes control of its historical destiny.[3] This was the national idea that dominated Europe for a century after 1830, inspiring the partition of empires, projects of linguistic and cultural unification, and the formation of a host of new states in East and West. Its quintessential statement was Giuseppe Mazzini's call in 1857: "Every nation a state" and "only one state for the entire nation."[4] The romantic principle, however, was sufficiently versatile to give play to diverse political visions, as may be gauged by the distance between Mazzini's projected map of Europe consisting of "a bare dozen states and federations" and the twenty six European states produced by the peace treaties following World War I under the influence of Woodrow Wilson's version of the nationality idea. Whereas Mazzini's romantic nationalism incorporated liberal-economic and progressivist notions inimical to the appearance of small states, President Wilson endorsed a purer strain of ethnic-linguistic nationhood sympathetic to the course of "Balkanization."

The constitution of all twenty-six new states as parliamentary democracies suggests the intimate relation between the romantic and the civic conceptions of the nation that existed in Europe from about 1870. In contrast to the ethnic-linguistic nation, the *civic nation* was regarded not as a prior cause of the state but as coterminous with it and, to some extent, a work of it. The civic nation comprises the unifying moral and affective bonds of the citizenry in a free, democratic polity; it comprises the ongoing moral-political reality of the "popular will" as a vital community of faith, sentiment, and devotion. A rational communion, the civic nation is formed over time through the operation of political and legal institutions according to universal principles of justice. But it is also a deliberate project of public education and mobilization: of educating citizens in the principles of liberal-democratic political culture and mobilizing them for political action.[5] Born in the crucible of late-eighteenth-century revo-

---

3. National self-consciousness in the romantic view may be consciousness of a past cultural-social-territorial integrity that has been lost and can be restored only through independent political action.

4. Cited in E. J. Hobsbawm, *Nations and Nationalism since 1780: Programme, Myth, Reality* (Cambridge: Cambridge University Press, 1990), p. 101.

5. Jacques Maritain in his post-war writing, *Man and the State* (Chicago: University of Chicago Press, 1951), presents the civic nation as both a spontaneous outgrowth of political activity and a conscious project of public education. While Maritain wrote as a Christian philosopher, his idea of the civic nation resonated with the modernist paradigms of other contemporary historians and social theorists, which set the stage for three decades of social-scientific theories of "modernization" (e.g., in the works of Ernest Gellner, Elie Kedourie, Daniel Lerner, Shmuel Eisenstadt, and Reinhard Bendix).

lutions, the civic nation has found its rational articulation in the equal rights of individual citizens: linguistic, cultural, and religious as well as civil and political rights. The civic nation requires that the state, understood as the permanent machinery and ongoing activity of government, be its subordinate agency, its instrument for defending and furthering the moral-juridical totality that it is.

In the inter-war years, this wedding of *romantic* and *civic* nations proved catastrophic, a harbinger of the century's worsening political miseries. In the first place, the nation-states produced by the Peace Treaties in eastern and southern Europe were defective on both ethnic-linguistic and civic grounds, lacking homogenous populations, rootedness in the soil, and a history of government. In the second place, the inevitable failure of the romantic-civic nation to produce justice for its minority peoples was conceded from the start by the imposition of Minority Treaties, transferring the protection of minority rights to the international *League of Nations*. Precipitating the rising tide of refugees across Europe was the conviction of members of minority "nations" that, without the "popular sovereignty" provided by "full national emancipation," they "were deprived of human rights."[6] With considerable penetration, some scholars have perceived Hitler's policies of invading neighboring countries with German-speaking populations, repatriating Germans living on foreign soils, and depriving undesirable minorities of citizen-rights as following through the Wilsonian logic of national, democratic self-determination.[7] And not only Hitler, we may add, but all subsequent revolutionary and dictatorial regimes that have aggressively sought to recover or emancipate "nationals" in foreign territories and/or have denationalized whole groups of citizens as beyond the pale of democratic rights.

It seems ironic, to say the least, that the post–World War II global political order defined by two decades of UN declarations should have as its twin planks the "equal and inalienable rights of individuals (including the 'right to a nationality')[8] and the equal and inalienable rights of 'peoples' to 'self-determination.'"[9] For the blend of civic and romantic nationalism has, arguably, been even less suited to the state-making of the decolonizing era. On the one hand, the liberal individualism of the UN's *Universal Declaration of Human Rights* (1948) has sat ill with the traditional social structures and political authorities of many decolonizing societies, and on the other, the tantalizingly ambiguous promise of self-

6. Hannah Arendt, *Origins of Totalitarianism* (London: André Deutsch, 1986 [orig. 1951]), p. 272.

7. Arendt, *Origins*, p. 275; Hobsbawm, *Nations and Nationalism*, p. 133.

8. *Universal Declaration of Human Rights, 1948*, Article 15 in I. Brownlie, ed., *Basic Documents on Human Rights*, 2nd ed. (Oxford: Oxford University Press, 1981), p. 24.

9. *Declaration on the Granting of Independence to Colonial Countries and Peoples, 1960* in Brownlie, ed., *Basic Documents*, p. 29.

determination for "peoples" has sat ill with the existing (colonial) boundaries of decolonized states. The combination of social disintegration under liberal ideological and economic pressures, mobilization of the political masses by 'democratic' dictators, and the absence of workable political institutions for incorporating traditional authorities and containing ethnic/tribal hostilities has contributed immeasurably to the unprecedented international problem of stateless refugees.[10] It is a most telling indictment of democratic nation-building that, by the 1980s, Africa could boast not only fifty new nation-states but a refugee population of over five million, "an estimated one-half of the world's total."[11] Moreover, even where traditional political and social arrangements have proved more stable, their deviation from international civic norms has been a nagging source of public resentment, cynicism, and polarization in these polities.

The relative persistence of colonial territorial boundaries in the post-colonial political order, despite the mooting of alternative visions of national emancipation, has reflected (among other factors) the continuing sway of the *functional* concept of the nation — the nation conceived as meeting such "functional" criteria as those of effective government, military capacity, constitutional order, unifying cultural traditions, social stability, and economic development. The functional concept of the nation is bound to reinforce any relatively successful geopolitical *status quo* and to favor territorial units with more rather than less potential across the criteria. Its importance in the post-colonial context has been to counterbalance the impetus given by the principle of national self-determination to the emergence of "paper states" ("juridical states"): functionally non-viable states that are nonetheless "guaranteed in their juridical sovereignty by the international community."[12] Unfortunately, ideological resistance and imperial ambitions within the international community have not always allowed this concept to carry its proper weight.

Moreover, the theoretical achievement of the functional nation has been marred by the long-standing liberal tendency to exaggerate the economic component. The tendency to understand and evaluate the nation chiefly as an economic organization, in terms of its benefits for industry, trade, and finance, is as strong as ever in both the developed and the developing world, to the detriment of political discussion and deliberation.[13] For instance, the seemingly in-

10. By the 1960s the prevailing Western (academic and popular) understanding of nation-building as a project of "modernization" was having an impact on post-colonial elites.

11. J. Mayall, *Nationalism and International Society* (Cambridge: Cambridge University Press, 1990), p. 55.

12. Mayall, *Nationalism and International Society*, p. 122.

13. Not surprisingly, defining the nation in terms of the exigencies of industrial and technological capitalism brings to the fore the elements of mass communication, mobility, stan-

terminable debate in Britain over the form of the European Community slogged on for many years without considerations beyond those of the national economy surfacing in any coherent political manner. Only defence policy attracted comparable attention from time to time — as, indeed, it should.[14] Even now there is little public appetite for a broader historical discussion of the distinctive political and legal traditions of European nations, and the consequences for them of the different avenues of European integration — whether federal, confederal, or more loosely associative.

Post-colonial polities have shown themselves to be, if anything, even more susceptible to the excessive identification of national with economic objectives, on account of (among other factors) the weakness of indigenous political traditions, widespread resentment over past economic exploitation, and the powerful models furnished by advanced industrial economies. Typically, rapid economic development has assumed disproportionate strategic and symbolic national importance in these countries, with the deleterious economic, social and environmental consequences of which we are now all too aware. The debt mountain of developing nations is one fairly predictable outcome of overly ambitious economic nation-making undertaken in the highly disadvantageous conditions of international trade and finance.

Thus have the prevailing concepts of the nation over the last two centuries — the "romantic," the "civic," and the "functional" — shown serious theoretical inadequacies in comprehending the *de facto* and *de iure* elements of concrete political order at the level of the nation-state. A Christian theological response to these failings has been made difficult by the eclipse of the historical development of Christian nations by the modern ideas and projects of "the nation." Confronted by these modern ideas and projects, Christian thinkers have been all too inclined to endorse or to reject them without considering the older biblically-based, theological tradition. And even when contemporary scholarship has conceded such a tradition, its researches have frequently not encouraged a sound theological-historical analysis of it, owing to the skeptical, relativist, reductionist, and historicist biases of sociological interpretations. These interpretations neither allow the decisive theological determinations of the nation to emerge out of the biblical tradition, nor understand the church's complex and wide-ranging historical role in the formation of nations, nor admit

---

dardized and specialized education. The liberal-economic nation has, therefore, intimate links to the "civic nation" through mass educational mobilization. The writings of Ernest Gellner over three decades has developed these ties, which have become a staple of the sociological literature.

14. However, the close linking within a national self-consciousness of military and economic ambitions is always a dangerous concoction.

the full extent of the tradition's possible engagement with, and transformation of, contemporary political theory and practice, in the advanced West as well as in the recently liberated East and in the post-colonial world.[15]

At the heart of the historical fatalism, or perhaps, "historical impenitence" (to use Chesterton's pointed epithet) of much contemporary scholarship is acquiescence in the hegemony of the civic nation in the advanced West — in the seemingly irreversible ideological and institutional settlement of liberal-democratic rights society. This settlement prescribes *an equality of individual right* to religious freedom that entails at best an equal representation of different religions in the public realm and at worst no religious representation at all, while it proscribes the national confession of Christian belief and the national establishment of one or more Christian churches. Running the gamut from deistic to agnostic to atheistic humanism, the advanced civic faith has already determined the unifying culture of political society and does not welcome theological intrusions into its self-understanding. Reinforcing its anti-theological bias is a fear of ethno-religious nationalism fed by the emergence in Africa and Asia of anti-Western Islamic and Buddhist nations and national movements that are, in fact, less "fundamentalist" (as they are commonly dubbed) than historically reactionary.[16] On their part, contemporary theologians have demonstrated too little appreciation of the theo-political matrices of the formation of nations, especially the wide-ranging influence of the Old Testament. It is to these scriptural theological themes and their historical elaborations that I now turn.

15. The methodological disregard for theological and ecclesial traditions in historical sociology has resulted in gross theoretical and historical misjudgments, the most glaring of which is that every idea of "the nation" is "nationalistic" in the sense that the nation is conceived as a "salvific community" and the supreme source of individual and collective identity; so that the history of the nation is the history of nationalism. Other misjudgments construe the nation as *primarily* the outcome of, or dependent on, a single political, social, and/or technological development, whether a vernacular culture or a "print" culture, parliamentary democracy or republican populism, or a capitalistic and industrial economy. Even the most assiduous scholars and capable theorists have fallen prey to one or the other of these misjudgments (e.g., Liah Greenfeld, Adrian Hastings, and Anthony Smith) which mar the soundness of their impressive analyses.

16. So-called Islamic fundamentalism, for example, is not an exegetical literalism in respect of the Koran but reversion to a restrictive medieval codification of Islamic law and spirituality.

The Nation as a Theological Construct

If we turn from the modern concepts of the nation to the revelation of God's kingship over Israel in the Old Testament, we are immediately struck by the theological articulation of all the ideas of "the nation" which we receive today in fragmentary and, dare I say, distorted formulations.[17] It becomes clear that Christian understandings of the nation have been, and must continue to be shaped by the divine revelation of political authority and political community in the history of Israel. In the first place, God's royal rule is revealed in his acts of delivering his people from their enemies, of giving them his law and of judging them, through the human mediation of warrior-leaders, kings, priests, and prophets. In the second place, the reality of God's kingdom is revealed in Israel's possession of the land as his gift and her possession of the law as the lasting record of God's royal judgments. In the third place, the Israelites are a people (ʻam) by virtue of their common ancestry, common language, and common historical memories: by God's election of the twelve tribes as his covenanted people in their forefather Abraham and in successive generations of patriarchs with whom he confirmed his covenantal promises, by their common sufferings in Egypt and deliverance from them, their wanderings in the desert and military conquest of Canaan for their promised homeland. In the fourth place, Israel perpetually receives her political identity through worshiping her divine Savior, Judge, Lawgiver, and Provider in public acts of thanksgiving, penitence, and petition. Finally, her historical vocation as God's uniquely favored people is to be a revelation of communal holiness to the gentile nations who themselves have a divinely ordained political vocation which they forsake at their peril.

Inevitably, the model of Israel played a leading role in the Christian formation of nations — not only in the emergence of modern Western nations from the fourteenth to the seventeenth centuries but in the emergence of their geopolitical predecessors — Ostrogothic and Burgundian kingdoms, Lombard Italy and Visigothic Spain, and the Western and Eastern Frankish realms. The reception of this model was invariably shaped by contemporary political traditions, whether indigenous Germanic or Roman imperial. Germanic Christian rulers and their European successors believed, with their subjects, that they held their thrones by divine appointment and by continuing divine favor. They cast themselves and were cast in the roles of Israelite rulers as they carried out their responsibilities of judging, legislating, and waging war. David and Solo-

---

17. See also Oliver O'Donovan, *The Desire of the Nations: Rediscovering the Roots of Political Theology* (Cambridge: Cambridge University Press, 1996), pp. 30-81.

mon provided the pervasive paradigm of royal rectitude by their knowledge of, and active obedience to, God's revealed law and their embodiment of divinely imparted wisdom. Christian rulers knew that their territorial kingdoms and their people's prosperity were not only given by God but removable by him in the event of their and/or their subjects' rebellion against his manifest will. They understood their realms to be bound together not only by historical, linguistic, and cultural ties, but preeminently by the ligaments of divine and human law. They saw their responsibility for public justice as extending to the public duty of rendering to God the worship of thankful, humble, obedient, and contrite hearts owing to him. Later Christian commonwealths, in the sixteenth and seventeenth centuries, rested their political vocations on divine-human covenantal foundations, after the Israelite pattern.

In modeling their political self-understanding on Israel's, Christian polities always tread a perilous theological route. Their ever-present temptation was so to identify with God's *one elect nation* as to deny the absolute historical uniqueness and universal representativeness of Israel's political vocation. Whenever they succumbed to this temptation, with its destructive political baggage of Holy War, theocratic legalism, and messianism, so-called Christian nations refused to be Christian, refused to be subject to the kingship of Christ and the advent of his kingdom. They refused to follow Israel into exile, unfulfilled restoration and messianic expectancy, and refused the fulfillment of Israel's vocation in the earthly ministry, death, resurrection, and exaltation of Jesus Christ, continued in the earthly witness of Christ's faithful people to his coming kingdom. They refused the confrontation of Christ's rule of righteousness and love with *the nation as such*, the judgment of his justice and peace on the sinful and alienated strivings after justice and peace of worldly polities. They refused to acknowledge the new meaning of the nation created by the earthly presence of christological power, judgment, law, and fellowship.

What is this new meaning of the nation? It is a meaning that takes shape in the penumbra of the church's eschatological witness in a sinful world. The nation is a concrete territorial order of political power, judgment, and tradition that sustains a space within the sinful human condition for the gathering of Christ's faithful people through the work of the Holy Spirit.[18] In a sense, the nation remains what Israel revealed it to be — its constitutive elements have not changed: a government that gives judgments, laws, and protection from enemies, a population inhabiting a homeland, linked by historical, linguistic, and cultural ties, and bound authoritatively by customs, laws, and political judg-

---

18. See also *Desire of the Nations*, pp. 146-57.

ments. But its theological significance has changed, its role in the divine economy *ad extra* has changed: it is no longer revealed to be the vehicle of salvation, but merely the guaranteed social space within which God's saving work proceeds. It is revealed to belong to the Father's sustaining governance of the world rather than his transforming governance through the Spirit of Christ. The nation is a reality of the old age which is passing away, but whose continuing sway serves the proclamatory mission of the renewed Israel.[19]

Only as the community of Pentecost, the Spirit-filled body of the exalted Christ, is grasped as the *telos* of earthly polity do the *inherent* deficiencies and limitations of the earthly nation come to light. These are the deficiencies, on the part of rulers, of coercive power, tragically inadequate judgment, and weak vision; on the part of the ruled, of inequitable laws, incomplete consent and merely external and episodic obedience; on the part of the ethnic/cultural community, of narrow and exclusive self-definition.[20] It is only as these deficiencies are judged by the church's fidelity to the worship and ministries appointed by Christ, for which she is empowered by the gifts of the Spirit, that their inevitability is manifest. Conversely, evidence of grave and widespread unfaithfulness in the church invariably provokes the nation to deny their inevitability. Whenever church institutions have adopted non-christological modes of judgment, sought worldly power and riches, cultivated worldly virtues, turned away from the intellectual and moral stringency of the revealed Word of Christ, civil rulers and commonwealths have correspondingly overstepped their vocations in defensive and offensive maneuvers in spiritual control. The conception of the church as the "nation at worship," which sprang up in the late Middle Ages in reaction to the exaggerated jurisdictional pretensions of the papal church, exemplifies such overstepping. For the nation can never coincide with the eschatological community of world-renunciation, suffering love, gospel proclamation and prophetic freedom that is the earthly bride of the risen Christ.

While recognizing all the natural and historical elements of the nation, the reappraisal opened up by the Christ-event reinforces a certain primacy that is already revealed in the political identity of Israel: the primacy of authoritative judgment and communal law, that together constitute the tradition of legal justice. In the light of the advent of Christ's kingdom, we can discern the defining aspect of the earthly nation to be the concrete rendering over time of legal justice, that is, the ongoing practice of judgment conducted through the medium

19. O'Donovan, *Desire of the Nations*, pp. 146-47.
20. Of course, these deficiencies are always susceptible of becoming the more extreme political perversions of tyranny, persecution, anarchy, factionalism, and nationalist aggression.

of law. It is this rather than permanent territorial boundaries or ethnic/linguistic homogeneity or economic power that gives political identity to a society. In the Christian political tradition the defining primacy of legal justice has been elaborated in the twin theological themes of (1) the divine vicariate of the ruler and (2) the commonwealth as a body of law, both of which have been central pillars of the Christian formation of nations. The supercession of these themes in the modern concepts of the nation goes some way to accounting for the proliferating perversions of the 'nation-state' in our time. Let us briefly indicate how their recovery in contemporary discussion may prove more efficacious in combating nationalist ideologies and averting their horrific consequences than any combination of the romantic and civic alternatives.

The Divine Vicariate of Civil Governors

To point out how inimical contemporary conceptions of the nation state have been to the Christian idea that governors have a divine vicariate is to state the obvious. It is, however, instructive to indicate the misrepresentation of the Christian idea invariably involved in this hostility. We can observe this misrepresentation in Jacques Maritain's 1948 treatise, *Man and the State,* where he associates the concept of the ruler as God's vicar with the divine right absolutism of the sixteenth and seventeenth centuries. Specifically he associates it with the theory of Bodin and Hobbes that "the people have absolutely deprived and divested themselves of their total power in order to transfer it to the Sovereign [prince]," thereby rendering him a superior subject of semi-divine power, accountable to the divine Sovereign alone.[21] Maritain views Hobbes's *mortal God* and Bodin's *puissance absolue* as the bedrock of the modern doctrine of state sovereignty (from Rousseau to Hegel) and its totalitarian extensions, which he repudiates for their hypostasizing of the symbolic representation of political society into a transcendent substance, "a metaphysical monad" or "person," a separate and independent carrier of absolute political right.[22]

Against the absolutizing "proprietary" or "transference" theory of political institution in which a substantial possession (namely, *power,* understood as the force by which persons are obliged to obey) is alienated from one owner to another, Maritain sets a delegative or fiduciary theory in which the political community entrusts its natural and inalienable right to govern itself to its chosen representative, who exercises that right by participation, without possessing

21. Maritain, *Man and the State,* pp. 13-17.
22. Maritain, *Man and the State,* p. 17.

it. On his fiduciary account, the government is the image not of God but of the people, subject and accountable to it, an active "instrument" of its will.[23]

From a theological and a historical point of view, Maritain's criticism of sixteenth-century sovereignty theory is both penetrating and misleading. On the one hand, it pinpoints the problematic aspects of the idea of transferring political power from the community to the ruler. For ever since the medieval recovery of the Roman law commentaries of early-third-century jurists, from which the idea arose,[24] civil lawyers had pondered the extent of this transference — whether it was total or partial — and its implications for the relative authority of different kinds of law: e.g., imperial decree as compared with popular custom. Invariably, their discussions veered toward either monarchial absolutism, attributing all communal power to the ruler, or dualism of sovereignty, dividing power between ruler and community: in the first instance, substituting the head for the body and in the second, locking head and body in a struggle for power. Manifestly, the democratic understanding of political authority as delegated by and vicariously exercised for the people is one way of overcoming the inadequacies of the transference model. On the other hand, Maritain's criticism fails to recognize that the transference theory of political authority was never intrinsic to the *theology* of the ruler's divine vicariate, which, for the better part of its history, aimed at circumscribing government within the boundaries set by law, justice, and the commonweal. Let me briefly dwell on the limiting and anti-despotic features of this theology.

The locus classicus for the divine vicariate of the ruler was biblical rather than Roman juristic: namely, St. Paul's exhortation to obedience in Rom. 13:1-7. This exhortation, it was commonly thought, acknowledged God's ordination of government as a social institution and his appointment of individual governors, for the purpose of rendering binding public judgment concerning matters of right and wrong, restraining evildoing by means of pun-

---

23. *Man and the State*, pp. 126-32. Maritain explicitly aligns his fiduciary account of political authority with the neo-scholastic natural-law thought of the Cardinals Cajetan and Bellarmine, and of Francisco Suárez (133), all three of whom, it should be remarked, were bent on maximizing the distance between the divine vicariate of the pope and the natural vicariate of all temporal rulers, in response to the conciliarist and Protestant 'heresies' of the time. It is noteworthy, however, that Maritain is more liberal than any of these Thomists, and especially Suárez, whose thought is closer to Bodin's than to Maritain's.

24. The *locus classicus* is the jurist Ulpian's observation in the *Digest* (1.4.1 pr., cf. *Inst.* 1.2.6) that what the prince pleases has the force of law because, by the royal law of the empire, the people have conferred on him all its political authority and power. (*Quod principi placuit, legis habet vigorem utpote cum lege regia, quae de imperio eius lata est, populus ei et in eum omne suum imperium et potestatem conferat.*)

ishment and the fear of punishment, and encouraging virtuous conduct by means of approval and other reward. From the New Testament's essentially juridical portrayal of government[25] developed the patristic systematization of rule as a postlapsarian divine ordinance that simultaneously manifested God's wrathful judgment on sinful humanity and his providential mercy toward it. In earthly government the Church Fathers saw God acting to protect the fragile goods of human life from the assault of sinful human passions by providing a limited judgment and punishment of human wrongdoing, in lieu of the limitlessness of both God's eschatological judgment and the unrestrained human passion for vengeance.[26]

Contrary to contemporary theological instincts, most pre-modern theologians considered it imperative that the one who executes public judgment be the earthly representative, or even "image," of the Heavenly Judge, in acknowledgment of two truths: first, of God's continuing sovereignty in judging his creatures, and second, of the radical equality of those created in his image, that forbade any of them coercively to judge his fellows. It was not enough for political authority to represent the whole community, the *universitas,* and express the common judgment of the people, as handed down in customary and statute law: for not even the whole community had the authority to take human life in punishment for crime, but God alone. Nevertheless, precisely as the human representative of a human community, the ruler received and exercised from God only delegated and participated power: "Whatever the prince can do," said John of Salisbury in the twelfth century, "is from God, so that power does not depart from God, but it is used as a substitute for His hand, making all things learn His justice and mercy."[27]

Moreover, it was *God's* justice and mercy and not the prince's capricious and tyrannous whim that the subject was to learn: delegated and participated authority was formed and directed by God's revelation of his will in nature and Scripture. Even the most Byzantine conception of the ruler as a "living law" *(lex animata, nomos empsuchos),* transcending the exactions of the positive law, still

---

25. This passage was heavily supported by 1 Pet. 2:13-15.

26. The tendency among patristic and later Christian writers to locate the historical origin of political authority in Cain's building of a city suggests the link (probably intended by the Genesis redactor) between God's establishment of political authority and, on the one hand, the substitution of communal justice for private vengeance, and on the other, God's merciful deferring of divine judgment. Instead of striking down the murderer Cain or giving him over to his avengers, God places the protective mark on him and allows him to take refuge in the city that he builds, away from God's presence (Gen. 4:9-17).

27. *Policraticus* 4.1; trans. C. Nederman (Cambridge: Cambridge University Press, 1990), p. 28. Also *IG,* p. 282.

cast him as interpreter of the divine Word in Christ and imitator of divine equity and virtue.[28] While not adequately expressing the fallibility and corruption of princely judgment, the Byzantine model did not remove it absolutely from prophetic counsel and admonition within the church. More consistently did the Western tradition of "theocratic kingship" hold in theo-political tension the public judgments of the ruler, judgments of the ruled formed and articulated independently of the ruler, and God's own judgments declared in his revealed Word by which both ruler and ruled are judged.

It is precisely this theo-political tension that modern democratic liberalism has collapsed by casting the government *exclusively* as vicar of the people, thereby providing a necessary historical condition of modern political tyranny and totalitarianism, as thinkers as far apart as Pope Leo XIII and Hannah Arendt have perceived. Whether "the people" that the government images is some fantastic racial essence or national folk spirit or avenging ethnic group or self-contained body of merely positive law or conflict of class interests and ideologies, or motor of economic development, it is a self-seeking, lawless, and idolatrous community, and not a community of divine law and right. It cannot be, to use late-medieval juristic language, a "community of the realm" *(communitas regni)* or a "mystical body of the commonweal" *(corpus reipublicae mysticum)*, not because there is lacking a monarch but because there is lacking the real moral bond of divine law between the governor and the governed that goes beyond the merely constitutional in the formal and procedural sense. Correspondingly, the modern totalitarian Vicar of the People is known by its emancipation from the divine commission to execute God's laws for the whole commonwealth, to give justice to *all* the persons within its territory.

Recognizing the divine vicariate of civil governors does not, of course, resolve the thorny problems of doing justice in the contemporary social setting. But it does dispel the dogma of popular sovereignty — that the popular will is the *source* of political authority and the *substance* of political judgment — which has infected the aggressive nationalisms of our time. It cannot be the nation, understood as either a prepolitical or a trans-governmental totality, that dispenses justice "under God" through the vicarious instrumentality of its elected governors, but rather the governors (whether elected or holding some other legitimate title) that by their political judgments "under God" constitute the nation as an ongoing reality. To grasp the dangerous theological error of the doctrine of self-government is to perceive its twin historical roots in late-medieval corporatist voluntarism (closely associated with the northern Italian

---

28. See the imperial panegyrics of Eusebius for Constantine I and of Agapetos in sixth-century Constantinople, *IG*, pp. 58-66, 181-88.

city states) and the spiritualist tradition of communal perfectionism and Messianism (especially in the Reformation period), which, amalgamated, produced a mystical totality of absolute communal right constituted by the free consensus of individual wills. Manifestly, this hybrid conforms neither to the heavenly communion of saints nor the earthly church militant nor the civil polities through which fallen humanity is ordered.

Political Society as a Body of Law in the 'Penumbra' of the Gospel

To focus the antipathy between the modern and the traditional Christian concepts of political society, let us return to the blend of romantic and civic nationalism characteristic of the twentieth century, and notice the subtle shift in perspective from the inter-war to the post-war years. Whereas in Wilsonian thinking the ethnic-linguistic and the civic nations seemed to compose a symbiotic and harmonious fit, post-war thought lost confidence in this fit. The staggering task of raising civil societies out of the ashes of dictatorial and totalitarian regimes implied an arduous transformation of the ethnic-linguistic into the civic nation. Particularist society and its machinery of government had to be reconstructed on rational, universal principles of freedom, equality, participation and plurality, applied to individuals and groups. Only such a political therapy would place and maintain government in the role of instrument rather than master of the governed.

The United Nations *Universal Declaration of Human Rights* embodied the international consensus on the post-war program of political renovation. This extensive catalogue of civil, political, and social rights attributed chiefly to individuals expressed the form of the civic nation as a coherent communal project — "a common standard of [communal] achievement."[29] In a comprehensive and universal moral-juridical code it articulated the unified communal will that was to constitute each and every society as a body politic or commonwealth, above and beyond its machinery of state and its whole fabric of statutory and customary laws. The opening proclamation made clear that the civic nation as a body of programmatic rights was first and foremost a project of

---

29. These rights not only included the venerable personal, political, and religious rights: to individual life, liberty, security, property, freedoms of association, speech, religious belief and practice, and equality before the law. They also included the "civic" right to equal political participation for all citizens, and the extensive catalogue of social rights that have become our public commonplaces: e.g., to humane employment, material security, medical care, suitable education, and cultural involvement.

public education and citizen mobilization. Fifty years on, we cannot fail to be astonished by the systematic indoctrination envisaged and the religious fervor conveyed:[30]

> The General Assembly proclaims *this universal declaration of human rights* as a common standard of achievement for all peoples and all nations to the end that every individual and every organ of society, keeping this Declaration constantly in mind, shall strive by teaching and education to promote respect for these rights and freedoms and by progressive measures, national and international, to secure their universal and effective recognition and observance. . . .

Thus were the civic nation and the civic community of nations to be constituted through the secular faith of the democratic creed. In the intervening years since the *Declaration* the creedal unity of the civic nation has, if anything, been intensified, especially with the welding of law and public ideology in constitutional Bills of Rights.[31] What has also become increasingly apparent is the debilitating effects on social moral agency of the abstract individualism and pluralism of the civil charter of rights — its frequent functioning in government legislation and judicial decision to undermine the legitimate representation of the moral and spiritual understandings within society.[32]

At the time of the UN *Declaration* and subsequently, there have been scholarly attempts to identify its moral-juridical content with the body of law or right that the pre-modern and early-modern juristic tradition called the *ius gentium* — the law of nations or law common to all peoples. But this identification, although attractive for its legal elevation of such international consensus, is highly problematic. And it is important to understand why. For the earlier jurists the *ius gentium* was preeminently customary or conventional law that covered a wide range of near-universal social practices and institu-

---

30. Brownlie, *Basic Documents,* p. 22.

31. We should remark that the American Bill of Rights does not support the public program of rights in its full social scope, in that it consists of constitutional amendments securing and extending the traditional liberties of British subjects for American citizens against the powers of government (especially the federal government) and an oppressive majority. For the role of the Bill of Rights within the American Constitution, see R. A. Goldwin, *From Parchment to Power: How James Madison Used the Bill of Rights to Save the Constitution* (Washington, D.C.: AEI Press, 1997).

32. Decisions of the Canadian judiciary in adjudicating cases under the *The Charter of Rights and Freedoms* (1982) provide spectacular examples of such undermining of moral and spiritual community. See articles in *University of British Columbia Law Review: Special Edition — Religion, Morality, and Law* 33 (2000).

tions — most notably, property and all the transactions dependent on it, and a host of customs observed everywhere by states and peoples in their dealings with one another, e.g., in navigating and trading, diplomacy, waging war, etc. The international aspect of the *ius gentium* was historically important in fostering the concept of a universal *political* as well as *moral* community: a community of all nations unified by juridically binding conventions as well as by moral sentiment.[33] It is hardly surprising, therefore, that some post-war internationalists (including Jacques Maritain) should look upon the United Nations *Declaration of Human Rights* as the unsurpassed historical achievement of the *ius gentium*.[34]

Nevertheless, the pre-modern juristic tradition never envisaged the *ius gentium* as a comprehensive, universal moral-juridical code. Rather it was seen to encompass diverse practices and institutions belonging to the civil and political organization of human society in its fallen and fragmented condition. Within the dominant Augustinian theology, such practices and institutions were viewed as accommodating human sinfulness, even as they restrained and punished it. Although they were seen to express the natural law of neighbor love given to mankind at his creation, they did so obliquely in a derivative and somewhat removed order of justice. Only ambiguously could they be described, as Maritain describes the *ius gentium* and the charter of rights belonging to it, as rational conceptualizations of an instinctively known natural law.[35] Moreover, the older juristic tradition never envisaged the *ius gentium* as the moral-juridical cement of individual political communities, the body of civic principles that, in articulating the popular will, constitutes societies as body politics — but this is the role assumed by the charter of rights.

33. Suárez provides the classic neo-scholastic account of how the *ius gentium* binds together sovereign states into a political-juridical community in *De legibus ac Deo legislatore* 2.19.

34. Although the Universal Declaration does not have the binding legal force on the ratifying states of a UN Covenant, it has been argued that "the emergence of a juridical consensus evidenced by state practice subsequent to its original proclamation has made the Declaration binding as part of the law of nations." J. W. Montgomery, *Human Rights and Human Dignity* (Dallas: Probe Books, 1986), p. 30.

35. Maritain, *Man and the State*, pp. 98-9. In identifying the Charter of Rights with the *ius gentium*, Maritain appealed to Thomas Aquinas's understanding of the latter's precepts as deriving from the natural law as conclusions from premises (*Summa Theologiae* 1a2ae 95.4) — a formulation which sat ill with later Thomists who failed to see how conclusions from natural law premises could be anything other than natural law. (Suárez, for example, proposed that the *ius gentium* was determined not by "self-evidence" but by "probability and human calculation" — *De legibus ac Deo legislatore* 2.19; translation from *IG*, p. 729.) Maritain intended to circumvent Thomas's problem with his own conception of the *ius gentium* (as rational conceptualizations of an instinctively known natural law).

On the contrary, against the ideological unification of the civil nation, the scriptural, theo-political tradition witnesses that the political unity of any society consists in its collective recognition of a governing authority and consent to a body of laws, and not in its subscription to a practical creed and plan of action. Through the judgments of its rulers accepted by the people and in their obedience to laws — in other words, in the actual execution of public justice — its common good or common weal takes on definition. The fourteenth-century English jurist, John Fortescue, gave expression to this insight, widespread among his European contemporaries, in referring to the legal constitution of the realm as "the nerves and sinews of the body [politic]."[36] In the feudal conception of the judge (whether king or lesser magistrate) as one who "found" the law rather than "made" it, and in the respect paid to the commonly "found" customs of communities, the close relationship between the law and the moral judgment of both the one and the many was affirmed. And therein was also affirmed the close relation between laws and the broader sentiments, tastes, manners and affections of communal life. Indeed, it is just this relationship between a society's political-legal definition and its cultural-moral continuity that the concept of "the nation" has chiefly expressed in the theo-political tradition.

Of course, beyond the ongoing achievement of public justice were the myriad articulations of the standards by which the achievement should be judged — by jurists, philosophers, theologians, bishops, and the chief bishop, all appealing to the authoritative revelation of God's justice and God's law for human community in the scriptural witness. Beyond the realized political unity of society were its myriad structures of solidarity, material and spiritual communities, goods, activities and institutions, all known to be equally ravaged by sin and equally objects of God's redemptive and sanctifying work. And finally all of redeemed society was known to be united within the body of Christ, the true *societas perfecta* of the universal church: one in Spirit, confession, and obedience.

The theological naiveté which has gripped Christians and non-Christians in the last century — particularly the latter half — is to think that two wholly unified and articulate common goods can coexist harmoniously and cooperatively: namely, the church of Christ and the civic nation united in the purely secular faith of the "democratic creed." For the most part, Christians have not perceived the inflation of what belongs to Caesar in democratic civil religion, its capacity to tyrannize society like some Jacobin-at-large. Both early critics of nationalism and totalitarianism like Jacques Maritain and later generations of

---

36. *A Treatise in Commendation of the Laws of England* 13; trans. F. Gregor in *The Works of John Fortescue, Knight: His Life, Works, and Family History*, 2 vols. (London: 1869), 2:346.

critics have failed to appreciate how the democratic creed itself functions as an ideology: i.e., a pseudo-religion justifying a false social totality. One early critic of totalitarianism, Hannah Arendt, always penetrating in her counter-suggestible historical and philosophical readings, approximated this insight in reflecting on the inability of modern states over the last two hundred years to protect the "rights of man."[37] Despite her penchant for regarding past beliefs as fatally anachronistic, and as such, unworkable in the present, she saw clearly that the advent of modern tyranny depended on the demise of a Christian political world where rulers were vicars of God rendering justice to "everyone within their territories" and commonwealths were "communities of obedience to divine and human law."[38] Arendt's resolution of the modern dilemma over the course of her distinguished career seems to have been to turn away from the unredeemable nation-state to small communities of heightened political participation,[39] whereas the reaction of many of her contemporaries has been to promote the idea of transnational political and economic communities and governments. But neither resolution has tapped the full resources of the Christian political tradition for addressing the problem of nationalism in our times.

37. Arendt, *Origins of Totalitarianism*, pp. 266-302.

38. Indeed, the bitter irony of modern anti-Semitism for Arendt was that it depended on the abandonment of the model of Israel — the chosen people manifesting God's law before the nations — not only by Christian polities but by secular and assimilated Jews who, by thinking of themselves as a depoliticized "chosen race," opened the floodgates of purely racial hatred on the part of European pan-national movements. *Origins of Totalitarianism*, pp. 72-74, 227-49.

39. See especially *On Revolution* (Harmondsworth, Middlesex: Penguin Books, 1973), pp. 215-81.

The Loss of a Sense of Place

OLIVER O'DONOVAN

Fremd bin ich eingezogen, fremd zieh' ich wieder aus, "A stranger came I hither, a stranger go I forth." Müller's "Gute Nacht" perfectly expresses the romantic conception of the artist as a wanderer, rootless, restless, driven from place to place by the compulsion of an ever-aspiring and never-satisfied spirit, unable to make a home within a settled community.[1] This brooding artistic self-consciousness infatuated the sensibilities of the early nineteenth century, and continues even now to provide a ready source of cliché. But history has taken an unkind revenge upon the poetic soul of the romantic era. *Homo oeconomicus,* that unspiritual clod, has become a wanderer *en masse,* as adept as any poet at breaking ties and moving on. In his extreme manifestations, as jet-set business-man or economic migrant, he circles the world in pursuit of gain, scatters his family over two or three continents and achieves a state of dislocation far beyond anything the poets dreamed of. In a more commonly encountered form, he treats overseas travel as a standard form of festive consumption, to be engaged in the spirit and with the regularity that his ancestors addressed their Christmas dinner.

Does this betray, it has been asked, a rootlessness of a more profound kind, the loss of a sense of place? What has made mobility possible is technology, and technology creates homogeneity, since it depends upon mass-production of interchangeable parts; homogeneity in turn numbs our sense of how one place differs from another, and so weakens our connection with the

---

1. This poem provides the opening of Schubert's *Winterreise.*

Originally delivered as the Church of Ireland Lecture at Queen's University, Belfast in 1986, and published in the *Irish Theological Quarterly* 55 (1989): 39-58. It is here revised extensively.

place we belong to, our "home." Every airport has always resembled every other; but as mercantile organization takes on the appearance of technological mass-production, every shopping street resembles every other, too. A Kentucky Fried Chicken outlet looks the same in Chicago and Shanghai. Only the architectural traces of past generations which survive on sufferance permit a sense of difference between one city center and another. To this problem, with its roots in the Industrial Revolution, there is a new dimension now, which has yet to make itself fully felt: the city itself is threatened with redundancy. Traditionally cities acted as a powerful localizing force, drawing us together by virtue of our need to communicate the resources of our culture, industrial, mercantile, educational, and artistic. But with computer terminals and good roads we can pursue cultural intercourse centrifugally. The loss of a sense of place has come to expression in a technology of placeless culture, mapped on the design of the worldwide web.

The major traditions of Western political thought have done little to help us understand the significance of place in political experience. From the Middle Ages political philosophy has aimed to provide a model for political relations that will be indefinitely portable. Ever since the constitution of kingdoms was conceived by civil lawyers in the twelfth century by extrapolation from the laws of the Roman empire, it has been a replicable form, a set of relations that could be established anywhere. Paradoxically, this idea grew from the conception of the Roman empire as eternal. If the kingdom of the Franks could be the eternal Rome in its own time and place, why could there not be many Romes simultaneously in different places? Each particular kingdom was demarcated, of course, by its territory; but the sole significance of the territorial limit was to provide a material basis for political relations that were in principle independent of it. Territory could even, it appeared, be treated as alienable property, capable of sale and purchase, transfer and acquisition, without loss to the identity of the political communities involved. The experience of colonialism reinforced these tendencies, and encouraged thinkers to conceive of each political community itself as mobile. Where there had once been one New Rome, there were now New England, New France, and New Spain. If constitutions, laws, and rights composed the state, they could be transported from the mountains, plains, rivers, and coasts among which they had evolved. In reaction to the French Revolution there developed a new line of conservative reflection on tradition; yet while this involved heightened attention to race and language, place remained an object of neglect. Had the American Revolution received the same philosophical attention as the French, it might not have been so. Did not that world-shaping event demonstrate that the Atlantic Ocean could not be denied? That the extension of a realm across an ocean onto a new continent was a pretence on which the constraints of locality would take their revenge?

In all this, philosophy showed itself inattentive to the poets, who, when they were not celebrating the wanderer's freedom, were celebrating his homesickness and patriotism. It was characteristic of the "age of sensibility," perhaps, that in dissociating feeling from reason, it disregarded poetry's claim to discern reality. By the middle of the twentieth century philosophy's antagonism to the poetic interest in place had been heightened to hostility, based on strong anti-romantic suspicions. Instincts attaching peoples to land and territory were held to be barbarous. This is well represented in two Christian contributions to political discussion that had considerable resonance in the 1940s. For the Protestant theologian Reinhold Niebuhr "the most urgent of all the issues which face our epoch" was "extending the principle of community to worldwide terms." Judaeo-Christianity, and to a lesser extent other religions, had contributed a universalism "in which the meaning of life and its obligations were interpreted above and beyond the limits of any particular community"; but it had seemed to be an inescapable constraint of history "that the effective human community should be much smaller than the universal community which was implied in any rigorous analysis of man's obligation to his fellow-man." And so particularities had always counted for too much. "In the whole long period of history the national and imperial communities which gave effective social cohesion to human life drew a considerable part of their power of cohesion from the power of particularity. Geographic boundary, ethnic homogeneity, and some common experience and tradition were the primary bases of their unity."[2] Local loyalties were a form of self-loving narrowness, a failure to embrace the demand for love of all mankind.

The Thomist Jacques Maritain, more conscious than Niebuhr that a universal community must rest on the foundation of smaller communities, had, nevertheless, only this to say about their geographical basis: "Living together does not mean occupying the same place in space. It does not mean, either, being subjected to the same physical or external conditions or pressures, or the same pattern of life. . . . Living together means sharing as men, not as beasts, that is, with a basic free acceptance, in certain common sufferings and in a certain human task."[3] The true human community will not be a town or a nation, but an International Society for accomplishing something. Loyalty based on the brute fact of geographical neighborhood is unworthy of rational human beings. It is for beasts to form their aggregations on the basis of proximity rather than projects.

2. *The Children of Light and the Children of Darkness* (London: Nisbet, 1945), pp. 105-7.
3. *Man and the State* (Chicago: University of Chicago Press, 1951), p. 207.

298

We must, of course, allow for the special historical circumstances that brought this tendency to a head. At the close of the Second World War liberals could be forgiven for overreacting to any hint of the naturism cultivated in the Nazi philosophy. Yet during the years when Niebuhr and Maritain were reasserting the universal, Simone Weil was making observations for the Free French forces on the phenomenon of "uprootedness." Writing of "a kind of uprootedness . . . one might call geographical, that is to say, concerned with human collectivities occupying clearly defined territorial limits," she concluded: "the actual significance of these collectivities has well nigh disappeared, except in one case only — that of the nation."[4] "The world requires at the present time," she proceeded, "a new patriotism" which would be different from the "pagan virtue" that had marked French history to that point, since in France patriotism had been based not on the past but on a violent break with the past.[5] This new patriotism was to be based on "compassion for our country."[6] Meanwhile Martin Heidegger, the twentieth-century thinker who was more ready than others to recognize such moments of truth as there may have been in National Socialism, as well as to learn from poetry, was feeling his way with the aid of Hölderlin from *Unheimlichkeit* ("homelessness") to *Heimkunft* ("homing"), from *Dasein* abroad in "the world" to "mortals" inhabiting "earth." To Heidegger has been credited the high distinction of initiating the philosophical enquiry into place.[7] Whatever the justice of this attribution, it is clear that religious writers of recent times who have urged our loss of a sense of place upon us have learned more from these idiosyncratic voices than from the mainstream of mid-century Christian universalism. These writers are mostly aligned with that late-twentieth century mood-change that has been dubbed 'postmodernism'. In this case a more precise designation might be "post-colonial," for much of it arises from first-hand encounter with indigenous cultures marginalized in the modern world.[8]

---

4. *The Need for Roots*, trans. Arthur Wills (New York: Harper, 1971), p. 99.

5. Weil, *Need for Roots*, pp. 110, 147.

6. Weil, *Need for Roots*, p. 170.

7. See Jean-Yves Lacoste, *Expérience et Absolu: Questions Disputées sur l'humanité de l'homme* (Paris: Presses Universitaires de France, 1994), and especially p. 9: "Les réalités les plus obvies ayant souvent le destin d'être les plus tardivement portées au concept, il revient à la localité, comme note transcendentale de l'humanité de l'homme, de ne pas avoir été vraiment pensée avant que Heidegger ne propose, en 1927, d'entendre ce que nous sommes sous le chiffre primordial de l'être-dans-le-monde — et ne procède ainsi à une imposante réorganisation de la *quaestio de homine*."

8. For example, Vine Deloria and Clifford M. Lytle, *The Nations Within: The Past and Future of American Indian Sovereignty* (New York: Pantheon, 1984); Vine Deloria, *For This Land: Writings on Religion in America* (New York: Routledge, 1999); Geoffrey R. Lilburne, *A Sense of*

If there is a "loss of the sense of place," what has been lost, and how? As a transcendental condition of humanity, place is what it has always been. As a theme of reflection, place is present as never before. And it was not the romantic wanderer, nor his modern successors, who actually lost their sense of place, for if they had, how could they have thought so much about wandering? Wandering is simply one pole of the sense of place, the dialectical opposite to homecoming, and it is hardly strange that the romantic poets brought the two themes to consciousness at the same time. One way of filling out the idea of loss is to suggest that it is home that has gone missing. If travel is the principal or only form in which the sense of place is now available to us, our sense of place is one-legged, no longer anchored in *our* place. But with the loss of the one pole the other is no longer experienced as its opposite and complement. Home and abroad become confounded; our sense of place that collapses in upon itself, reduced to a craving for travel. Wanderlust, like sexual lust, becomes constituted as an all-obliterating sense of need, blocking off the normal operation of desire to bring the strange into contact with the familiar. But this proposal, though plausible as a description of some well-known pathologies — types of mass-tourism, for example, or of international business — hardly does justice to the contemporary culture as a whole. The opposition of home and abroad is apparently meaningful enough to our contemporaries, who are not unable to identify the pathologies as pathologies. It would, at any rate, be strange to class those terms with the lost concepts of pre-modernity like "the sacred" or "nobility." Yet we are left with an intuition, which it would be wrong to dismiss, that these pathologies somehow reflect "where we have come," justifying a more far-reaching unease with ourselves.

What account can we give of this intuition? Clearly there is *a loss of moral confidence* in relation to place. Local difference has suffered a loss of moral dignity; however strongly local attachments make themselves felt, they are subjected to a kind of censorship at the point where they might weigh with us. But this reflects the *thematic absence* of place from our intellectual analysis and our political vernacular. We fail to articulate our local interests, to recognize the weight that they carry with us, and we are therefore incapa-

---

Place: a Christian Theology of the Land (Nashville: Abingdon Press, 1989) (influenced by aboriginal Australian culture). Some of the recent literature declares an interest in the sacredness of place and in the liturgical use of space. About this a caution is needed, well expressed by Jean-Yves Lacoste, whose own interests head in the same direction: "La liturgie est œuvre de liberté. Et à ce titre, elle n'appartient pas aux déterminations natives de la topologique de l'existence . . . c'est peut-être en la transgressant que la liturgie s'intègre à la topologie" (*Expérience et Absolu*, p. 27).

ble of subjecting them to ordered and rational criticism. We have no room for them in our canon of rational political appeals, so that a gap opens up between what we say and what we feel, between what we argue for and what we care for. The loyalty we guard for places shares the fate of certain other conservative instincts: it has hidden power, but can appear in civilized public discourse only in a dissimulated form, disguised in arguments ostensibly about other things. If forced into the open, it appears uncivil, as a kind of barbarian reaction. The thematic absence of place has been strongly reinforced by technological achievements that have brought the whole world nearer in one sense, though in other senses it has enhanced distances by redistributing them. The phenomenon of globalization may be held responsible for the immediate sense of crisis in our own time. Yet it is important to see that this is only an advanced phase, and a more extensive practical implementation, of ambitions deep-seated in our civilization. As generally with late-modernity, the features that strike us as most awkwardly newborn have been the longest time incubating.

II

The roots of Western place-denial are complex; but we may single out three leading elements of the philosophical and theological background that have fed it.

(1) In the first place we should notice the tendency in Platonism to speak of the spirit or intellect, divine or human, as transcending spatial definition because it transcends materiality. The most decisive formulations of this theme were those of Porphyry, who argued that intellect could not be "in space."[9] But in this he follows a line of thought opened up by Plotinus, for whom the spiritual realm is indivisibly one, *wholly* present wherever it is present, not "somewhere" but "one thing everywhere." Plotinus had said in a famous simile that the cosmos relates to the soul like a net floating in the sea.[10] The idea that the spiritual does not dwell in space but space in it, is extended also to the spiritual adept. Of the wise soul attentive to ultimate reality it was said in the circles of the young Augustine, deeply immersed in the influence of Plotinus: "He is not here among us, but in himself," "collected" (an image we still use in common parlance) out of the things of sense and dimension into that purely psychic

---

9. "The intellectual is not in space, but in itself, since it has not proceeded into mass." *Sentences* 33(35).4.

10. *Ennead* 4.3.3; 4.3.9.

space, which is not space at all.[11] Such an ideal for philosophical contemplation bred the conviction that local relations, which we necessarily have by virtue of being embodied souls, are to be transcended and left behind. In many curious ways the aspirations of idealist philosophy seem to be taken up by the projects of modern technology. To grasp what Plotinus meant by spirit transcending space, we may think of that oddest of contemporary phenomena, though we have now become entirely familiarized with it, the recorded voice of a dead person speaking to us. The speaker is all spirit and no body, nowhere and everywhere, without presence in our time yet communicating with us. In only one respect does this phenomenon fail to conform to the idealist conception: the disembodied state is, after all, no guarantee of wisdom.

(2) Alongside this philosophical tradition we should also notice the theological universalism promoted by Christianity. Believing existence is tied to no holy places: there is nowhere that God presents himself to faith more than anywhere else. All mankind is called to repent and believe the gospel; all places are equally consecrated as places of worship. In this conception we find the motivating conviction behind the early church's mission to the Gentile world. The gospel, as St. Luke shows us, spreads out from Jerusalem, which is a holy place only in the historical sense that what had been prophesied was accomplished there, and reaches to Judaea, to Samaria, and to the ends of the earth.[12] The revelation to Israel had been a situated revelation, in a land which YHWH had hallowed and in a city where he had chosen to dwell. But the revelation in Christ broke down this elective particularity, not only of race but also of place. This theme has been constantly recurrent in Western Christianity (no less before than after the Protestant Reformation), safeguarding Christian faith against a relapse into the concept of a situated place of divine presence.[13]

In laying side by side these two influences on our modern loss of a sense of place, we cannot fail to observe an important difference between them. The philosophical influence is concerned with abstraction from *space,* i.e., the extension of bodies as a feature of their materiality. The theological influence, on the other hand, has to do quite strictly with *place.* In Greek the word *topos* can do service for both, yet the implications are very different. Whereas abstraction

---

11. *De ordine* 2.6.19: *Etiamsi nos ipsam doceret sapientiam, non illum dicerem nobiscum esse, sed secum.*

12. Acts 1:8.

13. Cf. the charming little early-medieval Irish verse against pilgrimages, translated by Frank O'Connor in *Kings, Lords, and Commons* (London: Macmillan, 1961), p. 16: "To go to Rome is little profit, plenty pain. The master that you seek in Rome you find at home, or seek in vain."

from space is an *individualizing* movement of thought, attending to the phenomenon of consciousness by excluding the conditions of worldly interaction, abstraction from place is a *universalizing* movement of thought. When in the story from St. John's Gospel Jesus says to the Samaritan woman at the well: "The hour is coming and now is, when neither on this mountain nor in Jerusalem will you worship the Father. . . . But the hour is coming and now is when the true worshipers will worship the Father in spirit and truth," the most immediately striking feature of the saying is that it is cast in the philosophical language of spacelessness: neither here nor there, but "in spirit."[14] Yet the sentiment is at home not in philosophy but in biblical conceptions of salvation-history: the dawning of a moment in history at which the sectarian focus on contested holy places is to be supplanted by a universal worship that may be offered anywhere. The point is to comprehend the different peoples as a unity, leaping over the barrier that separates Jews from Samaritans. In a different idiom St. Peter will say: "Truly I perceive that God shows no particularity, but in every nation any one who fears him and does what is right is acceptable to him."[15]

To speak of "place" — it is a common enough observation — is to speak of a determinant of social identity. "Space" is an abstract notion, a dimension of mass; you can exist "in space," but not — except in a derived sense — "in this space," because there cannot be one or more distinct spaces. But you cannot exist "in place" without existing in some particular place different from all other places. Places, like human beings, have names. They are perceived in relation to human doings and actions. A place is a fruit of civilization, an area of space distinguished from others by the activities of a community. This does not only, of course, include human settlements, such as villages, towns, and cities, nor even developed lands; for widely-defined places such as countries are conceived as homes for their inhabitants, and empty places such as moorlands and mountains can be the object of affectionate recognition by those who move around or over them. Nor, if we say that places are socially constructed, do we mean that they are socially *posited;* for what places are constructed *out of* are natural features of the human environment. "The physical landscape is a partner, and an active rather than purely passive partner, in the conversation which creates the nature of a place," one commentator remarks judiciously, failing only, perhaps, in his choice of the term "landscape," which already supposes an aesthetic, and so highly selective, reading of the natural environment.[16] Not only

14. John 4:21, 23.
15. Acts 10:34-35.
16. Philip Sheldrake, *Spaces for the Sacred* (London: SCM, 2001), p. 15.

"landscapes" but climates and microclimates, mineral and vegetable resources, competitive ecosystems, and simple distances between one feature and the next, all comprise the material conditions for places, while the form is imposed by the human social capacity to organize and collaborate, a capacity which has its own natural shapes and styles of development. How far away is one place from the next? It will depend both on what there is on the ground — here a rock, there a swamp — and on how many people, doing what, are daily traversing that ground. To think of a place is simultaneously to think of a natural space on the one hand and of the community that is defined in relation to it on the other. It is to grasp the reciprocal relation between nature and culture: geographical space mediating a possibility for human community, community elevating dead space into the character and distinctiveness of place. A place is precisely a setting where a communication of some kind takes form.

To that extent every place is commonly owned. And here we confront a third major contributory factor to our contemporary loss of the sense of place, which is the economic doctrine, having its origins in the eighteenth century, that views land as a privately owned resource of industrial production. From Adam Smith's insight that the price of any commodity incorporates an element not only of wages and profit, but also of rent, there followed the conception that land was part of the fixed capital of any business enterprise, to be counted among the resources which are transformed, by the magic of production, into an ever-growing wealth of other kinds. Later thinkers such as Marx were to seize upon the incongruities of treating human labour as an industrial resource, and to protest against the implications of making this analytical abstraction the basis of industrial practice. Yet it is no less odd to regard land in this light. The illusion in the one case is the same as in the other: it appears to become *convertible*. "This city is built on coal!" the nineteenth-century industrialist could boast, with a satisfied assurance that with such a resource no city could ever lack wealth. But the very rhetorical pungency with which he expressed himself warns us of the difficulty: what a city needs to be built on is something that will hold up its buildings. Its land has a *prior* meaning for it, before it can be seen as an industrial resource; and no city has an interest in building on land that will shift and collapse as it is transformed into wealth. This is a parable for the general problem: to view land as a convertible resource is to ignore the primordial relationship which any human community has to its physical environment. By focusing exclusively on the productive relationship, the economic analysis carries political thought to a dangerous level of abstraction.

One rather obvious example of this is to be found in the high value placed since the industrial revolution on the private ownership of land. The philosophical culture of the eighteenth century made no allowance for local identification as a universal human need. (Of the poets, again, better things can be said: Goldsmith's *Deserted Village* understood exactly what the age was denying.) In the resulting vacuum of intelligibility, the sense of belonging was redirected to the only kind of relation with the land which the intellectual culture now understood: private ownership of it. In that same century, much of the common land which had survived from the Middle Ages was eroded. But private ownership of land simply will not bear the weight that the Lockean tradition of political thought placed upon it. Indeed, land can never be as entirely private as certain other possessions: it is among those things which are irreducibly public. It can be privately *worked*; and in order to facilitate its working, access may be restricted. Yet however high the fence, land is irreducibly public in that it forms a part of that extended place through, in, and around which the human community passes, and against the backdrop of which it conducts its life. A landowner can exclude the public from his land, but cannot, as it were, exclude his land from the public. His field is everyone else's scenery; his factory everyone else's civic building. You cannot withdraw two hundred acres from the map in the same way you might withdraw your telephone number from the public directory!

Simone Weil wrote: "Participation in collective possessions . . . is a no less important need. . . . Where a real civic life exists, each one feels he has a personal ownership in the public monuments, gardens, ceremonial pomp and circumstance; and a display of sumptuousness in which nearly all human beings seek fulfilment, is in this way placed within the reach of even the poorest."[17] She omitted to say that the public possession is not merely artefactual but natural. The identity of a city, no less than a village, is determined by its rivers, its stretches of open water, its hills, great or small, and its plains, not only by its monuments and parks. What would Hong Kong be without its mountain, its harbors, and its islands? With these features the citizen feels a stake of propriety, which is far more fundamental a datum of political reality than the administrative notion of ownership that assigns the hillside to a hundred thousand different proprietors and the harbor to a government agency. When we are unable to convert this sense of common propriety into any form of shared authority, then our natural political aspirations are frustrated; and out of such frustrations grow legal, political and sometimes military battles.

Consider, as a small example, the frustrations experienced in modern Britain, as in some other Western societies, at the planning process. Suppose that it is intended (as it usually is) to build a major roadway across a stretch of quiet countryside which forms, both socially and psychologically, a decisive ele-

17. Weil, *Need for Roots*, pp. 35f.

ment in the environment of neighboring communities. The route will sever a cluster of villages from their natural urban center, and will separate farms from the villages to which they properly belong. Compensation is offered to anyone with private property rights along the chosen route, but there is no compensation for the communities. Even a mechanism permitting them to make a contribution to the discussion of the plans has been difficult to establish; and much doubt is entertained about whether their contribution makes any difference. The law has a concept of "loss of amenity" to which an injured individual can appeal; but amenities are more truly common things, things we enjoy together or not at all.

Human existence evokes place out of space by a distinctive social pattern of mobility and rootedness that characterizes our species. Place is woven by the intertwining of human paths within a space that is shared. Human beings have need of artificial shelter and of community, and the combination of these two identifies their places. Even that most private place, the dwelling, is not a place of solitude, but of intimate community. Yet human beings are not stationary, like trees. They do not affirm their place by standing still in it. They have patterns of going out and coming in, of departure and return, identifying places as our own and other people's and identifying themselves and others as belonging to them. They move about and among each other, wending their ways in and out and around each others' places, so defining many places within their place, and defining between-place, through which they pass by negating it as place and restoring it to mere space. This common use of shared space as place is what defines all societies, a generalization which holds true not only for settled industrial or agricultural societies, but also for migrant societies; for though their ways take them further, from summer to winter pastures or hunting-grounds, their sense of belonging to their places and interacting with them is no less. By common experience of our place and common care for it we build up our sense of belonging to one another. And even, paradoxically, by quarrelling over it; for those who dispute over a parcel of land are fated to be as tightly bound to one another as any two people could be, linked by the fact that only they alone, of all the people in the world, care for that parcel of land to that extent.

Here, then, are the sources of our problem. The concept of place has been squeezed in a pincer-movement between a philosophical interest in consciousness and a theological interest in universality. The combination of these two antecedents has helped, at least, to foster a later economic conception of land as exploitable resource. The size of the problem we face, however, is apparent as soon as its antecedents are stated. For these conceptions are not simply mistaken. If we cherish the illusion that all we need to do to repair our loss is to unveil the Great False Turn in Western thought, which usually turns out to be Platonism, we shall be frustrated. It is hard to imagine how we could think about buying and selling, think about the reconciliation of nations, or think about thinking itself, without depending extensively on these very doctrines whose injurious effects we have observed. It is one thing to observe that there is a knot, quite another to untie it. Yet the problem may not be insuperable. For the effects, injurious as they may be, are not obviously *necessary*. Each strand of thought, when followed through attentively, is capable of generating its own qualifications, warning us of the limits of its application. If the spacelessness of the wise man is thought through as the fruitful philosophical paradox it is, it will be necessary to think it from both ends: not only that he is not here, but that he is with us. And if land can be private property, what does it imply for property that it can include land? We will surely find it subject to easements, those inescapable bridgeheads of public right that determine the character of real estate. If these two strands of thought seem, at a glance, to be open to development along other lines, what of the third strand, the theological one? In what follows we shall attempt to explore the question of place and theological universality a little more fully.

III

Let us begin from an impressionistic intuition, illustrate it, and then attempt to improve on it. The intuition is this: the Old Testament is full of the sense of place, but the New Testament is indifferent to it. The Old Testament is the story of a love affair between a tribe and its God, and a piece of land is the token of their affection and disaffection. The New Testament is the charter of a world faith with eternity in view, where neither race nor territory intervenes between God and mankind. In relating itself to the legacy of the Old Testament, the New systematically cancels its preoccupation with land and city. To explore this intuition, consider two texts between which the contrast might be thought to be most sharply drawn: the Book of Joshua and the Epistle to the Hebrews.

Nothing could be more affecting than the loving detail in which the Deuteronomistic authors of Joshua have gathered and preserved, between the thirteenth and nineteenth chapters, the ancient boundary-descriptions of each tribal territory, together with a list of villages and towns for each. From this section of the book, austerely forbidding to the casual reader, we form the most powerful impression of the bond which tied the people to the land. We are led, with the greatest geographical precision, up hills and down valleys, through tiny communities otherwise unknown to us, as many, no doubt, were unknown except by name to them. The contrast between the literary context, which is the narratives of conquest, and the historical occasion, which is the exile, is most poignant. If we let our imaginations rest upon the situation of the scribes (in Babylonia, I assume, not, as is sometimes alleged, in Judaea) carefully piecing together every geographical record that they had been able to lay hands on and carry with them into exile, we may perceive how the experience of loss has brought into the sharpest relief the importance of having once conquered. They draw the widest possible boundary, corresponding to the furthest limits of David's conquests, and ignore such major considerations as the presence of Philistine civilizations on the coastal plain. The land had been the gift of YHWH, and so every square mile must be held in the memory. Geography has become the object of that minute attention more normally reserved for genealogy and ritual.

To this preoccupation the anonymous New Testament letter (or, more exactly, speech) applies a typological style of interpretation (loosely, if not very helpfully, called "spiritualizing") that sees historical realities as pointing forward to eschatological ones. Its central interest is the Levitical priesthood and ritual, which, "annulled" by the more perfect priesthood of Christ, was therefore a mere "shadow of good things to come."[18] But Hebrews treats other features of Israel's culture, too, as somewhat shadowy, and this is markedly the case with the subject of our own interest. Joshua's conquest of Canaan, the author argues, is shown by the words of the 95th Psalm to have been insubstantial. For the Lord swore in his wrath, "They shall not enter into my rest," and if Joshua had actually given them rest there would have been no talk in the Psalm of another "today," when the invitation to enter is renewed.[19] When Abraham went forth in faith "to the place which he was to receive as an inheritance," he never settled, the author urges, but merely "sojourned," dwelling in tents. Why? Because he looked for the city which has foundations.[20] The patriarchal generation as a whole passed away without receiving any territorial possession, for their quest for a fatherland was really a quest for something "better, that is, something heavenly."[21] The patriarchal hope for a territory becomes transparent to an eschatological fulfillment. What is stated so explicitly by this author is implied elsewhere in the New Testament: the word "inheritance," for instance (Gk. *klēronomia*, translating the Hebrew

18. Heb. 10:1.
19. Heb. 4:1-8.
20. Heb. 11:8-10.
21. Heb. 11:13-16.

naḥªlāh, a dominant category for the land in the Pentateuchal and Deutero-nomic literature), is constantly used to represent the eschatological reality of salvation in Christ.

The confluence of this hermeneutic with the Platonic account of mind is the subject of an oft-told tale. Whether or not Hebrews itself is subject to Platonic influences, perhaps by way of Philo of Alexandria who anticipated certain aspects of its treatment of the promised land, the end result was to convert the territorial passion of Israel into a vision of salvation that was essentially spaceless and intellectual. Augustine represents this tradition at its height: "In the Old Testament, I say, are rehearsed earthly and temporal promises, which, whatever their figurative significance for the eternal and heavenly objects of the New Testament, are goods of this corruptible flesh. The good now promised, however, belongs to the very heart; it is an intellectual good."[22] When Jesus quoted the Psalm which said that "the meek shall inherit the land" *(terra)*, Augustine takes him to have meant "the solid stability, so to speak, of the eternal inheritance, where the soul possessed of good affection rests, as it were, in its proper place like a material body on the ground *(terra)*, and is nourished on its proper food like a body on the produce of the soil *(terra)*."[23]

The tale less often told is that of the continuity between the New Testament's interpretation of the conquest and the Deuteronomistic one. It was no arbitrary typological embroidery to look on Canaan as a heavenly possession; it sprang from a sensitivity to one strand in the thought of the historians, who had learned to see the land as a gift that pointed beyond itself. Always the gift of the land had been diaphanous. The land was the medium through which Yhwh gave himself to the people; it was theirs, because he was theirs. From the first moment that their feet touched the West Bank of the Jordan, the Book of Joshua tells us, the land was consecrated to worship, a place within which God and people would keep covenant. The most powerful symbol of this transparence is the landless status of the tribe of Levi: "Yhwh is their inheritance," the much-repeated tag declared. They were an eschatological sign, an arrow into heaven, which pointed beyond the land to what it signified.[24]

If Christianity spiritualized Old Testament territorial categories, then, it was because it found them already half-spiritualized. It took seriously the freight of commerce between God and man with which the land was charged.

22. *De spiritu et littera* 21.36.
23. *De sermone Domini in monte* 1.2.4.
24. Josh. 13:33; cf. Num. 18:20; Deut. 10:9; 18:2. The variation at 13:14, "the offerings by fire to Yhwh God of Israel are their inheritance" addresses more literally the question of how the tribe will live.

But it was precisely this freight that made it impossible to sustain and extend the Jewish sense of place. If commerce between God and man was to reach to the ends of the earth, these categories of salvation had to be freed from their over-determination. The nexus of land, covenant, and election had to be freed from particular designations in terms of Israel and Jerusalem. As we are reminded by St. John's story of Jesus and the Samaritan woman, there was no scope in orthodox Israel for a *class* of holy places with many members. What might have been the simplest answer to the woman's question about the Jerusalem temple and Jacob's well — that they were equally potent sanctuaries — was not available. Since the Deuteronomic reform worship had been organized around a central shrine, suitable for a monotheist obedience. The city, like the land and people, was elect. In the story of the Gileadite altar the historians found an illustration of how even within the tribal allotments local religious identifications could act as a threatening force of division.[25] Christianity, then, had either to uphold the unique status of Jerusalem, or announce that all holy places were now superseded. Its eschatological consciousness allowed it to take the latter course without denying the validity of what had been; the elect place was confined, we may say, within the parentheses of an elect history. The progress of the gospel to Samaria, the Gentile mission, the decision not to circumcise Gentile converts, all attest the same conception of that history: it was the elective purpose of God to move out from Jerusalem, the traditional focus of election, into every part of the world, without tying the universal church to a pilgrimage, either on foot or in spirit, to its local origins.

But even this radical move was not totally remote from the perspective of the Deuteronomistic historians. It was in their generation that the greatest of the prophets declared that Yhwh would make a new covenant "not like the covenant which I made with their fathers when I took them out of the land of Egypt,"[26] another text which features strongly in the argument of Hebrews. The historians, whose view runs from the conquest to the exile, have certainly made their own the prophet's negative verdict on that "old covenant" with law and land. Like Jeremiah, they understood the conquest as Yhwh's repudiation of it. And so they anticipated the negative verdict which the author to the Hebrews pronounced on the effects of Joshua's conquest: "If Joshua had given them rest, there would have been no talk of another day."[27] "The land had rest," they had told us; settlement had been achieved and resistance overcome. But the rest which it enjoyed was not exactly what was looked for, not the rest of total pos-

25. Josh. 22:10-34.
26. Jer. 31:31f.
27. Heb. 4:8.

session in the unqualified, unmediated rule of Yahweh, but rather a rest of partial success and qualified obedience.[28]

The decisive issue was Israel's relation to the surrounding communities. The settlement was to be a holy one, founded on a relation to YHWH wholly distinct from that of the Canaanite communities to their Baalim. Battle was the symbolic focus of this distinctness. The battle stories of the Book of Joshua are not tales of military prowess and heroism, but of miraculous delivery, always remarkable, sometimes even whimsical. They are stories of the initiatives of YHWH, not a local deity born in the land, but a warrior who entered it with his people. Yet they are also stories of ritual consecration, in which the community gives itself to receive the gift. The historians cherished the ritual traditions of Holy War, not as practices that they or their fathers or grandfathers had ever engaged in — the last serious attempt at revival, under the Northern reign of Jehu, had gone down into history as a moral disaster — but as a historical memory of self-consecration which the service of YHWH required. Everything to do with battle was charged with sanctity, everything was demanded in taking hold of that for which YHWH had taken hold of them. Yet this surrender was never fully made, for the tribes were slow to possess, they relaxed their warlike zeal, and they did not attempt the hard and mountainous territory. By the ninth chapter of the Book of Joshua they are entangled in an alliance, and in the tenth they are fighting for their alliance. The land was, indeed, *fully given,* for "not one of all the good promises which Yahweh had made to the house of Israel had failed."[29] But the gift fully given was not fully taken. It was a kind of Fall. And the occasion for the Fall was the very fact of settled existence and the unavoidable reality of neighbors. The gift itself contained the seeds of the failure. The tension between election and coexistence was never resolved. Precisely to this unresolved tension the Christian universalizing of election addressed itself.

IV

Once the exclusive claim for a holy place is set aside, is there anything left in the biblical tradition to be said more generally about place? There is, for biblical reflection upon place was never exhausted by the election of land and city. Here we may notice three contexts in which place comes into consideration.

(1) The election of Israel's holy places had a *background* in a general sensibility to the phenomena of migration and settlement. The first focus of Israel's

28. Josh. 11:23; 14:15.
29. Josh. 21:45.

belief in its election was Abraham. But in Abraham, as the author to the Hebrews shrewdly observed, not settlement but migration provides the topological reference. He is the wanderer of faith, who leaves the settled alienation of the city in search of a permanent home.[30] True, there are sites dotted all over the patriarchal narratives, which will have been known to the generations who recited them and wrote them down, but they are sites that commemorate the passage of Abraham through the land rather than its settlement. In Abraham Israel appreciated the bi-polar character of any sense of place. Even its holy place was not simply a function of inhabitation; the elect homeland presupposed an elect wandering. But if Israel's tenure of its land could not be aboriginal, neither could Abraham's migration. That, too, had its presuppositions: he began as a citizen of Ur, and the compilers of the Pentateuch, in prefacing the patriarchal narratives with a primeval history, were well aware of the importance of this background. If migration and settlement were to have a holy meaning for the descendents of Abraham, they must first have a general meaning for the descendents of Adam.

At the beginning of the primeval history we encounter the figure of Cain, who, being the first murderer, became also the first wanderer, cursed from the ground and condemned to be eternally a fugitive. But Cain is also the first founder of a city, and his children the first inventors of civilized arts.[31] These two traditions are combined in the subtle telling of the legend, suggesting that civic community, conducted behind the defensive barricades of city walls, is nothing but a form of institutionalized deracination. Neither migration nor settlement is original to human existence; neither reflects the state of innocence; each in its different way attests a more fundamental dislocation, and they are simply aspects of each other. Human history begins with a disrupted sense of place. Balancing the narrative of Cain at the end of the primeval history we find the story of the Tower of Babel, where settlement and migration appear in the reverse order. The fragility of civic order makes it subject to centrifugal forces. Loss of communication scatters its citizens abroad over the face of the earth.

Not only does Abraham's migration have its presuppositions; the migration of Israel under Moses and the conquest of the Holy Land under Joshua are set against the background both of patriarchal legend and of migration and settlement as a general phenomenon. The first speech of Deuteronomy puts forward the distinctive view that the displacement of the Canaanites by Israel was merely one case of YHWH's removal of degenerate autochthonous inhabitants

30. Gen. 12:1.
31. Gen. 4:17-24.

(the Rephaim) by civilized and law-abiding tribes. Migration was thus a tool of civilization in the divine plan. The force of this in the Deuteronomic narrative is to impose on Israel a recognition of Ammon, Moab, Edom, and even by implication the Philistines, who were held to have arrived from Crete, as neighbors who had a perfect right to exist free of attack.[32]

(2) The effect of the exile was to sharpen Israel's sense of a plurality of places. Precisely as it understood its holy place to have fallen under YHWH's condemnation, and was forced to consider the question of its future from a distance, it entertained a hope of restoration that would involve it in a new international context.

The sense of deracination was acute. Nowhere is it more expressively attested than in Psalm 137, where the exiles "by the waters of Babylon" find themselves cut off from the resources of their culture and their civilization. All that remains as a cultural memory is the bitter recollection of what they have suffered from Edom and Babylon, given voice in the wild curse with which the poem ends.[33] Yet the longer-term effect of the disruption was to create the conviction that Israel's future must be an international one. Most dramatically, of course, as Deutero-Isaiah and Ezra-Nehemiah demonstrate, the returning exiles saw their future as bound up in the triumph of the Medo-Persian empire. But there are other and earlier indications. The foreign oracles of the Book of Jeremiah, a collection probably of Babylonian origin, attend to the question of which nations will be part of a new world order that YHWH is bringing about when he overthrows the control of the oppressive Mesopotamian empire. Edom and Babylon will, as a matter of justice, disappear from the stage of history; but others have a role in the world that is coming to pass.[34] What is new is not the thought that other nations have a place in Israel's destiny: It had always been assumed that the leaders of the nations would be gathered to Jerusalem to worship YHWH. But which specific nations would be involved had hardly seemed to require consideration.[35] Now, however, the detailed shape of a post-imperial world order becomes important.

Disapora Jewry, always aware of its dislocation but learning to live in the

---

32. "I have given Esau the hill-country of Seir as his own" (Deut. 2:5; cf. 2:9; 2:19). Only the Rephaim are liable to attack, i.e., the Anakites in West Jordan, and the two East-Jordanian Amorite tribes. On the Philistines, cf. 2:23. This idea has a parallel in Amos 9:7.

33. The supreme skill with which the poet tears asunder the illusion of aesthetic grief which the opening lines create is, of course, lost on readers who decline to take its terrible conclusion as a serious testimony to the emotional extremes of dislocation.

34. Jer. 46-51. On this see my *The Desire of the Nations* (Cambridge: Cambridge University Press, 1996), p. 71.

35. Ps. 47:9.

midst of other peoples, assumes a great importance for Israel's sense of place. There is no longer one sacred land, to be distant from which is to be "cut off" from Yhwh. The immediate reality of the post-exilic situation was that Yhwh was worshiped, in all probability, by as many (or more) who lived outside Palestine as in it. The returned community could never be identified with the land quite as innocently as the pre-exilic community had been. Centuries later, when faced with the threat of the imposed assimilation of Israel to the Hellenistic patterns favored by the Seleucids, the faithful in Jerusalem would interpret their position through stories of a sixth-century Jewish exile in Babylon.

(3) The diaspora experience of place was created especially by two factors: the proximity in which Jew and non-Jew lived together, and the pilgrimage on which the pious Jew would visit Jerusalem for festivals. What held these two segments of experience together was the law, which conferred the national identity that was no longer established by residence. Pilgrimage repeated the wandering and migration of the ancient tribes, yet without ever resulting in settlement. The festival done, the obedient Jew turned back to where he dwelt "among those who hate peace." Pilgrimage was thus unending, and so replaced inhabitation as the dominant metaphor for life, as in the precious eighth stanza of Psalm 119:

> *My portion* is Yhwh; I promise to keep thy words.
> *I entreat* thy face with all my heart; be gracious to me
> according to thy promise.
> *I have considered* my way, and turn my feet to thy testimonies.
> *I hasten* and do not delay to keep thy commandments.
> *The cords* of the wicked ensnare me, but I do not forget thy law.
> *At midnight* I rise to praise thee because of thy righteous ordinances.
> *A companion* I am of all who fear thee, of those who keep thy precepts.
> *Thy steadfast love* fills the earth, Yhwh; thy statutes
> do thou teach me.[36]

The poet opens the stanza by telling us that he is without land, applying to himself the formula that used to be applied to the Levites: "their portion is Yhwh." In place of the tie to tribal or family allotment, the poet has made a covenant (1), and so is the archetype of the diaspora Israelite for whom the law is the true social reality of the divine gift. For the rest of the stanza we see him as a traveling pilgrim, "entreating thy face" (2). Fittingly, he breaks with his

---

36. Ps. 119:57-64. The opening words of each line, which carry a special emphasis by virtue of the alliterative composition of the poem — in this stanza beginning with the letter *ḥ* — are placed in their correct position and italicized.

usual custom of repeating at least one initial word in each stanza, so that this stanza never, as it were, finds a home. Pilgrimage involves him in planning a route (3), in traveling with urgency (4), in unwelcome delays which do not, however, force him to abandon his journey (5), and in night travel (6), when he does most of his poetic composition. Lacking a settled home, he has no regular society for support, but must fall in with those on the same God-fearing road (7). At the end of his journey, what awaits him? There is no mention of Jerusalem; rather, the point of arrival is the discovery that the whole earth is full of YHWH's steadfast love. The final three lines, six-stress rather than the usual five-stress lines, create a stately, processional feel: the way opens up before the large vista of the last line, with the whole earth stretched out before him. The simplicity of the final refrain is then especially powerful: what more has the poet to do at the climax of his journey than to learn, as he always does, YHWH's statutes?

From such a text it may appear that the sense of place has entirely evaporated into metaphor. Yet the seriousness with which diaspora Jews took the law as their guide forbade a simple spiritualization of it. Pilgrimage may be a metaphor for life, but that is because the law-governed life accords a major place to pilgrimage. The development, rather, occurs in two directions. First, there is an enhanced role for the city, as opposed to the land. Jerusalem still had its territory, though much less than the exilic Deuteronomists had thought it entitled to, but this hinterland now falls into the background. The metropolis, rather than the land, becomes the focus of Jewish loyalty.

So the preaching of Jesus, now seen to be much more of a piece with national expectations than it was once customary to admit, addressed a Jewish consciousness much less territorially defined than it had been and much more defined by reference to Jerusalem. The city is the negative focus of his most severe critiques, and the positive focus of his predictions of the coming Kingdom. The Gospels continually speak of his journeys to Jerusalem, especially (in St. John) those associated with the great pilgrim-feasts of the Jewish religious year. It was in Jerusalem, the apostles taught, that God vindicated his anointed, and in Jerusalem that the gift of the Holy Spirit was given. And Jerusalem was the focus of a further expectation of great importance, the gathering of the Gentiles to worship, taken to be the signal of the Kingdom's arrival. And so it was from Jerusalem, according to St. Luke, that the missionary message must go out, not only to Jews but also to Gentiles. The geographical consciousness of early Christianity, then, was precisely that which it inherited: that of a city at the center of the world.

In the second place, local particularities become generalized, as the project of law requires implementation in new local contexts. The law-collections that we know from the Pentateuch are impregnated with a sense of rural Palestine, and show little sign of adaptation. Yet they served Jews who may have lived their whole lives without needing to know how to reap fields, breed cattle, or plant trees, and provided them with local categories applicable in any situation. We may consider the summary law from the Holiness Code of Leviticus: "You shall love your neighbor as yourself."[37] Within its original context of Leviticus the word "neighbor" has evidently a local reference: here is the fellow-Jew who is bound to us by participation in a common local community, largely rural, and whose interests abut and sometimes conflict with our own.[38] But what becomes of it when it is read in Alexandria? Have we any reason to doubt that its local sense continues to be felt there, and that it is taken to impose obligations quite specifically to those "among whom I dwell," to the non-Jews who share a common city with the Jew who keeps the law?

The parable of the Merciful Samaritan in St. Luke's Gospel, with its profound rebuke to the spirit of Jewish exclusivism, shows us how far it was possible for the interpretation of this command to stretch. Christian exegesis of this parable has been mainly concerned to underline the rebuke it contains, and to stress the implication of universality. *Omni homini proximus est omnis homo*, wrote Augustine; "every man is neighbor to every man."[39] It is no part of my argument to suggest that this can be lightly dismissed: there are many societies where the rebuke of the parable strikes like a meteor against the complacency of racial or class self-love. Yet there are complacent forms of universalism, too, which may amount to not much more than universal indifference, for the universal claim of every human being upon every other is, after all, more of a critical principle than a substantial one, and to love everybody in the world equally is to love nobody very much. Once we have safeguarded our structures of society against unjust preferences, we may need to encounter the protest of the parable from the opposite side, drawing our attention to an urgent form of contingent proximity. "As it happened, a priest was going down the road. . . ."[40] As it happened! There is a nearness of contingency, a chancing upon, a nearness of pure place, unqualified by any relation or connection but simply a matter of finding yourself next to somebody; and it is that which the parable holds up to us as the context for the neighbor's claim. Far from denying the significance of

37. Lev. 19:18.
38. Our English word, of Germanic origin, is obviously derived from the word for "near"; and the same is true of the Latin *proximus* and the Greek *plēsion*. Of the Hebrew *rēaʿ* it is not possible to be so clear, but one etymological theory connects it with *rāʾāh*, "to pasture."
39. Sermon 299D.1.
40. Luke 10:31.

proximate relations, the parable discovers them where they are not looked for, nearer to us and under our very noses.

The story takes place on a road, the primary symbol of our capacity to weave place out of space by creating a non-place through which we pass on our way from place to place. The road is a space that exists only *between* one place and another. The traveler who takes to the road does not do so in order to be where he is, but to be where he is going to. Any point on the road may in fact be a place for someone else; but then the road is broken, as it were, at that point, and becomes two roads heading off in opposite directions. While we treat the road as a road, we suppress the possibility that there may be a place on it for us, and make every point on it a non-place that we pass through in order to arrive at *our* place. But at one point on the road in the story the wounded traveler presented an obstruction to this suppression of place — not a decisive obstruction, for it was open to the priest and the Levite to persist with it notwithstanding. But the mercy of the Samaritan restored that point on the road to the dignity of a real place, a place of meeting.

V

Read in this light, the parable of the Merciful Samaritan forces us to make a distinction between two opposed types of universalism. Universalism may be abstract, achieved by diverting attention from the place where we encounter the truth that interests us, by canceling place out as we grasp the truth. Alternatively, it may be concrete, achieved by denying the status of privileged places in order to concentrate on the actual place of encounter, wherever it may be. By suspending the privilege accorded to special places, we learn not to ignore the place nearest to us, not to let it be dissolved into a mere passage to somewhere else. In modern Western society our universalism is generally abstract, dissolving every place into a communications-network. To look out of a window onto a busy city street is to see pedestrians or cyclists wearing headphones to secure at least one of their five senses against engagement with the place through which they move, or talking on mobile telephones at a pitch that betrays their unawareness of people around them. We are at the end of a process which began in the modern world with the invention of the turnpike, which first took the road out of the place and situated the place on the road. The road we think of as a space where we do not belong, where propriety itself requires that we insulate ourselves against encounter, shrinking back from those who brush against us. Among the paradoxes of late-modern culture it must rank high that huge reservoirs of compassion can be released by television pictures of suffering in other parts of the world, while anyone who actually stops at a roadside to attend upon the plight of an accident victim, may expect to be treated as an eccentric. So it must be, no doubt, where the neutrality and openness of passageways has become a primary object of concern for those who defend public order.

Concrete universalism consists in seeing the particular place *as an instance of* the universal. The created world forms a universe of coordinated meaning, which it is our human vocation to comprehend as best we may. The world and the word are always universal, and a quest for truth (which includes a quest for justice) will always be a quest for intelligible principles. Not for nothing do we call our centers of intellectual endeavor "universities"; the scornful term "multiversity," coined to characterize the giant institutions of the North American continent, is meant to carry the accusation of intellectual failure. Who wants a local science, boasting of different experimental results from those reached elsewhere, or a local philosophy uninterested in what is thought in France or Germany? And who (as the Judaeo-Christian faith has always asked) wants a local religion, worshiping local gods? Love for God and man is not the object of a local cult. Yet it is practiced only in particular, intimate, and selective relations; the attempt to depict a form of human love without particularity, reciprocity or preference has never yielded anything but a cold-blooded monstrosity. It is not this proper attention to universal truths that diverts us from the particular relation in the particular place. Any particular place may be a scene on which many such truths are instantiated. It is the abstract universalism which shrinks from the direct experience of what presents itself here and now.

Yet for Christian theology it is not enough simply to declare for concrete rather than for abstract universals, since that overlooks the fact that God has made himself known in history. "The Word became flesh. . . ."[41] Among the paradoxes of that pregnant saying, there is, perhaps, none more startling than this: that the divine Word, the intelligibility of God, communicated its universal truth through a unique act of election. The flesh of Jesus was particular as was no other flesh, and not simply as one among many instances of a universal rule. A universalism that responds to God's initiative has taken its beginning from the historical fact of an elect man in an elect place. If it transcends holy places, then, it does so not by subsuming them into a universal, but by proceeding from their unique, once-for-all role to new general possibilities in the history that follows them. The elect places of history are the matrix in which meetings between God and mankind are shaped. It is *because* the holy land was elect

41. John 1:14.

that the meeting-place between a Jew and a Samaritan, the two historic inhabitants of that land, could be a place of reconciliation, looking forward to a new holy land. Similarly, when the community which worships in spirit and in truth is revealed from heaven, the name it is given is "Jerusalem."[42] This is the key to understanding the catholicity of the church.

In concluding, one last observation is in place about the "new patriotism" called for by Simone Weil, a patriotism based on compassion. "The compassion felt for fragility is always associated with love for real beauty, because we are keenly conscious of the fact that the existence of the really beautiful things ought to be assured forever, and is not."[43] The importance of Weil's observation is that it calls to the aid of the nation-state precisely that acceptance of the contingent which is essential to an evangelical conception of locality. The claim of the nation-state is not founded on racial solidarity or on cultural homogeneity or on the logic of territorial separation — e.g., the claim of an island to be separate from its mainland, or of a mainland to govern its island. It is founded on the acknowledgment that whatever the limits, racial, cultural, or territorial, of any given nation-state, they could have been quite different. Contingent historical circumstances have thrown the nation together in *this* form, which is at once infinitely open to challenge and yet the only form available to us. Compassion for the nation-state is bred of the knowledge that it is neither necessary nor inevitable, yet mediates good. Whether compassion is always safe, I strongly doubt. But it is certainly the case that if national patriotism is to have any moral claim on us, it will have to be based on this recognition: "The nation is a fact, and a fact is not an absolute value."[44] That there should be any form of solidarity is something for which we have to take moral responsibility; it requires our will to recover the particular out of the universal. Perhaps only compassion can draw the gifted and the able back from the great world capitals and universities to the regional and local communities from which they sprang, to put the gifts and skills which they possess at the service of their neighbors.

It is generally true of European intelligentsia, at least, that the nation-state has come to seem incredible — a perspective encouraged, no doubt, by the European wars of the last century, but essentially a judgment of theory rather than of experience. Yet the good of the nation-state is seen in its absence, when conflicts arise apart from defined solidarities and state organizations. The conflicts of the dissolving Yugoslavia were of this order. That now raging in the holy land itself is another: Israel's great tragedy is not that Palestinians want a

42. Rev. 21:2.
43. Weil, *Need for Roots*, pp. 147, 170, 172.
44. Weil, *Need for Roots*, p. 131.

[handwritten marginalia:] Is it true of the diff intelligentsia. There seems a reaction back to a kind of nationalism which demands a Balkr, or an faith etc

nation-state, but that they are not one. Evil are the conflicts of nations, but many times more evil are the conflicts that oppose communities without the identities or disciplines of nations. The "war against terrorism" on which a rhetorically inebriated Western leadership has engaged the civilized world has forced us to contemplate the scope and nature of armed struggle when neither nationality nor any other unit of local identity will count in distinguishing friends from enemies. We may well shed tears for the nation-state and lament the fragility of its good.[45]

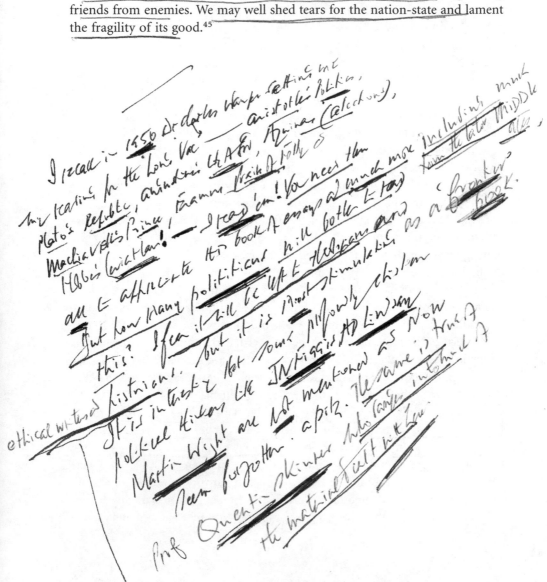

45. For further exploration of these suggestions, see pp. 276-95 above.

Index of Names

Agapetos, 210
Albertus Magnus, 108-9, 110n., 112
Alciato, Andrea, 152n.
Alexander III, Pope, 102
Alexander of Hales, 83, 105n., 108n.
Almain, Jacques, 76n., 151n., 152
Althusius, Johannes, 68, 77
Ambrose, Bp. of Milan, 77n., 79n., 104, 105n., 107n.
Anselm, Abp. of Canterbury, 83
Arendt, Hannah, 280n., 290, 295
Aristotle, 8, 11-16, 97-99, 108-12, 113-14, 116, 129-30, 157-58, 167-70, 175-84, 186-87, 190-94, 195, 198-202, 211, 226-29, 232, 239-45, 258
Apollinaris (Apollinarius), 266
Attwood, David, 246, 262
Augustijn, Cornelis, 123
Augustine, Bp. of Hippo, 4-6, 15-16, 18, 42, 48-72, 79-81, 83-85, 88-91, 104, 105n., 106, 112, 114, 122, 191, 239, 242-43, 253, 270-71, 293, 301, 309, 316
Ayala, Balthazar, 174n., 196

Bainton, Roland, 133
Bardy, G., 49n.
Barrow, R. H., 48n., 55n., 69n.
Barth, Karl, 17-18, **246-75**
Basil, 'the Great', Bp. of Caesarea, 78n., 79n., 104, 105n., 107n.

Bauckham, Richard 25-26, 29-31, 36n., 37n., 39n., 41n.
Baylor, Michael G., 147n.
Bellarmine, Robert, 288n.
Belli, Pierino, 196
Bentham, Jeremy, 137
Bernard of Clairvaux, 127
Berman, Harold, 155n.
Betz, Hans-Dieter, 27, 28n.
Beza, Theodore, 174
Biggar, Nigel, 247n., 249n., 250n.
Black, Antony, 155n., 160n.
Bodin, Jean, 287-88
Bonagratia of Bergamo, 149
Bonaventure (Giovanni di Fidanza), 6, 8, 73, 83-86, 88-89, 91, 92-94, 108n., 109n., 149n.
Boniface VIII, Pope, 86, 100n.
Borschberg, Peter, 174n.
Bretherton, Luke, 276n.
Brett, Annabel, 150n., 151n., 197n.
Brown, Peter, 62, 64
Brunner, Emil, 169n., 265
Bucer, Martin, 144, 163
Buridan, Jean, 197
Burt, Donald X., 56

Cajetan, Thomas de Vio, 158n., 174, 288n.
Calvin, John, 144-47, 154, 163-64, 173
Capito, Wolfgang, 146n.